CENGAGE
Learning

**Shelly Cashman Microsoft Office 365 &
Outlook 2016: Introductory**
Corinne Hoisington

SVP, GM Skills & Global Product Management:
Dawn Gerrain

Product Director: Kathleen McMahon

Senior Product Team Manager: Lauren Murphy

Product Team Manager: Andrea Topping

Associate Product Manager: Melissa Stehler

Senior Director, Development: Marah
Bellegarde

Product Development Manager: Leigh Hefferon

Senior Content Developer: Alyssa Pratt

Developmental Editor: Lisa Ruffolo

Product Assistant: Erica Chapman

Manuscript Quality Assurance Project Leader:
Jeffrey Schwartz

Senior Production Director: Wendy Troeger

Production Director: Patty Stephan

Content Project Manager: Arul Joseph Raj,
Lumina

Manufacturing Planner: Julio Esperas

Designer: Diana Graham

Text Design: Joel Sadagursky

Cover Template Designer: Diana Graham

Cover images: Mario7/Shutterstock.com; Mrs.
Opossum/Shutterstock.com

Compositor: Lumina Datamatics

Vice President, Marketing: Brian Joyner

Marketing Director: Michele McTighe

Marketing Manager: Stephanie Albracht

For product information and technology assistance, contact us at
Cengage Learning Customer & Sales Support, 1-800-354-9706

For permission to use material from this text or product,
submit all requests online at www.cengage.com/permissions.
Further permissions questions can be e-mailed to
permissionrequest@cengage.com

Library of Congress Control Number: 2015957837

ISBN: 978-1-305-87113-7

Cengage Learning
20 Channel Center Street
Boston, MA 02210
USA

Cengage Learning is a leading provider of customized learning solutions with employees residing in nearly 40 different countries and sales in more than 125 countries around the world. Find your local representative at **www.cengage.com.**

Cengage Learning products are represented in Canada by Nelson Education, Ltd.

To learn more about Cengage Learning, visit **www.cengage.com**

Purchase any of our products at your local college store or at our preferred online store **www.cengagebrain.com**

Printed at CLDPC, USA, 11-16

Microsoft® Office 365™
OUTLOOK® 2016

INTRODUCTORY

D0206472

Microsoft® Office 365™
OUTLOOK® 2016

INTRODUCTORY

HOISINGTON

CENGAGE
Learning®

SHELLY CASHMAN SERIES®

Australia • Brazil • Japan • Korea • Mexico • Singapore • Spain • United Kingdom • United States

Microsoft® Office 365™
OUTLOOK® 2016

Contents

Productivity Apps for School and Work

Introduction to OneNote 2016	**PA 2**
Introduction to Sway	**PA 6**
Introduction to Office Mix	**PA 10**
Introduction to Microsoft Edge	**PA 14**

Microsoft Office 2016 and Windows 10

Office 2016 and Windows 10: Essential Concepts and Skills

Objectives	**OFF 1**
Roadmap	OFF 1
Introduction to the Windows 10 Operating System	**OFF 2**
Using a Touch Screen and a Mouse	OFF 3
Scrolling	OFF 4
Keyboard Shortcuts	OFF 5
Starting Windows	OFF 5
To Sign In to an Account	OFF 6
The Windows Desktop	OFF 7
Introduction to Microsoft Office 2016	**OFF 7**
Microsoft Office 2016 Apps	OFF 7
Microsoft Office 2016 Suites	OFF 8
Running and Using an App	**OFF 9**
Word	OFF 9
To Run an App Using the Start Menu and Create a Blank Document	OFF 9
To Maximize a Window	OFF 11
Word Document Window, Ribbon, and Elements Common to Office Apps	OFF 12
To Display a Different Tab on the Ribbon	OFF 16
To Collapse and Expand the Ribbon and Use Full Screen Mode	OFF 17
To Use a Shortcut Menu to Relocate the Quick Access Toolbar	OFF 19
To Customize the Quick Access Toolbar	OFF 20
To Enter Text in a Document	OFF 21
Document Properties	**OFF 22**
To Change Document Properties	OFF 22
Printing, Saving, and Organizing Files	**OFF 23**
Printing a Document	OFF 23
To Print a Document	OFF 23
Organizing Files and Folders	OFF 25
To Create a Folder	OFF 26
Folder Windows	OFF 27
To Create a Folder within a Folder	OFF 28
To Create the Remaining Folders	OFF 28
To Expand a Folder, Scroll through Folder Contents, and Collapse a Folder	OFF 29
To Switch from One App to Another	OFF 30
To Save a File in a Folder	OFF 31
Navigating in Dialog Boxes	OFF 34
To Minimize and Restore a Window	OFF 34
To Save a File on OneDrive	OFF 35
To Sign Out of a Microsoft Account	OFF 37
Screen Resolution	**OFF 38**
To Change the Screen Resolution	OFF 39
To Exit an Office App with One Document Open	OFF 41
To Copy a Folder to OneDrive	OFF 42
To Unlink a OneDrive Account	OFF 44
Additional Microsoft Office Apps	**OFF 45**
PowerPoint	OFF 46
To Run an App Using the Search Box	OFF 47
The PowerPoint Window and Ribbon	OFF 48
To Enter Content in a Title Slide	OFF 49
To Save a File in a Folder	OFF 49
To Create a New Office Document from the Backstage View	OFF 50
To Enter Content in a Title Slide of a Second PowerPoint Presentation	OFF 51
To Save a File in a Folder	OFF 51
To Close an Office File Using the Backstage View	OFF 52
To Open a Recent Office File Using the Backstage View	OFF 52
To Exit an Office App	OFF 53
Excel	OFF 53
To Create a New Blank Office Document from File Explorer	OFF 54
To Run an App from File Explorer and Open a File	OFF 55
Unique Features of Excel	OFF 56
To Enter a Worksheet Title	OFF 57
To Save an Existing Office File with the Same File Name	OFF 58
To Save a File with a New File Name	OFF 59
To Exit an Office App	OFF 59

Access	OFF 59
To Run an App	OFF 59
Unique Elements in Access	OFF 60
To Create an Access Database	OFF 61
To Close an Office File	OFF 62
To Open an Existing Office File	OFF 63
To Exit an Office App	OFF 63
Other Office Apps	**OFF 64**
Outlook	OFF 64
Publisher	OFF 65
OneNote	OFF 66
Renaming, Moving, and Deleting Files	**OFF 67**
To Rename a File	OFF 68
To Move a File	OFF 68
To Delete a File	OFF 69
Microsoft Office and Windows Help	**OFF 70**
To Open the Help Window in an Office App	OFF 70
Moving and Resizing Windows	OFF 70
To Move a Window by Dragging	OFF 70
To Resize a Window by Dragging	OFF 71
Using Office Help	OFF 72
To Obtain Help Using the Search Text Box	OFF 72
Obtaining Help while Working in an Office App	OFF 73
To Obtain Help Using the Tell Me Box	OFF 74
Using the Windows Search Box	OFF 74
To Use the Windows Search Box	OFF 74
Summary	**OFF 75**
Apply Your Knowledge	**OFF 76**
Extend Your Knowledge	**OFF 77**
Expand Your World	**OFF 78**
In the Labs	**OFF 78**

Microsoft **Office 365 & Outlook 2016**

MODULE ONE
Managing Email Messages with Outlook

Objectives	**OUT 1**
Roadmap	OUT 1
Introduction to Outlook	**OUT 2**
Project — Composing and Sending	
Email Messages	**OUT 2**
Setting Up Outlook	**OUT 3**
Parts of an Email Address	OUT 4
To Run Outlook	OUT 5
To Change the Navigation Bar Options	OUT 6
To Open an Outlook Data File	OUT 7
To Set Language Preferences	OUT 9
To Set the Sensitivity Level	
for All New Messages	OUT 10
Composing and Sending Email messages	**OUT 11**
To Compose an Email Message	OUT 11
To Apply a Theme	OUT 14
To Send an Email Message	OUT 15
How Email Messages Travel from	
Sender to Receiver	OUT 15
Working with Incoming Messages	**OUT 16**
To View an Email Message	
in the Reading Pane	OUT 17
To Open an Email Message in a Window	OUT 18
Opening Attachments	OUT 19

To Preview and Save an Attachment	OUT 19
To Open an Attachment	OUT 21
To Print an Email Message	OUT 21
Using the Outlook People Pane	OUT 22
To Change the View of the People Pane	OUT 22
To Reposition the Reading Pane Using	
the Tell Me Search Tool	OUT 24
Responding to Messages	**OUT 26**
To Reply to an Email Message	OUT 26
Message Formats	OUT 29
To Change the Message Format	OUT 29
Checking Spelling and Grammar	OUT 31
To Check the Spelling of a Correctly Typed Word	OUT 31
To Check the Spelling of Misspelled Text	OUT 32
Saving and Closing an Email Message	OUT 33
To Save and Close an Email Message	
without Sending It	OUT 33
To Open a Saved Email Message	OUT 35
To Attach a File to an Email Message	OUT 36
To Set Message Importance and	
Send the Message	OUT 37
To Forward an Email Message	OUT 38
Organizing Messages with Outlook Folders	**OUT 40**
To Create a New Folder in the Inbox Folder	OUT 40
To Move an Email Message to a Folder	OUT 41
Outlook Quick Steps	OUT 43
To Move an Email Message Using Quick Steps	OUT 43
To Delete an Email Message	OUT 45
Working with the Mailbox	OUT 46
To View Mailbox Size	OUT 46
Summary	**OUT 48**
Apply Your Knowledge	**OUT 49**
Extend Your Knowledge	**OUT 50**
Expand Your World: Cloud and Web Technologies	**OUT 51**
In the Labs	**OUT 53**

MODULE TWO
Managing Calendars with Outlook

Objectives	**OUT 57**
Managing Calendars with Outlook	**OUT 57**
Roadmap	OUT 57
Introduction to the Outlook Calendar	**OUT 58**
Project — Appointments, Events, and	
Meetings in Calendar	**OUT 58**
Configuring the Outlook Calendar	OUT 59
Calendar Window	OUT 59
Calendar Items	OUT 60
To Create a Calendar Folder	OUT 61
To Add a City to the Calendar Weather Bar	OUT 64
Navigating the Calendar	OUT 65
To Go to a Specific Date	OUT 65
To Display the Calendar in Work Week View	OUT 66
To Display the Calendar in Week View	OUT 67
To Display the Calendar in Month View	OUT 68
To Display the Calendar in Schedule View	OUT 68
To Add Holidays to the Default Calendar	OUT 70
Creating and Editing Appointments	**OUT 72**
Creating Appointments in the Appointment Area	OUT 73
To Create a One-Time Appointment	
Using the Appointment Area	OUT 73
Organize the Calendar with Color Categories	OUT 75

To Add Color Categories — OUT 75
To Assign a Color Category to an Appointment — OUT 77
Creating Appointments Using the
    Appointment Window — OUT 77
To Create an Appointment
    Using the Appointment Window — OUT 78
Setting Appointment Options — OUT 80
To Change the Status
    of an Appointment — OUT 81
To Set a Reminder for an Appointment — OUT 81
Creating Recurring Appointments — OUT 83
To Set Recurrence Options
    for an Appointment — OUT 83
To Save an Appointment — OUT 84
To Add More Recurring Appointments — OUT 86
Using Natural Language Phrasing — OUT 87
To Create an Appointment Date and
    Time Using Natural Language Phrases — OUT 88
Editing Appointments — OUT 89
To Move an Appointment to a Different
    Time on the Same Day — OUT 89
To Move an Appointment to a
    Different Date — OUT 90
To Delete a Single Occurrence
    of a Recurring Appointment — OUT 91
Scheduling Events — **OUT 92**
To Create a One-Time Event in the
    Appointment Window — OUT 92
To Delete a One-Time Event — OUT 95

To Create a Recurring Event Using the
    Appointment Window — OUT 95
To Move a Recurring Event to a
    Different Day — OUT 98
Scheduling Meetings — **OUT 100**
To Import an iCalendar File — OUT 101
To View Calendars in the Overlay Mode — OUT 102
To View and Dock the Peek Calendar — OUT 103
To Create and Send a Meeting Request — OUT 104
To Change the Time of a Meeting
    and Send an Update — OUT 106
To Reply to a Meeting Request — OUT 107
Printing Calendars in Different Views — **OUT 108**
To Print the Calendar in Weekly
    Calendar Style — OUT 109
To Change the Calendar View
    to List View — OUT 110
To Print the Calendar in List View — OUT 111
Saving and Sharing the Calendar — **OUT 112**
To Save a Calendar as an iCalendar File — OUT 112
To Share a Calendar — OUT 113
Summary — **OUT 114**
Apply Your Knowledge — **OUT 115**
Extend Your Knowledge — **OUT 116**
Expand Your World: Cloud and Web Technologies — **OUT 117**
In the Labs — **OUT 118**

Index — **IND 1**

Productivity Apps for School and Work

Corinne Hoisington

Lochlan keeps track of his class notes, football plays, and internship meetings with OneNote.

Zoe is using the annotation features of Microsoft Edge to take and save web notes for her research paper.

Nori is creating a Sway site to highlight this year's activities for the Student Government Association.

Hunter is adding interactive videos and screen recordings to his PowerPoint resume.

© Rawpixel/Shutterstock.com

Being computer literate no longer means mastery of only Word, Excel, PowerPoint, Outlook, and Access. To become technology power users, Hunter, Nori, Zoe, and Lochlan are exploring Microsoft OneNote, Sway, Mix, and Edge in Office 2016 and Windows 10.

In this Module

Introduction to OneNote 2016 2
Introduction to Sway 6
Introduction to Office Mix 10
Introduction to Microsoft Edge............. 14

Learn to use productivity apps!
Links to companion **Sways**, featuring **videos** with hands-on instructions, are located on www.cengagebrain.com.

Introduction to OneNote 2016

notebook | section tab | To Do tag | screen clipping | note | template | Microsoft OneNote Mobile app | sync | drawing canvas | inked handwriting | Ink to Text

Bottom Line

- OneNote is a note-taking app for your academic and professional life.
- Use OneNote to get organized by gathering your ideas, sketches, webpages, photos, videos, and notes in one place.

As you glance around any classroom, you invariably see paper notebooks and notepads on each desk. Because deciphering and sharing handwritten notes can be a challenge, Microsoft OneNote 2016 replaces physical notebooks, binders, and paper notes with a searchable, digital notebook. OneNote captures your ideas and schoolwork on any device so you can stay organized, share notes, and work with others on projects. Whether you are a student taking class notes as shown in **Figure 1** or an employee taking notes in company meetings, OneNote is the one place to keep notes for all of your projects.

Figure 1: OneNote 2016 notebook

Each **notebook** is divided into sections, also called **section tabs**, by subject or topic.

Use **To Do tags**, icons that help you keep track of your assignments and other tasks.

Type on a page to add a **note**, a small window that contains text or other types of information.

Personalize a page with a **template**, or stationery.

Write or draw directly on the page using drawing tools.

Pages can include pictures such as **screen clippings**, images from any part of a computer screen.

Attach files and enter equations so you have everything you need in one place.

Creating a OneNote Notebook

OneNote is divided into sections similar to those in a spiral-bound notebook. Each OneNote notebook contains sections, pages, and other notebooks. You can use One-Note for school, business, and personal projects. Store information for each type of project in different notebooks to keep your tasks separate, or use any other organization that suits you. OneNote is flexible enough to adapt to the way you want to work.

When you create a notebook, it contains a blank page with a plain white background by default, though you can use templates, or stationery, to apply designs in categories such as Academic, Business, Decorative, and Planners. Start typing or use the buttons on the Insert tab to insert notes, which are small resizable windows that can contain text, equations, tables, on-screen writing, images, audio and video recordings, to-do lists, file attachments, and file printouts. Add as many notes as you need to each page.

Learn to use OneNote!

Links to companion **Sways**, featuring **videos** with hands-on instructions, are located on www.cengagebrain.com.

Syncing a Notebook to the Cloud

OneNote saves your notes every time you make a change in a notebook. To make sure you can access your notebooks with a laptop, tablet, or smartphone wherever you are, OneNote uses cloud-based storage, such as OneDrive or SharePoint. **Microsoft OneNote Mobile app**, a lightweight version of OneNote 2016 shown in **Figure 2**, is available for free in the Windows Store, Google Play for Android devices, and the AppStore for iOS devices.

If you have a Microsoft account, OneNote saves your notes on OneDrive automatically for all your mobile devices and computers, which is called **syncing**. For example, you can use OneNote to take notes on your laptop during class, and then open OneNote on your phone to study later. To use a notebook stored on your computer with your OneNote Mobile app, move the notebook to OneDrive. You can quickly share notebook content with other people using OneDrive.

Figure 2: Microsoft OneNote Mobile app

Notes synced to OneDrive and displayed on a smartphone

Taking Notes

Use OneNote pages to organize your notes by class and topic or lecture. Beyond simple typed notes, OneNote stores drawings, converts handwriting to searchable text and mathematical sketches to equations, and records audio and video.

OneNote includes drawing tools that let you sketch freehand drawings such as biological cell diagrams and financial supply-and-demand charts. As shown in **Figure 3**, the Draw tab on the ribbon provides these drawing tools along with shapes so you can insert diagrams and other illustrations to represent your ideas. When you draw on a page, OneNote creates a **drawing canvas**, which is a container for shapes and lines.

On the Job Now

OneNote is ideal for taking notes during meetings, whether you are recording minutes, documenting a discussion, sketching product diagrams, or listing follow-up items. Use a meeting template to add pages with content appropriate for meetings.

Figure 3: Tools on the Draw tab

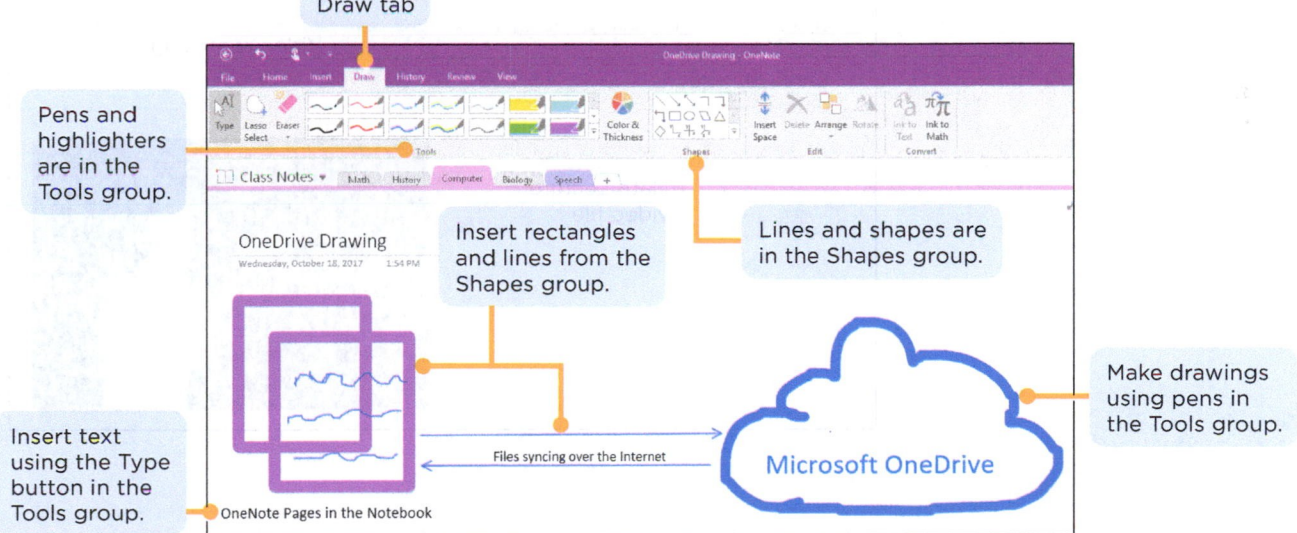

Draw tab

Pens and highlighters are in the Tools group.

Insert rectangles and lines from the Shapes group.

Lines and shapes are in the Shapes group.

Insert text using the Type button in the Tools group.

Make drawings using pens in the Tools group.

Converting Handwriting to Text

When you use a pen tool to write on a notebook page, the text you enter is called **inked handwriting**. OneNote can convert inked handwriting to typed text when you use the **Ink to Text** button in the Convert group on the Draw tab, as shown in **Figure 4**. After OneNote converts the handwriting to text, you can use the Search box to find terms in the converted text or any other note in your notebooks.

Figure 4: Converting handwriting to text

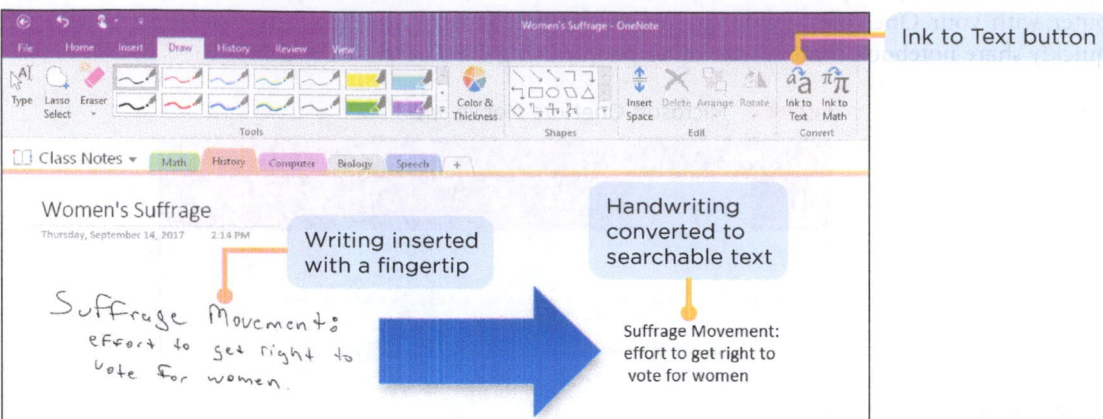

Ink to Text button

Women's Suffrage
Thursday, September 14, 2017 2:14 PM

Writing inserted with a fingertip

Suffrage Movement: effort to get right to vote for women.

Handwriting converted to searchable text

Suffrage Movement: effort to get right to vote for women

Recording a Lecture

If your computer or mobile device has a microphone or camera, OneNote can record the audio or video from a lecture or business meeting as shown in **Figure 5**. When you record a lecture (with your instructor's permission), you can follow along, take regular notes at your own pace, and review the video recording later. You can control the start, pause, and stop motions of the recording when you play back the recording of your notes.

Figure 5: Video inserted in a notebook

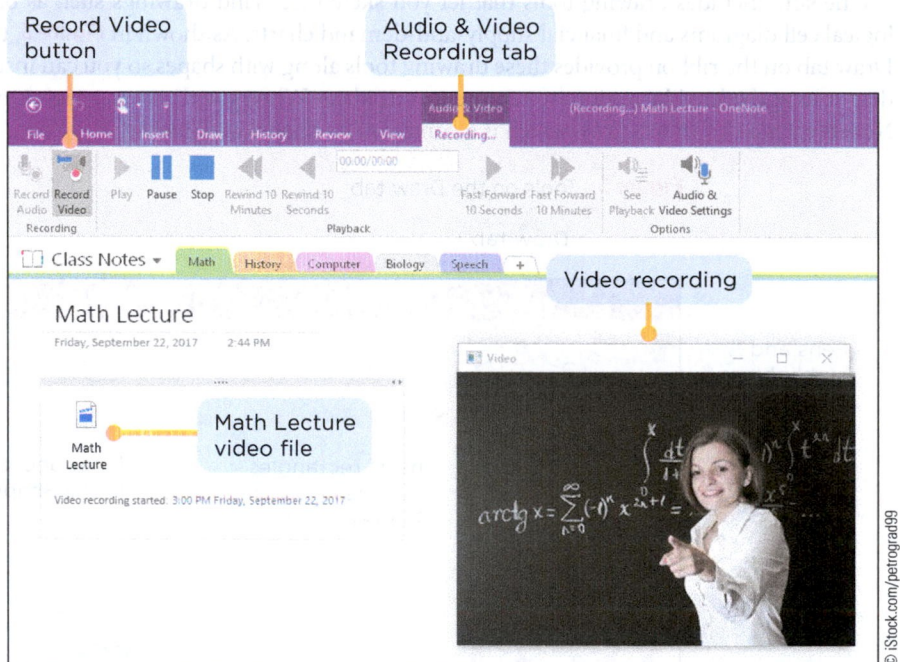

Record Video button

Audio & Video Recording tab

Video recording

Math Lecture
Friday, September 22, 2017 2:44 PM

Math Lecture video file

Video recording started: 3:00 PM Friday, September 22, 2017

Try This Now

Learn to use OneNote!
Links to companion **Sways**, featuring **videos** with hands-on instructions, are located on www.cengagebrain.com.

1: Taking Notes for a Week

As a student, you can get organized by using OneNote to take detailed notes in your classes. Perform the following tasks:

    a. Create a new OneNote notebook on your Microsoft OneDrive account (the default location for new notebooks). Name the notebook with your first name followed by "Notes," as in **Caleb Notes**.

    b. Create four section tabs, each with a different class name.

    c. Take detailed notes in those classes for one week. Be sure to include notes, drawings, and other types of content.

    d. Sync your notes with your OneDrive. Submit your assignment in the format specified by your instructor.

2: Using OneNote to Organize a Research Paper

You have a research paper due on the topic of three habits of successful students. Use OneNote to organize your research. Perform the following tasks:

    a. Create a new OneNote notebook on your Microsoft OneDrive account. Name the notebook **Success Research**.

    b. Create three section tabs with the following names:

- **Take Detailed Notes**
- **Be Respectful in Class**
- **Come to Class Prepared**

    c. On the web, research the topics and find three sources for each section. Copy a sentence from each source and paste the sentence into the appropriate section. When you paste the sentence, OneNote inserts it in a note with a link to the source.

    d. Sync your notes with your OneDrive. Submit your assignment in the format specified by your instructor.

3: Planning Your Career

Note: This activity requires a webcam or built-in video camera on any type of device.

Consider an occupation that interests you. Using OneNote, examine the responsibilities, education requirements, potential salary, and employment outlook of a specific career. Perform the following tasks:

    a. Create a new OneNote notebook on your Microsoft OneDrive account. Name the notebook with your first name followed by a career title, such as **Kara - App Developer**.

    b. Create four section tabs with the names **Responsibilities, Education Requirements, Median Salary**, and **Employment Outlook**.

    c. Research the responsibilities of your career path. Using OneNote, record a short video (approximately 30 seconds) of yourself explaining the responsibilities of your career path. Place the video in the Responsibilities section.

    d. On the web, research the educational requirements for your career path and find two appropriate sources. Copy a paragraph from each source and paste them into the appropriate section. When you paste a paragraph, OneNote inserts it in a note with a link to the source.

    e. Research the median salary for a single year for this career. Create a mathematical equation in the Median Salary section that multiplies the amount of the median salary times 20 years to calculate how much you will possibly earn.

    f. For the Employment Outlook section, research the outlook for your career path. Take at least four notes about what you find when researching the topic.

    g. Sync your notes with your OneDrive. Submit your assignment in the format specified by your instructor.

Introduction to Sway

Sway site | responsive design | Storyline | card | Creative Commons license | animation emphasis effects | Docs.com

Expressing your ideas in a presentation typically means creating PowerPoint slides or a Word document. Microsoft Sway gives you another way to engage an audience. Sway is a free Microsoft tool available at Sway.com or as an app in Office 365. Using Sway, you can combine text, images, videos, and social media in a website called a **Sway site** that you can share and display on any device. To get started, you create a digital story on a web-based canvas without borders, slides, cells, or page breaks. A Sway site organizes the text, images, and video into a **responsive design**, which means your content adapts perfectly to any screen size as shown in **Figure 6**. You store a Sway site in the cloud on OneDrive using a free Microsoft account.

Figure 6: Sway site with responsive design

You can display a Sway presentation in a web browser.

Sway uses responsive design to make sure pages fit perfectly on any device.

© iStock.com/marinello, © iStock.com/marekuliasz

Creating a Sway Presentation

You can use Sway to build a digital flyer, a club newsletter, a vacation blog, an informational site, a digital art portfolio, or a new product rollout. After you select your topic and sign into Sway with your Microsoft account, a **Storyline** opens, providing tools and a work area for composing your digital story. See **Figure 7**. Each story can include text, images, and videos. You create a Sway by adding text and media content into a Storyline section, or **card**. To add pictures, videos, or documents, select a card in the left pane and then select the Insert Content button. The first card in a Sway presentation contains a title and background image.

Figure 7: Creating a Sway site

Design and create Sway presentations.

Share and play published Sway sites.

Arrange content in a Storyline, which contains all the text, pictures, videos, and other media in a Sway presentation.

To add content, select a card, which is designed to hold a particular type of information.

After selecting a card, click the Insert Content button to add the content to the Sway presentation.

Adding Content to Build a Story

As you work, Sway searches the Internet to help you find relevant images, videos, tweets, and other content from online sources such as Bing, YouTube, Twitter, and Facebook. You can drag content from the search results right into the Storyline. In addition, you can upload your own images and videos directly in the presentation. For example, if you are creating a Sway presentation about the market for commercial drones, Sway suggests content to incorporate into the presentation by displaying it in the left pane as search results. The search results include drone images tagged with a **Creative Commons license** at online sources as shown in **Figure 8**. A Creative Commons license is a public copyright license that allows the free distribution of an otherwise copyrighted work. In addition, you can specify the source of the media. For example, you can add your own Facebook or OneNote pictures and videos in Sway without leaving the app.

On the Job Now

If you have a Microsoft Word document containing an outline of your business content, drag the outline into Sway to create a card for each topic.

Figure 8: Images in Sway search results

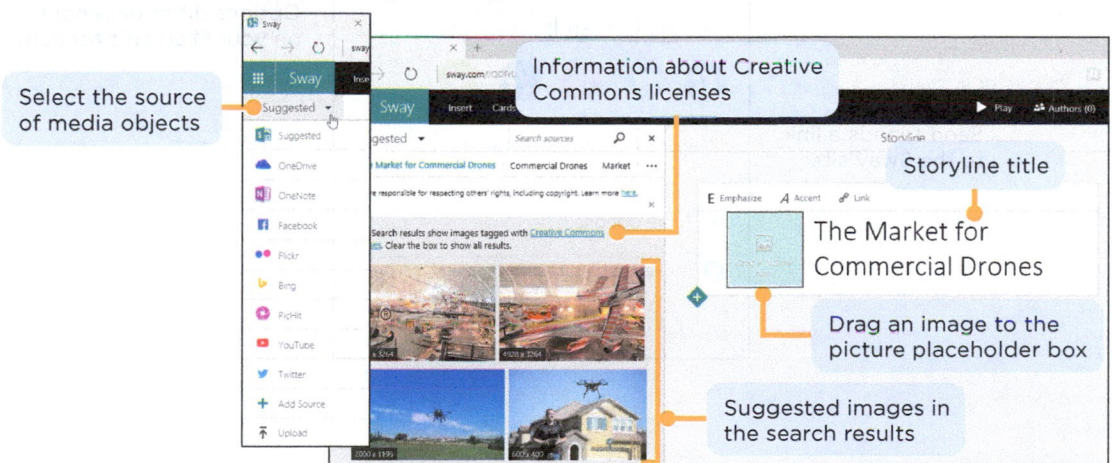

Select the source of media objects

Information about Creative Commons licenses

Storyline title

The Market for Commercial Drones

Drag an image to the picture placeholder box

Suggested images in the search results

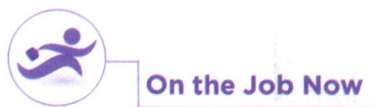

Designing a Sway

Sway professionally designs your Storyline content by resizing background images and fonts to fit your display, and by floating text, animating media, embedding video, and removing images as a page scrolls out of view. Sway also evaluates the images in your Storyline and suggests a color palette based on colors that appear in your photos. Use the Design button to display tools including color palettes, font choices, **animation emphasis effects**, and style templates to provide a personality for a Sway presentation. Instead of creating your own design, you can click the Remix button, which randomly selects unique designs for your Sway site.

Publishing a Sway

Use the Play button to display your finished Sway presentation as a website. The Address bar includes a unique web address where others can view your Sway site. As the author, you can edit a published Sway site by clicking the Edit button (pencil icon) on the Sway toolbar.

Sharing a Sway

When you are ready to share your Sway website, you have several options as shown in **Figure 9**. Use the Share slider button to share the Sway site publically or keep it private. If you add the Sway site to the Microsoft **Docs.com** public gallery, anyone worldwide can use Bing, Google, or other search engines to find, view, and share your Sway site. You can also share your Sway site using Facebook, Twitter, Google+, Yammer, and other social media sites. Link your presentation to any webpage or email the link to your audience. Sway can also generate a code for embedding the link within another webpage.

Figure 9: Sharing a Sway site

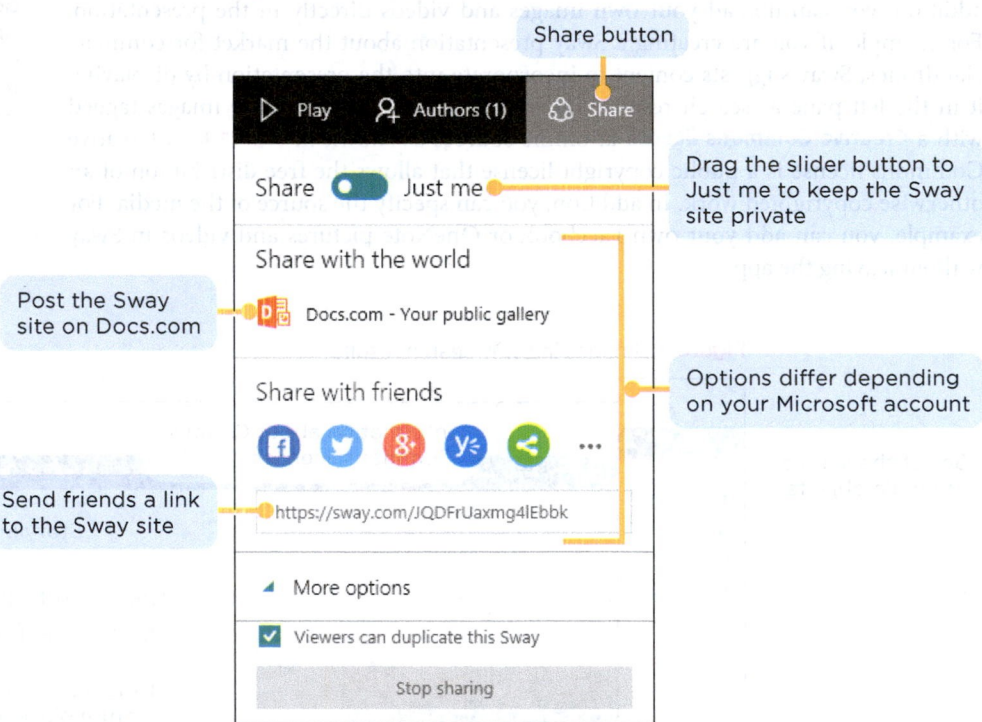

Try This Now

Learn to use Sway!
Links to companion **Sways**, featuring **videos** with hands-on instructions, are located on www.cengagebrain.com.

1: Creating a Sway Resume

Sway is a digital storytelling app. Create a Sway resume to share the skills, job experiences, and achievements you have that match the requirements of a future job interest. Perform the following tasks:

   a. Create a new presentation in Sway to use as a digital resume. Title the Sway Storyline with your full name and then select a background image.
   b. Create three separate sections titled **Academic Background, Work Experience**, and **Skills**, and insert text, a picture, and a paragraph or bulleted points in each section. Be sure to include your own picture.
   c. Add a fourth section that includes a video about your school that you find online.
   d. Customize the design of your presentation.
   e. Submit your assignment link in the format specified by your instructor.

2: Creating an Online Sway Newsletter

Newsletters are designed to capture the attention of their target audience. Using Sway, create a newsletter for a club, organization, or your favorite music group. Perform the following tasks:

   a. Create a new presentation in Sway to use as a digital newsletter for a club, organization, or your favorite music group. Provide a title for the Sway Storyline and select an appropriate background image.
   b. Select three separate sections with appropriate titles, such as Upcoming Events. In each section, insert text, a picture, and a paragraph or bulleted points.
   c. Add a fourth section that includes a video about your selected topic.
   d. Customize the design of your presentation.
   e. Submit your assignment link in the format specified by your instructor.

3: Creating and Sharing a Technology Presentation

To place a Sway presentation in the hands of your entire audience, you can share a link to the Sway presentation. Create a Sway presentation on a new technology and share it with your class. Perform the following tasks:

   a. Create a new presentation in Sway about a cutting-edge technology topic. Provide a title for the Sway Storyline and select a background image.
   b. Create four separate sections about your topic, and include text, a picture, and a paragraph in each section.
   c. Add a fifth section that includes a video about your topic.
   d. Customize the design of your presentation.
   e. Share the link to your Sway with your classmates and submit your assignment link in the format specified by your instructor.

Introduction to Office Mix

add-in | clip | slide recording | Slide Notes | screen recording | free-response quiz

To enliven business meetings and lectures, Microsoft adds a new dimension to presentations with a powerful toolset called Office Mix, a free add-in for PowerPoint. (An **add-in** is software that works with an installed app to extend its features.) Using Office Mix, you can record yourself on video, capture still and moving images on your desktop, and insert interactive elements such as quizzes and live webpages directly into PowerPoint slides. When you post the finished presentation to OneDrive, Office Mix provides a link you can share with friends and colleagues. Anyone with an Internet connection and a web browser can watch a published Office Mix presentation, such as the one in **Figure 10**, on a computer or mobile device.

Figure 10: Office Mix presentation

Adding Office Mix to PowerPoint

To get started, you create an Office Mix account at the website mix.office.com using an email address or a Facebook or Google account. Next, you download and install the Office Mix add-in (see **Figure 11**). Office Mix appears as a new tab named Mix on the PowerPoint ribbon in versions of Office 2013 and Office 2016 running on personal computers (PCs).

Figure 11: Getting started with Office Mix

Capturing Video Clips

A **clip** is a short segment of audio, such as music, or video. After finishing the content on a PowerPoint slide, you can use Office Mix to add a video clip to animate or illustrate the content. Office Mix creates video clips in two ways: by recording live action on a webcam and by capturing screen images and movements. If your computer has a webcam, you can record yourself and annotate the slide to create a **slide recording** as shown in **Figure 12**.

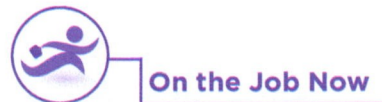
Figure 12: Making a slide recording

Record your voice; also record video if your computer has a camera.

Use the Slide Notes button to display notes for your narration.

For best results, look directly at your webcam while recording video.

Choose a video and audio device to record images and sound.

Use inking tools to write and draw on the slide as you record.

When you are making a slide recording, you can record your spoken narration at the same time. The **Slide Notes** feature works like a teleprompter to help you focus on your presentation content instead of memorizing your narration. Use the Inking tools to make annotations or add highlighting using different pen types and colors. After finishing a recording, edit the video in PowerPoint to trim the length or set playback options.

The second way to create a video is to capture on-screen images and actions with or without a voiceover. This method is ideal if you want to show how to use your favorite website or demonstrate an app such as OneNote. To share your screen with an audience, select the part of the screen you want to show in the video. Office Mix captures everything that happens in that area to create a **screen recording**, as shown in **Figure 13**. Office Mix inserts the screen recording as a video in the slide.

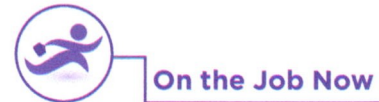
Figure 13: Making a screen recording

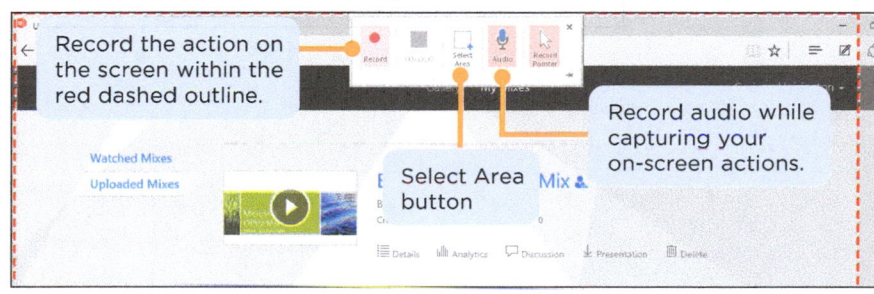

Record the action on the screen within the red dashed outline.

Record audio while capturing your on-screen actions.

Select Area button

Inserting Quizzes, Live Webpages, and Apps

To enhance and assess audience understanding, make your slides interactive by adding quizzes, live webpages, and apps. Quizzes give immediate feedback to the user as shown in **Figure 14**. Office Mix supports several quiz formats, including a **free-response quiz** similar to a short answer quiz, and true/false, multiple-choice, and multiple-response formats.

Figure 14: Creating an interactive quiz

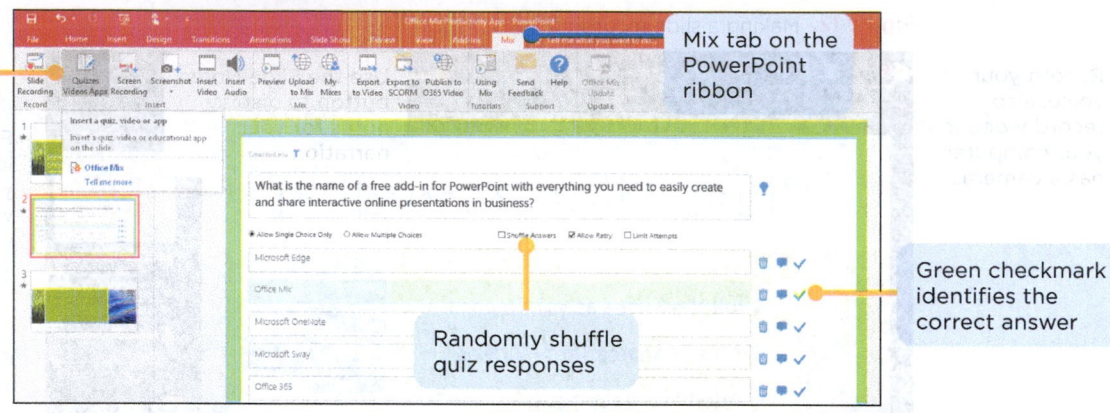

Quizzes Videos Apps button

Mix tab on the PowerPoint ribbon

Green checkmark identifies the correct answer

Randomly shuffle quiz responses

Sharing an Office Mix Presentation

When you complete your work with Office Mix, upload the presentation to your personal Office Mix dashboard as shown in **Figure 15**. Users of PCs, Macs, iOS devices, and Android devices can access and play Office Mix presentations. The Office Mix dashboard displays built-in analytics that include the quiz results and how much time viewers spent on each slide. You can play completed Office Mix presentations online or download them as movies.

Figure 15: Sharing an Office Mix presentation

Office Mix dashboard displays the quiz analytics.

Try This Now

1: Creating an Office Mix Tutorial for OneNote

Learn to use Office Mix!
Links to companion **Sways**, featuring **videos** with hands-on instructions, are located on www.cengagebrain.com.

Note: This activity requires a microphone on your computer.

Office Mix makes it easy to record screens and their contents. Create PowerPoint slides with an Office Mix screen recording to show OneNote 2016 features. Perform the following tasks:

a. Create a PowerPoint presentation with the Ion Boardroom template. Create an opening slide with the title **My Favorite OneNote Features** and enter your name in the subtitle.
b. Create three additional slides, each titled with a new feature of OneNote. Open OneNote and use the Mix tab in PowerPoint to capture three separate screen recordings that teach your favorite features.
c. Add a fifth slide that quizzes the user with a multiple-choice question about OneNote and includes four responses. Be sure to insert a checkmark indicating the correct response.
d. Upload the completed presentation to your Office Mix dashboard and share the link with your instructor.
e. Submit your assignment link in the format specified by your instructor.

2: Teaching Augmented Reality with Office Mix

Note: This activity requires a webcam or built-in video camera on your computer.

A local elementary school has asked you to teach augmented reality to its students using Office Mix. Perform the following tasks:

a. Research augmented reality using your favorite online search tools.
b. Create a PowerPoint presentation with the Frame template. Create an opening slide with the title **Augmented Reality** and enter your name in the subtitle.
c. Create a slide with four bullets summarizing your research of augmented reality. Create a 20-second slide recording of yourself providing a quick overview of augmented reality.
d. Create another slide with a 30-second screen recording of a video about augmented reality from a site such as YouTube or another video-sharing site.
e. Add a final slide that quizzes the user with a true/false question about augmented reality. Be sure to insert a checkmark indicating the correct response.
f. Upload the completed presentation to your Office Mix dashboard and share the link with your instructor.
g. Submit your assignment link in the format specified by your instructor.

3: Marketing a Travel Destination with Office Mix

Note: This activity requires a webcam or built-in video camera on your computer.

To convince your audience to travel to a particular city, create a slide presentation marketing any city in the world using a slide recording, screen recording, and a quiz. Perform the following tasks:

a. Create a PowerPoint presentation with any template. Create an opening slide with the title of the city you are marketing as a travel destination and your name in the subtitle.
b. Create a slide with four bullets about the featured city. Create a 30-second slide recording of yourself explaining why this city is the perfect vacation destination.
c. Create another slide with a 20-second screen recording of a travel video about the city from a site such as YouTube or another video-sharing site.
d. Add a final slide that quizzes the user with a multiple-choice question about the featured city with five responses. Be sure to include a checkmark indicating the correct response.
e. Upload the completed presentation to your Office Mix dashboard and share your link with your instructor.
f. Submit your assignment link in the format specified by your instructor.

Introduction to Microsoft Edge

Reading view | Hub | Cortana | Web Note | Inking | sandbox

Bottom Line

- Microsoft Edge is the name of the new web browser built into Windows 10.
- Microsoft Edge allows you to search the web faster, take web notes, read webpages without distractions, and get instant assistance from Cortana.

Microsoft Edge is the default web browser developed for the Windows 10 operating system as a replacement for Internet Explorer. Unlike its predecessor, Edge lets you write on webpages, read webpages without advertisements and other distractions, and search for information using a virtual personal assistant. The Edge interface is clean and basic, as shown in **Figure 16**, meaning you can pay more attention to the webpage content.

Figure 16: Microsoft Edge tools

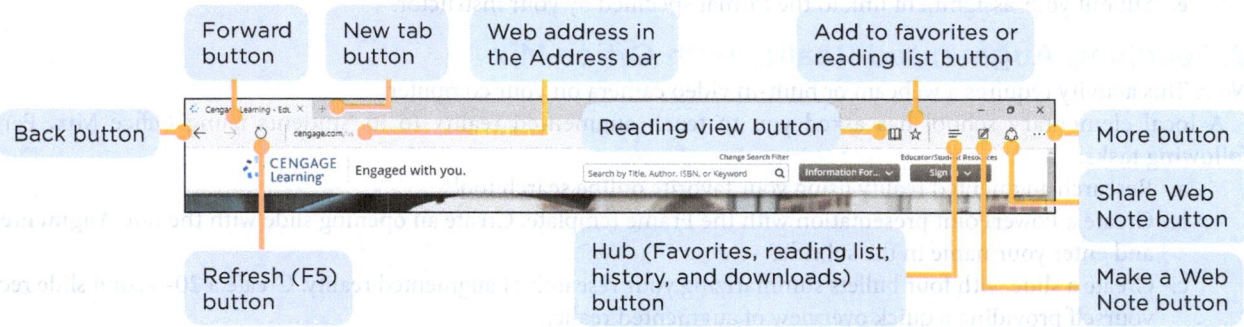

Forward button · New tab button · Web address in the Address bar · Add to favorites or reading list button · Back button · Reading view button · More button · Refresh (F5) button · Hub (Favorites, reading list, history, and downloads) button · Share Web Note button · Make a Web Note button

Learn to use Edge!

Links to companion **Sways**, featuring **videos** with hands-on instructions, are located on www.cengagebrain.com.

Browsing the Web with Microsoft Edge

One of the fastest browsers available, Edge allows you to type search text directly in the Address bar. As you view the resulting webpage, you can switch to **Reading view**, which is available for most news and research sites, to eliminate distracting advertisements. For example, if you are catching up on technology news online, the webpage might be difficult to read due to a busy layout cluttered with ads. Switch to Reading view to refresh the page and remove the original page formatting, ads, and menu sidebars to read the article distraction-free.

Consider the **Hub** in Microsoft Edge as providing one-stop access to all the things you collect on the web, such as your favorite websites, reading list, surfing history, and downloaded files.

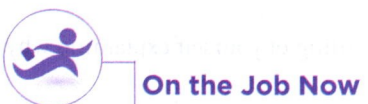

On the Job Now

Businesses started adopting Internet Explorer more than 20 years ago simply to view webpages. Today, Microsoft Edge has a different purpose: to promote interaction with the web and share its contents with colleagues.

Locating Information with Cortana

Cortana, the Windows 10 virtual assistant, plays an important role in Microsoft Edge. After you turn on Cortana, it appears as an animated circle in the Address bar when you might need assistance, as shown in the restaurant website in **Figure 17**. When you click the Cortana icon, a pane slides in from the right of the browser window to display detailed information about the restaurant, including maps and reviews. Cortana can also assist you in defining words, finding the weather, suggesting coupons for shopping, updating stock market information, and calculating math.

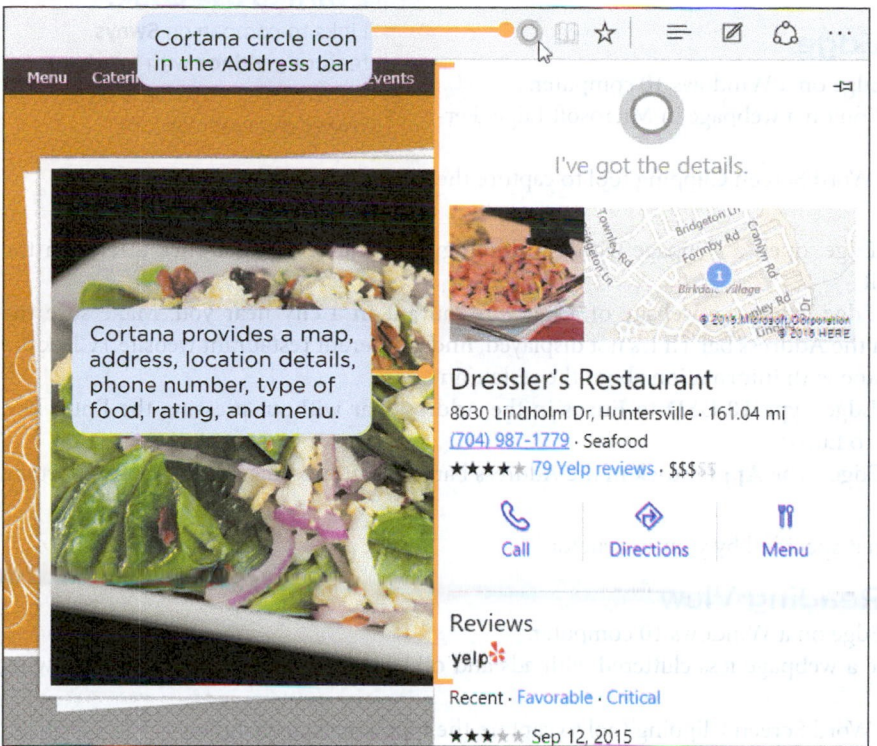

Annotating Webpages

One of the most impressive Microsoft Edge features are the **Web Note** tools, which you use to write on a webpage or to highlight text. When you click the Make a Web Note button, an **Inking** toolbar appears, as shown in **Figure 18**, that provides writing and drawing tools. These tools include an eraser, a pen, and a highlighter with different colors. You can also insert a typed note and copy a screen image (called a screen clipping). You can draw with a pointing device, fingertip, or stylus using different pen colors. Whether you add notes to a recipe, annotate sources for a research paper, or select a product while shopping online, the Web Note tools can enhance your productivity. After you complete your notes, click the Save button to save the annotations to OneNote, your Favorites list, or your Reading list. You can share the inked page with others using the Share Web Note button.

On the Job Now

To enhance security, Microsoft Edge runs in a partial sandbox, an arrangement that prevents attackers from gaining control of your computer. Browsing within the **sandbox** protects computer resources and information from hackers.

Figure 18: Web Note tools in Microsoft Edge

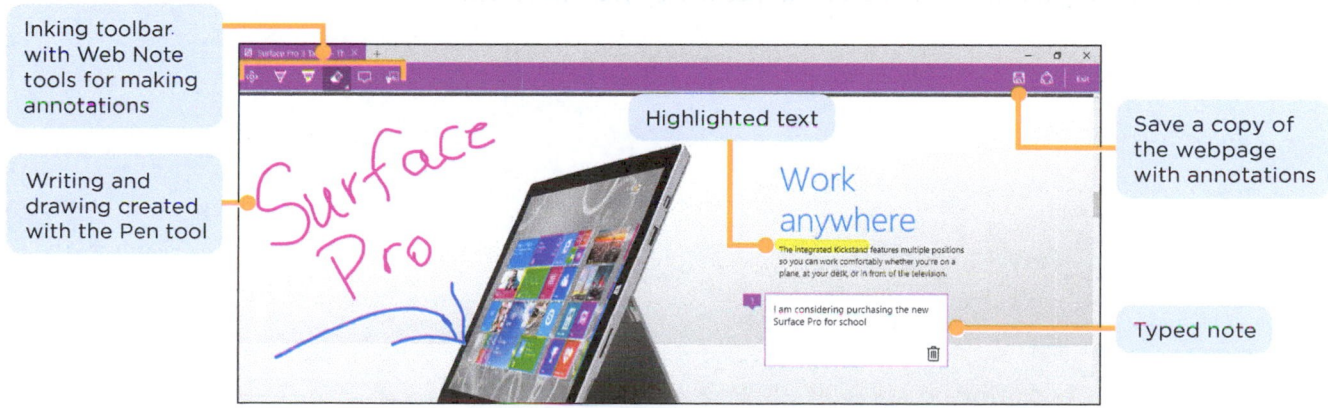

Try This Now

Learn to use Edge!
Links to companion **Sways**, featuring **videos** with hands-on instructions, are located on www.cengagebrain.com.

1: Using Cortana in Microsoft Edge

Note: This activity requires using Microsoft Edge on a Windows 10 computer.

Cortana can assist you in finding information on a webpage in Microsoft Edge. Perform the following tasks:

a. Create a Word document using the Word Screen Clipping tool to capture the following screenshots.

- Screenshot A—Using Microsoft Edge, open a webpage with a technology news article. Right-click a term in the article and ask Cortana to define it.
- Screenshot B—Using Microsoft Edge, open the website of a fancy restaurant in a city near you. Make sure the Cortana circle icon is displayed in the Address bar. (If it's not displayed, find a different restaurant website.) Click the Cortana circle icon to display a pane with information about the restaurant.
- Screenshot C—Using Microsoft Edge, type **10 USD to Euros** in the Address bar without pressing the Enter key. Cortana converts the U.S. dollars to Euros.
- Screenshot D—Using Microsoft Edge, type **Apple stock** in the Address bar without pressing the Enter key. Cortana displays the current stock quote.

b. Submit your assignment in the format specified by your instructor.

2: Viewing Online News with Reading View

Note: This activity requires using Microsoft Edge on a Windows 10 computer.

Reading view in Microsoft Edge can make a webpage less cluttered with ads and other distractions. Perform the following tasks:

a. Create a Word document using the Word Screen Clipping tool to capture the following screenshots.

- Screenshot A—Using Microsoft Edge, open the website **mashable.com**. Open a technology article. Click the Reading view button to display an ad-free page that uses only basic text formatting.
- Screenshot B—Using Microsoft Edge, open the website **bbc.com**. Open any news article. Click the Reading view button to display an ad-free page that uses only basic text formatting.
- Screenshot C—Make three types of annotations (Pen, Highlighter, and Add a typed note) on the BBC article page displayed in Reading view.

b. Submit your assignment in the format specified by your instructor.

3: Inking with Microsoft Edge

Note: This activity requires using Microsoft Edge on a Windows 10 computer.

Microsoft Edge provides many annotation options to record your ideas. Perform the following tasks:

a. Open the website **wolframalpha.com** in the Microsoft Edge browser. Wolfram Alpha is a well-respected academic search engine. Type **US$100 1965 dollars in 2015** in the Wolfram Alpha search text box and press the Enter key.

b. Click the Make a Web Note button to display the Web Note tools. Using the Pen tool, draw a circle around the result on the webpage. Save the page to OneNote.

c. In the Wolfram Alpha search text box, type the name of the city closest to where you live and press the Enter key. Using the Highlighter tool, highlight at least three interesting results. Add a note and then type a sentence about what you learned about this city. Save the page to OneNote. Share your OneNote notebook with your instructor.

d. Submit your assignment link in the format specified by your instructor.

Office 2016 and Windows 10: Essential Concepts and Skills

Objectives

You will have mastered the material in this module when you can:

- Use a touch screen
- Perform basic mouse operations
- Start Windows and sign in to an account
- Identify the objects on the Windows 10 desktop
- Identify the apps in and versions of Microsoft Office 2016
- Run an app
- Identify the components of the Microsoft Office ribbon

- Create folders
- Save files
- Change screen resolution
- Perform basic tasks in Microsoft Office apps
- Manage files
- Use Microsoft Office Help and Windows Help

This introductory module covers features and functions common to Office 2016 apps, as well as the basics of Windows 10.

Roadmap

In this module, you will learn how to perform basic tasks in Windows and the Office apps. The following roadmap identifies general activities you will perform as you progress through this module:

1. SIGN IN to an account
2. USE WINDOWS
3. USE Office APPS
4. FILE and Folder MANAGEMENT
5. SWITCH between APPS

6. **SAVE** and Manage **FILES**

7. **CHANGE SCREEN RESOLUTION**

8. **EXIT** Office **APPS**

9. **USE ADDITIONAL** Office **APPS**

10. **USE** Office and Windows **HELP**

At the beginning of the step instructions throughout each module, you will see an abbreviated form of this roadmap. The abbreviated roadmap uses colors to indicate module progress: gray means the module is beyond that activity, blue means the task being shown is covered in that activity, and black means that activity is yet to be covered. For example, the following abbreviated roadmap indicates the module would be showing a task in the USE APPS activity.

1 SIGN IN | 2 USE WINDOWS | **3 USE APPS** | 4 FILE MANAGEMENT | 5 SWITCH APPS | 6 SAVE FILES

7 CHANGE SCREEN RESOLUTION | 8 EXIT APPS | 9 USE ADDITIONAL APPS | 10 USE HELP

Use the abbreviated roadmap as a progress guide while you read or step through the instructions in this module.

Introduction to the Windows 10 Operating System

Windows 10 is the newest version of Microsoft Windows, which is a popular and widely used operating system (Figure 1). An **operating system (OS)** is a set of programs that coordinate all the activities among computer or mobile device hardware.

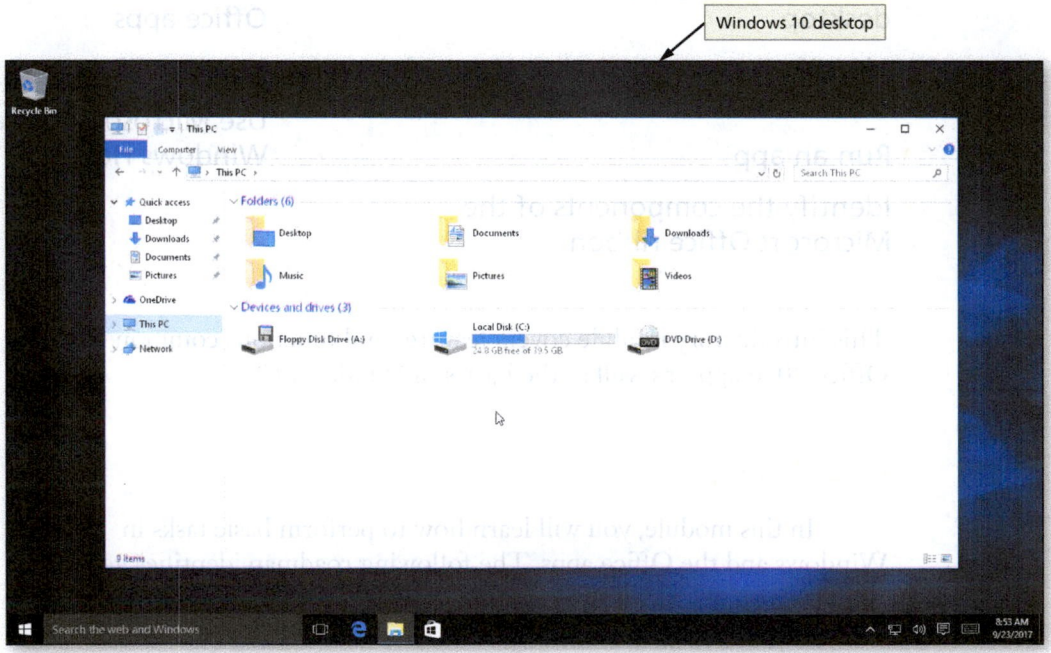

Figure 1

The Windows operating system simplifies the process of working with documents and apps by organizing the manner in which you interact with the computer. Windows is used to run apps. An application, or **app**, consists of programs designed to make users more productive and/or assist them with personal tasks, such as word processing or browsing the web.

Using a Touch Screen and a Mouse

Windows users who have computers or devices with touch screen capability can interact with the screen using gestures. A **gesture** is a motion you make on a touch screen with the tip of one or more fingers or your hand. Touch screens are convenient because they do not require a separate device for input. Table 1 presents common ways to interact with a touch screen.

Table 1 Touch Screen Gestures			
Motion	**Description**	**Common Uses**	**Equivalent Mouse Operation**
Tap	Quickly touch and release one finger one time.	Activate a link (built-in connection). Press a button. Run a program or an app.	Click
Double-tap	Quickly touch and release one finger two times.	Run a program or an app. Zoom in (show a smaller area on the screen, so that contents appear larger) at the location of the double-tap.	Double-click
Press and hold	Press and hold one finger to cause an action to occur, or until an action occurs.	Display a shortcut menu (immediate access to allowable actions). Activate a mode enabling you to move an item with one finger to a new location.	Right-click
Drag, or slide	Press and hold one finger on an object and then move the finger to the new location.	Move an item around the screen. Scroll.	Drag
Swipe	Press and hold one finger and then move the finger horizontally or vertically on the screen.	Select an object. Swipe from edge to display a bar such as the Action Center, Apps bar, and Navigation bar (all discussed later).	Drag
Stretch	Move two fingers apart.	Zoom in (show a smaller area on the screen, so that contents appear larger).	None
Pinch	Move two fingers together.	Zoom out (show a larger area on the screen, so that contents appear smaller).	None

Windows users who do not have touch screen capabilities typically work with a mouse that has at least two buttons. For a right-handed user, the left button usually is

If you are using your finger on a touch screen and are having difficulty completing the steps in this module, consider using a stylus. Many people find it easier to be precise with a stylus than with a finger. In addition, with a stylus you see the pointer. If you still are having trouble completing the steps with a stylus, try using a mouse.

CONSIDER THIS

BTW
Pointer
If you are using a touch screen, the pointer may not appear on the screen as you perform touch gestures. The pointer will reappear when you begin using the mouse.

the primary mouse button, and the right mouse button is the secondary mouse button. Left-handed people, however, can reverse the function of these buttons.

Table 2 explains how to perform a variety of mouse operations. Some apps also use keys in combination with the mouse to perform certain actions. For example, when you hold down the CTRL key while rolling the mouse wheel, text on the screen may become larger or smaller based on the direction you roll the wheel. The function of the mouse buttons and the wheel varies depending on the app.

Table 2 Mouse Operations

Operation	Mouse Action	Example*	Equivalent Touch Gesture
Point	Move the mouse until the pointer on the desktop is positioned on the item of choice.	Position the pointer on the screen.	None
Click	Press and release the primary mouse button, which usually is the left mouse button.	Select or deselect items on the screen or run an app or app feature.	Tap
Right-click	Press and release the secondary mouse button, which usually is the right mouse button.	Display a shortcut menu.	Press and hold
Double-click	Quickly press and release the primary mouse button twice without moving the mouse.	Run an app or app feature.	Double-tap
Triple-click	Quickly press and release the primary mouse button three times without moving the mouse.	Select a paragraph.	Triple-tap
Drag	Point to an item, hold down the primary mouse button, move the item to the desired location on the screen, and then release the mouse button.	Move an object from one location to another or draw pictures.	Drag or slide
Right-drag	Point to an item, hold down the right mouse button, move the item to the desired location on the screen, and then release the right mouse button.	Display a shortcut menu after moving an object from one location to another.	Press and hold, then drag
Rotate wheel	Roll the wheel forward or backward.	Scroll vertically (up and down).	Swipe
Free-spin wheel	Whirl the wheel forward or backward so that it spins freely on its own.	Scroll through many pages in seconds.	Swipe
Press wheel	Press the wheel button while moving the mouse.	Scroll continuously.	None
Tilt wheel	Press the wheel toward the right or left.	Scroll horizontally (left and right).	None
Press thumb button	Press the button on the side of the mouse with your thumb.	Move forward or backward through webpages and/or control media, games, etc.	None

*Note: The examples presented in this column are discussed as they are demonstrated in this chapter.

Scrolling

A **scroll bar** is a horizontal or vertical bar that appears when the contents of an area may not be visible completely on the screen (Figure 2). A scroll bar contains **scroll arrows** and a **scroll box** that enable you to view areas that currently cannot be seen on the screen. Clicking the up and down scroll arrows moves the screen content up or down one line. You also can click above or below the scroll box to move up or down a section, or drag the scroll box up or down to move to a specific location.

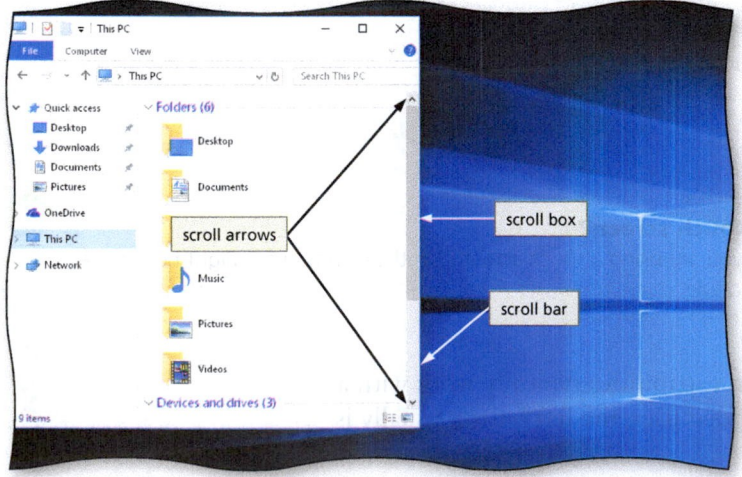

Figure 2

Keyboard Shortcuts

In many cases, you can use the keyboard instead of the mouse to accomplish a task. To perform tasks using the keyboard, you press one or more keyboard keys, sometimes identified as a **keyboard shortcut**. Some keyboard shortcuts consist of a single key, such as the F1 key. For example, to obtain help in many apps, you can press the F1 key. Other keyboard shortcuts consist of multiple keys, in which case a plus sign separates the key names, such as CTRL+ESC. This notation means to press and hold down the first key listed, press one or more additional keys, and then release all keys. For example, to display the Start menu, press CTRL+ESC, that is, hold down the CTRL key, press the ESC key, and then release both keys.

Starting Windows

It is not unusual for multiple people to use the same computer in a work, educational, recreational, or home setting. Windows enables each user to establish a **user account**, which identifies to Windows the resources, such as apps and storage locations, a user can access when working with the computer.

Each user account has a user name and may have a password and an icon, as well. A **user name** is a unique combination of letters or numbers that identifies a specific user to Windows. A **password** is a private combination of letters, numbers, and special characters associated with the user name that allows access to a user's account resources. An icon is a small image that represents an object; thus, a **user icon** is a picture associated with a user name.

When you turn on a computer, Windows starts and displays a **lock screen** consisting of the time and date (Figure 3). To unlock the screen, click the lock screen. Depending on your computer's settings, Windows may or may not display a sign-in screen that shows the user names and user icons for users who have accounts on the computer. This **sign-in screen** enables you to sign in to your user account and makes the computer available for use. Clicking the user icon begins the process of signing in, also called logging on, to your user account.

BTW

Minimize Wrist Injury
Computer users frequently switch between the keyboard and the mouse during a word processing session; such switching strains the wrist. To help prevent wrist injury, minimize switching. For instance, if your fingers already are on the keyboard, use keyboard keys to scroll. If your hand already is on the mouse, use the mouse to scroll. If your hand is on the touch screen, use touch gestures to scroll.

lock screen

current date and time

2:57
Wednesday, September 23

Figure 3

At the bottom of the sign-in screen is the 'Connect to Internet' button, 'Ease of access' button, and a Shut down button. Clicking the 'Connect to Internet' button displays a list of each network connection and its status. You also can connect to or disconnect from a network. Clicking the 'Ease of access' button displays the Ease of access menu, which provides tools to optimize a computer to accommodate the needs of the mobility, hearing, and vision impaired users. Clicking the Shut down button displays a menu containing commands related to putting the computer or mobile device in a low-power state, shutting it down, and restarting the computer or mobile device. The commands available on your computer or mobile device may differ.

- The Sleep command saves your work, turns off the computer fans and hard drive, and places the computer in a lower-power state. To wake the computer from sleep mode, press the power button or lift a laptop's cover, and sign in to your account.

- The Shut down command exits running apps, shuts down Windows, and then turns off the computer.

- The Restart command exits running apps, shuts down Windows, and then restarts Windows.

To Sign In to an Account

1 SIGN IN | 2 USE WINDOWS | 3 USE APPS | 4 FILE MANAGEMENT | 5 SWITCH APPS | 6 SAVE FILES
7 CHANGE SCREEN RESOLUTION | 8 EXIT APPS | 9 USE ADDITIONAL APPS | 10 USE HELP

The following steps, which use SCSeries as the user name, sign in to an account based on a typical Windows installation. *Why? After starting Windows, you might be required to sign in to an account to access the computer or mobile device's resources.* You may need to ask your instructor how to sign in to your account.

- Click the lock screen (shown in Figure 3) to display a sign-in screen.

- Click the user icon (for SCSeries, in this case) on the sign-in screen, which depending on settings, either will display a second sign-in screen that contains a Password text box (Figure 4) or will display the Windows desktop (Figure 5).

Note: To help you locate screen elements that are referenced in the step instructions, such as buttons and commands, this book uses red boxes to point to these screen elements.

SCSeries

Submit button

Password text box

SCSeries user icon

Shut down button

'Connect to Internet' button

'Ease of access' button

Figure 4

Q&A

Why do I not see a user icon?
Your computer may require you to type a user name instead of clicking an icon.

What is a text box?
A text box is a rectangular box in which you type text.

Why does my screen not show a Password text box?
Your account does not require a password.

- If Windows displays a sign-in screen with a Password text box, type your password in the text box.

2

- Click the Submit button (shown in Figure 4) to sign in to your account and display the Windows desktop (Figure 5).

Q&A

Why does my desktop look different from the one in Figure 5?
The Windows desktop is customizable, and your school or employer may have modified the desktop to meet its needs. Also, your screen resolution, which affects the size of the elements on the screen, may differ from the screen resolution used in this book. Later in this module, you learn how to change screen resolution.

How do I type if my tablet has no keyboard?
You can use your fingers to press keys on a keyboard that appears on the screen, called an on-screen keyboard, or you can purchase a separate physical keyboard that attaches to or wirelessly communicates with the tablet.

Figure 5

The Windows Desktop

The Windows 10 desktop (Figure 5) and the objects on the desktop emulate a work area in an office. Think of the Windows desktop as an electronic version of the top of your desk. You can perform tasks such as placing objects on the desktop, moving the objects around the desktop, and removing items from the desktop.

When you run an app in Windows 10, it appears on the desktop. Some icons also may be displayed on the desktop. For instance, the icon for the **Recycle Bin**, the location of files that have been deleted, appears on the desktop by default. A **file** is a named unit of storage. Files can contain text, images, audio, and video. You can customize your desktop so that icons representing programs and files you use often appear on your desktop.

Introduction to Microsoft Office 2016

Microsoft Office 2016 is the newest version of Microsoft Office, offering features that provide users with better functionality and easier ways to work with the various files they create. This version of Office also is designed to work more optimally on mobile devices and online.

Microsoft Office 2016 Apps

Microsoft Office 2016 includes a wide variety of apps, such as Word, PowerPoint, Excel, Access, Outlook, Publisher, and OneNote:

- **Microsoft Word 2016**, or Word, is a full-featured word processing app that allows you to create professional-looking documents and revise them easily.

- **Microsoft PowerPoint 2016**, or PowerPoint, is a complete presentation app that enables you to produce professional-looking presentations and then deliver them to an audience.
- **Microsoft Excel 2016**, or Excel, is a powerful spreadsheet app that allows you to organize data, complete calculations, make decisions, graph data, develop professional-looking reports, publish organized data to the web, and access real-time data from websites.
- **Microsoft Access 2016**, or Access, is a database management system that enables you to create a database; add, change, and delete data in the database; ask questions concerning the data in the database; and create forms and reports using the data in the database.
- **Microsoft Outlook 2016**, or Outlook, is a communications and scheduling app that allows you to manage email accounts, calendars, contacts, and access to other Internet content.
- **Microsoft Publisher 2016**, or Publisher, is a desktop publishing app that helps you create professional-quality publications and marketing materials that can be shared easily.
- **Microsoft OneNote 2016**, or OneNote, is a note taking app that allows you to store and share information in notebooks with other people.

Microsoft Office 2016 Suites

A **suite** is a collection of individual apps available together as a unit. Microsoft offers a variety of Office suites, including a stand-alone desktop app, Microsoft Office 365, and Microsoft Office Online. **Microsoft Office 365**, or Office 365, provides plans that allow organizations to use Office in a mobile setting while also being able to communicate and share files, depending upon the type of plan selected by the organization. **Microsoft Office Online** includes apps that allow you to edit and share files on the web using the familiar Office interface.

During the Office 365 installation, you select a plan, and depending on your plan, you receive different apps and services. Office Online apps do not require a local installation and can be accessed through OneDrive and your browser. **OneDrive** is a cloud storage service that provides storage and other services, such as Office Online, to computer users.

CONSIDER THIS

How do you sign up for a OneDrive account?

- Use your browser to navigate to onedrive.live.com.
- Create a Microsoft account by clicking the Sign up button and then entering your information to create the account.
- Sign in to OneDrive using your new account or use it in Office to save your files on OneDrive.

Apps in a suite, such as Microsoft Office, typically use a similar interface and share features. Once you are comfortable working with the elements and the interface and performing tasks in one app, the similarity can help you apply the knowledge and skills you have learned to another app(s) in the suite. For example, the process for saving a file in Word is the same in PowerPoint, Excel, and some of the other Office apps. While briefly showing how to use several Office apps, this module illustrates some of the common functions across the apps and identifies the characteristics unique to these apps.

Running and Using an App

To use an app, you must instruct the operating system to run the app. Windows provides many different ways to run an app, one of which is presented in this section (other ways to run an app are presented throughout this module). After an app is running, you can use it to perform a variety of tasks. The following pages use Word to discuss some elements of the Office interface and to perform tasks that are common to other Office apps.

Word

Word is a full-featured word processing app that allows you to create many types of personal and business documents, including flyers, letters, memos, resumes, reports, fax cover sheets, mailing labels, and newsletters. Word also provides tools that enable you to create webpages and save these webpages directly on a web server. Word has many features designed to simplify the production of documents and add visual appeal. Using Word, you easily can change the shape, size, and color of text. You also can include borders, shading, tables, images, pictures, charts, and web addresses in documents.

To Run an App Using the Start Menu and Create a Blank Document

1 SIGN IN | **2 USE WINDOWS** | 3 USE APPS | 4 FILE MANAGEMENT | 5 SWITCH APPS | 6 SAVE FILES
7 CHANGE SCREEN RESOLUTION | 8 EXIT APPS | 9 USE ADDITIONAL APPS | 10 USE HELP

Across the bottom of the Windows 10 desktop is the taskbar. The taskbar contains the **Start button**, which you use to access apps, files, folders, and settings. A **folder** is a named location on a storage medium that usually contains related documents.

Clicking the Start button displays the Start menu. The **Start menu** allows you to access programs, folders, and files on the computer or mobile device and contains commands that allow you to start programs, store and search for documents, customize the computer or mobile device, and sign out of a user account or shut down the computer or mobile device. A **menu** is a list of related items, including folders, programs, and commands. Each **command** on a menu performs a specific action, such as saving a file or obtaining help. *Why? When you install an app, for example, the app's name will be added to the All apps list on the Start menu.*

The following steps, which assume Windows is running, use the Start menu to run an Office app and create a blank document based on a typical installation. You may need to ask your instructor how to run an Office app on your computer. Although the steps illustrate running the Word app, the steps to run any Office app are similar.

1

- Click the Start button on the Windows 10 taskbar to display the Start menu (Figure 6).

Figure 6

2

- Click All apps at the bottom of the left pane of the Start menu to display a list of apps installed on the computer or mobile device. If necessary, scroll to display the app you wish to run (Figure 7).

Figure 7

3

- If the app you wish to run is located in a folder, click or scroll to and then click the folder in the All apps list to display a list of the folder's contents.
- Click, or scroll to and then click, the program name (Microsoft Word 2016, in this case) in the list to run the selected program (Figure 8).

Figure 8

4

- Click the Blank document thumbnail on the Word start screen to create a blank Word document in the Word window (Figure 9).

Q&A What happens when you run an app?

Some apps provide a means for you to create a blank document, as shown in Figure 8; others immediately display a blank document in an app window, such as the Word window shown in Figure 9. A **window** is a rectangular area that displays data and information. The top of a window has a **title bar**, which is a horizontal space that contains the window's name.

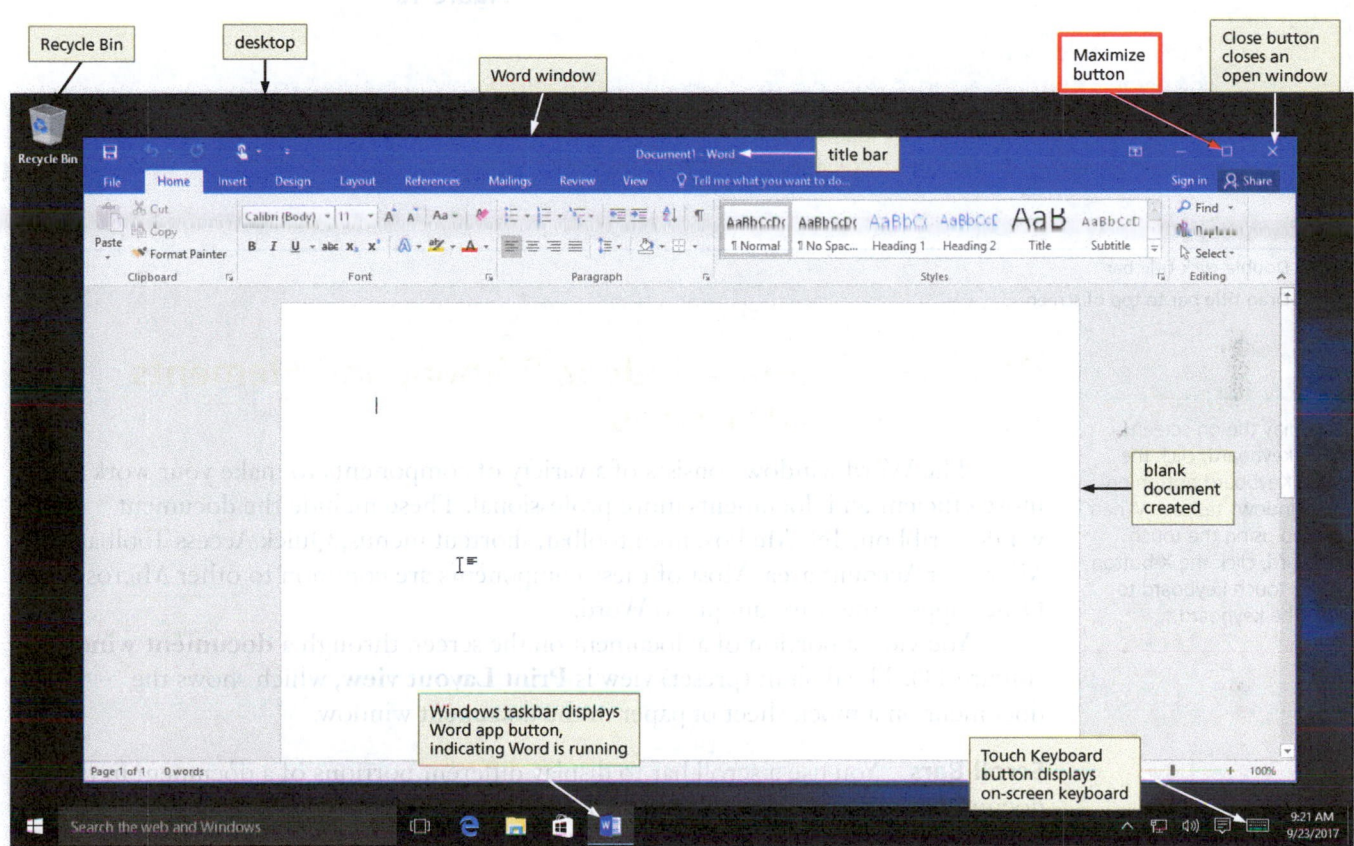

Figure 9

Other Ways

1. Type app name in search box, click app name in results list
2. Double-click file created in app you want to run

To Maximize a Window

Sometimes content is not visible completely in a window. One method of displaying the entire contents of a window is to **maximize** it, or enlarge the window so that it fills the entire screen. The following step maximizes the Word window; however, any Office app's window can be maximized using this step. *Why? A maximized window provides the most space available for using the app.*

- If the app window is not maximized already, click the Maximize button (shown in Figure 9) next to the Close button on the window's title bar (the Word window title bar, in this case) to maximize the window (Figure 10).

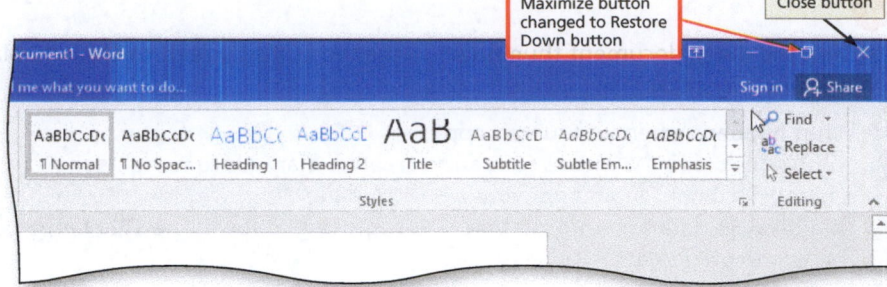

Figure 10

Q&A

What happened to the Maximize button?

It changed to a Restore Down button, which you can use to return a window to its size and location before you maximized it.

How do I know whether a window is maximized?

A window is maximized if it fills the entire display area and the Restore Down button is displayed on the title bar.

Other Ways

1. Double-click title bar
2. Drag title bar to top of screen

Word Document Window, Ribbon, and Elements Common to Office Apps

The Word window consists of a variety of components to make your work more efficient and documents more professional. These include the document window, ribbon, Tell Me box, mini toolbar, shortcut menus, Quick Access Toolbar, and Microsoft Account area. Most of these components are common to other Microsoft Office apps; others are unique to Word.

You view a portion of a document on the screen through a **document window** (Figure 11). The default (preset) view is **Print Layout view**, which shows the document on a mock sheet of paper in the document window.

Scroll Bars   You use a scroll bar to display different portions of a document in the document window. At the right edge of the document window is a vertical scroll bar. If a document is too wide to fit in the document window, a horizontal scroll bar also appears at the bottom of the document window. On a scroll bar, the position of the scroll box reflects the location of the portion of the document that is displayed in the document window.

Status Bar   The **status bar**, located at the bottom of the document window above the Windows taskbar, presents information about the document, the progress of current tasks, and the status of certain commands and keys; it also provides controls for viewing the document. As you type text or perform certain tasks, various indicators and buttons may appear on the status bar.

The left side of the status bar in Figure 11 shows the current page followed by the total number of pages in the document, the number of words in the document, and an icon to check spelling and grammar. The right side of the status bar includes buttons and controls you can use to change the view of a document and adjust the size of the displayed document.

Ribbon   The ribbon, located near the top of the window below the title bar, is the control center in Word and other Office apps (Figure 12). The ribbon provides easy, central access to the tasks you perform while creating a document. The ribbon consists

Figure 11

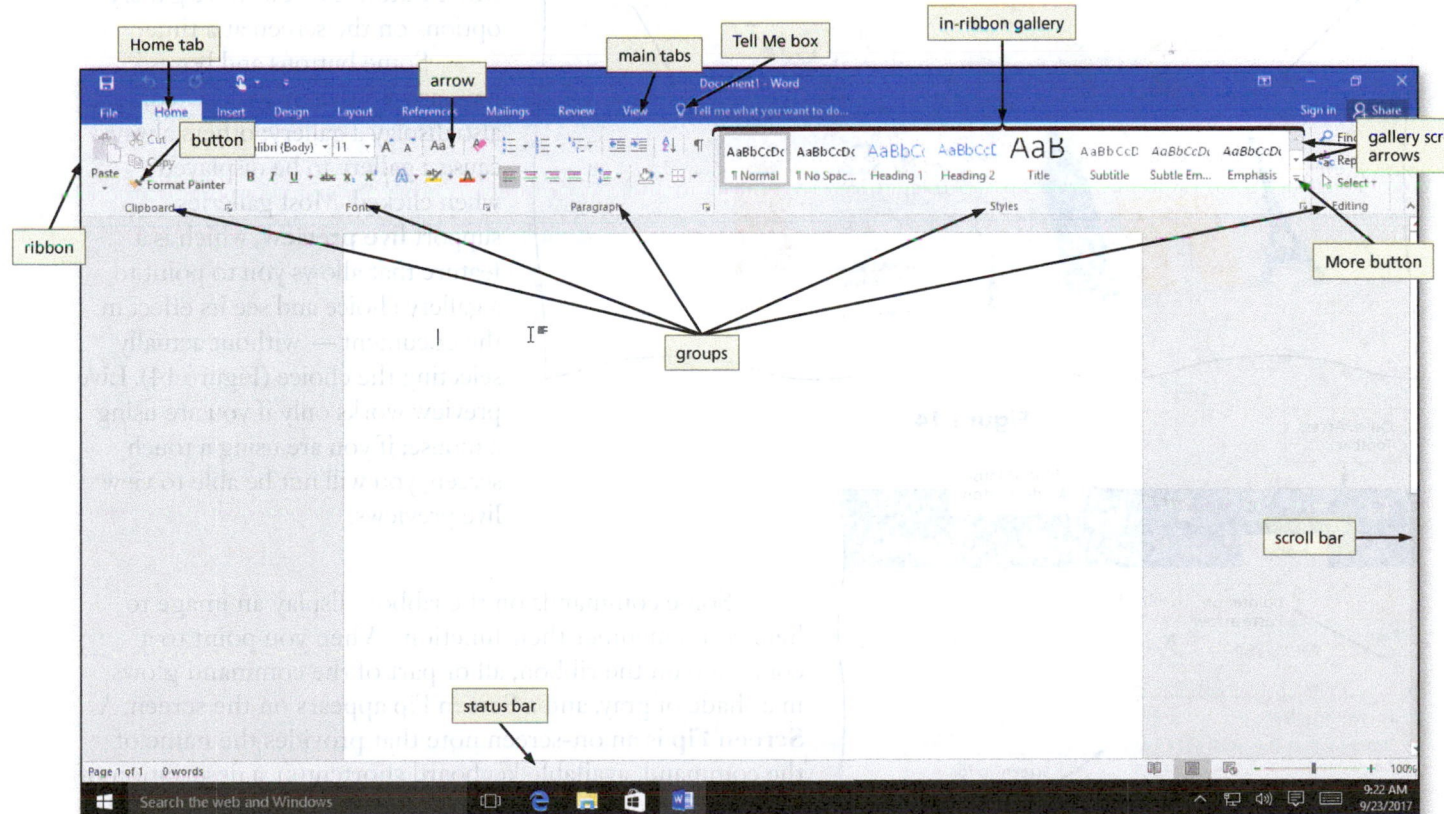

Figure 12

of tabs, groups, and commands. Each **tab** contains a collection of groups, and each **group** contains related commands. When you run an Office app, such as Word, it initially displays several main tabs, also called default or top-level tabs. All Office apps have a Home tab, which contains the more frequently used commands.

Figure 13

In addition to the main tabs, the Office apps display **tool tabs**, also called contextual tabs (Figure 13), when you perform certain tasks or work with objects such as pictures or tables. If you insert a picture in a Word document, for example, the Picture Tools tab and its related subordinate Format tab appear, collectively referred to as the Picture Tools Format tab. When you are finished working with the picture, the Picture Tools Format tab disappears from the ribbon. Word and other Office apps determine when tool tabs should appear and disappear based on tasks you perform. Some tool tabs, such as the Table Tools tab, have more than one related subordinate tab.

Figure 14

Items on the ribbon include buttons, boxes, and galleries (shown in Figure 12). A **gallery** is a set of choices, often graphical, arranged in a grid or in a list. You can scroll through choices in an in-ribbon gallery by clicking the gallery's scroll arrows. Or, you can click a gallery's More button to view more gallery options on the screen at a time.

Some buttons and boxes have arrows that, when clicked, also display a gallery; others always cause a gallery to be displayed when clicked. Most galleries support **live preview**, which is a feature that allows you to point to a gallery choice and see its effect in the document — without actually selecting the choice (Figure 14). Live preview works only if you are using a mouse; if you are using a touch screen, you will not be able to view live previews.

Some commands on the ribbon display an image to help you remember their function. When you point to a command on the ribbon, all or part of the command glows in a shade of gray, and a ScreenTip appears on the screen. A **ScreenTip** is an on-screen note that provides the name of the command, available keyboard shortcut(s), a description of the command, and sometimes instructions for how to obtain help about the command (Figure 15).

Figure 15

Some groups on the ribbon have a small arrow in the lower-right corner, called a **Dialog Box Launcher**, that when clicked, displays a dialog box or a task pane with additional options for the group (Figure 16). When presented with a dialog box, you make selections and must close the dialog box before returning to the document. A **task pane**, in contrast to a dialog box, is a window that can remain open and visible while you work in the document.

BTW
Touch Mode
The Office and Windows interfaces may vary if you are using touch mode. For this reason, you might notice that the function or appearance of your touch screen differs slightly from this module's presentation.

Figure 16

Tell Me Box   The **Tell Me box**, which appears to the right of the tabs on the ribbon, is a type of search box that helps you to perform specific tasks in an Office app (Figure 17). As you type in the Tell Me box, the word-wheeling feature displays search results that are refined as you type. For example, if you want to center text in a document, you can type "center" in the Tell Me box and then select the appropriate command. The Tell Me box also lists the last five commands accessed from the box.

Mini Toolbar   The **mini toolbar**, which appears automatically based on tasks you perform, contains commands related to changing the appearance of text in a document (Figure 18). If you do not use the mini toolbar, it disappears from the screen. The buttons, arrows, and boxes on the mini toolbar vary, depending on whether you are using Touch mode versus Mouse mode. If you right-click an item in the document window, Word displays both the mini toolbar and a shortcut menu, which is discussed in a later section in this module.

All commands on the mini toolbar also exist on the ribbon. The purpose of the mini toolbar is to minimize hand or mouse movement.

Figure 17

BTW
Turning Off the Mini Toolbar
If you do not want the mini toolbar to appear, click File on the ribbon to open the Backstage view, click the Options tab in the Backstage view, if necessary, click General (Options dialog box), remove the check mark from the 'Show Mini Toolbar on selection' check box, and then click the OK button.

Figure 18

Quick Access Toolbar The **Quick Access Toolbar**, located initially (by default) above the ribbon at the left edge of the title bar, provides convenient, one-click access to frequently used commands (shown in Figure 15). The commands on the Quick Access Toolbar always are available, regardless of the task you are performing. The Touch/Mouse Mode button on the Quick Access Toolbar allows you to switch between Touch mode and Mouse mode. If you primarily are using touch gestures, Touch mode will add more space between commands in menus and on the ribbon so that they are easier to tap. While touch gestures are convenient ways to interact with Office apps, not all features are supported when you are using Touch mode. If you are using a mouse, Mouse mode will not add the extra space between buttons and commands. The Quick Access Toolbar is discussed in more depth later in the module.

KeyTips If you prefer using the keyboard instead of the mouse, you can press the ALT key on the keyboard to display **KeyTips**, or keyboard code icons, for certain commands (Figure 19). To select a command using the keyboard, press the letter or number displayed in the KeyTip, which may cause additional KeyTips related to the selected command to appear. To remove KeyTips from the screen, press the ALT key or the ESC key until all KeyTips disappear, or click anywhere in the app window.

Microsoft Account Area In this area, you can use the Sign in link to sign in to your Microsoft account. Once signed in, you will see your account information, as well as a picture if you have included one in your Microsoft account.

Figure 19

To Display a Different Tab on the Ribbon

1 SIGN IN | 2 USE WINDOWS | 3 USE APPS | 4 FILE MANAGEMENT | 5 SWITCH APPS | 6 SAVE FILES
7 CHANGE SCREEN RESOLUTION | 8 EXIT APPS | 9 USE ADDITIONAL APPS | 10 USE HELP

When you run Word, the ribbon displays nine main tabs: File, Home, Insert, Design, Layout, References, Mailings, Review, and View. The tab currently displayed is called the **active tab**.

The following step displays the Insert tab, that is, makes it the active tab. *Why? When working with an Office app, you may need to switch tabs to access other options for working with a document.*

- Click Insert on the ribbon to display the Insert tab (Figure 20).

 Experiment

- Click the other tabs on the ribbon to view their contents. When you are finished, click Insert on the ribbon to redisplay the Insert tab.

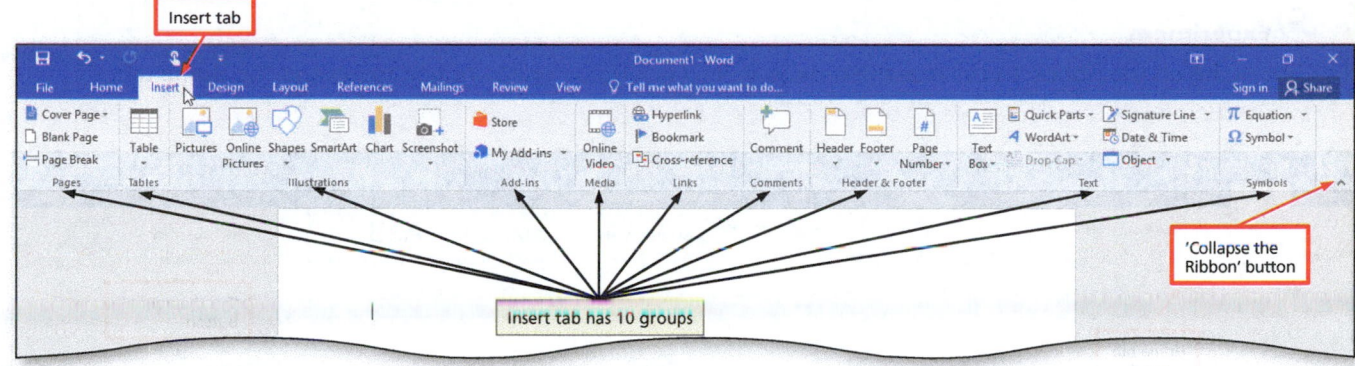

Figure 20

Other Ways

1. Press ALT, press letter corresponding to tab to display
2. Press ALT, press LEFT ARROW or RIGHT ARROW until desired tab is displayed

To Collapse and Expand the Ribbon and Use Full Screen Mode

1 SIGN IN | 2 USE WINDOWS | 3 USE APPS | 4 FILE MANAGEMENT | 5 SWITCH APPS | 6 SAVE FILES
7 CHANGE SCREEN RESOLUTION | 8 EXIT APPS | 9 USE ADDITIONAL APPS | 10 USE HELP

To display more of a document or other item in the window of an Office app, some users prefer to collapse the ribbon, which hides the groups on the ribbon and displays only the main tabs, or to use **Full Screen mode**, which hides all the commands and just displays the document. Each time you run an Office app, the ribbon appears the same way it did the last time you used that Office app. The modules in this book, however, begin with the ribbon appearing as it did at the initial installation of the software.

The following steps collapse, expand, and restore the ribbon in an Office app and then switch to Full Screen mode. **Why?** *If you need more space on the screen to work with your document, you may consider collapsing the ribbon or switching to Full Screen mode to gain additional workspace.*

- Click the 'Collapse the Ribbon' button on the ribbon (shown in Figure 20) to collapse the ribbon (Figure 21).

Q&A What happened to the 'Collapse the Ribbon' button?

The 'Pin the ribbon' button replaces the 'Collapse the Ribbon' button when the ribbon is collapsed. You will see the 'Pin the ribbon' button only when you expand a ribbon by clicking a tab.

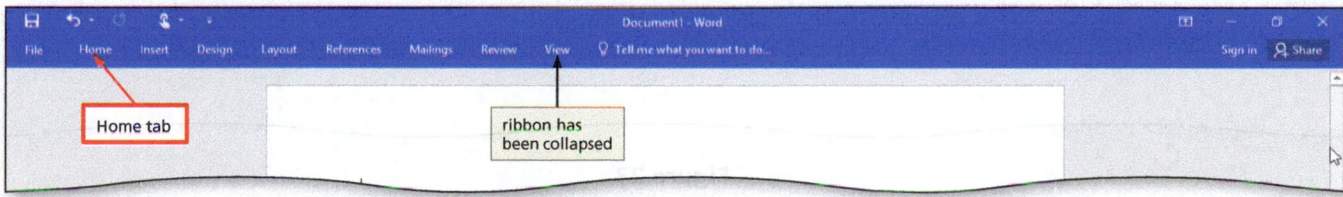

Figure 21

2

- Click Home on the ribbon to expand the Home tab (Figure 22).

Q&A Why would I click the Home tab?

If you want to use a command on a collapsed ribbon, click the main tab to display the groups for that tab. After you select a command on the ribbon and resume working in the document, the groups will be collapsed once again. If you decide not to use a command on the ribbon, you can collapse the groups by clicking the same main tab or clicking in the app window.

Experiment

- Click Home on the ribbon to collapse the groups again. Click Home on the ribbon to expand the Home tab.

Figure 22

3

- Click the 'Pin the ribbon' button on the expanded Home tab to restore the ribbon.
- Click the 'Ribbon Display Options' button to display the Ribbon Display Options menu (Figure 23).

Figure 23

4

- Click Auto-hide Ribbon to hide all the commands from the screen (Figure 24).
- Click the ellipsis to temporarily display the ribbon.
- Click the 'Ribbon Display Options' button to display the Ribbon Display Options menu (shown in Figure 23).
- Click 'Show Tabs and Commands' to exit Full Screen mode.

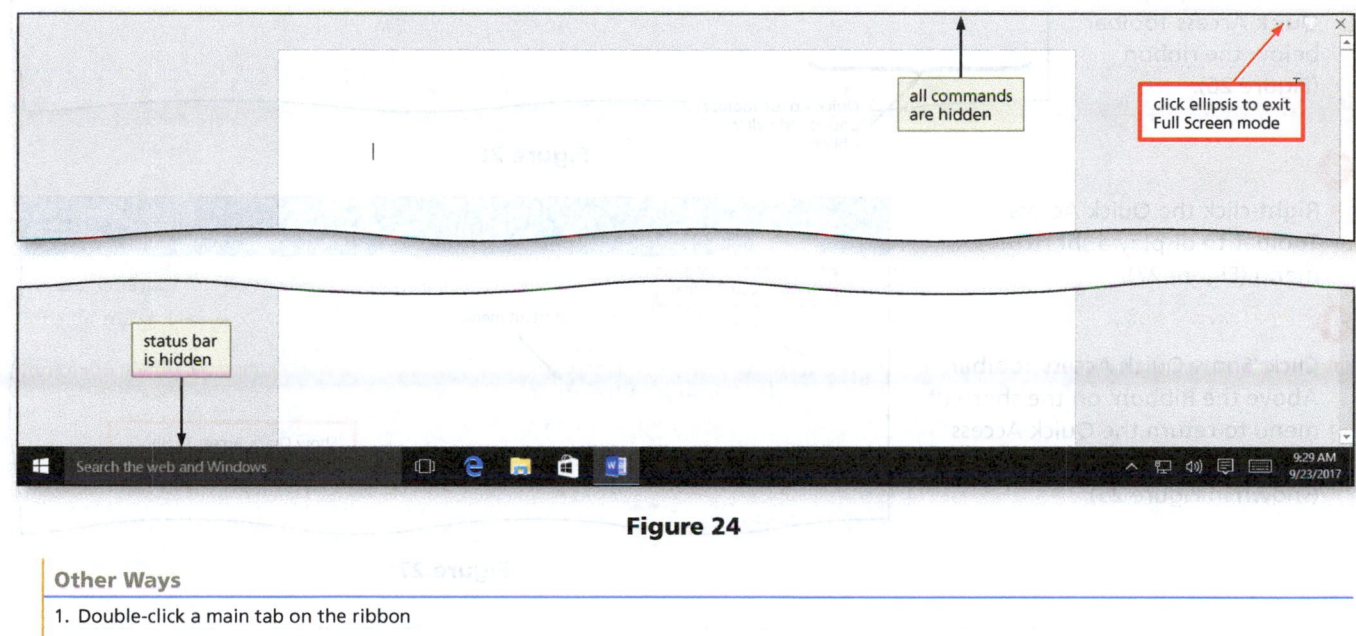

Figure 24

Other Ways

1. Double-click a main tab on the ribbon
2. Press CTRL+F1

To Use a Shortcut Menu to Relocate the Quick Access Toolbar

1 SIGN IN | 2 USE WINDOWS | **3 USE APPS** | **4 FILE MANAGEMENT** | **5 SWITCH APPS** | **6 SAVE FILES**
7 CHANGE SCREEN RESOLUTION | **8 EXIT APPS** | **9 USE ADDITIONAL APPS** | **10 USE HELP**

When you right-click certain areas of the Word and other Office app windows, a shortcut menu will appear. A **shortcut menu** is a list of frequently used commands that relate to an object. *Why? You can use shortcut menus to access common commands quickly.* When you right-click the status bar, for example, a shortcut menu appears with commands related to the status bar. When you right-click the Quick Access Toolbar, a shortcut menu appears with commands related to the Quick Access Toolbar. The following steps use a shortcut menu to move the Quick Access Toolbar, which by default is located on the title bar.

1

- Right-click the Quick Access Toolbar to display a shortcut menu that presents a list of commands related to the Quick Access Toolbar (Figure 25).

Figure 25

- Click 'Show Quick Access Toolbar Below the Ribbon' on the shortcut menu to display the Quick Access Toolbar below the ribbon (Figure 26).

Figure 26

- Right-click the Quick Access Toolbar to display a shortcut menu (Figure 27).

- Click 'Show Quick Access Toolbar Above the Ribbon' on the shortcut menu to return the Quick Access Toolbar to its original position (shown in Figure 25).

Figure 27

Other Ways

1. Click 'Customize Quick Access Toolbar' button on Quick Access Toolbar, click 'Show Below the Ribbon' or 'Show Above the Ribbon'

To Customize the Quick Access Toolbar

1 SIGN IN | 2 USE WINDOWS | 3 USE APPS | 4 FILE MANAGEMENT | 5 SWITCH APPS | 6 SAVE FILES
7 CHANGE SCREEN RESOLUTION | 8 EXIT APPS | 9 USE ADDITIONAL APPS | 10 USE HELP

The Quick Access Toolbar provides easy access to some of the more frequently used commands in the Office apps. By default, the Quick Access Toolbar contains buttons for the Save, Undo, and Redo commands. If your computer or mobile device has a touch screen, the Quick Access Toolbar also might display the Touch/Mouse Mode button. You can customize the Quick Access Toolbar by changing its location in the window, as shown in the previous steps, and by adding more buttons to reflect commands you would like to access easily. The following steps add the Quick Print button to the Quick Access Toolbar. *Why? Adding the Quick Print button to the Quick Access Toolbar speeds up the process of printing.*

- Click the 'Customize Quick Access Toolbar' button to display the Customize Quick Access Toolbar menu (Figure 28).

Q&A Which commands are listed on the Customize Quick Access Toolbar menu?

It lists commands that commonly are added to the Quick Access Toolbar.

Figure 28

2

- Click Quick Print on the Customize Quick Access Toolbar menu to add the Quick Print button to the Quick Access Toolbar (Figure 29).

Q&A How would I remove a button from the Quick Access Toolbar?
You would right-click the button you wish to remove and then click 'Remove from Quick Access Toolbar' on the shortcut menu or click the 'Customize Quick Access Toolbar' button on the Quick Access Toolbar and then click the button name in the Customize Quick Access Toolbar menu to remove the check mark.

Figure 29

To Enter Text in a Document

1 SIGN IN | 2 USE WINDOWS | **3 USE APPS** | 4 FILE MANAGEMENT | 5 SWITCH APPS | 6 SAVE FILES
7 CHANGE SCREEN RESOLUTION | 8 EXIT APPS | 9 USE ADDITIONAL APPS | 10 USE HELP

The first step in creating a document is to enter its text by typing on the keyboard. By default, Word positions text at the left margin as you type. The following steps type this first line of a flyer. *Why? To begin creating a flyer, for example, you type the headline in the document window.*

1

- Type **VISIT NATIONAL MONUMENTS** as the text (Figure 30).

Q&A What is the blinking vertical bar to the right of the text?
The blinking bar is the insertion point, which indicates where text, graphics, and other items will be inserted in the document. As you type, the insertion point moves to the right, and when you reach the end of a line, it moves down to the beginning of the next line.

What if I make an error while typing?
You can press the BACKSPACE key until you have deleted the text in error and then retype the text correctly.

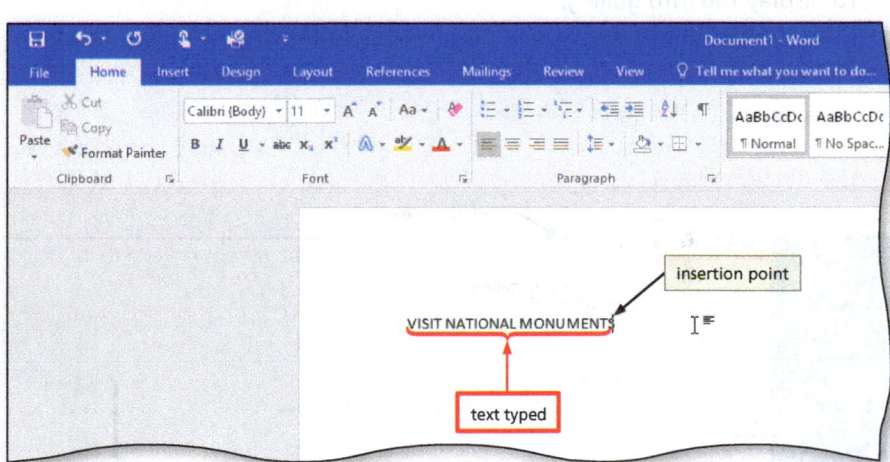

Figure 30

2

- Press the ENTER key to move the insertion point to the beginning of the next line (Figure 31).

Q&A Why did blank space appear between the entered text and the insertion point?
Each time you press the ENTER key, Word creates a new paragraph and inserts blank space between the two paragraphs. Depending on your settings, Office may or may not insert a blank space between the two paragraphs.

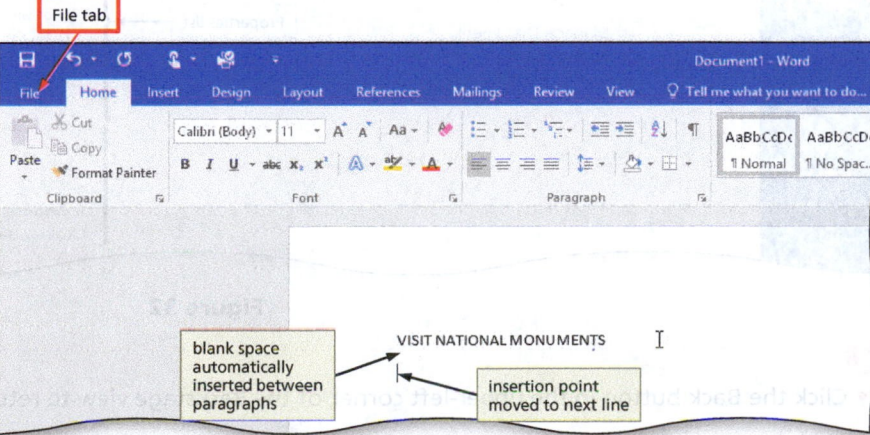

Figure 31

Document Properties

You can organize and identify your files by using **document properties**, which are the details about a file, such as the project author, title, and subject. For example, a class name or document topic can describe the file's purpose or content.

CONSIDER THIS

Why would you want to assign document properties to a document?
Document properties are valuable for a variety of reasons:

- Users can save time locating a particular file because they can view a file's document properties without opening the file.

- By creating consistent properties for files having similar content, users can better organize their files.

- Some organizations require users to add document properties so that other employees can view details about these files.

To Change Document Properties

1 SIGN IN | 2 USE WINDOWS | 3 USE APPS | **4 FILE MANAGEMENT** | 5 SWITCH APPS | 6 SAVE FILES
7 CHANGE SCREEN RESOLUTION | 8 EXIT APPS | 9 USE ADDITIONAL APPS | 10 USE HELP

You can change the document properties while working with the file in an Office app. When you save the file, the Office app (Word, in this case) will save the document properties with the file. The following steps change document properties. *Why? Adding document properties will help you identify characteristics of the file without opening it.*

1

- Click File on the ribbon to open the Backstage view and then, if necessary, click the Info tab in the Backstage view to display the Info gallery.
- Click to the right of the Comments property in the Properties list, and type `CIS 101 Assignment` in the text box (Figure 32).

Q&A What is the Backstage view?
The **Backstage view** contains a set of commands that enable you to manage documents and provides data about the documents.

Figure 32

2

- Click the Back button in the upper-left corner of the Backstage view to return to the document window.

Printing, Saving, and Organizing Files

BTW
File Type
Depending on your Windows settings, the file type .docx may be displayed immediately to the right of the file name after you save the file. The file type .docx is a Word 2016 document.

While you are creating a document, the computer or mobile device stores it in memory. When you save a document, the computer or mobile device places it on a storage medium, such as a hard disk, solid state drive (SSD), USB flash drive, or optical disc. The storage medium can be permanent in your computer, may be portable where you remove it from your computer, or may be on a web server you access through a network or the Internet.

A saved document is referred to as a file. A **file name** is the name assigned to a file when it is saved. When saving files, you should organize them so that you easily can find them later. Windows provides tools to help you organize files.

Printing a Document

After creating a document, you may want to print it. Printing a document enables you to distribute it to others in a form that can be read or viewed but typically not edited.

CONSIDER THIS

What is the best method for distributing a document?

The traditional method of distributing a document uses a printer to produce a hard copy. A **hard copy** or **printout** is information that exists on a physical medium, such as paper. Hard copies can be useful for the following reasons:

- Some people prefer proofreading a hard copy of a document rather than viewing it on the screen to check for errors and readability.

- Hard copies can serve as a backup reference if your storage medium is lost or becomes corrupted and you need to recreate the document.

Instead of distributing a hard copy of a document, users can distribute the document as an electronic image that mirrors the original document's appearance. The electronic image of the document can be sent as an email attachment, posted on a website, or copied to a portable storage medium, such as a USB flash drive. Two popular electronic image formats, sometimes called fixed formats, are PDF by Adobe Systems and XPS by Microsoft. In Word, you can create electronic image files through the Save As dialog box and the Export, Share, and Print tabs in the Backstage view. Electronic images of documents, such as PDF and XPS, can be useful for the following reasons:

- Users can view electronic images of documents without the software that created the original document (e.g., Word). For example, to view a PDF file you use a program called Adobe Reader, which can be downloaded free from Adobe's website.

- Sending electronic documents saves paper and printer supplies. Society encourages users to contribute to **green computing**, which involves reducing the electricity consumed and environmental waste generated when using computers, mobile devices, and related technologies.

To Print a Document

1 SIGN IN | 2 USE WINDOWS | 3 USE APPS | **4 FILE MANAGEMENT** | 5 SWITCH APPS | 6 SAVE FILES
7 CHANGE SCREEN RESOLUTION | 8 EXIT APPS | 9 USE ADDITIONAL APPS | 10 USE HELP

With the document opened, you may want to print it. *Why? Because you want to see how the text will appear on paper; you want to print a hard copy on a printer.* The following steps print a hard copy of the contents of the document.

- Click File on the ribbon to open the Backstage view.
- Click the Print tab in the Backstage view to display the Print gallery (Figure 33).

Q&A How can I print multiple copies of my document?
Increase the number in the Copies box in the Print gallery.

What if I decide not to print the document at this time?
Click the Back button in the upper-left corner of the Backstage view to return to the document window.

2

- Verify that the selected printer will print a hard copy of the document. If necessary, click the Printer Status button to display a list of available printer options and then click the desired printer to change the currently selected printer.

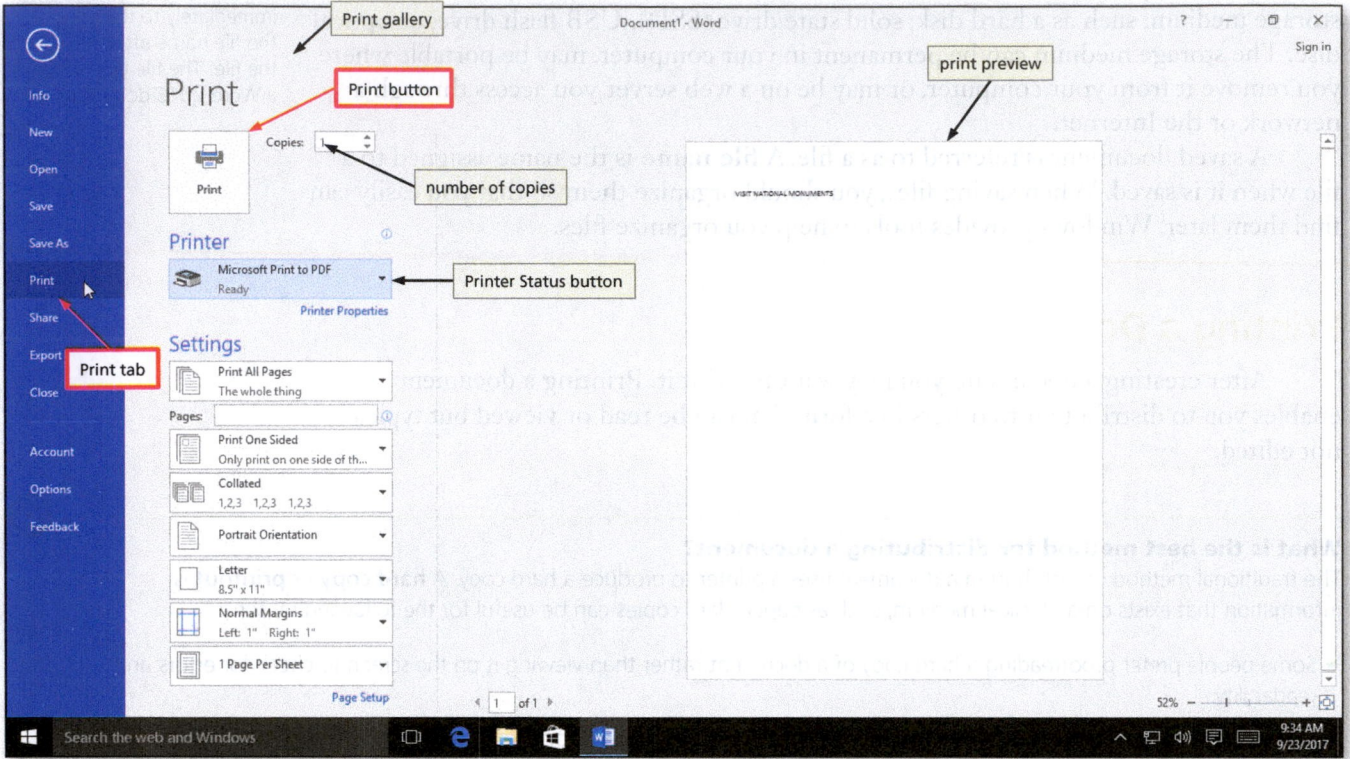

Figure 33

3

- Click the Print button in the Print gallery to print the document on the currently selected printer.
- When the printer stops, retrieve the hard copy (Figure 34).

Q&A What if I want to print an electronic image of a document instead of a hard copy?
You would click the Printer Status button in the Print gallery and then select the desired electronic image option, such as Microsoft XPS Document Writer, which would create an XPS file.

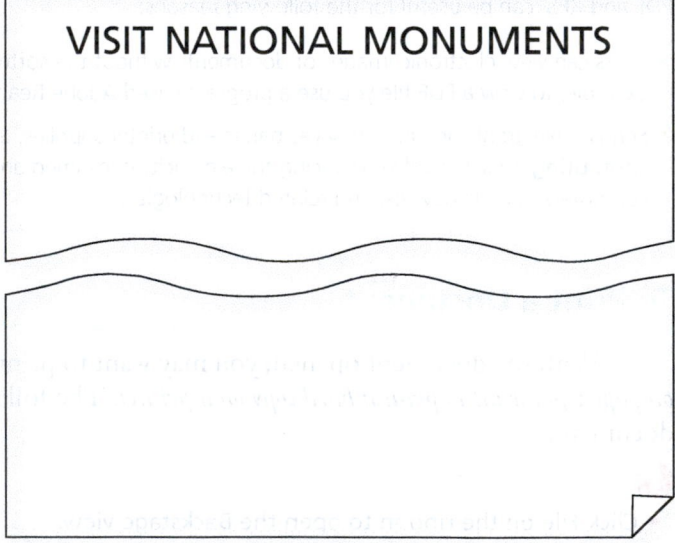

Figure 34

Other Ways

1. Press CTRL+P

Organizing Files and Folders

A file contains data. This data can range from a research paper to an accounting spreadsheet to an electronic math quiz. You should organize and store files in folders to avoid misplacing a file and to help you find a file quickly.

If you are taking an introductory computer class (CIS 101, for example), you may want to design a series of folders for the different subjects covered in the class. To accomplish this, you can arrange the folders in a hierarchy for the class, as shown in Figure 35.

Figure 35

The hierarchy contains three levels. The first level contains the storage medium, such as a hard drive. The second level contains the class folder (CIS 101, in this case), and the third level contains seven folders, one each for a different Office app that will be covered in the class (Word, PowerPoint, Excel, Access, Outlook, Publisher, and OneNote).

When the hierarchy in Figure 35 is created, the storage medium is said to contain the CIS 101 folder, and the CIS 101 folder is said to contain the separate Office folders (i.e., Word, PowerPoint, Excel, etc.). In addition, this hierarchy easily can be expanded to include folders from other classes taken during additional semesters.

The vertical and horizontal lines in Figure 35 form a pathway that allows you to navigate to a drive or folder on a computer or network. A **path** consists of a drive letter (preceded by a drive name when necessary) and colon, to identify the storage device, and one or more folder names. A hard disk typically has a drive letter of C. Each drive or folder in the hierarchy has a corresponding path.

By default, Windows saves documents in the Documents folder, music in the Music folder, photos in the Pictures folder, videos in the Videos folder, and downloads in the Downloads folder.

The following pages illustrate the steps to organize the folders for this class and save a file in one of those folders:

1. Create the folder identifying your class.
2. Create the Word folder in the folder identifying your class.
3. Create the remaining folders in the folder identifying your class (one each for PowerPoint, Excel, Access, Outlook, Publisher, and OneNote).
4. Save a file in the Word folder.
5. Verify the location of the saved file.

To Create a Folder

When you create a folder, such as the CIS 101 folder shown in Figure 35, you must name the folder. A folder name should describe the folder and its contents. A folder name can contain spaces and any uppercase or lowercase characters, except a backslash (\), slash (/), colon (:), asterisk (*), question mark (?), quotation marks ("), less than symbol (<), greater than symbol (>), or vertical bar (|). Folder names cannot be CON, AUX, COM1, COM2, COM3, COM4, LPT1, LPT2, LPT3, PRN, or NUL. The same rules for naming folders also apply to naming files.

The following steps create a class folder (CIS 101, in this case) in the Documents folder. *Why? When storing files, you should organize the files so that it will be easier to find them later.*

1

- Click the File Explorer button on the taskbar to run the File Explorer.
- If necessary, double-click This PC in the navigation pane to expand the contents of your computer.
- Click the Documents folder in the navigation pane to display the contents of the Documents folder in the file list (Figure 36).

Figure 36

2

- Click the New folder button on the Quick Access Toolbar to create a new folder with the name, New folder, selected in a text box (Figure 37).

Q&A   Why is the folder icon displayed differently on my computer or mobile device?
Windows might be configured to display contents differently on your computer or mobile device.

Figure 37

- The **ribbon** contains four tabs used to accomplish various tasks on the computer related to organizing and managing the contents of the open window. This ribbon works similarly to the ribbon in the Office apps.
- The **navigation pane** on the left contains the Quick access area, the OneDrive area, the This PC area, and the Network area.
- The **Quick Access area** shows locations you access frequently. By default, this list contains links only to your Desktop, Downloads, Documents, and Pictures.

To Create a Folder within a Folder

1 SIGN IN | 2 USE WINDOWS | 3 USE APPS | **4 FILE MANAGEMENT** | 5 SWITCH APPS | 6 SAVE FILES
7 CHANGE SCREEN RESOLUTION | 8 EXIT APPS | 9 USE ADDITIONAL APPS | 10 USE HELP

With the class folder created, you can create folders that will store the files you create using each Office app. The following step creates a Word folder in the CIS 101 folder (or the folder identifying your class). *Why? To be able to organize your files, you should create a folder structure.*

1

- Double-click the icon or folder name for the CIS 101 folder (or the folder identifying your class) in the file list to open the folder.
- Click the New folder button on the Quick Access Toolbar to create a new folder with the name, New folder, selected in a text box folder.
- Type **Word** in the text box as the new folder name.
- Press the ENTER key to rename the folder (Figure 39).

Figure 39

Other Ways

1. Press CTRL+SHIFT+N
2. Click the New folder button (Home tab | New group)

To Create the Remaining Folders

The following steps create the remaining folders in the folder identifying your class (in this case, CIS 101).

1 Click the New folder button on the Quick Access Toolbar to create a new folder with the name, New folder, selected in a text box.

2 Type **PowerPoint** in the text box as the new folder name.

3 Press the ENTER key to rename the folder.

4 Repeat Steps 1 through 3 to create each of the remaining folders, using Excel, Access, Outlook, Publisher, and OneNote as the folder names (Figure 40).

Figure 40

3

- Type **CIS 101** (or your class code) in the text box as the new folder name.
- If requested by your instructor, add your last name to the end of the folder name.
- Press the ENTER key to change the folder name from New folder to a folder name identifying your class (Figure 38).

Q&A What happens when I press the ENTER key?

The class folder (CIS 101, in this case) is displayed in the file list, which contains the folder name, date modified, type, and size.

Figure 38

Other Ways

1. Press CTRL+SHIFT+N
2. Click the New folder button (Home tab | New group)

Folder Windows

The File Explorer window (shown in Figure 38) is called a folder window. Recall that a folder is a specific named location on a storage medium that contains related files. Most users rely on **folder windows** for finding, viewing, and managing information on their computers. Folder windows have common design elements, including the following (shown in Figure 38).

- The **address bar** provides quick navigation options. The arrows on the address bar allow you to visit different locations on the computer or mobile device.
- The buttons to the left of the address bar allow you to navigate the contents of the navigation pane and view recent pages.
- The **Previous Locations arrow** displays the locations you have visited.
- The **Refresh button** on the right side of the address bar refreshes the contents of the folder list.
- The **Search box** contains the dimmed words, Search Documents. You can type a term in the search box for a list of files, folders, shortcuts, and elements containing that term within the location you are searching.

To Expand a Folder, Scroll through Folder Contents, and Collapse a Folder

1 SIGN IN | 2 USE WINDOWS | 3 USE APPS | **4 FILE MANAGEMENT** | 5 SWITCH APPS | 6 SAVE FILES
7 CHANGE SCREEN RESOLUTION | 8 EXIT APPS | 9 USE ADDITIONAL APPS | 10 USE HELP

Folder windows display the hierarchy of items and the contents of drives and folders in the file list. You might want to expand a folder in the navigation pane to view its contents, scroll through its contents, and collapse it when you are finished viewing its contents. *Why? When a folder is expanded, you can see all the folders it contains. By contrast, a collapsed folder hides the folders it contains.* The following steps expand, scroll through, and then collapse the folder identifying your class (CIS 101, in this case).

 1

- Double-click the Documents folder in the This PC area of the navigation pane, which expands the folder to display its contents and displays a black arrow to the left of the Documents folder icon (Figure 41).

Figure 41

 2

- Double-click the CIS 101 folder, which expands the folder to display its contents and displays a black arrow to the left of the folder icon (Figure 42).

Experiment

- Drag the scroll box down or click the down scroll arrow on the vertical scroll bar to display additional folders at the bottom of the navigation pane. Drag the scroll box up or click the scroll bar above the scroll box to move the scroll box to the top of the navigation pane. Drag the scroll box down the scroll bar until the scroll box is halfway down the scroll bar.

Figure 42

3

- Double-click the folder identifying your class (CIS 101, in this case) to collapse the folder (Figure 43).

Q&A Why are some folders indented below others?
A folder contains the indented folders below it.

Figure 43

Other Ways

1. Point to display arrows in navigation pane, click arrow to expand or collapse
2. Select folder to expand or collapse using arrow keys, press RIGHT ARROW to expand; press LEFT ARROW to collapse

---

To Switch from One App to Another

1 SIGN IN | 2 USE WINDOWS | 3 USE APPS | 4 FILE MANAGEMENT | **5 SWITCH APPS** | **6 SAVE FILES**
7 CHANGE SCREEN RESOLUTION | 8 EXIT APPS | 9 USE ADDITIONAL APPS | 10 USE HELP

The next step is to save the Word file containing the headline you typed earlier. Word, however, currently is not the active window. You can use the button on the taskbar and live preview to switch to Word and then save the document in the Word document window.

Why? *By clicking the appropriate app button on the taskbar, you can switch to the open app you want to use.* The steps below switch to the Word window; however, the steps are the same for any active Office app currently displayed as a button on the taskbar.

1

- Point to the Word app button on the taskbar to see a live preview of the open document(s) or the window title(s) of the open document(s), depending on your computer's configuration (Figure 44).

Q&A What if I am using a touch screen?
Live preview will not work if you are using a touch screen. If you are using a touch screen and do not have a mouse, proceed to Step 2.

Figure 44

2

- Click the button or the live preview to make the app associated with the app button the active window (Figure 45).

Q&A What if multiple documents are open in an app?
Click the desired live preview to switch to the window you want to use.

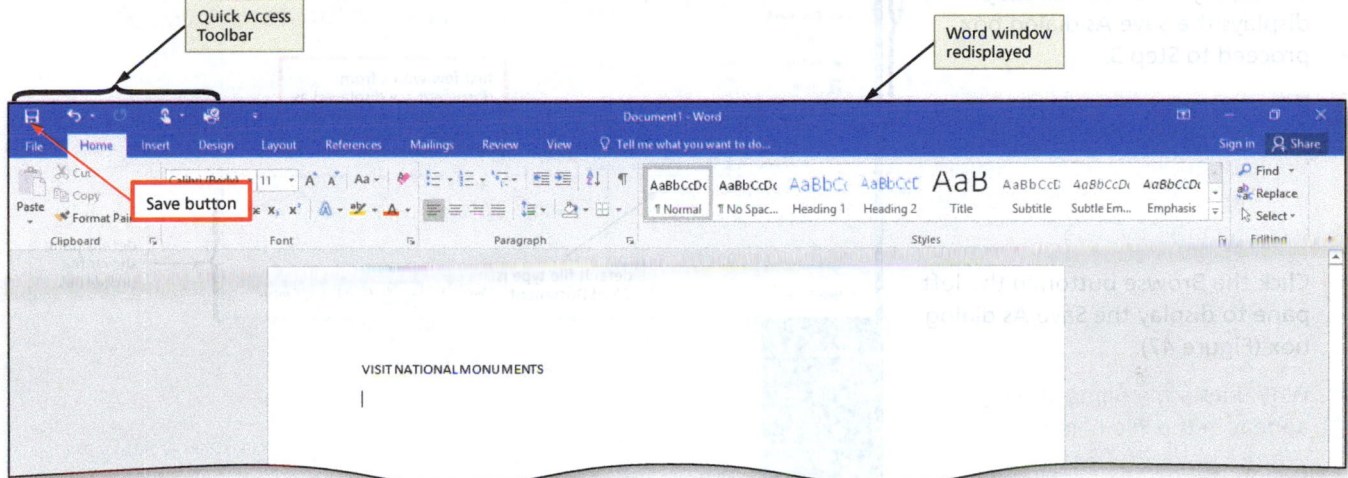

Figure 45

Other Ways

1. Press ALT+TAB until app you wish to display is selected

To Save a File in a Folder

1 SIGN IN | 2 USE WINDOWS | 3 USE APPS | 4 FILE MANAGEMENT | 5 SWITCH APPS | **6 SAVE FILES**
7 CHANGE SCREEN RESOLUTION | 8 EXIT APPS | 9 USE ADDITIONAL APPS | 10 USE HELP

With the folders for storing your files created, you can save the Word document. *Why? Without saving a file, you may lose all the work you have done and will be unable to reuse or share it with others later.* The following steps save a file in the Word folder contained in your class folder (CIS 101, in this case) using the file name, National Monuments.

1

- Click the Save button (shown in Figure 45) on the Quick Access Toolbar, which depending on settings, will display either the Save As gallery in the Backstage view (Figure 46) or the Save As dialog box (Figure 47).

Q&A What if the Save As gallery is not displayed in the Backstage view?
Click the Save As tab to display the Save As gallery.

How do I close the Backstage view?
Click the Back button in the upper-left corner of the Backstage view to return to the app window.

Figure 46

2

- If your screen displays the Backstage view, click This PC, if necessary, to display options in the right pane related to saving on your computer or mobile device; if your screen already displays the Save As dialog box, proceed to Step 3.

Q&A
What if I wanted to save on OneDrive instead?
You would click OneDrive. Saving on OneDrive is discussed in a later section in this module.

- Click the Browse button in the left pane to display the Save As dialog box (Figure 47).

Q&A
Why does a file name already appear in the File name box?
Word automatically suggests a file name the first time you save a document. The file name normally consists of the first few words contained in the document. Because the suggested file name is selected, you do not need to delete it; as soon as you begin typing, the new file name replaces the selected text.

navigation pane (your list may differ)

Save As dialog box

first few words from document are displayed as default file name and are selected in File name box

details pane shows file properties

default file type is Word Document

Figure 47

3

- Type **National Monuments** in the File name box (Save As dialog box) to change the file name. Do not press the ENTER key after typing the file name because you do not want to close the dialog box at this time (Figure 48).

Q&A
What characters can I use in a file name?
The only invalid characters are the backslash (\), slash (/), colon (:), asterisk (*), question mark (?), quotation mark ("), less than symbol (<), greater than symbol (>), and vertical bar (|).

new file name replaces highlighted text in File name box

Figure 48

- Navigate to the desired save location (in this case, the Word folder in the CIS 101 folder [or your class folder] in the Documents folder) by performing the tasks in Steps 4a and 4b.

- If the Documents folder is not displayed in the navigation pane, drag the scroll bar in the navigation pane until Documents appears.

- If the Documents folder is not expanded in the navigation pane, double-click Documents to display its folders in the navigation pane.

- If your class folder (CIS 101, in this case) is not expanded, double-click the CIS 101 folder to select the folder and display its contents in the navigation pane (Figure 49).

Figure 49

Q&A What if I do not want to save in a folder?

Although storing files in folders is an effective technique for organizing files, some users prefer not to store files in folders. If you prefer not to save this file in a folder, select the storage device on which you wish to save the file and then proceed to Step 5.

- Click the Word folder in the navigation pane to select it as the new save location and display its contents in the file list (Figure 50).

Figure 50

5

- Click the Save button (Save As dialog box) to save the document in the selected folder in the selected location with the entered file name (Figure 51).

Q&A

How do I know that the file is saved?
While an Office app is saving a file, it briefly displays a message on the status bar indicating the amount of the file saved. In addition, the file name appears on the title bar.

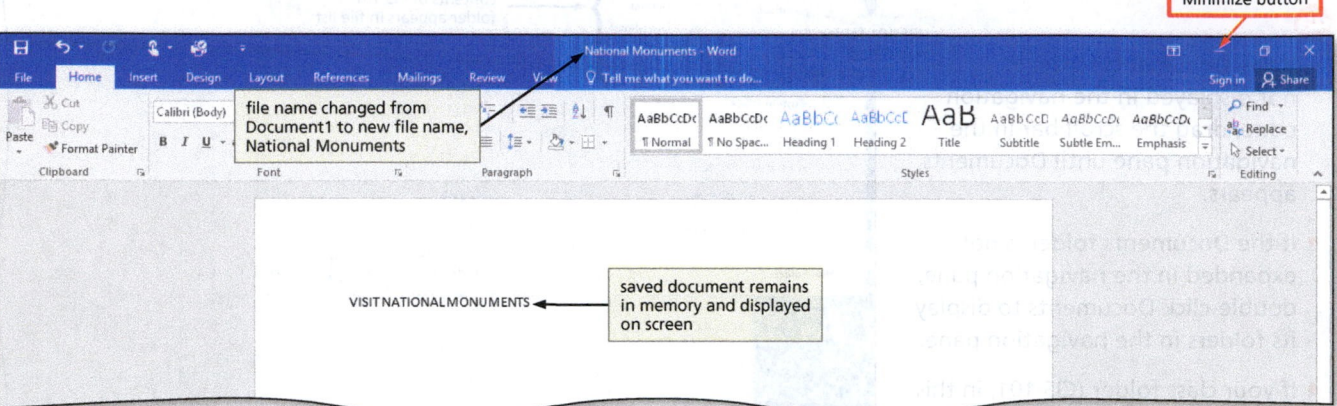

Figure 51

Other Ways

1. Click File on ribbon, click Save As in Backstage view, click This PC, click Browse button, type file name (Save As dialog box), navigate to desired save location, click Save button

2. Press F12, type file name (Save As dialog box), navigate to desired save location, click Save button

How often should you save a document?

It is important to save a document frequently for the following reasons:

- The document in memory might be lost if the computer is turned off or you lose electrical power while an app is running.

- If you run out of time before completing a project, you may finish it at a future time without starting over.

Navigating in Dialog Boxes

Navigating is the process of finding a location on a storage device. While saving the National Monuments file, for example, Steps 4a and 4b navigated to the Word folder located in the CIS 101 folder in the Documents folder. When performing certain functions in Windows apps, such as saving a file, opening a file, or inserting a picture in an existing document, you most likely will have to navigate to the location where you want to save the file or to the folder containing the file you want to open or insert. Most dialog boxes in Windows apps requiring navigation follow a similar procedure; that is, the way you navigate to a folder in one dialog box, such as the Save As dialog box, is similar to how you might navigate in another dialog box, such as the Open dialog box. If you chose to navigate to a specific location in a dialog box, you would follow the instructions in Steps 4a and 4b.

To Minimize and Restore a Window

1 SIGN IN | **2 USE WINDOWS** | 3 USE APPS | 4 FILE MANAGEMENT | 5 SWITCH APPS | 6 SAVE FILES
7 CHANGE SCREEN RESOLUTION | 8 EXIT APPS | 9 USE ADDITIONAL APPS | 10 USE HELP

Before continuing, you can verify that the Word file was saved properly. To do this, you will minimize the Word window and then open the CIS 101 window so that you can verify the file is stored in the CIS 101 folder on the hard drive. A **minimized window** is an open window that is hidden from view but can be displayed quickly by clicking the window's button on the taskbar.

In the following example, Word is used to illustrate minimizing and restoring windows; however, you would follow the same steps regardless of the Office app you are using. ***Why?*** *Before closing an app, you should make sure your file saved correctly so that you can find it later.*

The following steps minimize the Word window, verify that the file is saved, and then restore the minimized window.

1

- Click the Minimize button on the app's title bar (shown in Figure 51) to minimize the window (Figure 52).

Q&A Is the minimized window still available?
The minimized window, Word in this case, remains available but no longer is the active window. It is minimized as a button on the taskbar.

- If the File Explorer window is not open on the screen, click the File Explorer button on the taskbar to make the File Explorer window the active window.

Figure 52

2

- Double-click the Word folder in the file list to select the folder and display its contents (Figure 53).

Q&A Why does the File Explorer button on the taskbar change?
A selected app button indicates that the app is active on the screen. When the button is not selected, the app is running but not active.

3

- After viewing the contents of the selected folder, click the Word button on the taskbar to restore the minimized window (as shown in Figure 51).

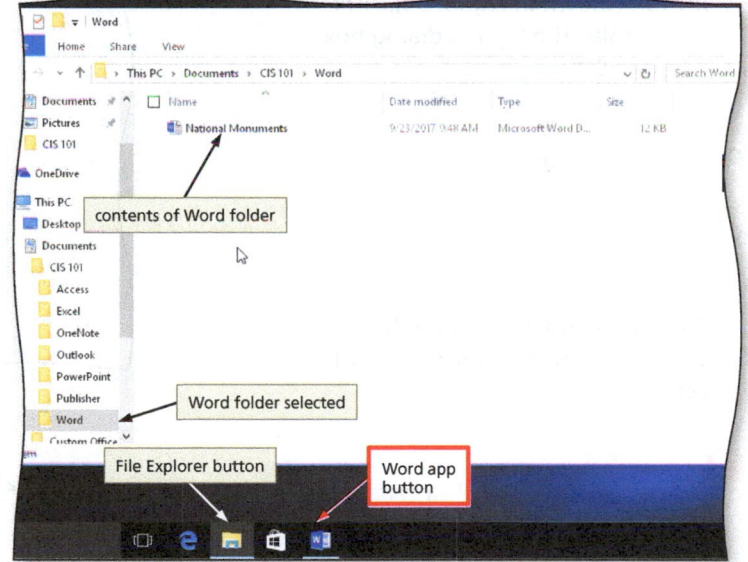

Figure 53

Other Ways

1. Right-click title bar, click Minimize on shortcut menu, click taskbar button in taskbar button area
2. Press WINDOWS+M, press WINDOWS+SHIFT+M
3. Click Word app button on taskbar to minimize window. Click Word app button again to restore window.

To Save a File on OneDrive

1 SIGN IN | 2 USE WINDOWS | 3 USE APPS | 4 FILE MANAGEMENT | 5 SWITCH APPS | **6 SAVE FILES**
7 CHANGE SCREEN RESOLUTION | 8 EXIT APPS | 9 USE ADDITIONAL APPS | 10 USE HELP

One of the features of Office is the capability to save files on OneDrive so that you can use the files on multiple computers or mobile devices without having to use an external storage device, such as a USB flash drive. Storing files on OneDrive also enables you to share files more efficiently with others, such as when using Office Online and Office 365.

In the following example, Word is used to save a file on OneDrive. *Why? Storing files on OneDrive provides more portability options than are available from storing files in the Documents folder.*

You can save files directly on OneDrive from within an Office app. The following steps save the current Word file on OneDrive. These steps require you have a Microsoft account and an Internet connection.

1

- Click File on the ribbon to open the Backstage view.

Q&A What is the purpose of the File tab?
The File tab opens the Backstage view for each Office app.

- Click the Save As tab in the Backstage view to display the Save As gallery.
- Click OneDrive to display OneDrive saving options or a Sign In button, if you are not signed in already to your Microsoft account (Figure 54).

Figure 54

2

- If your screen displays a Sign In button (shown in Figure 54), click it to display the Sign in dialog box (Figure 55).

Q&A What if the Sign In button does not appear?
If you already are signed into your Microsoft account, the Sign In button will not be displayed. In this case, proceed to Step 3.

- Follow the instructions on the screen to sign in to your Microsoft account.

Figure 55

3

- If necessary, click OneDrive in the left pane.
- In the Backstage view, click the Documents folder in the right pane to display the Save As dialog box (Figure 56).

4

- Click the Save button (Save As dialog box) to save the file on OneDrive.

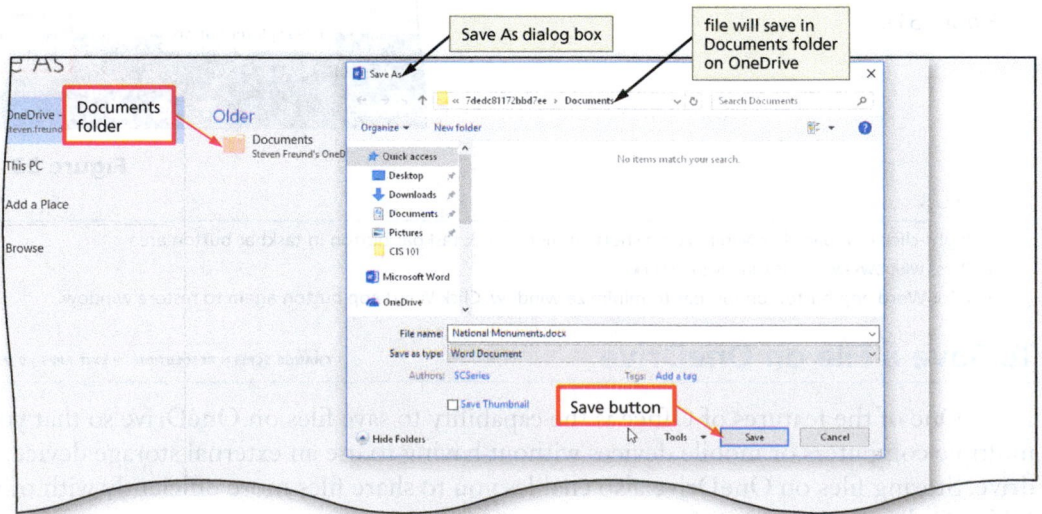

Figure 56

To Sign Out of a Microsoft Account

If you are using a public computer or otherwise wish to sign out of your Microsoft account, you should sign out of the account from the Accounts gallery in the Backstage view. Signing out of the account is the safest way to make sure that nobody else can access online files or settings stored in your Microsoft account. ***Why?*** *For security reasons, you should sign out of your Microsoft account when you are finished using a public or shared computer. Staying signed in to your Microsoft account might enable others to access your files.*

The following steps sign out of a Microsoft account from Word. You would use the same steps in any Office app. If you do not wish to sign out of your Microsoft account, read these steps without performing them.

1 Click File on the ribbon to open the Backstage view.

2 Click the Account tab to display the Account gallery (Figure 57).

3 Click the Sign out link, which displays the Remove Account dialog box. If a Can't remove Windows accounts dialog box appears instead of the Remove Account dialog box, click the OK button and skip the remaining steps.

Q&A Why does a Can't remove Windows accounts dialog box appear?
If you signed in to Windows using your Microsoft account, then you also must sign out from Windows, rather than signing out from within Word. When you are finished using Windows, be sure to sign out at that time.

4 Click the Yes button (Remove Account dialog box) to sign out of your Microsoft account on this computer.

Q&A Should I sign out of Windows after removing my Microsoft account?
When you are finished using the computer, you should sign out of Windows for maximum security.

5 Click the Back button in the upper-left corner of the Backstage view to return to the document.

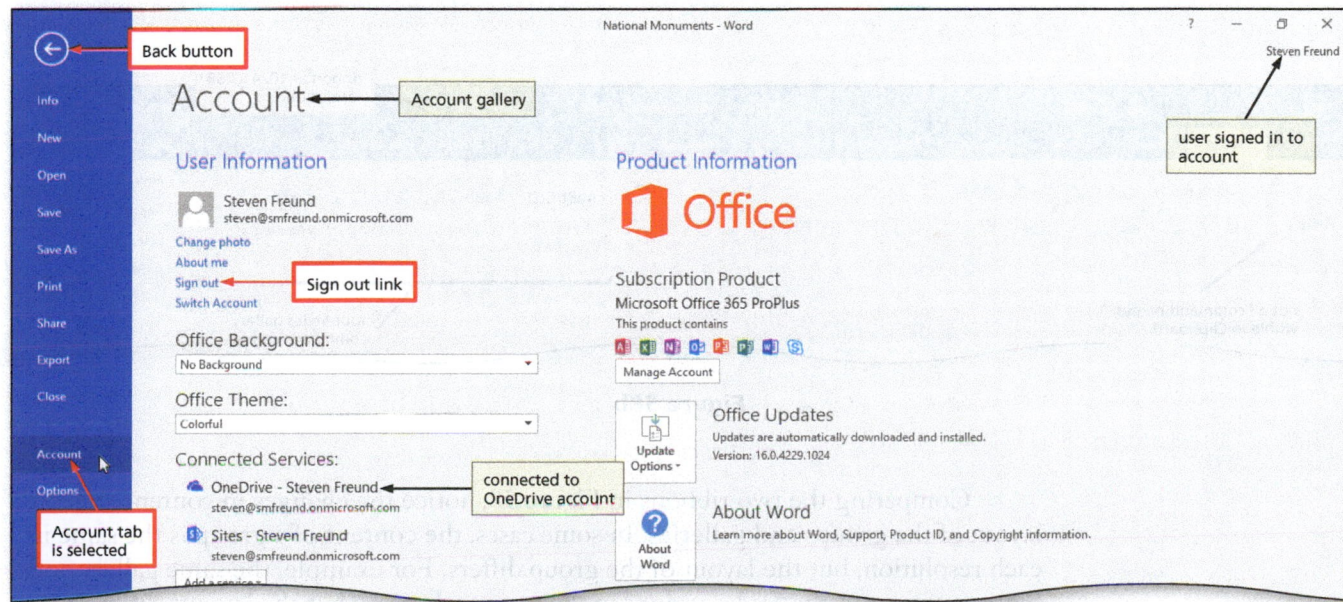

Figure 57

Screen Resolution

Screen resolution indicates the number of pixels (dots) that the computer uses to display the letters, numbers, graphics, and background you see on the screen. When you increase the screen resolution, Windows displays more information on the screen, but the information decreases in size. The reverse also is true: as you decrease the screen resolution, Windows displays less information on the screen, but the information increases in size.

Screen resolution usually is stated as the product of two numbers, such as 1366 × 768 (pronounced "thirteen sixty-six by seven sixty-eight"). A 1366 × 768 screen resolution results in a display of 1366 distinct pixels on each of 768 lines, or about 1,050,624 pixels. Changing the screen resolution affects how the ribbon appears in Office apps and some Windows dialog boxes. Figure 58 shows the Word ribbon at screen resolutions of 1366 × 768 and 1024 × 768. All of the same commands are available regardless of screen resolution. The app (Word, in this case), however, makes changes to the groups and the buttons within the groups to accommodate the various screen resolutions. The result is that certain commands may need to be accessed differently depending on the resolution chosen. A command that is visible on the ribbon and available by clicking a button at one resolution may not be visible and may need to be accessed using its Dialog Box Launcher at a different resolution.

Figure 58a

Figure 58b

Comparing the two ribbons in Figure 58, notice the changes in content and layout of the groups and galleries. In some cases, the content of a group is the same in each resolution, but the layout of the group differs. For example, the same gallery and buttons appear in the Styles groups in the two resolutions, but the layouts differ. In other cases, the content and layout are the same across the resolution, but the level of detail differs with the resolution.

To Change the Screen Resolution

If you are using a computer to step through the modules in this book and you want your screen to match the figures, you may need to change your screen's resolution. *Why? The figures in this book use a screen resolution of 1366 × 768.* The following steps change the screen resolution to 1366 × 768. Your computer already may be set to 1366 × 768. Keep in mind that many computer labs prevent users from changing the screen resolution; in that case, read the following steps for illustration purposes.

1

- Click the Show desktop button, which is located at the far-right edge of the taskbar, to display the Windows desktop.

- Right-click an empty area on the Windows desktop to display a shortcut menu that contains a list of commands related to the desktop (Figure 59).

Q&A Why does my shortcut menu display different commands?
Depending on your computer's hardware and configuration, different commands might appear on the shortcut menu.

Figure 59

2

- Click Display settings on the shortcut menu to open the Settings app window. If necessary, scroll to display the 'Advanced display settings' link (Figure 60).

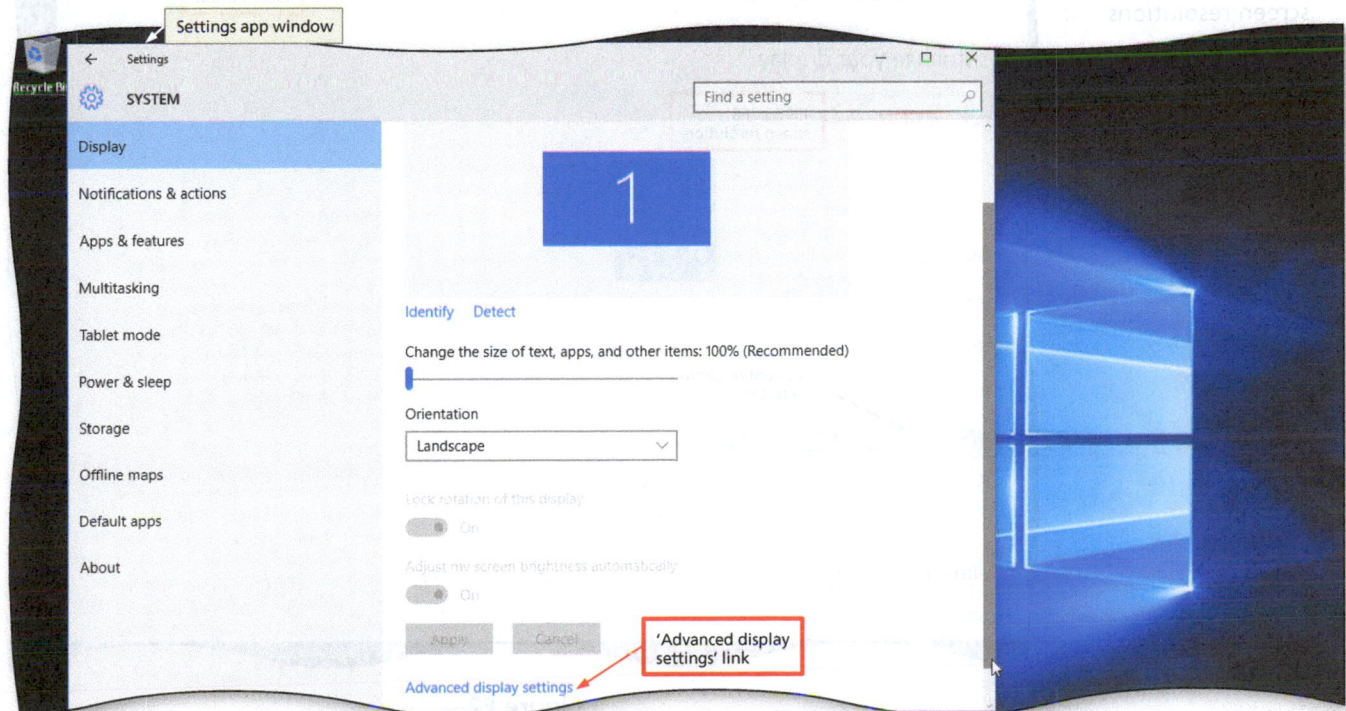

Figure 60

3

- Click 'Advanced display settings' in the Settings window to display the advanced display settings.
- If necessary, scroll to display the Resolution box (Figure 61).

Figure 61

4

- Click the Resolution box to display a list of available screen resolutions (Figure 62).
- If necessary, scroll to and then click 1366 × 768 to select the screen resolution.

Q&A

What if my computer does not support the 1366 × 768 resolution? Some computers do not support the 1366 × 768 resolution. In this case, select a resolution that is close to the 1366 × 768 resolution.

Figure 62

- Click the Apply button (Advanced Display Settings window) (shown in Figure 61) to change the screen resolution and display a confirmation message (Figure 63).
- Click the Keep changes button to accept the new screen resolution.
- Click the Close button (shown in Figure 62) to close the Settings app window.

Figure 63

Other Ways

1. Click Start button, click Settings, click System, click Display, click 'Advanced display settings,' select desired resolution in Resolution box, click Apply button, click Keep changes button

2. Type `screen resolution` in search box, click 'Change the screen resolution,' select desired resolution in Resolution box, click Apply, click Keep changes

To Exit an Office App with One Document Open

1 SIGN IN | 2 USE WINDOWS | 3 USE APPS | 4 FILE MANAGEMENT | 5 SWITCH APPS | 6 SAVE FILES
7 CHANGE SCREEN RESOLUTION | 8 EXIT APPS | 9 USE ADDITIONAL APPS | 10 USE HELP

When you exit an Office app, such as Word, if you have made changes to a file since the last time the file was saved, the Office app displays a dialog box asking if you want to save the changes you made to the file before it closes the app window. **Why?** *The dialog box contains three buttons with these resulting actions: the Save button saves the changes and then exits the Office app, the Don't Save button exits the Office app without saving changes, and the Cancel button closes the dialog box and redisplays the file without saving the changes.*

If no changes have been made to an open document since the last time the file was saved, the Office app will close the window without displaying a dialog box.

The following steps exit an Office app. In the following example, Word is used to illustrate exiting an Office app; however, you would follow the same steps regardless of the Office app you were using.

- If necessary, click the Word app button on the taskbar to display the Word window on the desktop (Figure 64).

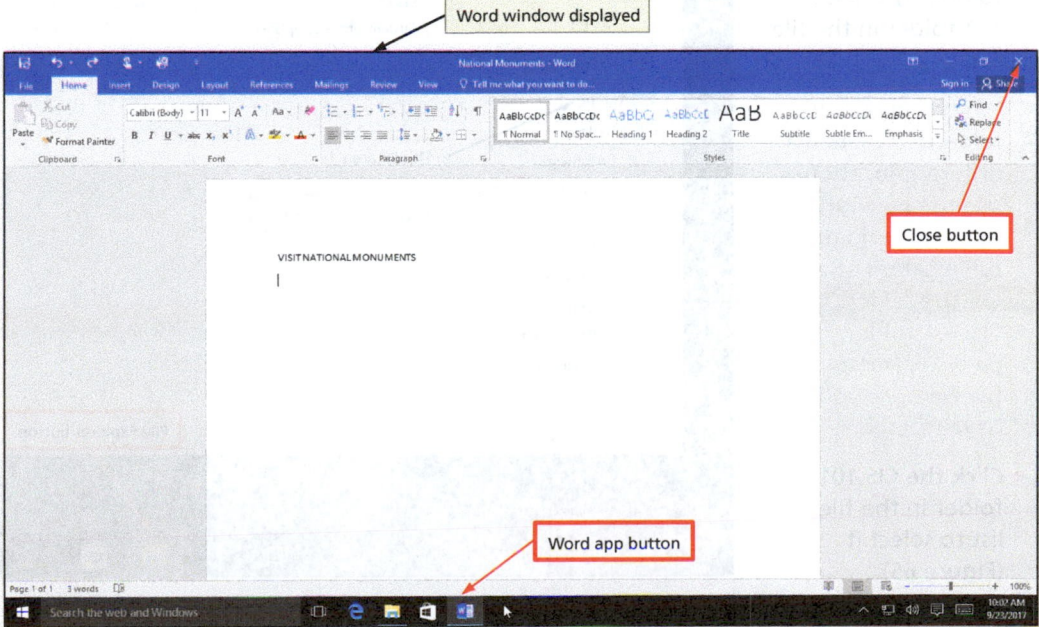

Figure 64

2

- Click the Close button to close the document and exit Word. If a Microsoft Word dialog box appears, click the Save button to save any changes made to the document since the last save.

Q&A What if I have more than one document open in an Office app?
You could click the Close button for each open document. When you click the last open document's Close button, you also exit the Office app. As an alternative that is more efficient, you could right-click the app button on the taskbar and then click 'Close all windows' on the shortcut menu, or press ALT+F4 to close all open documents and exit the Office app.

Other Ways

1. Right-click the Office app button on Windows taskbar, click Close window on shortcut menu
2. Press ALT + F4

To Copy a Folder to OneDrive

1 SIGN IN | 2 USE WINDOWS | 3 USE APPS | **4 FILE MANAGEMENT** | 5 SWITCH APPS | 6 SAVE FILES
7 CHANGE SCREEN RESOLUTION | 8 EXIT APPS | **9 USE ADDITIONAL APPS** | 10 USE HELP

To back up your files or easily make them available on another computer or mobile device, you can copy them to OneDrive. The following steps copy your CIS 101 folder to OneDrive. If you do not have access to a OneDrive account, read the following steps without performing them. *Why? It often is good practice to have a backup of your files so that they are available in case something happens to your original copies.*

1

- Click the File Explorer button on the taskbar to make the folder window the active window.
- Click Documents in the This PC area of the navigation pane to display the CIS 101 folder in the file list.

Q&A What if my CIS 101 folder is stored in a different location?
Use the navigation pane to navigate to the location of your CIS 101 folder. The CIS 101 folder should be displayed in the file list once you have located it.

- Click the CIS 101 folder in the file list to select it (Figure 65).

Figure 65

- Click Home on the ribbon to display the Home tab.
- Click the Copy to button (Home tab | Organize group) to display the Copy to menu (Figure 66).

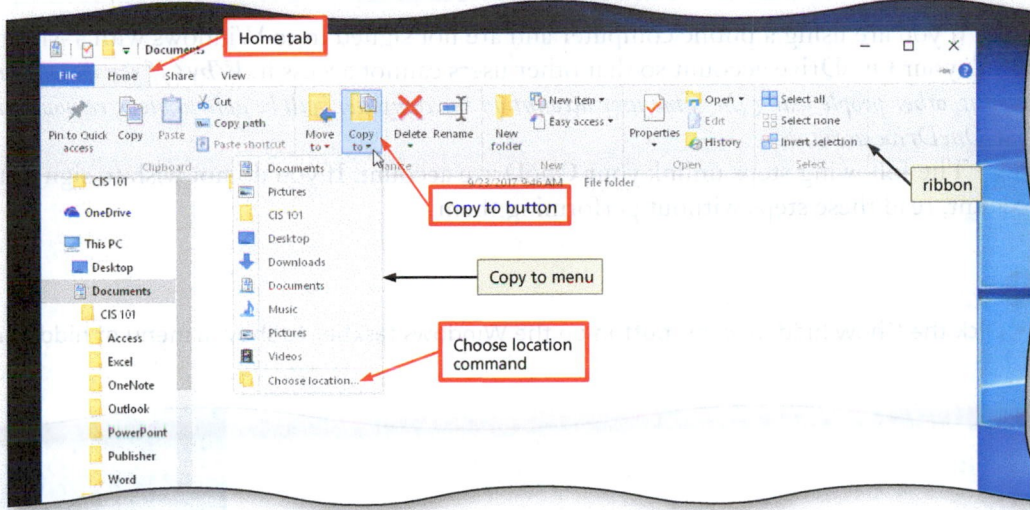

Figure 66

- Click Choose location on the Copy to menu to display the Copy Items dialog box.
- Click OneDrive (Copy Items dialog box) to select it (Figure 67).

Figure 67

- Click the Copy button (Copy Items dialog box) to copy the selected folder to OneDrive.
- Click OneDrive in the navigation pane to verify the CIS 101 folder displays in the file list (Figure 68).

Q&A Why does a Microsoft OneDrive dialog box display when I click OneDrive in the navigation pane?

If you are not currently signed in to Windows using a Microsoft account, you will manually need to sign in to a Microsoft account to save files to OneDrive. Follow the instructions on the screen to sign in to your Microsoft account.

Figure 68

Other Ways

1. In File Explorer, select folder to copy, click Copy button (Home tab | Clipboard group), display contents of OneDrive in file list, click Paste button (Home tab | Clipboard group)

2. In File Explorer, select folder to copy, press CTRL+C, display contents of OneDrive in file list, press CTRL+V

3. Drag folder to copy to OneDrive in navigation pane

To Unlink a OneDrive Account

If you are using a public computer and are not signed in to Windows with a Microsoft account, you should unlink your OneDrive account so that other users cannot access it. *Why? If you do not unlink your OneDrive account, other people using the same user account on the computer will be able to view, remove, and add to files stored in your OneDrive account.*

The following steps unlink your OneDrive account. If you do not wish to sign out of your Microsoft account, read these steps without performing them.

1

- Click the 'Show hidden icons' button on the Windows taskbar to show a menu of hidden icons (Figure 69).

Figure 69

2

- Right click the OneDrive icon (shown in Figure 69) to display a shortcut menu (Figure 70).

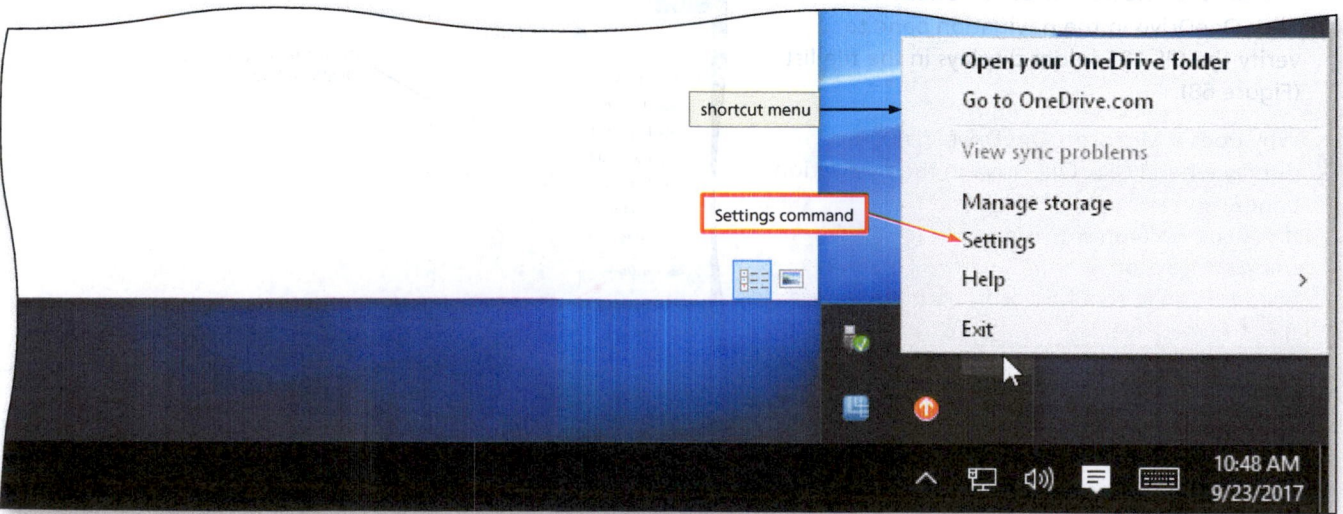

Figure 70

3

- Click Settings on the shortcut menu to display the Microsoft OneDrive dialog box (Figure 71).

Figure 71

4

- If necessary, click the Settings tab.
- Click the Unlink OneDrive button (Microsoft OneDrive dialog box) to unlink the OneDrive account (Figure 72).
- When the Microsoft OneDrive dialog box appears with a Welcome to OneDrive message, click the Close button.
- Minimize the File Explorer window.

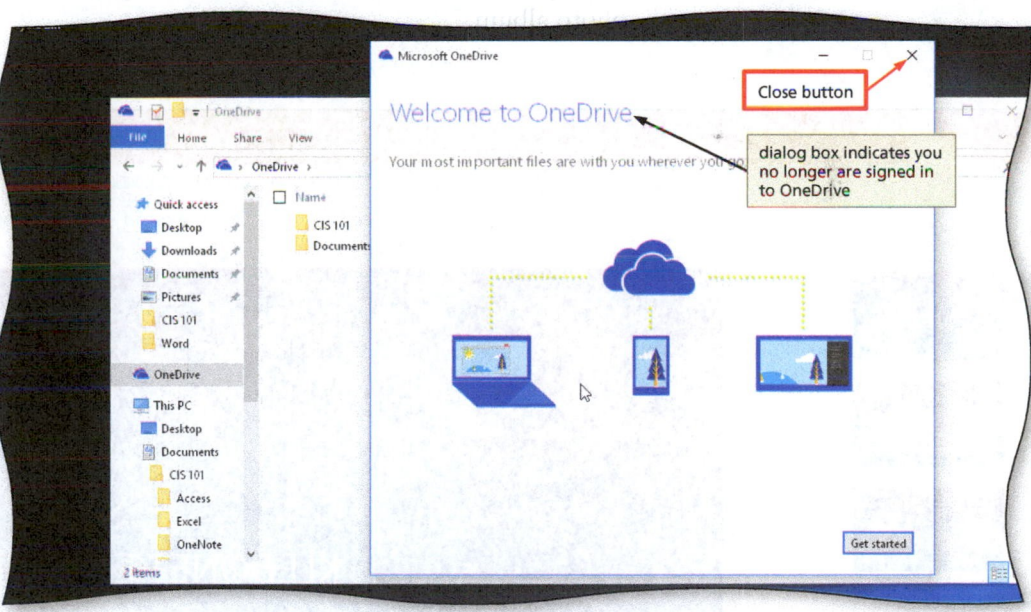

Figure 72

Break Point: If you wish to take a break, this is a good place to do so. To resume at a later time, continue to follow the steps from this location forward.

Additional Microsoft Office Apps

The previous section used Word to illustrate common features of Office and some basic elements unique to Word. The following sections present elements unique to PowerPoint, Excel, and Access, as well as illustrate additional common features of Office.

In the following pages, you will learn how to do the following:

1. Run an Office app (PowerPoint) using the search box.
2. Create two small documents in the same Office app (PowerPoint).
3. Close one of the documents.
4. Reopen the document just closed.
5. Create a document in a different Office app (Excel).
6. Save the document with a new file name.
7. Create a file in a different Office app (Access).
8. Close the file and then open the file.

PowerPoint

PowerPoint is a full-featured presentation app that allows you to produce compelling presentations to deliver and share with an audience (Figure 73). A PowerPoint **presentation** also is called a **slide show**. PowerPoint contains many features to design, develop, and organize slides, including formatting text, adding and editing video and audio clips, creating tables and charts, applying artistic effects to pictures, animating graphics, and collaborating with friends and colleagues. You then can turn your presentation into a video, broadcast your slide show on the web, or create a photo album.

Figure 73

To Run an App Using the Search Box

The following steps, which assume Windows is running, use the search box to run the PowerPoint app based on a typical installation; however, you would follow similar steps to run any Office app. *Why? Some people prefer to use the search box to locate and run an app, as opposed to searching through a list of all apps on the Start menu.* You may need to ask your instructor how to run apps for your computer.

1

- Type **PowerPoint 2016** as the search text in the search box and watch the search results appear in the search results (Figure 74).

Q&A

Do I need to type the complete app name or use correct capitalization?

No, you need to type just enough characters of the app name for it to appear in the search results. For example, you may be able to type PowerPoint or powerpoint, instead of PowerPoint 2016.

2

- Click the app name, PowerPoint 2016 in this case, in the search results to run PowerPoint (Figure 75).

Figure 74

Figure 75

- Click the Blank Presentation thumbnail to create a blank presentation and display it in the PowerPoint window.
- If the app window is not maximized, click the Maximize button on its title bar to maximize the window (Figure 76).

Figure 76

The PowerPoint Window and Ribbon

The PowerPoint window consists of a variety of components to make your work more efficient and documents more professional: the window, ribbon, mini toolbar, shortcut menus, Quick Access Toolbar, and Microsoft Account area. Many of these components are common to other Office apps and have been discussed earlier in this module. Other components, discussed in the following paragraphs and later in subsequent modules, are unique to PowerPoint.

The basic unit of a PowerPoint presentation is a **slide**. A slide may contain text and objects, such as graphics, tables, charts, and drawings. **Layouts** are used to position this content on the slide. When you create a new presentation, the default **Title Slide** layout appears (shown in Figure 76). The purpose of this layout is to introduce the presentation to the audience. PowerPoint includes several other built-in standard layouts.

The default slide layouts are set up in **landscape orientation**, where the slide width is greater than its height. In landscape orientation, the slide size is preset to 13.3 inches wide and 7.5 inches high when printed on a standard sheet of paper measuring 11 inches wide and 8.5 inches high.

Placeholders　**Placeholders** are boxes with dashed or solid borders that are displayed when you create a new slide. All layouts except the Blank slide layout contain placeholders. Depending on the particular slide layout selected, title and subtitle placeholders are displayed for the slide title and subtitle; a content placeholder is displayed for text or a table, chart, picture, graphic, or movie. The title slide in Figure 76 has two text placeholders for the main heading, or title, and the subtitle.

Ribbon　The ribbon in PowerPoint is similar to the one in Word and the other Microsoft Office apps. When you run PowerPoint, the ribbon displays nine main tabs: File, Home, Insert, Design, Transitions, Animations, Slide Show, Review, and View.

To Enter Content in a Title Slide

With the exception of a blank slide, PowerPoint assumes every new slide has a title. Many of PowerPoint's layouts have both a title text placeholder and at least one content placeholder. To make creating a presentation easier, any text you type after a new slide appears becomes title text in the title text placeholder. As you begin typing text in the title text placeholder, the title text also is displayed in the Slide 1 thumbnail in the Thumbnail pane. The title for this presentation is Mara's Marbles. The following step enters a presentation title on the title slide. *Why? In general, every presentation should have a title to describe what the presentation will be covering.*

1
- Click the 'Click to add title' label located inside the title text placeholder (shown in Figure 76) to select the placeholder.
- Type **Mara's Marbles** in the title text placeholder. Do not press the ENTER key because you do not want to create a new line of text (Figure 77).

Figure 77

To Save a File in a Folder

The following steps save the presentation in the PowerPoint folder in the class folder (CIS 101, in this case) in the Documents folder using the file name, Mara's Marbles.

1 Click the Save button on the Quick Access Toolbar (shown in Figure 77), which depending on settings will display either the Save As gallery in the Backstage view or the Save As dialog box.

2 If your screen displays the Backstage view, click This PC, if necessary, to display options in the right pane related to saving on your computer; if your screen already displays the Save As dialog box, proceed to Step 4.

3 Click the Browse button in the left pane to display the Save As dialog box.

4 If necessary, type **Mara's Marbles** in the File name box (Save As dialog box) to change the file name. Do not press the ENTER key after typing the file name because you do not want to close the dialog box at this time.

5 Navigate to the desired save location (in this case, the PowerPoint folder in the CIS 101 folder [or your class folder] in the Documents folder). For specific instructions, perform the tasks in Steps 5a through 5e.

5a If the Documents folder is not displayed in the navigation pane, slide to scroll or drag the scroll bar in the navigation pane until Documents appears.

5b If the Documents folder is not expanded in the navigation pane, double-click Documents to display its folders in the navigation pane.

5c If the Documents folder is not expanded in the navigation pane, double-click Documents to display its folders in the navigation pane.

5d If your class folder (CIS 101, in this case) is not expanded, double-click the CIS 101 folder to select the folder and display its contents in the navigation pane.

5e Click the PowerPoint folder in the navigation pane to select it as the new save location and display its contents in the file list.

6 Click the Save button (Save As dialog box) to save the presentation in the selected folder in the selected location with the entered file name.

To Create a New Office Document from the Backstage View

1 SIGN IN | 2 USE WINDOWS | 3 USE APPS | 4 FILE MANAGEMENT | 5 SWITCH APPS | 6 SAVE FILES
7 CHANGE SCREEN RESOLUTION | 8 EXIT APPS | **9 USE ADDITIONAL APPS** | **10 USE HELP**

As discussed earlier, the Backstage view contains a set of commands that enable you to manage documents and data about the documents. ***Why? From the Backstage view in PowerPoint, for example, you can create, open, print, and save presentations. You also can share documents, manage versions, set permissions, and modify document properties. In other Office 2016 apps, the Backstage view may contain features specific to those apps.*** The following steps create a file, a blank presentation in this case, from the Backstage view.

1

- Click File on the ribbon to open the Backstage view (Figure 78).

Q&A What is the purpose of the Info tab in the Backstage view?
The Info tab, which is selected by default when you click File on the ribbon, allows you to protect your document, inspect your document, and manage versions of your document as well as view all the file properties, such as when the file was created.

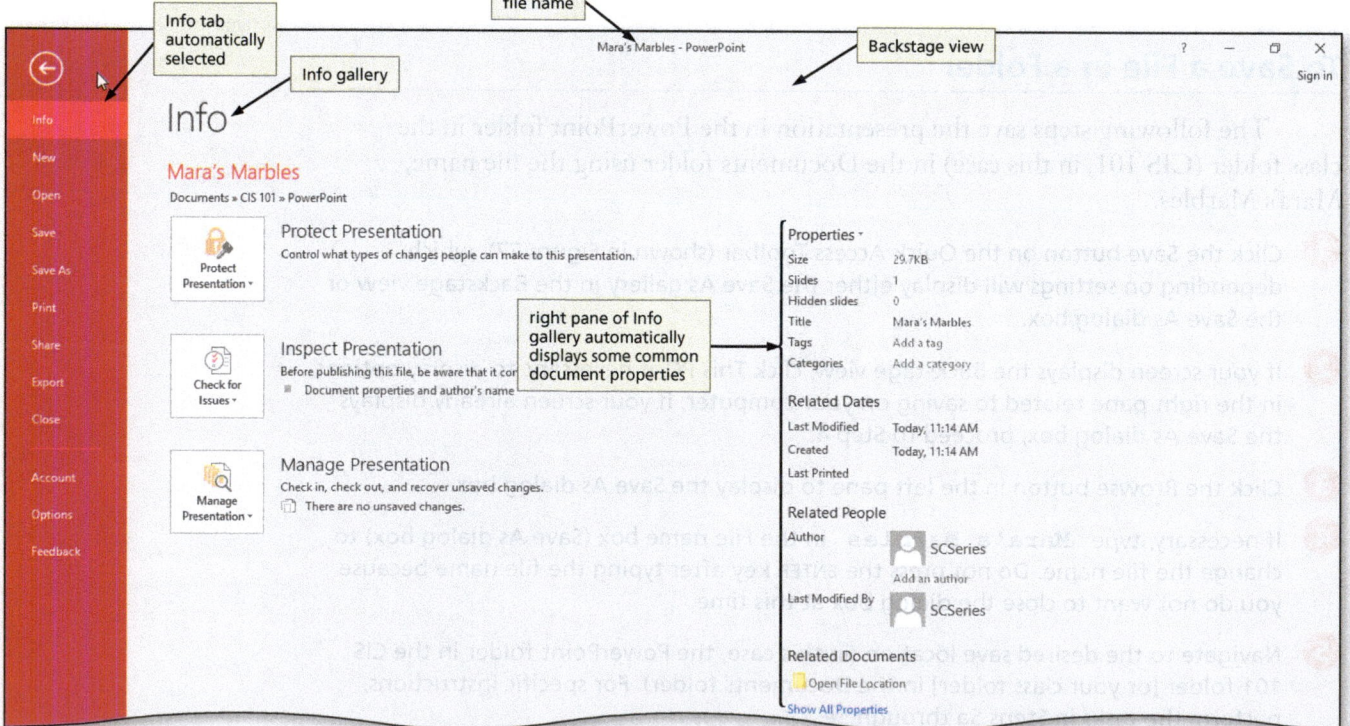

Figure 78

2

- Click the New tab in the Backstage view to display the New gallery (Figure 79).

Q&A

Can I create documents through the Backstage view in other Office apps?
Yes. If the Office app has a New tab in the Backstage view, the New gallery displays various options for creating a new file.

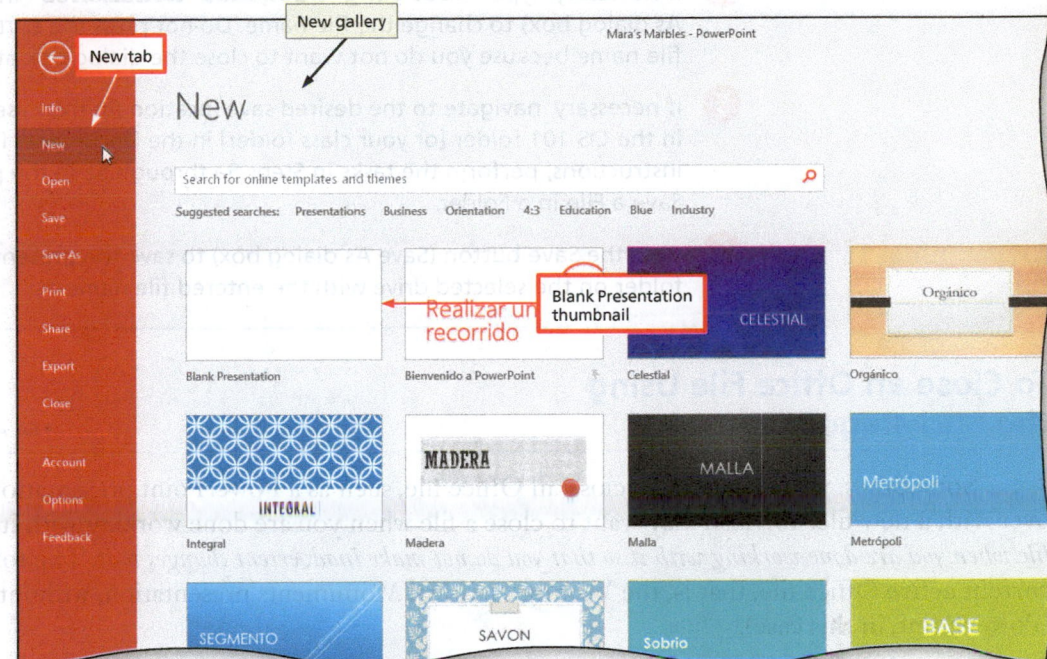

Figure 79

3

- Click the Blank Presentation thumbnail in the New gallery to create a new presentation.

Other Ways

1. Press CTRL+N

To Enter Content in a Title Slide of a Second PowerPoint Presentation

The presentation title for this presentation is Visiting National Monuments. The following steps enter a presentation title on the title slide.

1 Click the title text placeholder to select it.

2 Type **Visiting National Monuments** in the title text placeholder. Do not press the ENTER key.

To Save a File in a Folder

The following steps save the second presentation in the PowerPoint folder in the class folder (CIS 101, in this case) in the Documents folder using the file name, Visiting National Monuments.

1 Click the Save button on the Quick Access Toolbar, which depending on settings will display either the Save As gallery in the Backstage view or the Save As dialog box.

2 If your screen displays the Backstage view, click This PC, if necessary, to display options in the right pane related to saving on your computer; if your screen already displays the Save As dialog box, proceed to Step 4.

3 Click the Browse button in the left pane to display the Save As dialog box.

4 If necessary, type `Visiting National Monuments` in the File name box (Save As dialog box) to change the file name. Do not press the ENTER key after typing the file name because you do not want to close the dialog box at this time.

5 If necessary, navigate to the desired save location (in this case, the PowerPoint folder in the CIS 101 folder [or your class folder] in the Documents folder). For specific instructions, perform the tasks in Steps 5a through 5e in the previous section titled To Save a File in a Folder.

6 Click the Save button (Save As dialog box) to save the presentation in the selected folder on the selected drive with the entered file name.

To Close an Office File Using the Backstage View

1 SIGN IN | 2 USE WINDOWS | 3 USE APPS | 4 FILE MANAGEMENT | 5 SWITCH APPS | 6 SAVE FILES
7 CHANGE SCREEN RESOLUTION | 8 EXIT APPS | **9 USE ADDITIONAL APPS** | 10 USE HELP

Sometimes, you may want to close an Office file, such as a PowerPoint presentation, entirely and start over with a new file. You also may want to close a file when you are done working with it. *Why? You should close a file when you are done working with it so that you do not make inadvertent changes to it.* The following steps close the current active Office file, that is, the Visiting National Monuments presentation, without exiting the active app (PowerPoint, in this case).

1

- Click File on the ribbon to open the Backstage view (Figure 80).

2

- Click Close in the Backstage view to close the open file (Visiting National Monuments, in this case) without exiting the active app.

Q&A What if the Office app displays a dialog box about saving?
Click the Save button if you want to save the changes, click the Don't Save button if you want to ignore the changes since the last time you saved, and click the Cancel button if you do not want to close the document.

Can I use the Backstage view to close an open file in other Office apps, such as Word and Excel?
Yes.

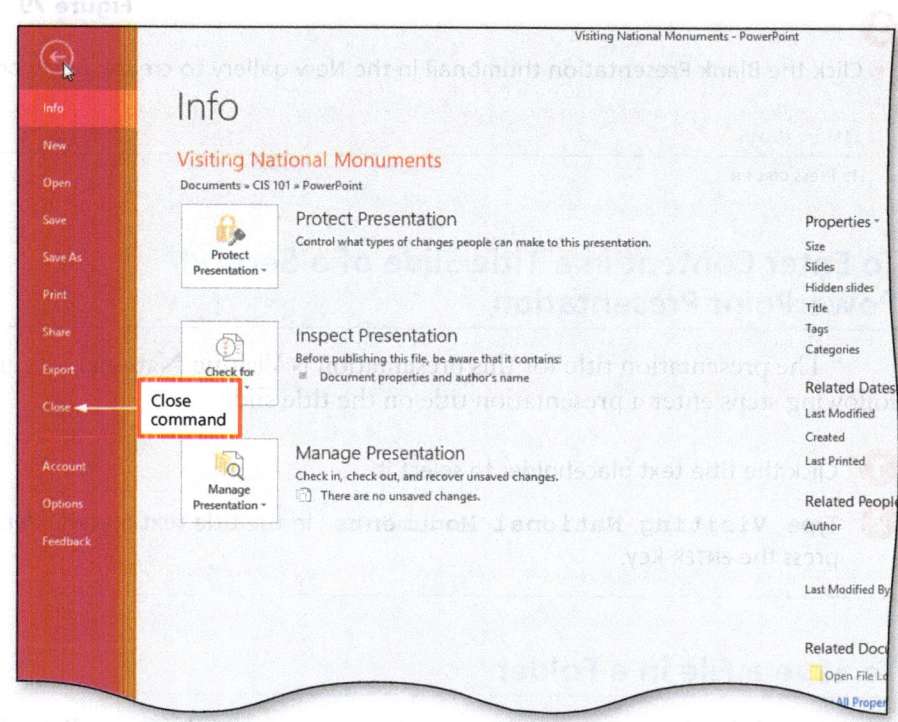

Figure 80

Other Ways

1. Press CTRL+F4

To Open a Recent Office File Using the Backstage View

1 SIGN IN | 2 USE WINDOWS | 3 USE APPS | 4 FILE MANAGEMENT | 5 SWITCH APPS | 6 SAVE FILES
7 CHANGE SCREEN RESOLUTION | 8 EXIT APPS | **9 USE ADDITIONAL APPS** | 10 USE HELP

You sometimes need to open a file that you recently modified. *Why? You may have more changes to make, such as adding more content or correcting errors.* The Backstage view allows you to access recent files easily. The following steps reopen the Visiting National Monuments file just closed.

1

- Click File on the ribbon to open the Backstage view.
- Click the Open tab in the Backstage view to display the Open gallery (Figure 81).

2

- Click the desired file name in the Recent list, Visiting National Monuments in this case, to open the file.

Q&A Can I use the Backstage view to open a recent file in other Office apps, such as Word and Excel?

Yes, as long as the file name appears in the list of recent files.

Figure 81

Other Ways

1. Click File on ribbon, click Open in Backstage view, click This PC, click Browse button, navigate to file (Open dialog box), click Open button

To Exit an Office App

You are finished using PowerPoint. Thus, you should exit this Office app. The following steps exit PowerPoint.

1 If you have one Office document open, click the Close button on the right side of the title bar to close the document and exit the Office app; or if you have multiple Office documents open, right-click the app button on the taskbar and then click 'Close all windows' on the shortcut menu, or press ALT+F4 to close all open documents and exit the Office app.

Q&A If I am using a touch screen, could I press and hold the Close button until all windows close and the app exits?

Yes.

2 If a dialog box appears, click the Save button to save any changes made to the document since the last save.

Excel

Excel is a powerful spreadsheet app that allows users to organize data, complete calculations, make decisions, graph data, develop professional-looking reports (Figure 82), publish organized data to the web, and access real-time data from websites. The four major parts of Excel are:

- **Workbooks and Worksheets:** A **workbook** is like a notebook. Inside the workbook are sheets, each of which is called a **worksheet**. Thus, a workbook is a collection of worksheets. Worksheets allow users to enter, calculate, manipulate, and analyze data, such as numbers and text. The terms worksheet and spreadsheet are interchangeable.

- **Charts:** Excel can draw a variety of charts, such as column charts and pie charts.

- **Tables:** Tables organize and store data within worksheets. For example, once a user enters data into a worksheet, an Excel table can sort the data, search for specific data, and select data that satisfies defined criteria.

- **Web Support:** Web support allows users to save Excel

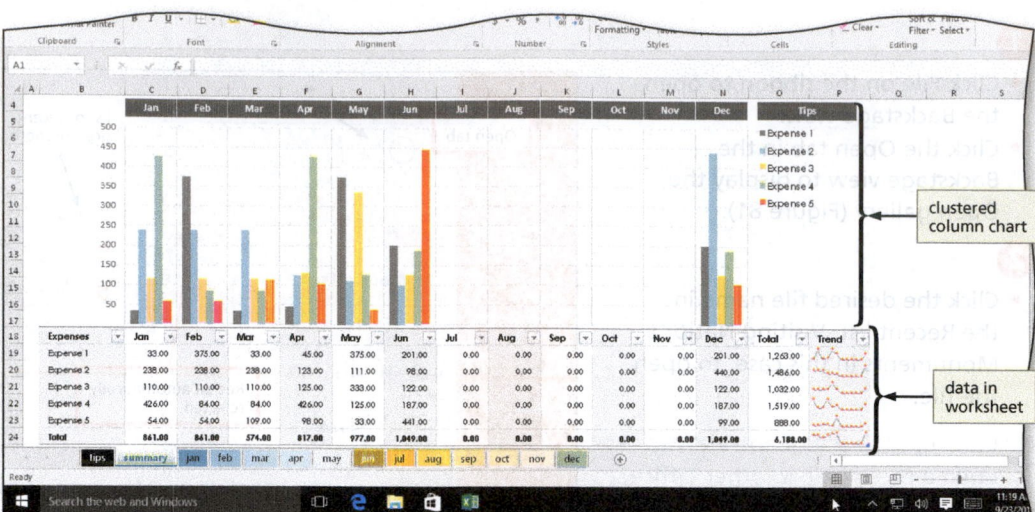

Figure 82

worksheets or parts of a worksheet in a format that a user can view in a browser, so that a user can view and manipulate the worksheet using a browser. Excel web support also provides access to real-time data, such as stock quotes, using web queries.

To Create a New Blank Office Document from File Explorer

1 SIGN IN | 2 USE WINDOWS | 3 USE APPS | 4 FILE MANAGEMENT | 5 SWITCH APPS | 6 SAVE FILES
7 CHANGE SCREEN RESOLUTION | 8 EXIT APPS | 9 USE ADDITIONAL APPS | 10 USE HELP

File Explorer provides a means to create a blank Office document without running an Office app. The following steps use File Explorer to create a blank Excel document. *Why? Sometimes you might need to create a blank document and then return to it later for editing.*

1

- If necessary, click the File Explorer button on the taskbar to make the folder window the active window.

- If necessary, double-click the Documents folder in the navigation pane to expand the Documents folder.

- If necessary, double-click your class folder (CIS 101, in this case) in the navigation pane to expand the folder.

- Click the Excel folder in the navigation pane to display its contents in the file list.

- With the Excel folder selected, right-click an open area in the file list to display a shortcut menu.

- Point to New on the shortcut menu to display the New submenu (Figure 83).

Figure 83

- Click 'Microsoft Excel Worksheet' on the New submenu to display an icon and text box for a new file in the current folder window with the file name, New Microsoft Excel Worksheet, selected (Figure 84).

Figure 84

- Type **Silver Sky Hardware** in the text box and then press the ENTER key to assign a new file name to the new file in the current folder (Figure 85).

Figure 85

To Run an App from File Explorer and Open a File

1 SIGN IN | 2 USE WINDOWS | 3 USE APPS | 4 FILE MANAGEMENT | 5 SWITCH APPS | 6 SAVE FILES
7 CHANGE SCREEN RESOLUTION | 8 EXIT APPS | **9 USE ADDITIONAL APPS** | 10 USE HELP

Previously, you learned how to run an Office app using the Start menu and the search box. The following steps, which assume Windows is running, use File Explorer to run the Excel app based on a typical installation. *Why? Another way to run an Office app is to open an existing file from File Explorer, which causes the app in which the file was created to run and then open the selected file.* You may need to ask your instructor how to run Office apps for your computer.

- If necessary, display the file to open in the folder window in File Explorer (shown in Figure 85).
- Right-click the file icon or file name (Silver Sky Hardware, in this case) to display a shortcut menu (Figure 86).

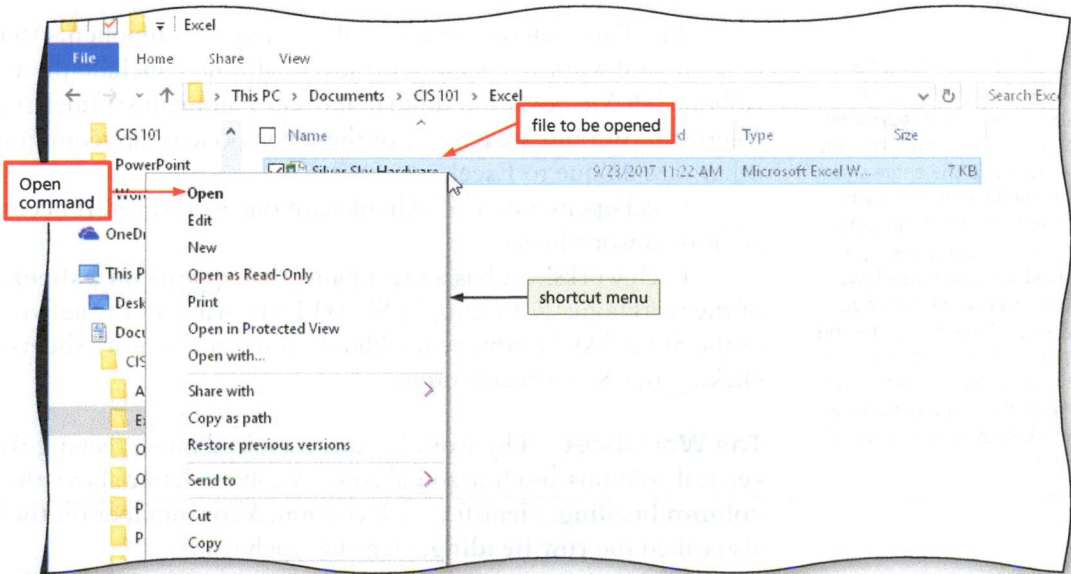

Figure 86

2
- Click Open on the shortcut menu to open the selected file in the app used to create the file, Excel in this case (Figure 87).
- If the window is not maximized, click the Maximize button on the title bar to maximize the window.

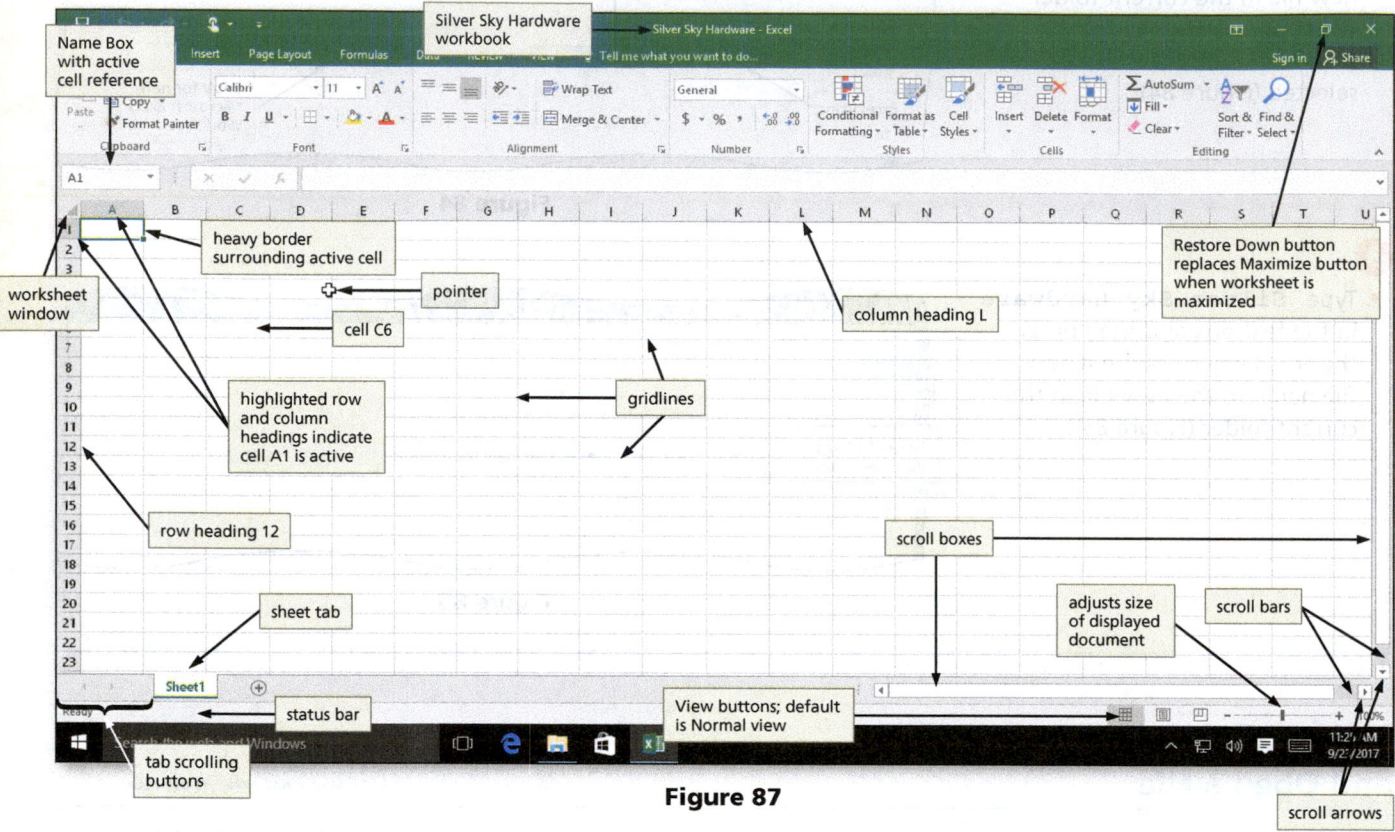

Figure 87

Q&A Instead of using File Explorer, can I run Excel using the same method shown previously for Word and PowerPoint?
Yes, you can use any method of running an Office app to run Excel.

BTW
The Worksheet Size and Window
The 16,384 columns and 1,048,576 rows in Excel make for a huge worksheet that — if you could imagine — takes up the entire side of a building to display in its entirety. Your computer screen, by comparison, is a small window that allows you to view only a minute area of the worksheet at one time. While you cannot see the entire worksheet, you can move the window over the worksheet to view any part of it.

Unique Features of Excel

The Excel window consists of a variety of components to make your work more efficient and worksheets more professional. These include the worksheet window, ribbon, Tell Me box, mini toolbar and shortcut menus, Quick Access Toolbar, and Microsoft Account area. Some of these components are common to other Office apps; others are unique to Excel.

Excel opens a new workbook with one worksheet. If necessary, you can add additional worksheets.

Each worksheet has a sheet name that appears on a **sheet tab** at the bottom of the workbook. For example, Sheet1 is the name of the active worksheet displayed in the Silver Sky Hardware workbook. You can add more sheets to the workbook by clicking the New sheet button.

The Worksheet The worksheet is organized into a rectangular grid containing vertical columns and horizontal rows. A column letter above the grid, also called the **column heading**, identifies each column. A row number on the left side of the grid, also called the **row heading**, identifies each row.

The intersection of each column and row is a cell. A **cell** is the basic unit of a worksheet into which you enter data. Each worksheet in a workbook has 16,384 columns and 1,048,576 rows for a total of 17,179,869,184 cells. Only a small fraction of the active worksheet appears on the screen at one time.

A cell is referred to by its unique address, or **cell reference**, which is the coordinates of the intersection of a column and a row. To identify a cell, specify the column letter first, followed by the row number. For example, cell reference C6 refers to the cell located at the intersection of column C and row 6 (Figure 87).

One cell on the worksheet, designated the **active cell**, is the one into which you can enter data. The active cell in Figure 87 is A1. The active cell is identified in three ways. First, a heavy border surrounds the cell; second, the active cell reference shows immediately above column A in the Name box; and third, the column heading A and row heading 1 are highlighted so that it is easy to see which cell is active (Figure 87).

The horizontal and vertical lines on the worksheet itself are called **gridlines**. Gridlines make it easier to see and identify each cell in the worksheet. If desired, you can turn the gridlines off so that they do not show on the worksheet. While learning Excel, gridlines help you to understand the structure of the worksheet.

The pointer in Figure 87 has the shape of a block plus sign. The pointer appears as a block plus sign whenever it is located in a cell on the worksheet. Another common shape of the pointer is the block arrow. The pointer turns into the block arrow when you move it outside the worksheet or when you drag cell contents between rows or columns.

Ribbon   When you run Excel, the ribbon displays eight main tabs: File, Home, Insert, Page Layout, Formulas, Data, Review, and View. The Formulas and Data tabs are specific to Excel. The Formulas tab allows you to work with Excel formulas, and the Data tab allows you to work with data processing features such as importing and sorting data.

Formula Bar   As you type, Excel displays the entry in the **formula bar**, which appears below the ribbon (Figure 88). You can make the formula bar larger by dragging the sizing handle at the bottom of the formula bar or clicking the expand button to the right of the formula bar. Excel also displays the active cell reference in the **Name box** on the left side of the formula bar.

BTW
Customizing the Ribbon
In addition to customizing the Quick Access Toolbar, you can add items to and remove items from the ribbon. To customize the ribbon, click File on the ribbon to open the Backstage view, click the Options tab in the Backstage view, and then click Customize Ribbon in the left pane of the Options dialog box. More information about customizing the ribbon is presented in a later module.

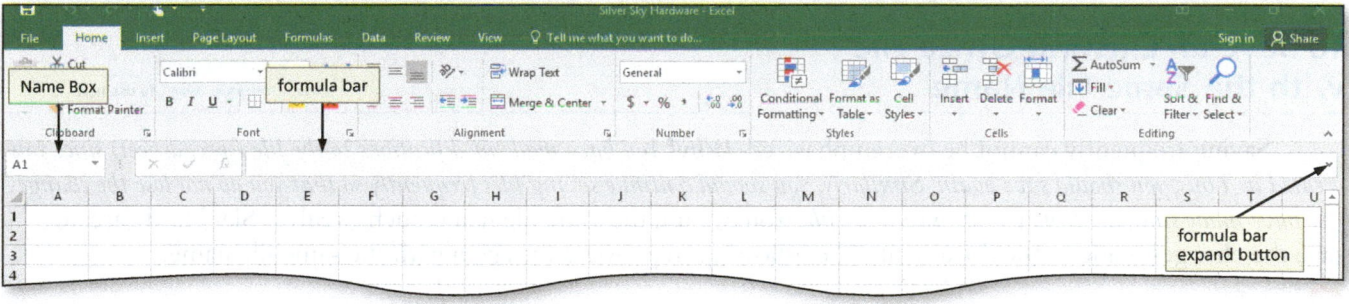

Figure 88

To Enter a Worksheet Title

1 SIGN IN | 2 USE WINDOWS | 3 USE APPS | 4 FILE MANAGEMENT | 5 SWITCH APPS | 6 SAVE FILES
7 CHANGE SCREEN RESOLUTION | 8 EXIT APPS | 9 USE ADDITIONAL APPS | 10 USE HELP

To enter data into a cell, you first must select it. The easiest way to select a cell (make it active) is to use the mouse to move the block plus sign pointer to the cell and then click. An alternative method is to use the arrow keys that are located just to the right of the typewriter keys on the keyboard. An arrow key selects the cell adjacent to the active cell in the direction of the arrow on the key.

In Excel, any set of characters containing a letter, hyphen (as in a telephone number), or space is considered text. **Text** is used to place titles, such as worksheet titles, column titles, and row titles, on the worksheet. The following steps enter the worksheet title in cell A1. *Why? A title informs others as to the contents of the worksheet, such as information regarding a company.*

1

- If it is not already the active cell, click cell A1 to make it the active cell.
- Type **Silver Sky Hardware** in cell A1 (Figure 89).

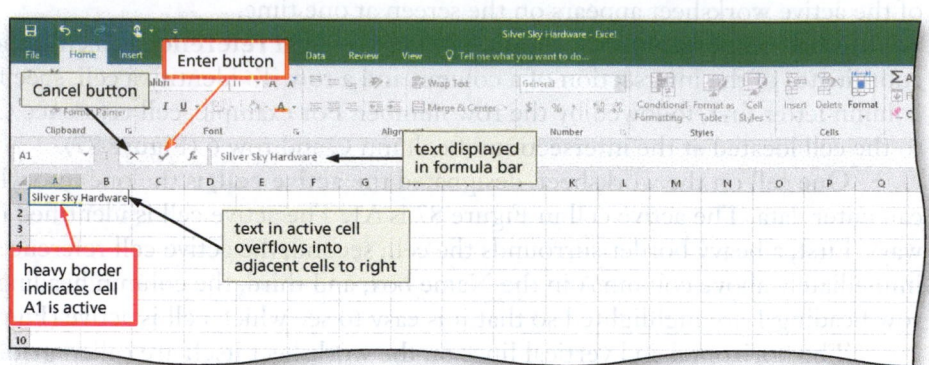

Figure 89

2

- Click the Enter button to complete the entry and enter the worksheet title in cell A1 (Figure 90).

Q&A

Why do some commands on the ribbon appear dimmed?

Excel dims the commands that are unavailable for use at the current time.

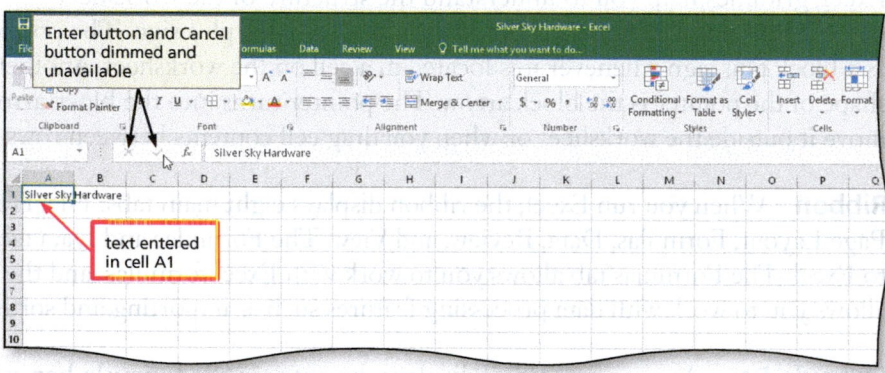

Figure 90

Other Ways

1. To complete entry, click any cell other than active cell

2. To complete entry, press ENTER, HOME, PAGE UP, PAGE DOWN, END, UP ARROW, DOWN ARROW, LEFT ARROW, or RIGHT ARROW

To Save an Existing Office File with the Same File Name

1 SIGN IN | 2 USE WINDOWS | 3 USE APPS | 4 FILE MANAGEMENT | 5 SWITCH APPS | 6 SAVE FILES
7 CHANGE SCREEN RESOLUTION | 8 EXIT APPS | **9 USE ADDITIONAL APPS** | 10 USE HELP

Saving frequently cannot be overemphasized. *Why? You have made modifications to the file (spreadsheet) since you created it. Thus, you should save again. Similarly, you should continue saving files frequently so that you do not lose the changes you have made since the time you last saved the file.* You can use the same file name, such as Silver Sky Hardware, to save the changes made to the document. The following step saves a file again with the same file name.

1

- Click the Save button on the Quick Access Toolbar to overwrite the previously saved file (Silver Sky Hardware, in this case) in the Excel folder (Figure 91).

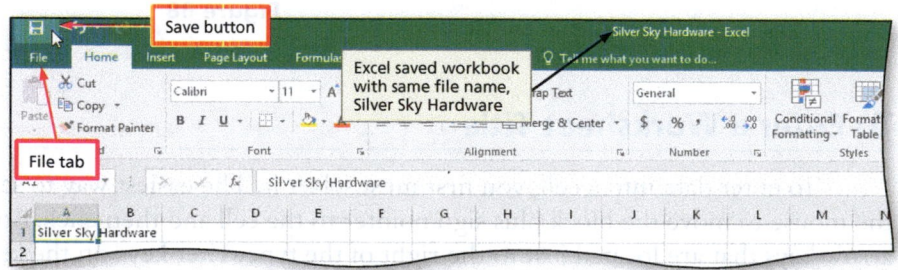

Figure 91

Other Ways

1. Press CTRL+S

2. Press SHIFT+F12

To Save a File with a New File Name

You might want to save a file with a different file name or to a different location. For example, you might start a homework assignment with a data file and then save it with a final file name for submission to your instructor, saving it to a location designated by your instructor. The following steps save a file with a different file name.

1 Click the File tab to open the Backstage view.

2 Click the Save As tab to display the Save As gallery.

3 If necessary, click This PC to display options in the right pane related to saving on your computer.

4 Click the Browse button in the left pane to display the Save As dialog box.

5 Type `Silver Sky Hardware Sales Summary` in the File name box (Save As dialog box) to change the file name. Do not press the ENTER key after typing the file name because you do not want to close the dialog box at this time.

6 If necessary, navigate to the desired save location (in this case, the Excel folder in the CIS 101 folder [or your class folder] in the Documents folder). For specific instructions, perform the tasks in Steps 5a through 5e in the previous section titled To Save a File in a Folder, replacing the PowerPoint folder with the Excel folder.

7 Click the Save button (Save As dialog box) to save the worksheet in the selected folder on the selected drive with the entered file name.

To Exit an Office App

You are finished using Excel. The following steps exit Excel.

1 If you have one Office document open, click the Close button on the right side of the title bar to close the document and exit the Office app; or if you have multiple Office documents open, right-click the app button on the taskbar and then click 'Close all windows' on the shortcut menu, or press ALT + F4 to close all open documents and exit the Office app.

2 If a dialog box appears, click the Save button to save any changes made to the file since the last save.

Access

The term **database** describes a collection of data organized in a manner that allows access, retrieval, and use of that data. **Access** is a database management system. A **database management system** is software that allows you to use a computer to create a database; add, change, and delete data in the database; create queries that allow you to ask questions concerning the data in the database; and create forms and reports using the data in the database.

To Run an App

The following steps, which assume Windows is running, run the Access app based on a typical installation. You may need to ask your instructor how to run apps for your computer.

1 Type **Access 2016** as the search text in the search box and watch the search results appear in the search results.

2 Click the app name, Access 2016 in this case, in the search results to run Access.

3 If the window is not maximized, click the Maximize button on its title bar to maximize the window (Figure 92).

Q&A Do I have to run Access using these steps?

No. You can use any previously discussed method of running an Office app to run Access.

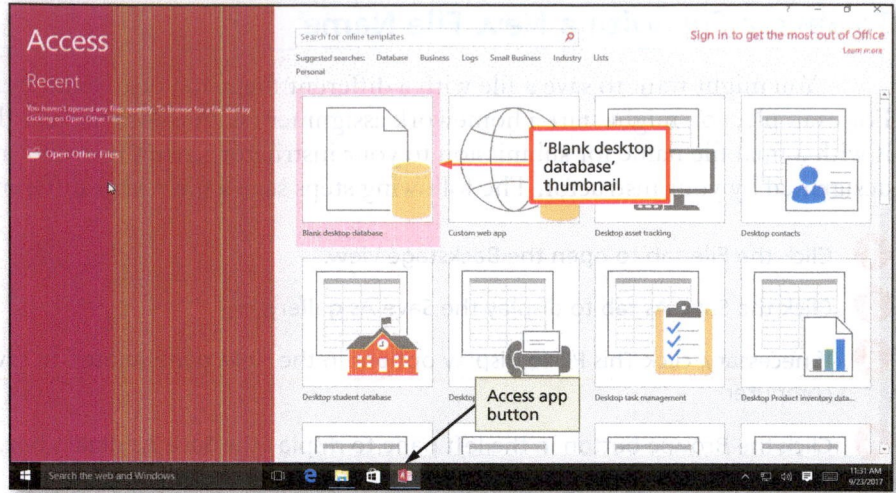

Figure 92

Unique Elements in Access

You work on objects such as tables, forms, and reports in the **Access work area**. Figure 93 shows a work area with multiple objects open. **Object tabs** for the open objects appear at the top of the work area. You select an open object by clicking its tab. In the figure, the Customer List table is the selected object. To the left of the work area is the Navigation Pane, which contains a list of all the objects in the database. You use this pane to open an object. You also can customize the way objects are displayed in the Navigation Pane.

Because the Navigation Pane can take up space in the window, you may not have as much open space for working as you would with Word or Excel. You can use the 'Shutter Bar Open/Close Button' to minimize the Navigation Pane when you are not using it, which allows more space to work with tables, forms, reports, and other database elements.

Figure 93

Ribbon When you run Access, the ribbon displays five main tabs: File, Home, Create, External Data, and Database Tools. Access has unique groupings such as Sort & Filter and Records that are designed specifically for working with databases. Many of the formatting options are reserved for the tool tabs that appear when you are working with forms and reports.

To Create an Access Database

Unlike the other Office apps, Access saves a database when you first create it. When working in Access, you will add data to an Access database. As you add data to a database, Access automatically saves your changes rather than waiting until you manually save the database or exit Access. Recall that in Word and Excel, you entered the data first and then saved it.

Because Access automatically saves the database as you add and change data, you do not always have to click the Save button on the Quick Access Toolbar. Instead, the Save button in Access is used for saving the objects (including tables, queries, forms, reports, and other database objects) a database contains. You can use either the 'Blank desktop database' option or a template to create a new database. If you already know the organization of your database, you would use the 'Blank desktop database' option. If not, you can use a template. Templates can guide you by suggesting some commonly used database organizations.

The following steps use the 'Blank desktop database' option to create a database named Rimitoein Electronics in the Access folder in the class folder (CIS 101, in this case) in the Documents folder. *Why? You have decided to use Microsoft Access to maintain large amounts of data.*

- Click the 'Blank desktop database' thumbnail (shown in Figure 92) to select the database type.
- Type **Rimitoein Electronics** in the File Name text box (Blank desktop database dialog box) to enter the new file name. Do not press the ENTER key after typing the file name because you do not want to create the database at this time (Figure 94).

Figure 94

- Click the 'Browse for a location to put your database' button to display the File New Database dialog box.
- Navigate to the location for the database, that is, the Documents folder, then to the folder identifying your class (CIS 101, in this case), and then to the Access folder (Figure 95). For specific instructions, perform the tasks in Steps 5a through 5e in the previous section titled To Save a File in a Folder, replacing the PowerPoint folder with the Access folder.

Q&A
Why does the 'Save as type' box say Microsoft Access 2007-2016 Databases?
Microsoft Access database formats change with some new versions of Microsoft Access. The most recent format is the Microsoft Access 2007-2016 Databases format, which was released with Access 2007.

Figure 95

3

- Click the OK button (File New Database dialog box) to select the Access folder as the location for the database and close the dialog box (Figure 96).

4

- Click the Create button (Blank desktop database dialog box) to create the database on the selected drive in the selected folder with the file name, Rimitoein Electronics (Figure 97).

Q&A How do I know that the Rimitoein Electronics database is created?
The file name of the database appears on the title bar.

Figure 96

Figure 97

To Close an Office File

Assume you need to close the Access database and return to it later. The following step closes an Office file.

1 Click File on the ribbon to open the Backstage view and then click Close in the Backstage view to close the open file (Rimitoein Electronics, in this case) without exiting the active app.

Q&A Why is Access still on the screen?
When you close a database, the app remains running.

To Open an Existing Office File

Assume you wish to continue working on an existing file, that is, a file you previously saved. Earlier in this module, you learned how to open a recently used file through the Backstage view. The following step opens a database, specifically the Rimitoein Electronics database, that recently was saved. *Why? Because the file has been created already, you just need to reopen it.*

- Click File on the ribbon to open the Backstage view and then click Open in the Backstage view to display the Open gallery in the Backstage view.
- Click This PC to display recent folders accessed on your computer.
- Click the Browse button to display the Open dialog box.
- If necessary, navigate to the location of the file to open.
- Click the file to open, Rimitoein Electronics in this case, to select the file (Figure 98).
- Click the Open button (Open dialog box) to open the file. If necessary, click the Enable Content button.

Q&A
Why did the Security Warning appear?
The Security Warning appears when you open an Office file that might contain harmful content. The files you create in this module are not harmful, but you should be cautious when opening files from other people.

Figure 98

Other Ways

1. Press CTRL+O	2. Navigate to file in File Explorer window, double-click file name

To Exit an Office App

You are finished using Access. The following step exits Access.

1 Click the Close button on the right side of the title bar to close the file and exit the Office app.

Other Office Apps

In addition to the Office apps discussed thus far, three other apps are useful when collaborating and communicating with others: Outlook, Publisher, and OneNote.

Outlook

Outlook is a powerful communications and scheduling app that helps you communicate with others, keep track of contacts, and organize your calendar. Apps such as Outlook provide a way for individuals and workgroups to organize, find, view, and share information easily. Outlook allows you to send and receive email messages and provides a means to organize contacts. Users can track email messages, meetings, and notes related to a particular contact. Outlook's Calendar, People, Tasks, and Notes components aid in this organization. Contact information readily is available from the Outlook Calendar, Mail, People, and Tasks components by accessing the Search Contacts feature.

Email is the transmission of messages and files over a computer network. Email has become an important means of exchanging information and files between business associates, classmates and instructors, friends, and family. Businesses find that using email to send documents electronically saves both time and money. Parents with students away at college or relatives who live across the country find that communicating by email is an inexpensive and easy way to stay in touch with their family members. Exchanging email messages is a widely used service of the Internet.

The Outlook Window   Figure 99 shows an Outlook window, which is divided into three panes: the Navigation pane, the message pane to the left of center, and the Reading pane to the right of center.

Figure 99

When an email message is open in Outlook, it is displayed in a Message window (Figure 100). When you open a message, the Message tab on the ribbon appears, which contains the more frequently used commands.

Figure 100

Publisher

BTW

Running Publisher
When you first run Publisher, the New templates gallery usually is displayed in the Backstage view. If it is not displayed, click File on the ribbon, click the Options tab in the Backstage view, click General (Publisher Options dialog box), and then click 'Show the New template gallery when starting Publisher' to select the check box in the right pane.

Publisher is a powerful desktop publishing (DTP) app that assists you in designing and producing professional-quality documents that combine text, graphics, illustrations, and photos. DTP software provides additional tools beyond those typically found in word processing apps, including design templates, graphic manipulation tools, color schemes or libraries, advanced layout and printing tools, and web components. For large jobs, businesses use DTP software to design publications that are camera ready, which means the files are suitable for outside commercial printing. In addition, DTP software can be used to create webpages and interactive web forms.

Publisher is used by people who regularly produce high-quality color publications, such as newsletters, brochures, flyers, logos, signs, catalogs, cards, and business forms. Publisher has many features designed to simplify production and make publications visually appealing. Using Publisher, you easily can change the shape, size, and color of text and graphics. You can include many kinds of graphical objects, including mastheads, borders, tables, images, pictures, charts, and web objects in publications, as well as integrate spreadsheets and databases.

The Publisher Window Publisher initially displays a list of publication types. **Publication types** are typical publications used by desktop publishers. The more popular types are displayed in the center of the window.

Once you select a publication type, a dialog box is displayed to allow you to create the publication (Figure 101). Some templates are installed with Publisher, and others are available online. In Figure 101, the Business newsletter publication dialog box is displayed.

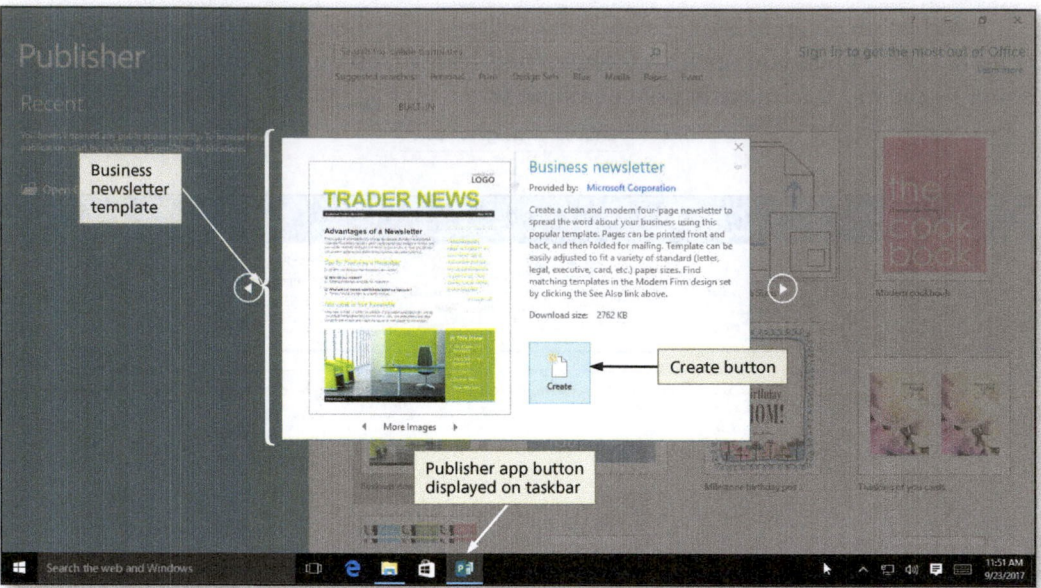

Figure 101

When you select the desired template, Publisher creates the publication and sets it up for you to edit. Figure 102 shows the Business newsletter publication that Publisher creates when default options are selected.

Figure 102

OneNote

OneNote is a note taking app that assists you in entering, saving, organizing, searching, and using notes. It enables you to create pages, which are organized in sections, just as in a physical notebook. In OneNote, you can type notes anywhere on a page and then easily move the notes around on the page. You can create lists and outlines, use handwriting to enter notes, and create drawings. If you use a tablet to add handwritten notes to a document, OneNote can convert the handwriting to text. It also can perform searches on the handwritten entries. Pictures and data from other apps easily are incorporated in your notes.

In addition to typing and handwriting, you can take audio notes. For example, you could record conversations during a meeting or lecture. As you record, you can take additional notes. When you play back the audio notes, you can synchronize the additional notes you took; that is, OneNote will show you during playback the exact points at which you added the notes. A variety of note flags, which are symbols that call your attention to notes on a page, enable you to flag notes as being important. You then can use the Note Flags summary to view the flagged notes, which can be sorted in a variety of ways.

OneNote includes tools to assist you with organizing a notebook and navigating its contents. It also includes a search feature, making it easy to find the specific notes in which you are interested. For short notes that you always want to have available readily, you can use Side Notes, which are used much like the sticky notes that you might use in a physical notebook.

OneNote Window   All activity in OneNote takes place in the **notebook** (Figure 103). Like a physical notebook, the OneNote notebook consists of notes that are placed on **pages**. The pages are grouped into **sections**, which can be further grouped into **folders**. (No folders are shown in the notebook in the figure.) You can use the Search box to search for specific text in your notes.

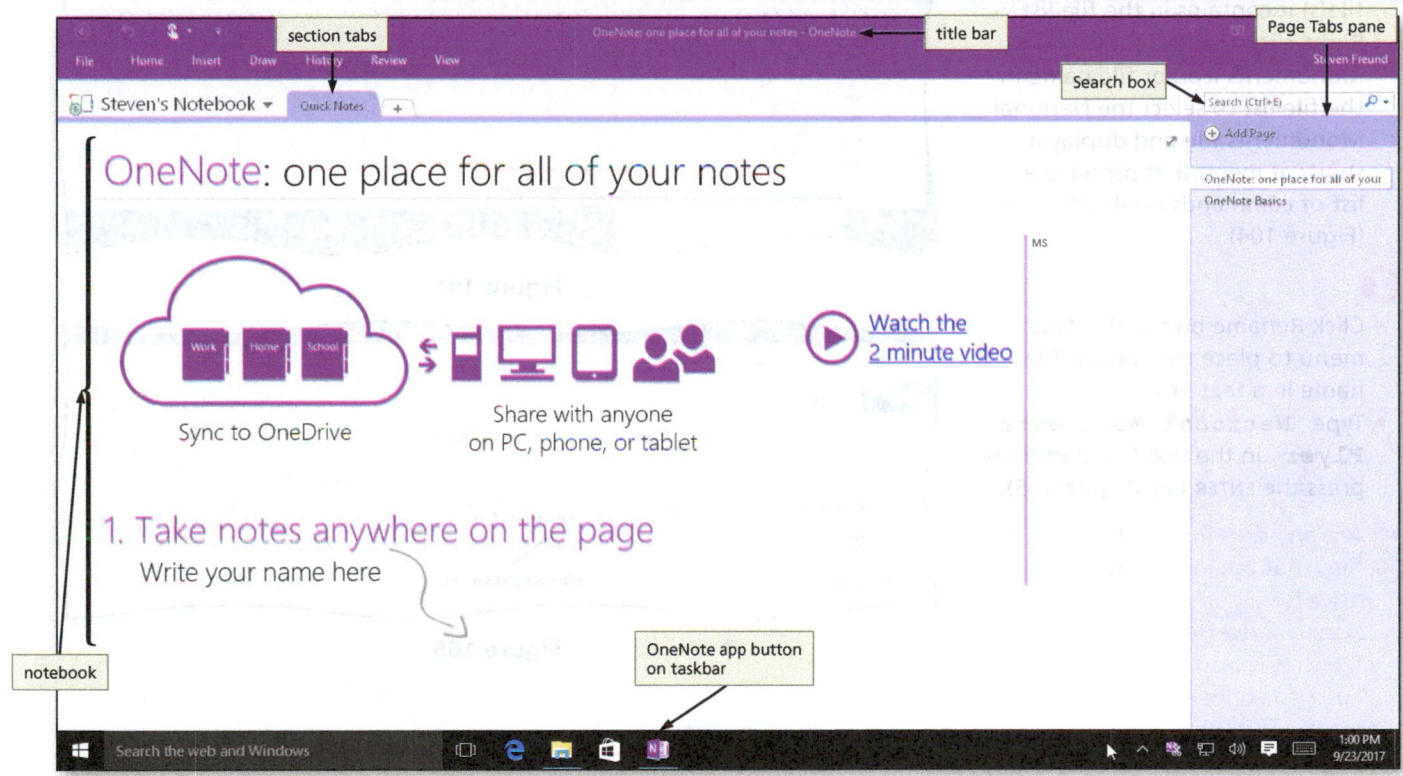

Figure 103

You can add pages to the notebook using the Add Page button in the Page Tabs pane. If page tabs are displayed, you can switch to a page by clicking its tab. Figure 103 shows the Quick Notes page being displayed for the notebook.

Break Point: If you wish to take a break, this is a good place to do so. To resume at a later time, continue to follow the steps from this location forward.

Renaming, Moving, and Deleting Files

Earlier in this module, you learned how to organize files in folders, which is part of a process known as **file management**. The following sections cover additional file management topics including renaming, moving, and deleting files.

To Rename a File

In some circumstances, you may want to change the name of, or rename, a file or a folder. **Why?** *You may want to distinguish a file in one folder or drive from a copy of a similar file, or you may decide to rename a file to better identify its contents.* The following steps change the name of the National Monuments file in the Word folder to National Monuments Flyer.

- If necessary, click the File Explorer button on the taskbar to make the folder window the active window.
- Navigate to the location of the file to be renamed (in this case, the Word folder in the CIS 101 [or your class folder] folder in the Documents folder) to display the file(s) it contains in the file list.
- Right-click the National Monuments icon or file name in the file list to select the National Monuments file and display a shortcut menu that presents a list of commands related to files (Figure 104).

Figure 104

- Click Rename on the shortcut menu to place the current file name in a text box.
- Type **National Monuments Flyer** in the text box and then press the ENTER key (Figure 105).

Q&A

Are any risks involved in renaming files that are located on a hard drive?

If you inadvertently rename a file that is associated with certain apps, the apps may not be able to find the file and, therefore, may not run properly. Always use caution when renaming files.

Can I rename a file when it is open?

No, a file must be closed to change the file name.

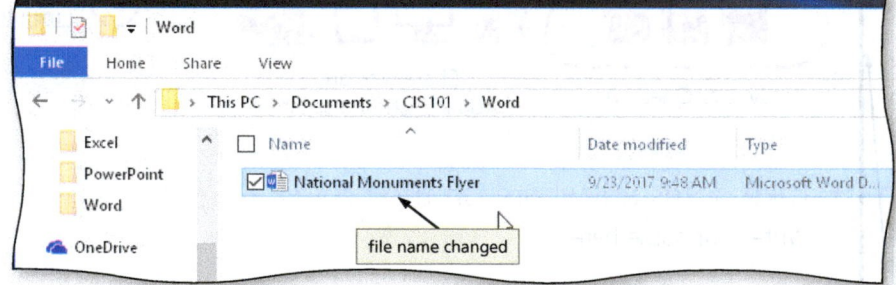

Figure 105

Other Ways

1. Select file, press F2, type new file name, press ENTER   2. Select file, click Rename (Home tab | Organize group), type new file name, press ENTER

To Move a File

Why? *At some time, you may want to move a file from one folder, called the source folder, to another, called the destination folder.* When you move a file, it no longer appears in the original folder. If the destination and the source folders are on the same media, you can move a file by dragging it. If the folders are on different media, then you will need to right-drag the file, and then click Move here on the shortcut menu. The following step moves the Silver Sky Hardware Sales Summary file from the Excel folder to the OneNote folder.

1

- In File Explorer, navigate to the location of the file to be moved (in this case, the Excel folder in the CIS 101 folder [or your class folder] in the Documents folder).
- Click the Excel folder in the navigation pane to display the files it contains in the right pane (Figure 106).
- Drag the Silver Sky Hardware Sales Summary file in the right pane to the OneNote folder in the navigation pane.

Figure 106

Other Ways

1. Right-click file to move, click Cut on shortcut menu, right-click destination folder, click Paste on shortcut menu

2. Select file to move, press CTRL+X, select destination folder, press CTRL+V

To Delete a File

1 SIGN IN | 2 USE WINDOWS | 3 USE APPS | **4 FILE MANAGEMENT** | 5 SWITCH APPS | 6 SAVE FILES
7 CHANGE SCREEN RESOLUTION | 8 EXIT APPS | 9 USE ADDITIONAL APPS | **10 USE HELP**

A final task you may want to perform is to delete a file. Exercise extreme caution when deleting a file or files. When you delete a file from a hard drive, the deleted file is stored in the Recycle Bin where you can recover it until you empty the Recycle Bin. If you delete a file from removable media, such as a USB flash drive, the file is deleted permanently. The next steps delete the Visiting National Monuments file from the PowerPoint folder. *Why? When a file no longer is needed, you can delete it to conserve space on your storage location.*

1

- In File Explorer, navigate to the location of the file to be deleted (in this case, the PowerPoint folder in the CIS 101 folder [or your class folder] in the Documents folder).
- Click the Visiting National Monuments icon or file name in the right pane to select the file.
- Right-click the selected file to display a shortcut menu (Figure 107).

2

- Click Delete on the shortcut menu to delete the file.
- If a dialog box appears, click the Yes button to delete the file.

Q&A Can I use this same technique to delete a folder?

Figure 107

Yes. Right-click the folder and then click Delete on the shortcut menu. When you delete a folder, all of the files and folders contained in the folder you are deleting, together with any files and folders on lower hierarchical levels, are deleted as well. For example, if you delete the CIS 101 folder, you will delete all folders and files inside the CIS 101 folder.

Other Ways

1. Select file, press DELETE

Microsoft Office and Windows Help

At any time while you are using one of the Office apps, you can use Office Help to display information about all topics associated with the app. To illustrate the use of Office Help, this section uses Word. Help in other Office apps operates in a similar fashion.

In Office, Help is presented in a window that has browser-style navigation buttons. Each Office app has its own Help home page, which is the starting Help page that is displayed in the Help window. If your computer is connected to the Internet, the contents of the Help page reflect both the local help files installed on the computer and material from Microsoft's website.

To Open the Help Window in an Office App

1 SIGN IN | 2 USE WINDOWS | 3 USE APPS | 4 FILE MANAGEMENT | 5 SWITCH APPS | 6 SAVE FILES
7 CHANGE SCREEN RESOLUTION | 8 EXIT APPS | 9 USE ADDITIONAL APPS | 10 USE HELP

The following step opens the Word Help window. *Why? You might not understand how certain commands or operations work in Word, so you can obtain the necessary information using help.*

- Run an Office app, in this case Word.
- Click the Blank document thumbnail to display a blank document.
- Press F1 to open the app's Help window (Figure 108).

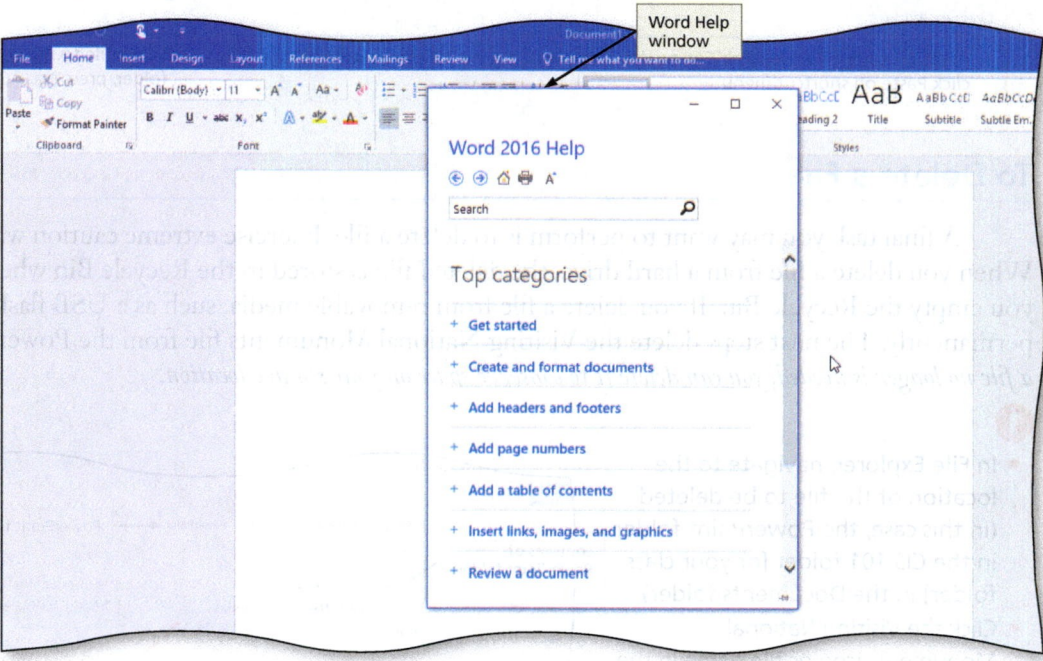

Figure 108

Moving and Resizing Windows

At times, it is useful, or even necessary, to have more than one window open and visible on the screen at the same time. You can resize and move these open windows so that you can view different areas of and elements in the window. In the case of the Help window, for example, it could be covering document text in the Word window that you need to see.

To Move a Window by Dragging

1 SIGN IN | **2 USE WINDOWS** | 3 USE APPS | 4 FILE MANAGEMENT | 5 SWITCH APPS | 6 SAVE FILES
7 CHANGE SCREEN RESOLUTION | 8 EXIT APPS | 9 USE ADDITIONAL APPS | 10 USE HELP

You can move any open window that is not maximized to another location on the desktop by dragging the title bar of the window. *Why? You might want to have a better view of what is behind the window or just want to move the window so that you can see it better.* The following step drags the Word Help window to the upper-left corner of the desktop.

- Drag the window title bar (the Word Help window title bar, in this case) so that the window moves to the upper-left corner of the desktop, as shown in Figure 109.

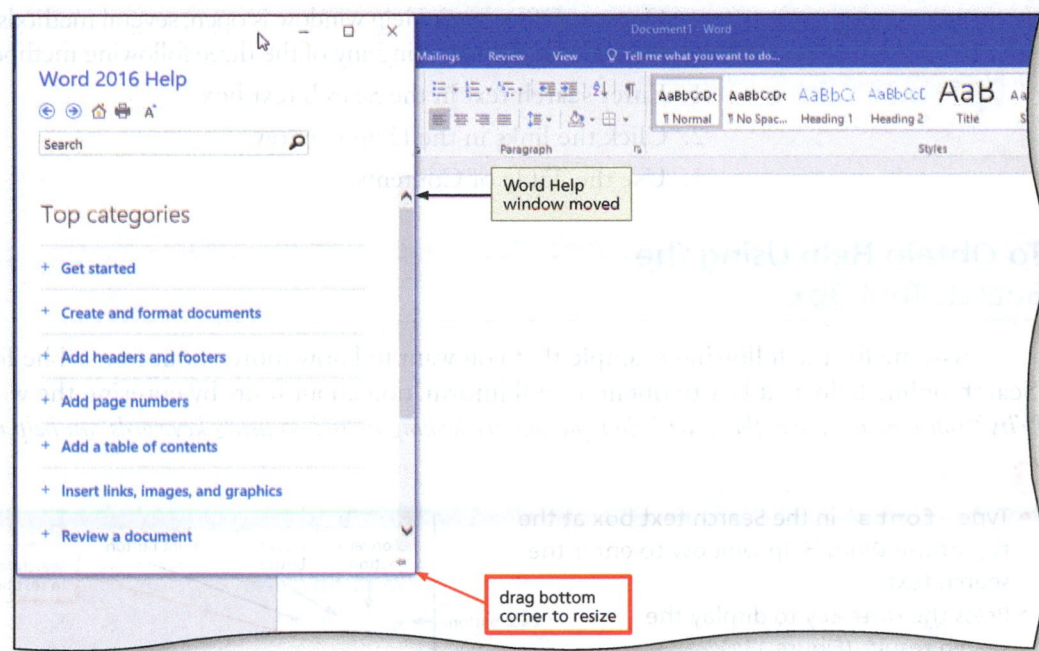

Figure 109

To Resize a Window by Dragging

1 SIGN IN | **2 USE WINDOWS** | 3 USE APPS | 4 FILE MANAGEMENT | 5 SWITCH APPS | 6 SAVE FILES
7 CHANGE SCREEN RESOLUTION | 8 EXIT APPS | 9 USE ADDITIONAL APPS | 10 USE HELP

A method used to change the size of the window is to drag the window borders. The following step changes the size of the Word Help window by dragging its borders. *Why? Sometimes, information is not visible completely in a window, and you want to increase the size of the window.*

- If you are using a mouse, point to the lower-right corner of the window (the Word Help window, in this case) until the pointer changes to a two-headed arrow.
- Drag the bottom border downward to display more of the active window (Figure 110).

Q&A Can I drag other borders on the window to enlarge or shrink the window?
Yes, you can drag the left, right, and top borders and any window corner to resize a window.

Q&A Will Windows remember the new size of the window after I close it?
Yes. When you reopen the window, Windows will display it at the same size it was when you closed it.

Figure 110

Using Office Help

Once an Office app's Help window is open, several methods exist for navigating Help. You can search for help by using any of the three following methods from the Help window:

1. Enter search text in the Search text box.
2. Click the links in the Help window.
3. Use the Table of Contents.

To Obtain Help Using the Search Text Box

1 SIGN IN | 2 USE WINDOWS | 3 USE APPS | 4 FILE MANAGEMENT | 5 SWITCH APPS | 6 SAVE FILES
7 CHANGE SCREEN RESOLUTION | 8 EXIT APPS | 9 USE ADDITIONAL APPS | 10 USE HELP

Assume for the following example that you want to know more about fonts. The following steps use the 'Search online help' text box to obtain useful information about fonts by entering the word, fonts, as search text. *Why?* *You may not know the exact help topic you are looking to find, so using keywords can help narrow your search.*

- Type **fonts** in the Search text box at the top of the Word Help window to enter the search text.
- Press the ENTER key to display the search results (Figure 111).

Q&A Why do my search results differ?
If you do not have an Internet connection, your results will reflect only the content of the Help files on your computer. When searching for help online, results also can change as material is added, deleted, and updated on the online Help webpages maintained by Microsoft.

Q&A Why were my search results not very helpful?
When initiating a search, be sure to check the spelling of the search text; also, keep your search specific to return the most accurate results.

Figure 111

- Click the 'Change the font color (text color)' link to display the Help information associated with the selected topic (Figure 112).

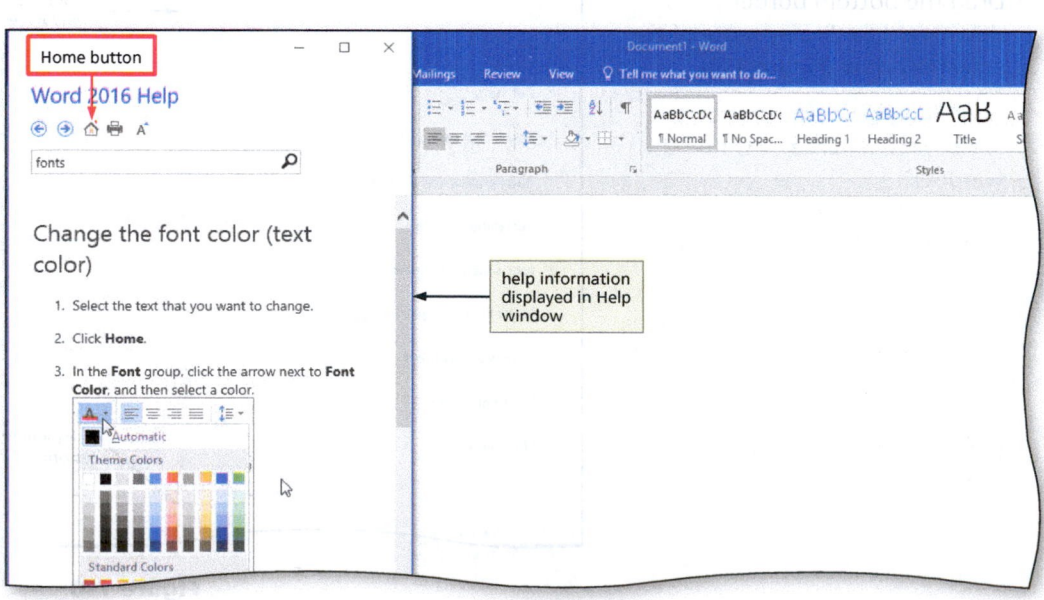

Figure 112

3

- Click the Home button in the Help window to clear the search results and redisplay the Help home page (Figure 113).
- Click the Close button in the Word 2016 Help window to close the window.

Figure 113

Obtaining Help while Working in an Office App

Help in the Office apps provides you with the ability to obtain help directly, without opening the Help window and initiating a search. For example, you may be unsure about how a particular command works, or you may be presented with a dialog box that you are not sure how to use.

Figure 114 shows one option for obtaining help while working in an Office app. If you want to learn more about a command, point to its button and wait for the ScreenTip to appear. If the Help icon and 'Tell me more' link appear in the ScreenTip, click the 'Tell me more' link or press the F1 key while pointing to the button to open the Help window associated with that command.

Figure 115 shows a dialog box that contains a Help button. Clicking the Help button or pressing the F1 key while the dialog box is displayed opens a Help window. The Help window contains help about that dialog box, if available. If no help file is available for that particular dialog box, then the main Help window opens.

As mentioned previously, the Tell Me box is available in most Office apps and can perform a variety of functions. One of these functions is to provide easy access to commands by typing a description of the command.

Figure 114

Figure 115

To Obtain Help Using the Tell Me Box

If you are having trouble finding a command in an Office app, you can use the Tell Me box to search for the function you are trying to perform. As you type, the Tell Me box will suggest commands that match the search text you are entering. *Why? You can use the Tell Me box to quickly access commands you otherwise may be unable to find on the ribbon.* The following step finds information about margins.

- Type **margins** in the Tell Me box and watch the search results appear.
- Point to Adjust Margins to display a submenu displaying the various margin settings (Figure 116).
- Click an empty area of the document window to close the search results.

- Exit Microsoft Word.

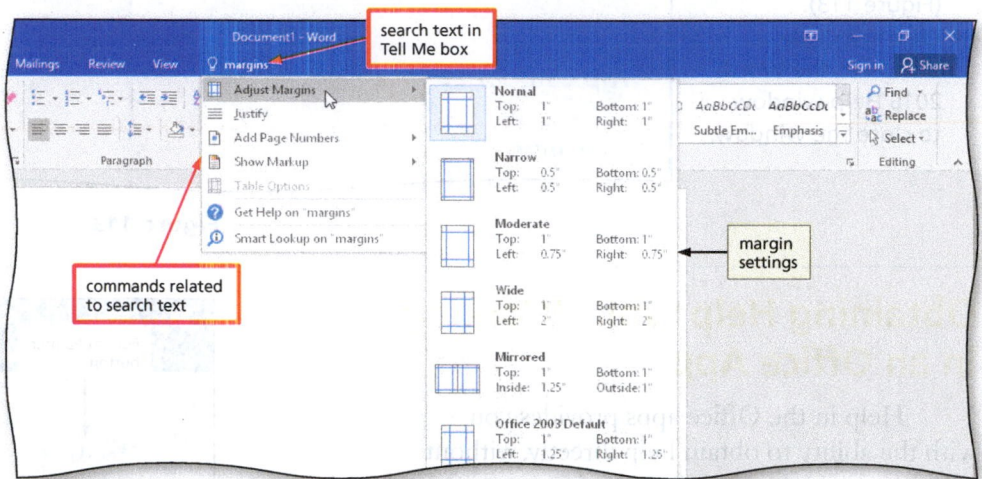

Figure 116

Using the Windows Search Box

One of the more powerful Windows features is the Windows search box. The search box is a central location from where you can type search text and quickly access related Windows commands or web search results. In addition, **Cortana** is a new search tool in Windows that you can access using the search box. It can act as a personal assistant by performing functions such as providing ideas; searching for apps, files, and folders; and setting reminders. In addition to typing search text in the search box, you also can use your computer or mobile device's microphone to give verbal commands.

To Use the Windows Search Box

The following step uses the Windows search box to search for a Windows command. *Why? Using the search box to locate apps, settings, folders, and files can be faster than navigating windows and dialog boxes to search for the desired content.*

- Type **notification** in the search box to display the search results. The search results include related Windows settings, Windows Store apps, and web search results (Figure 117).
- Click an empty area of the desktop to close the search results.

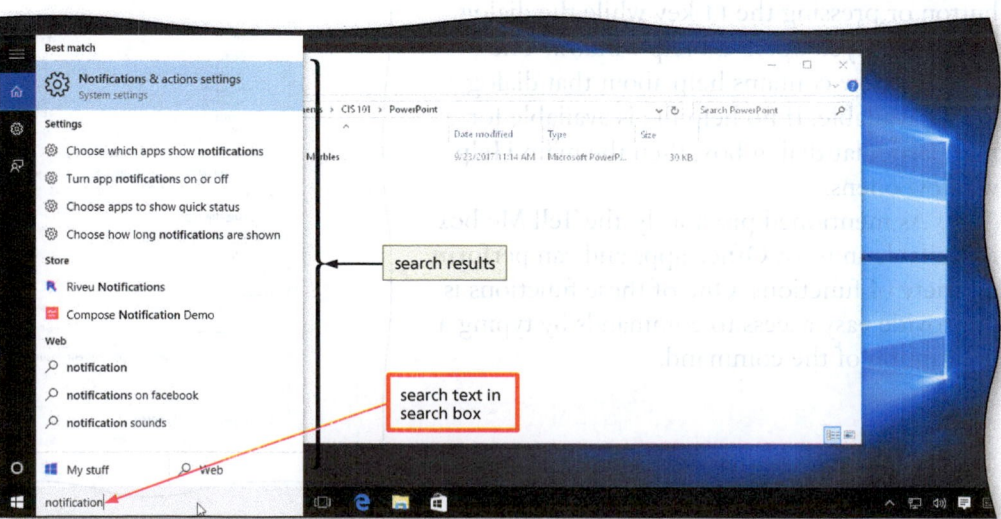

Figure 117

Summary

In this module, you learned how to use the Windows interface, several touch screen and mouse operations, file and folder management, some basic features of some Microsoft Office apps (including Word, PowerPoint, Excel, and Access), and discovered the common elements that exist among these different Office apps. You also were introduced to additional Office apps, including Outlook, Publisher, and OneNote. Topics covered included signing in, using Windows, using apps, file management, switching between apps, saving files, changing screen resolution, exiting apps, using additional apps, and using help.

CONSIDER THIS: PLAN AHEAD

What guidelines should you follow to plan your projects?

The process of communicating specific information is a learned, rational skill. Computers and software, especially Microsoft Office 2016, can help you develop ideas and present detailed information to a particular audience and minimize much of the laborious work of drafting and revising projects. No matter what method you use to plan a project, it is beneficial to follow some specific guidelines from the onset to arrive at a final product that is informative, relevant, and effective. Use some aspects of these guidelines every time you undertake a project, and others as needed in specific instances.

1. Determine the project's purpose.

    a) Clearly define why you are undertaking this assignment.

    b) Begin to draft ideas of how best to communicate information by handwriting ideas on paper; composing directly on a laptop, tablet, or mobile device; or developing a strategy that fits your particular thinking and writing style.

2. Analyze your audience.

    a) Learn about the people who will read, analyze, or view your work.

    b) Determine their interests and needs so that you can present the information they need to know and omit the information they already possess.

    c) Form a mental picture of these people or find photos of people who fit this profile so that you can develop a project with the audience in mind.

3. Gather possible content.

    a) Locate existing information that may reside in spreadsheets, databases, or other files.

    b) Conduct a web search to find relevant websites.

    c) Read pamphlets, magazine and newspaper articles, and books to gain insights of how others have approached your topic.

    d) Conduct personal interviews to obtain perspectives not available by any other means.

    e) Consider video and audio clips as potential sources for material that might complement or support the factual data you uncover.

4. Determine what content to present to your audience.

    a) Write three or four major ideas you want an audience member to remember after reading or viewing your project.

    b) Envision your project's endpoint, the key fact you wish to emphasize, so that all project elements lead to this final element.

    c) Determine relevant time factors, such as the length of time to develop the project, how long readers will spend reviewing your project, or the amount of time allocated for your speaking engagement.

    d) Decide whether a graph, photo, or artistic element can express or enhance a particular concept.

    e) Be mindful of the order in which you plan to present the content, and place the most important material at the top or bottom of the page, because readers and audience members generally remember the first and last pieces of information they see and hear.

How should you submit solutions to questions in the assignments identified with a **symbol?**
Every assignment in this book contains one or more questions with a symbol. These questions require you to think beyond the assigned file. Present your solutions to the question in the format required by your instructor. Possible formats may include one or more of these options: write the answer; create a document that contains the answer; present your answer to the class; discuss your answer in a group; record the answer as audio or video using a webcam, smartphone, or portable media player; or post answers on a blog, wiki, or website.

CONSIDER THIS

Apply Your Knowledge

Reinforce the skills and apply the concepts you learned in this module.

Creating a Folder and a Document

Instructions: You will create a PowerPoint Assignments folder and then create a PowerPoint presentation and save it in the folder.

Perform the following tasks:

1. Open the File Explorer window and then double-click to open the Documents folder.

2. Click the New folder button on the Quick Access Toolbar to display a new folder icon and text box for the folder name.

3. Type **PowerPoint Assignments** in the text box to name the folder. Press the ENTER key to create the folder in the Documents folder.

4. Run PowerPoint and create a new blank presentation.

5. Enter **Technology Update** in the title text placeholder (Figure 118).

6. Click the Save button on the Quick Access Toolbar. Navigate to the PowerPoint folder in the Documents folder and then save the document using the file name, Apply 1 Presentation.

7. If your Quick Access Toolbar does not show the Quick Print button, add the Quick Print button to the Quick Access Toolbar. Print the presentation using the Quick Print button on the Quick Access Toolbar. When you are finished printing, remove the Quick Print button from the Quick Access Toolbar.

8. Submit the printout to your instructor.

9. Exit PowerPoint.

10. ✺ What other commands might you find useful to include on the Quick Access Toolbar?

Figure 118

Extend Your Knowledge

Extend the skills you learned in this module and experiment with new skills. You will use Help to complete the assignment.

Using Help

Instructions: Use Office Help to perform the following tasks.

Perform the following tasks:

1. Run Word.
2. Click the Microsoft Word Help button to open the Word Help window (Figure 119).
3. Search Word Help to answer the following questions.

    a. What are the steps to create a hanging indent?

    b. What is mail merge?
4. With the Word app still running, run PowerPoint.
5. Click the Microsoft PowerPoint Help button on the title bar to open the PowerPoint Help window.
6. Search PowerPoint Help to answer the following questions.

    a. How can you create a Venn diagram?

    b. How do you add slide numbers to each slide?
7. Exit PowerPoint.
8. Run Excel.
9. Click the Microsoft Excel Help button to open the Excel Help window.
10. Search Excel Help to answer the following questions.

    a. What different types of charts are available in Excel?

    b. What is Flash Fill?

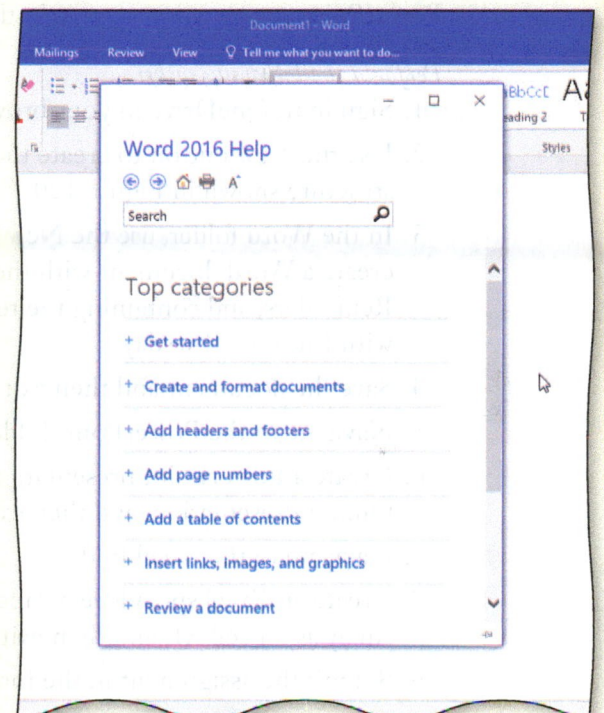

Figure 119

11. Exit Excel.
12. Run Access.
13. Click the Microsoft Access Help button to open the Access Help window.
14. Search Access Help to answer the following questions.

    a. What is a query?

    b. What are data types?
15. Exit Access.
16. Type the answers from your searches in a new blank Word document. Save the document with a new file name and then submit it in the format specified by your instructor.
17. Exit Word.
18. 🌐 What search text did you use to perform the searches above? Did it take multiple attempts to search and locate the exact information for which you were searching?

Expand Your World
Creating Office Online Documents

Create a solution that uses cloud or web technologies by learning and investigating on your own from general guidance.

Instructions: Create the folders shown in Figure 120. Then, using the respective Office Online app, create a small file to save in each folder (i.e., create a Word document to save in the Word folder, a PowerPoint presentation to save in the PowerPoint folder, and so on).

Perform the following tasks:

1. Sign in to OneDrive in your browser.

2. Use the New button to create the folder structure shown in Figure 120.

3. In the Word folder, use the New button to create a Word document with the file name, Reminders, and containing the text, Lunch with Lucas on Tuesday.

4. Save the document and then exit the app.

5. Navigate to the PowerPoint folder.

Figure 120

6. Create a PowerPoint presentation called Widget Sales with one slide containing the title text, Online Presentation, and then exit the app.

7. Navigate to the Excel folder.

8. Create an Excel spreadsheet called Widget Sales Analysis containing the text, Sales Cost Analysis, in cell A1, and then exit the app.

9. Submit the assignment in the format specified by your instructor.

10. ✺ Based on your current knowledge of OneDrive, do you think you will use it? What about the Office Online apps?

In the Labs

Design, create, modify, and/or use files following the guidelines, concepts, and skills presented in this module. Labs 1 and 2, which increase in difficulty, require you to create solutions based on what you learned in the module; Lab 3 requires you to apply your creative thinking and problem-solving skills to design and implement a solution.

Lab 1: Creating Folders for a Bookstore

Problem: Your friend works for a local bookstore. He would like to organize his files in relation to the types of books available in the store. He has seven main categories: fiction, biography, children, humor, social science, nonfiction, and medical. You are to create a folder structure similar to Figure 121.

Perform the following tasks:

1. Click the File Explorer button on the taskbar and display the contents of the Documents folder.

2. In the Documents folder, create the main folder and name it Book Categories.

3. Navigate to the Book Categories folder.

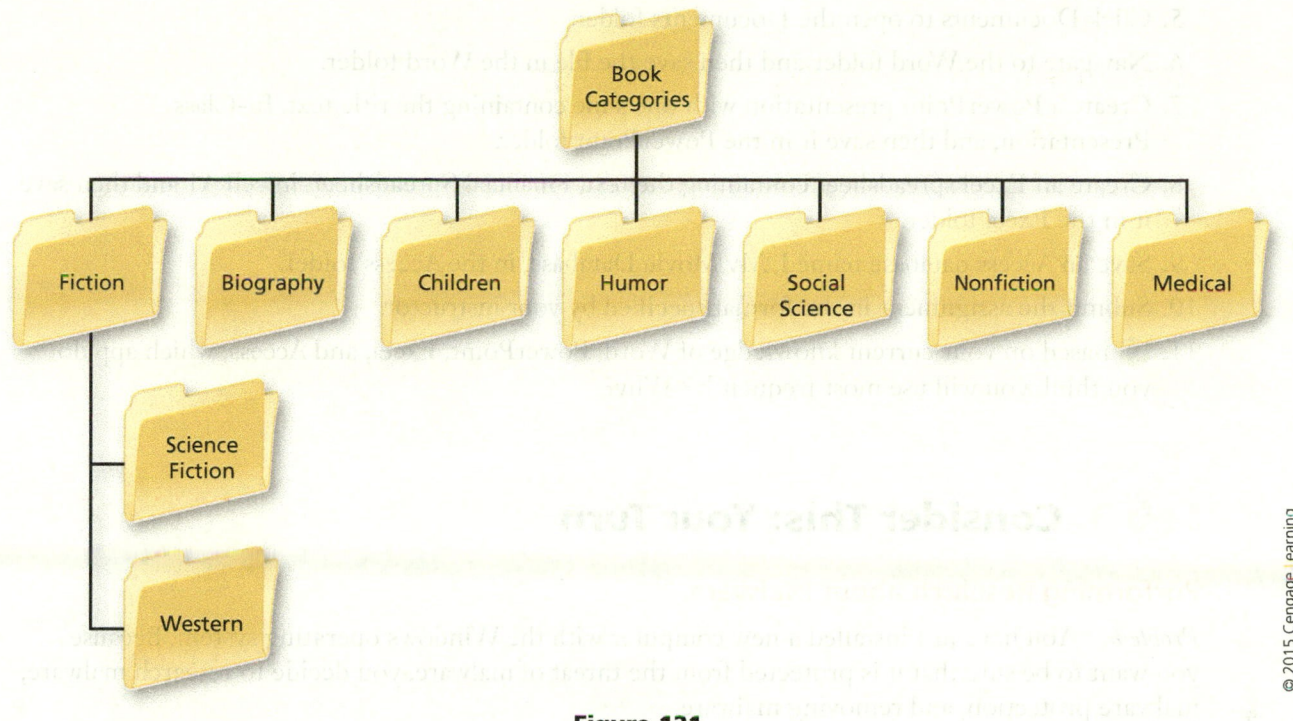

© 2015 Cengage Learning

Figure 121

4. Within the Book Categories folder, create a folder for each of the following: Fiction, Biography, Children, Humor, Social Science, Nonfiction, and Medical.

5. Within the Fiction folder, create two additional folders, one for Science Fiction and the second for Western.

6. Submit the assignment in the format specified by your instructor.

7. ✹ Think about how you use your computer for various tasks (consider personal, professional, and academic reasons). What folders do you think will be required on your computer to store the files you save?

Lab 2: **Creating Office Documents and Saving Them in Appropriate Folders**

Problem: You are taking a class that requires you to create a Word, PowerPoint, Excel, and Access file. You will save these files to folders named for four different Office apps (Figure 122).

Perform the following tasks:

1. Create the folders shown in Figure 122.

2. Create a Word document containing the text, Week 1 Notes.

3. In the Backstage view, click Save As and then click This PC.

4. Click the Browse button to display the Save As dialog box.

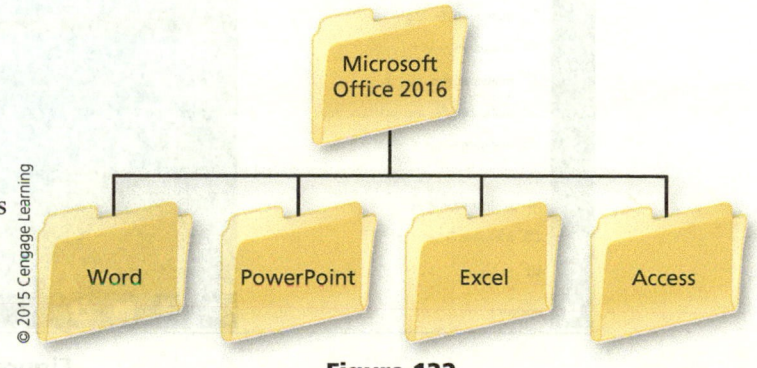

© 2015 Cengage Learning

Figure 122

5. Click Documents to open the Documents folder.

6. Navigate to the Word folder and then save the file in the Word folder.

7. Create a PowerPoint presentation with one slide containing the title text, In-Class Presentation, and then save it in the PowerPoint folder.

8. Create an Excel spreadsheet containing the text, Financial Spreadsheet, in cell A1 and then save it in the Excel folder.

9. Save an Access database named, My Movie Database, in the Access folder.

10. Submit the assignment in the format specified by your instructor.

11. ✳ Based on your current knowledge of Word, PowerPoint, Excel, and Access, which app do you think you will use most frequently? Why?

Lab 3: **Consider This: Your Turn**

Performing Research about Malware

Problem: You have just installed a new computer with the Windows operating system. Because you want to be sure that it is protected from the threat of malware, you decide to research malware, malware protection, and removing malware.

Part 1:   Research the following three topics: malware, malware protection, and removing malware. Use the concepts and techniques presented in this module to use the search box to find information regarding these topics. Create a Word document that contains steps to properly safeguard a computer from malware, ways to prevent malware, as well as the different ways to remove malware or a virus should your computer become infected. Submit your assignment in the format specified by your instructor.

Part 2:   You made several decisions while searching for this assignment. What decisions did you make? What was the rationale behind these decisions? How did you locate the required information about malware?

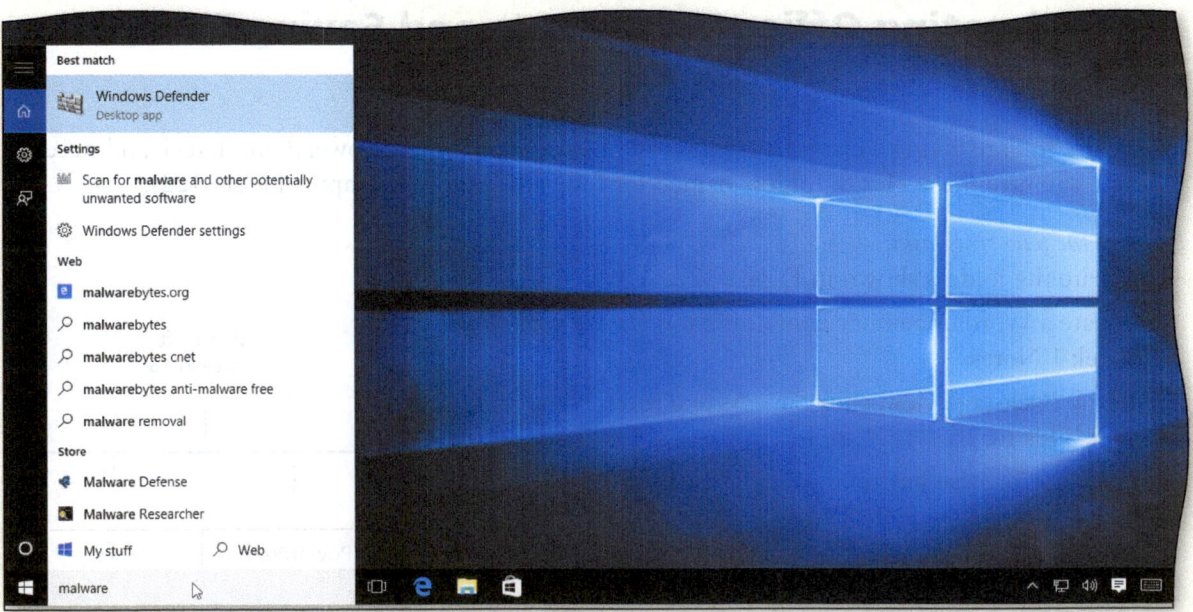

Figure 123

Inbox - Outlook Data File - Outlook
Microsoft Outlook 2016

File   Home   Send / Receive   Folder   View   ♀ Tell me what you want to do...

1 | Managing Email Messages with Outlook

Objectives

You will have mastered the material in this module when you can:

- Add a Microsoft account to Outlook
- Set language preferences and sensitivity levels
- Apply a theme
- Compose, address, and send an email message
- Open, read, print, and close an email message
- Preview and save a file attachment
- Display the People Pane
- Reply to an email message

- Check spelling as you type an email message
- Attach a file to an outgoing email message
- Forward an email message
- Copy another person when sending an email message
- Create and move messages into a folder
- Delete an email message
- View the mailbox size

This introductory module covers features and functions common to managing email messages in Outlook 2016.

Roadmap

In this module, you will learn how to perform basic email messaging tasks. The following roadmap identifies general activities you will perform as you progress through this module:

1. CONFIGURE the ACCOUNT OPTIONS
2. COMPOSE AND SEND an email message
3. VIEW AND PRINT an email message
4. REPLY to an email message
5. ATTACH a FILE to an email message
6. ORGANIZE email MESSAGES in folders

At the beginning of the step instructions throughout each module, you will see an abbreviated form of this roadmap. The abbreviated roadmap uses colors to indicate module progress: gray means the module is beyond that activity, blue means the task being shown is covered in that activity, and black means that activity is yet to be covered. For example, the following abbreviated roadmap indicates the module would be showing a task in the View and Print activity.

1 CONFIGURE ACCOUNT OPTIONS | 2 COMPOSE & SEND | **3 VIEW & PRINT** | **4 REPLY**

5 ATTACH FILE | 6 ORGANIZE MESSAGES

Use the abbreviated roadmap as a progress guide while you read or step through the instructions in this module.

Introduction to Outlook

Outlook 2016 helps you organize and manage your communications, contacts, schedules, and tasks. **Email** (short for **electronic mail**) is the transmission of messages and files between computers or smart devices over a network. An **email client**, such as Microsoft Outlook 2016, is an app that allows you to compose, send, receive, store, and delete email messages. Outlook can access mail servers in a local network, such as your school's network, or on a remote network, such as the Internet. Finally, you can use Outlook to streamline your messages so that you easily can find and respond to them later.

To use Outlook, you must have an email account. An **email account** is an electronic mailbox you receive from an **email service provider**, which is an organization that provides servers for routing and storing email messages. Your employer or school could set up an email account for you, or you can do so yourself through your Internet service provider (ISP) or using a web application such as a Microsoft account, Google Gmail, Yahoo! Mail, or iCloud Mail. Outlook does not create or issue email accounts; it merely provides you with access to them. When you have an email account, you also have an **email address**, which identifies your email account on a network so you can send and receive email messages.

Project — Composing and Sending Email Messages

The project in this module follows the general guidelines for using Outlook to compose, open, and reply to email messages, as shown in Figure 1–1. To communicate with individuals and groups, you typically send or receive some kind of message. Phone calls, letters, texting, and email are examples of ways to communicate a message. Email is a convenient way to send information to multiple people at once.

A work study student in the Pathways Internship Office at Langford College, Sophia Garza, uses Outlook to communicate with faculty and fellow students. This module uses Microsoft Outlook 2016 to compose, send, read, reply to, and forward email messages regarding an upcoming Internship Fair. Sophia has been asked by Ms. Ella Pauley, the director of the internship program, to coordinate the marketing of the Pathways Internship Fair this October. Using Outlook, Sophia reads email messages from her director and students regarding internship opportunities. She replies to email messages and includes a document containing a flyer about the Internship Fair. To organize messages, she also creates folders and then stores the messages in the folders.

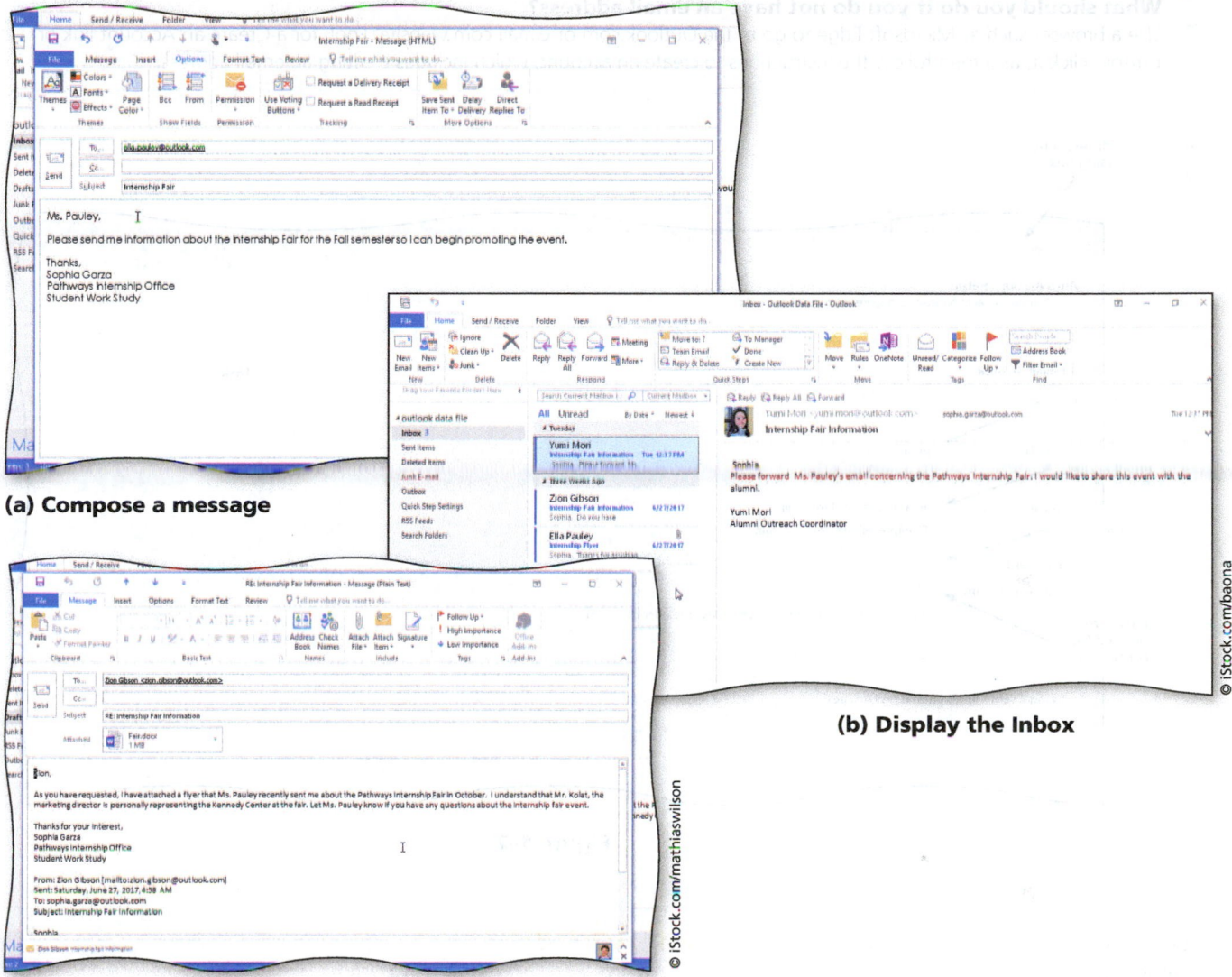

(a) Compose a message

(b) Display the Inbox

(c) Reply and attach a file to a message

Figure 1–1

Setting Up Outlook

Many computer users have an email account from an online email service provider such as Outlook.com or Gmail.com and another email account at work or school. Instead of using a web app for your online email account and another app for your school account, you can use Outlook 2016 to access all of your email messages in a single location. When you access your email in Outlook 2016, you can take advantage of a full set of features that include social networking, translation services, and file management. You can read your downloaded messages offline and set options to organize your messages in a way that is logical and convenient for you.

The first time you start Outlook on a personal computer, the Auto Account Setup feature guides you to provide information that Outlook needs to send and receive email messages (Figure 1–2). First, the setup feature prompts you to provide your name, which will appear in email messages that you send to other people. Next, the setup feature requests your email address and a password.

CONSIDER THIS

What should you do if you do not have an email address?
Use a browser such as Microsoft Edge to go to the Outlook.com or Gmail.com website. Look for a Create an Account link or button, click it, and then follow the instructions to create an account, which includes creating an email address.

Figure 1–2

For an introduction to Windows and instructions about how to perform basic Windows tasks, read the Office and Windows module at the beginning of this book, where you can learn how to resize windows, change screen resolution, create folders, move and rename files, use Windows Help, and much more.

Parts of an Email Address

An email address is divided into two parts. The first part contains a **user name**, which is a combination of characters, such as letters of the alphabet and numbers, that identifies a specific user. The last part is a **domain name**, which is the name associated with a specific Internet address and is assigned by your email service provider. A user name must be different from other user names in the same domain. For example, the outlook.com domain can have only one user named Sophia.Garza. An email address contains an @ (pronounced *at*) symbol to separate the user name from the domain name. Figure 1–3 shows an email address for Sophia Garza, which would be read as sophia dot garza at outlook dot com.

Figure 1–3

To Run Outlook

If you are using a computer or mobile device to step through the project in this module and you want your screens to match the figures in this book, you should change your screen's resolution to 1366 × 768. For information about how to change a computer's resolution, refer to the Office and Windows module at the beginning of this book.

The following steps, which assume Windows 10 is running, use the Start menu to run Outlook based on a typical installation. You may need to ask your instructor how to run Outlook on your computer. For a detailed example of the procedure summarized below, refer to the Office and Windows module.

1 Click the Start button on the Windows 10 taskbar to display the Start menu.

2 Click All apps at the bottom of the left pane of the Start menu to display a list of apps installed on the computer or mobile device.

3 Scroll to and then click Outlook 2016 in the All apps list to run Outlook.

4 If the Outlook window is not maximized, click the Maximize button on its title bar to maximize the window.

> One of the few differences between Windows 8 and Windows 10 occur in the steps to run Outlook. If you are using Windows 8, scroll the Start screen and then click the Outlook 2016 tile.

To Add an Email Account

You can add one or more of your personal email accounts to Outlook. For most accounts, Outlook automatically detects and configures the account after you type your name, email address, and password. Add an email account to Outlook when you are working on your personal or home computer only. You do not want your personal information or email messages on a public computer. Although most people add an email account the first time Outlook runs, you can add email accounts at any time. This module assumes you already set up an email account in Outlook. If you choose to add an email account to Outlook, you would use the following steps.

1. If you started Outlook for the first time, click the Next button to set up an email account. Otherwise, click the File tab, and then click Add Account.

2. If necessary, click the Yes button to add an email account, and then click the Next button to display the Add Account window.

3. Click the Your Name text box, and then type your first and last name to associate your name with the account.

4. Click the E-mail Address text box, and then type your full email address to associate your email address with the account.

5. Click the Password text box, and then type your password to verify the password to your email account.

6. Click the Retype Password text box, and then type your password again to confirm your password.

7. Click the Next button to configure your account settings and sign in to your mail server.

8. Click the Finish button to add your email account.

BTW
The Ribbon and Screen Resolution
Outlook may change how the groups and buttons within the groups appear on the ribbon, depending on the computer or mobile device's screen resolution. Thus, your ribbon may look different from the ones in this book if you are using a screen resolution other than 1366 × 768.

CONSIDER THIS

Will your screen look different if you are using a touch screen?

The Office and Windows interfaces may vary if you are using a touch screen. For this reason, you might notice that the function or appearance of your touch screen differs slightly from this module's presentation.

CONSIDER THIS

How do you remove an email account?

- To remove an email account in Outlook, click the File tab on the ribbon.
- If necessary, click the Info tab in the Backstage view.
- Click the Account Settings button, and then click Account Settings to display the Account Settings dialog box.
- Click the account you want to remove, and then click Remove.
- In the Account Settings dialog box, click the Yes button.

To Change the Navigation Bar Options

1 CONFIGURE ACCOUNT OPTIONS | 2 COMPOSE & SEND | 3 VIEW & PRINT
4 REPLY | 5 ATTACH FILE | 6 ORGANIZE MESSAGES

The first time you start Outlook, the lower-left corner of the screen provides compact navigation by default. To change the Navigation bar from displaying small icons representing Mail, Calendar, Contacts, and Task to a text view, you can disable the compact navigation setting on the Navigation bar. The following steps change the Navigation bar options. *Why? Instead of small icons, you can display the Mail, Calendar, Contacts, and Task text labels.*

1

- Click the Navigation Options button (three dots) on the Navigation bar to display a list of Navigation bar options (Figure 1–4).

Q&A

The left pane in my Outlook window is not expanded as it is in Figure 1–4. What should I do?
Click the Expand the Folder Pane button, which is a small arrow button to the left of today's date in the Outlook window.

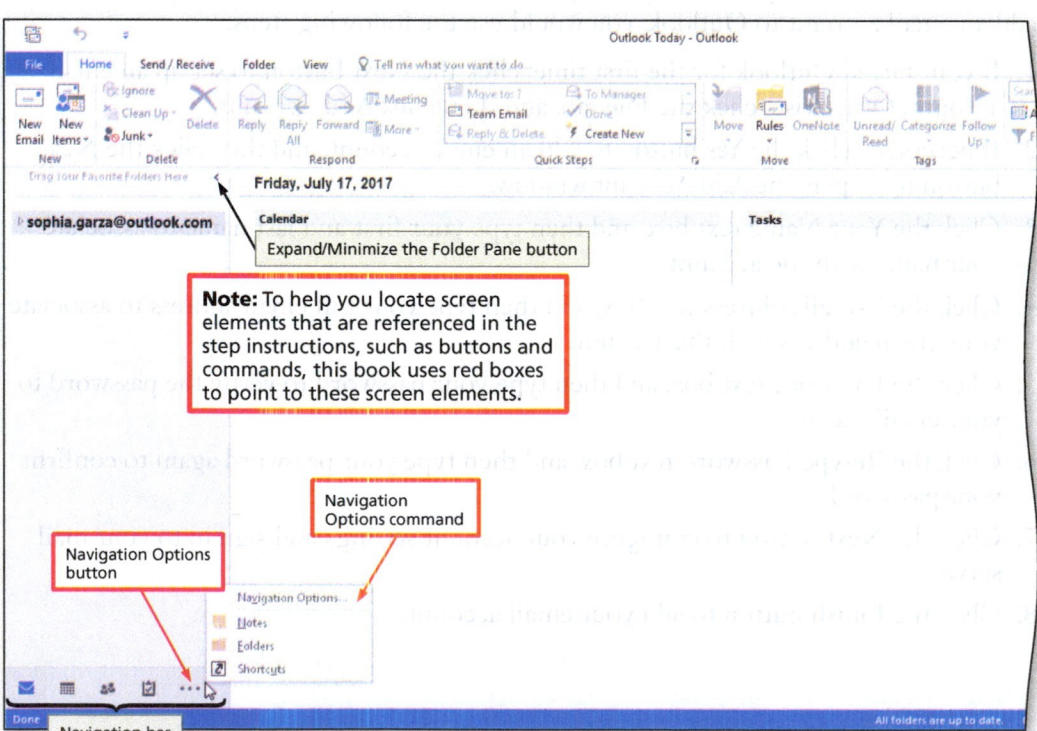

Figure 1–4

2

- Click Navigations Options to display the Navigation Options dialog box.

- If necessary, click the Compact Navigation check box (Navigation Options dialog box) to remove the check mark and disable the compact navigation setting on the Navigation bar (Figure 1–5).

Figure 1–5

3

- Click the OK button to change the Navigation bar so it displays text labels instead of icons (Figure 1–6).

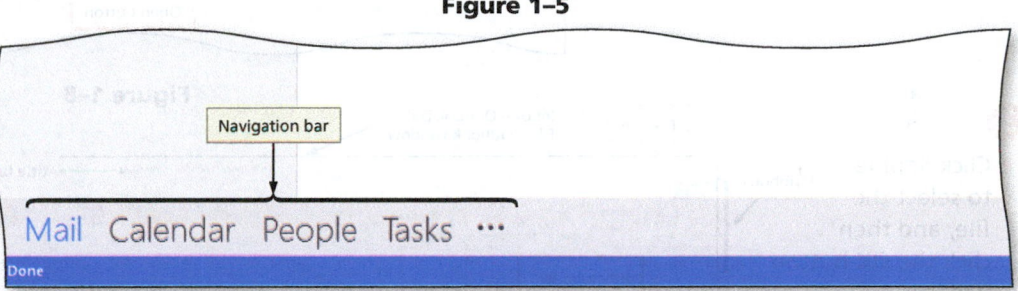

Figure 1–6

To Open an Outlook Data File

Microsoft Outlook uses a special file format called a **personal storage table (.pst file)** to save your email files, calendar entries, and contacts. The email messages with which you work in this module are stored in a personal storage table file named Sophia.pst, which is an Outlook mailbox located with the Data Files. To complete this assignment, you will be required to use the Data Files. Please contact your instructor for information about accessing the Data Files. In this example, the Sophia mailbox is located in the Module 01 folder in the Outlook folder in the Data Files folder. The following steps open the Sophia.pst file in Outlook, display the Inbox for the Sophia file, and then make your Sophia mailbox match the figures in this module. *Why? Opening or importing a .pst file allows you to move your email and other Outlook information to another computer.*

1

- Click File on the ribbon to open the Backstage view.

- Click the Open & Export tab in the Backstage view to display the Open gallery (Figure 1–7).

Figure 1–7

2

- Click Open Outlook Data File to display the Open Outlook Data File dialog box.

- Navigate to the mailbox location (in this case, the Module 01 folder in the Outlook folder in the Data Files folder) (Figure 1–8).

For an introduction to Office and instructions about how to perform basic tasks in Office apps, read the Office and Windows module at the beginning of this book, where you can learn how to run an application, use the ribbon, save a file, open a file, exit an application, use Help, and much more.

Figure 1–8

3

- Click Sophia to select the file, and then click the OK button (Open Outlook Data File dialog box) to open the Sophia mailbox in your Outlook window.

- If necessary, click the white triangle next to the outlook data file mailbox in the Navigation Pane to expand the folders.

- Click the Inbox folder below the outlook data file heading in the Navigation Pane to view Sophia's Inbox (Figure 1–9).

Figure 1–9

Q&A

What is the Navigation Pane?
The **Navigation Pane** is a pane along the left side of the Outlook window that contains shortcuts to your Outlook folders and gives you quick access to them. You use the Navigation Pane to browse all your Outlook folders using one of its views: Mail, Calendar, People, or Tasks.

What is the Inbox?
The **Inbox** is the Outlook folder that contains incoming email messages.

The contact photo shown in Figure 1–9 does not appear in my Outlook window. What should I do?
Outlook needs to synchronize the contact photos with the email addresses in the Sophia data file. Click the Close button to close Outlook, restart it, and then expand the outlook data file in the Navigation Pane to have the photos appear. You also might need to import the data file rather than opening it. In Step 2 on this page, click Import/Export instead of Open Outlook Data File.

To Set Language Preferences

You can use the Outlook Options dialog box to set the Office Language Preferences. ***Why?*** *You can specify the editing and display languages, such as the languages used in the dictionaries, grammar checking, and sorting.* Usually, Outlook configures the language settings to match your operating system; however, if you want to change those settings, you can adjust the Language preferences. The following steps set the Language preferences.

1

- Click File on the ribbon to open the Backstage view (Figure 1–10).

Q&A Why does my account information appear in the Backstage view?
If you have already set up an email account in Outlook, it appears on the Info tab in the Backstage view. Other options, such as Rules and Alerts, might also appear.

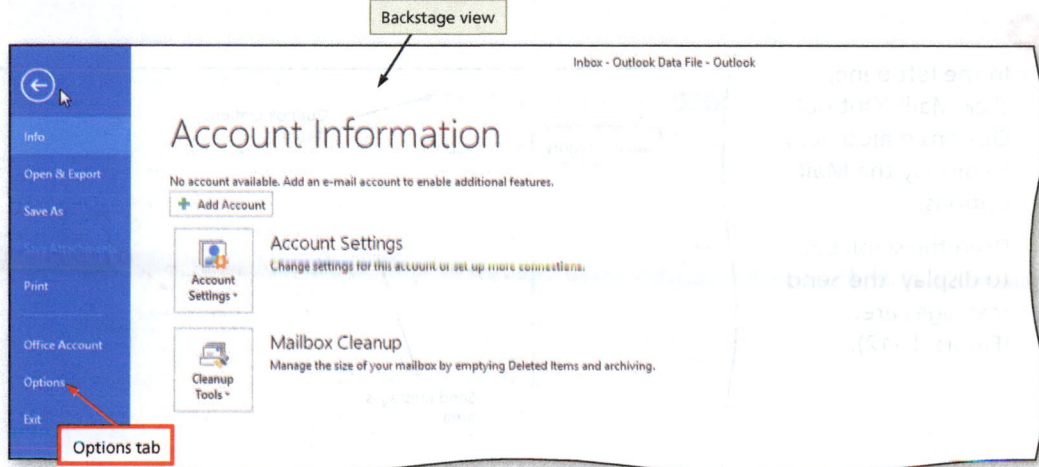

Figure 1–10

2

- Click the Options tab in the Backstage view to display the Outlook Options dialog box.

- In the left pane, click Language (Outlook Options dialog box) to display the Language options.

- Click the '[Add additional editing languages]' arrow to display a list of editing languages that can be added to Outlook (Figure 1–11).

Q&A How do I set a default language?
After selecting an editing language that you want to use, click the name of the language and then click the 'Set as Default' button.

Figure 1–11

3

- If necessary, scroll the list and then click English (United States) to set the default editing language. Otherwise, click the '[Add additional editing languages]' arrow again to close the list.

To Set the Sensitivity Level for All New Messages

The **Sensitivity level** of a message advises the recipient on how to treat the contents of the message. Sensitivity levels are Normal, Personal, Private, and Confidential. Changing the Sensitivity setting in the Outlook Options dialog box changes the default Sensitivity level of all messages created afterward. *Why? For example, if you set the Sensitivity level of a message to Confidential, the information should not be disclosed to anyone except the recipient.* The following steps set the default Sensitivity level.

1

- In the left pane, click Mail (Outlook Options dialog box) to display the Mail options.

- Drag the scroll bar to display the Send messages area (Figure 1–12).

Figure 1–12

2

- Click the 'Default Sensitivity level' arrow to display a list of Sensitivity levels (Figure 1–13).

Q&A

Can I set one message to an individual Sensitivity level such as private?

Yes, you can set the Sensitivity level for a single message using the More Options Dialog Box Launcher (Options tab | More Options group) to open the Properties dialog box. Click the Sensitivity button and then click Private to change the sensitivity of a single message to private.

Figure 1–13

- If necessary, click Normal to set the default Sensitivity level of all new messages.
- Click the OK button to close the Outlook Options dialog box.

Q&A | What should I do if the ribbon does not stay open?
Click any tab on the ribbon, and then click the 'Pin the ribbon' button (thumbtack icon) in the lower-right corner of the ribbon to keep the ribbon open.

Composing and Sending Email messages

Composing an email message is the most frequent personal and business task you perform in Microsoft Outlook. Composing an email message consists of four basic steps: open a new message window, enter message header information, enter the message text, and add a signature. When composing an email message, it is best to keep your message text concise and to the point. If you must write a longer, detailed message, break up your message into bullet points or into separate emails each with a clear summary of action.

An email message is organized into two areas: the message header and the message area. The information in the **message header** routes the message to its recipients and identifies the subject of the message. The message header identifies the primary recipient(s) in the To box. If you have multiple recipients in the To box, you can separate each email address with a semicolon. Recipients in the Cc (courtesy copy or carbon copy) and Bcc (blind courtesy copy) boxes, if displayed, also receive the message; however, the names of the recipients in the Bcc box are not visible to other recipients. The **subject line** states the purpose of the message.

The **message area**, where you type an email message, consists of a greeting line or salutation, the message text, an optional closing, and one or more signature lines as shown in Table 1–1.

BTW
Inserting Hyperlinks
To insert a web address in an email message, click where you want to insert the hyperlink, and then click the Hyperlink button (Insert tab | Links group) to display the Insert Hyperlink dialog box. In the Address text box, type the web address you want to insert as a hyperlink, and then click the OK button to insert the hyperlink into the message body.

Table 1–1 Message Area Parts	
Part	**Description**
Greeting line or salutation	Sets the tone of the message and can be formal or informal, depending on the nature of the message. You can use a colon (:) or comma (,) at the end of the greeting line.
Message text	Informs the recipient or requests information.
Closing	Informs the recipient or requests information. A closing signals an end to the message using courtesy words such as *Thank you* or *Regards*. Because the closing is most appropriate for formal email messages, it is optional.
Signature line(s)	Identifies the sender and may contain additional information, such as a job title, business name, and phone number(s). In a signature, the name usually is provided on one line followed by other information listed on separate lines.

To Compose an Email Message

1 CONFIGURE ACCOUNT OPTIONS | **2 COMPOSE & SEND** | 3 VIEW & PRINT
4 REPLY | 5 ATTACH FILE | 6 ORGANIZE MESSAGES

An email message from Sophia Garza, the work study student in the Pathways Internship Office, requests information about the Internship Fair from the director named Ella Pauley. The following steps compose a new email message. **Why?** *Composing email messages is a direct and efficient method to connect with personal and professional contacts.*

1

- Click the New Email button (Home tab | New group) to open the Untitled – Message (HTML) window (Figure 1–14).

Q&A

What does HTML mean in the title bar?

HTML is the format for the new email message. Outlook messages can use two other formats: Rich Text Format (RTF) and Plain Text. All of these formats are discussed later in this module.

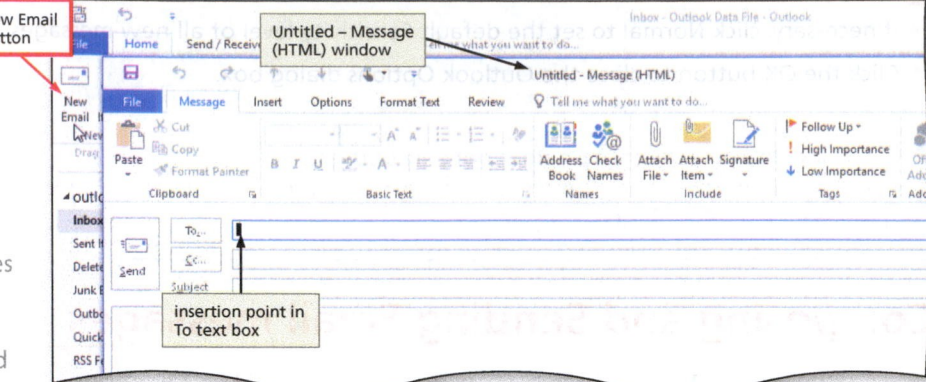

Figure 1–14

2

- Type **ella.pauley@ outlook.com** (with no spaces) in the To text box to enter the email address of the recipient.

- Click the Subject text box, and then type **Internship Fair** to enter the subject line.

- Press the TAB key to move the insertion point into the message area (Figure 1–15).

Figure 1–15

3

- Type **Ms. Pauley,** as the greeting line.

- Press the ENTER key to move the insertion point to the beginning of the next line.

- Press the ENTER key again to insert a blank line between the greeting line and the message text (Figure 1–16).

Q&A

What does it mean if I use all capital letters in my email message?

Writing in all capital letters is considered the same as shouting. Use proper capitalization as you compose your email.

Figure 1–16

- Type `Please send me information about the Internship Fair for the Fall semester so I can begin promoting the event.` to enter the message text.

- Press the ENTER key two times to insert a blank line below the message text (Figure 1–17).

Figure 1–17

- Type `Thanks,` to enter the closing for the message.

- Press the ENTER key to move the insertion point to the next line.

- Type `Sophia Garza` as the first line of the signature.

- Press the ENTER key to move the insertion point to the next line.

- Type `Pathways Internship Office` as the second line of the signature.

- Press the ENTER key to move the insertion point to the next line.

- Type `Student Work Study` as the third line of the signature (Figure 1–18).

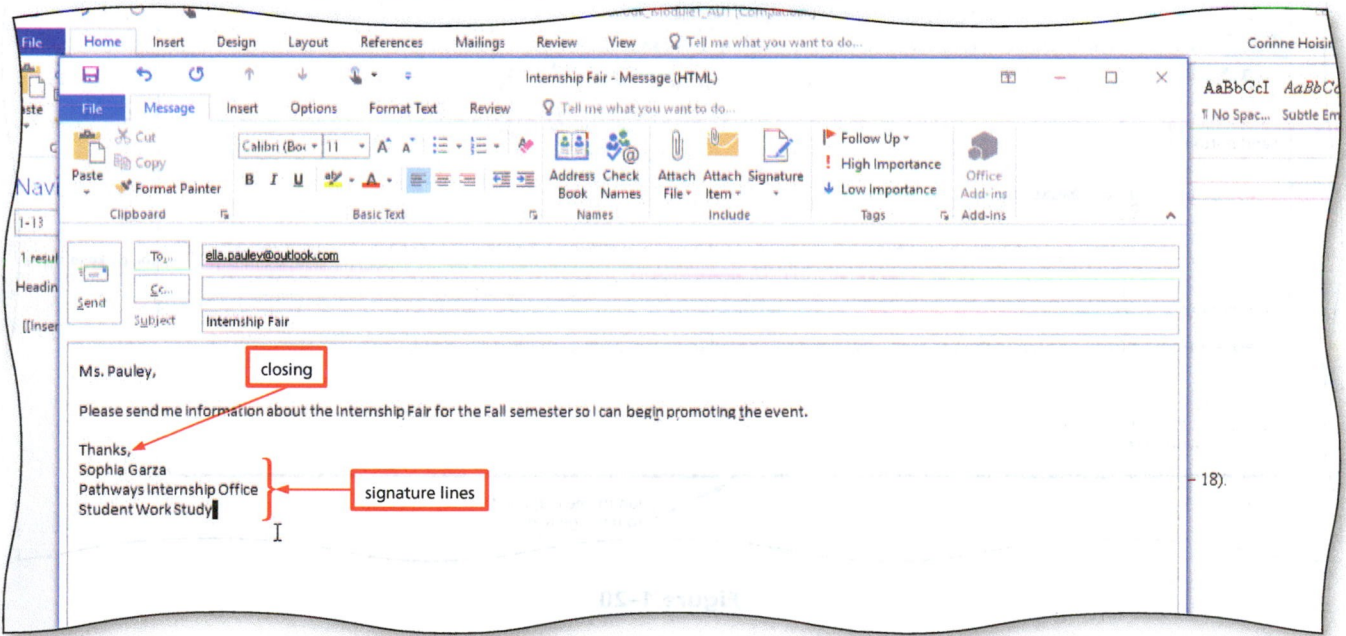

Figure 1–18

Q&A

What if I make an error while typing an email message?

Press the BACKSPACE key until you have deleted the error and then retype the text correctly. You also can click the Undo button on the Quick Access Toolbar to undo your most recent action.

Do I always need to type my last name in the signature of an email message?

No. If you and your recipient know each other, you can type only your first name as the signature.

Other Ways

1. Click Inbox folder, press CTRL+N

To Apply a Theme

An Outlook theme can give an email message instant style and personality. Each theme provides a unique set of colors, fonts, and effects. *Why? Themes give your organization's communications a modern, professional look using subtle styles.* The following steps apply a theme to the message.

 1

- Click Options on the ribbon to display the Options tab.

- Click the Themes button (Options tab | Themes group) to display the Themes gallery (Figure 1–19).

Figure 1–19

 2

- Click Ion in the Themes gallery to change the theme of the message (Figure 1–20).

Figure 1–20

How can you create your own theme for your messages to strengthen your company's brand?

- Format a message with a customized font, colors, and background.
- Click the Themes button (Options tab | Themes group) to display the Themes gallery.
- Click Save Current Theme to display the Save Current Theme dialog box.
- Type a name in the File name text box to name your new theme.
- Click the Save button to save your new theme.

CONSIDER THIS

To Send an Email Message

Why? *After you complete a message, send it to the recipient, who typically receives the message in seconds.* The following step sends the completed email message to the recipient.

• Click the Send button in the message header to send the email message and close the message window.

Q&A What happened to the email message?
Outlook automatically sends email messages to their recipient(s) when you click Send in a new message window if you have your own email account set up.

Why did I get an error message that stated that 'No valid email accounts are configured. Add an account to send email'?
If you do not have an email account set up in Outlook, you cannot connect to the Internet to send the email. Click Cancel to close the error message.

Other Ways

1. Press ALT+S

How Email Messages Travel from Sender to Receiver

When you send someone an email message, it travels across the Internet to the computer at your email service provider that handles outgoing email messages. This computer, called the **outgoing email server**, examines the email address on your message, selects the best route for sending the message across the Internet, and then sends the email message. Many outgoing email servers use **SMTP (Simple Mail Transfer Protocol)**, which is a communications protocol, or set of rules for communicating with other computers. An email program such as Outlook contacts the outgoing email server and then transfers the email message(s) in its Outbox to that server. If the email program cannot contact the outgoing email server, the email message(s) remains in the Outbox until the program can connect to the server.

As an email message travels across the Internet, routers direct the email message to a computer at your recipient's email service provider that handles incoming email messages. A **router** is a device that forwards data on a network. The computer handling incoming email messages, called the incoming email server, stores the email message(s) until your recipient uses an email program such as Outlook to retrieve the email message(s). Some email servers use **POP3**, the latest version of **Post Office Protocol (POP)**, a communications protocol for incoming email. Figure 1–21 shows how an email message may travel from a sender to a receiver.

In most cases, the Auto Account Setup feature does not require you to enter the name of your POP or SMTP server, but many businesses require that you manually enter these server settings. You can verify these Internet email settings in the Change Account dialog box, which is displayed by tapping or clicking the File tab on the ribbon to open the Backstage view, tapping or clicking the Account Settings button in the Backstage view, tapping or clicking Account Settings to display the Account Settings dialog box, selecting your email address, and then tapping or clicking the Change button. Figure 1–22 shows the Change Account dialog box for Sophia Garza. Notice that this account uses a mail server named m.hotmail.com.

Figure 1–21

Figure 1–22

Working with Incoming Messages

When you receive email messages, Outlook directs them to your Inbox and displays them in the **message pane**, which lists the contents of the selected folder (Figure 1–23). The list of messages displayed in the message pane is called the **message list**. An unread (unopened) email message in the message list includes a blue vertical bar in front of the message and displays the subject text and time of arrival in a blue bold font. An open envelope icon indicates a previously read (opened) message.

The blue number next to the Inbox folder shows how many unread messages are stored in the Inbox. The email messages on your computer may be different.

You can read incoming messages in three ways: in an open window, in the Reading Pane, or as a hard copy. A **hard copy (printout)** is information presented on a physical medium such as paper.

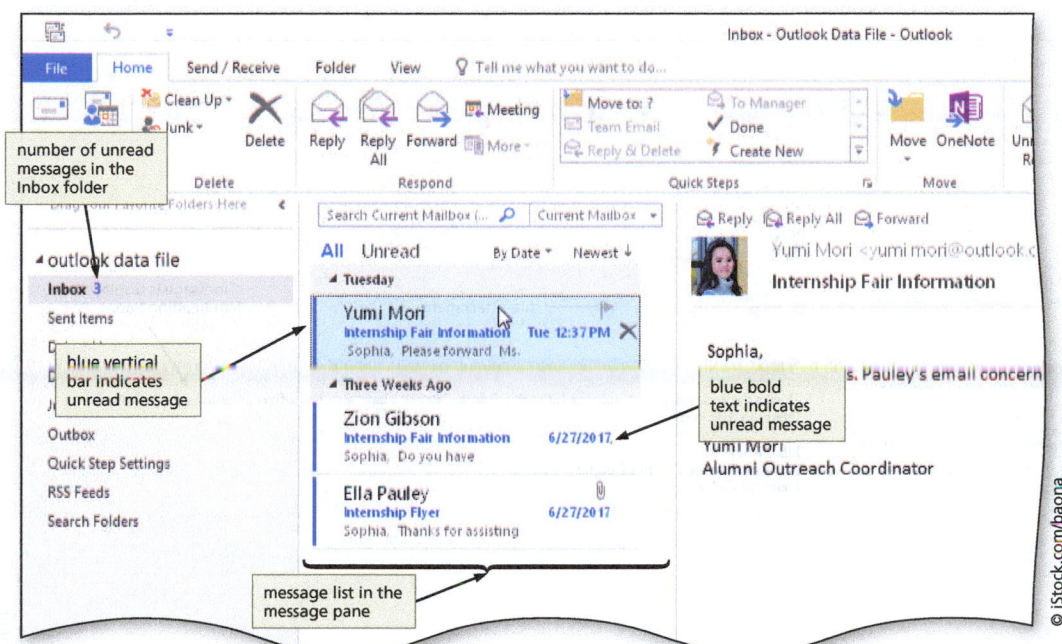

Figure 1–23

BTW
Know the Sender

If you receive an email message from someone you do not know, you should not open it because it might trigger a virus. Unsolicited email messages, known as **spam** or **junk email**, are email messages sent from an unknown sender to many email accounts, usually advertising a product or service such as low-cost medication, low-interest loans, or free credit reports. Do not click a hyperlink in an email message from an unknown sender. A **hyperlink** is a word, phrase, symbol, or picture in an email message or on a webpage that, when tapped or clicked, directs you to another document or website.

To View an Email Message in the Reading Pane

1 CONFIGURE ACCOUNT OPTIONS | 2 COMPOSE & SEND | 3 VIEW & PRINT
4 REPLY | 5 ATTACH FILE | 6 ORGANIZE MESSAGES

Why? *You can preview messages in your Inbox without opening them by using the Reading Pane.* The **Reading Pane** appears on the right side of the Outlook window by default and displays the contents of a message without requiring you to open the message. An advantage of viewing messages in the Reading Pane is that if a message includes content that could be harmful to your computer, such as a malicious script or an attachment containing a virus, the Reading Pane does not activate the harmful content. An **attachment** is a file such as a document or picture you send along with an email message. The attached document can be a file saved to your local computer or from OneDrive, as long as you have Microsoft's cloud service account connected. The instructor Ella Pauley has sent a response to Sophia concerning the Internship Fair. The following step displays an email message from a sender.

1

- Click the message header from Ella Pauley in the Inbox message list to select the email message and display its contents in the Reading Pane (Figure 1–24).

Q&A What happens to the message header when I select another message?

Outlook automatically marks messages as read after you preview the message in the Reading Pane and select another message to view. A read message is displayed in the message list without a vertical blue line or bold text.

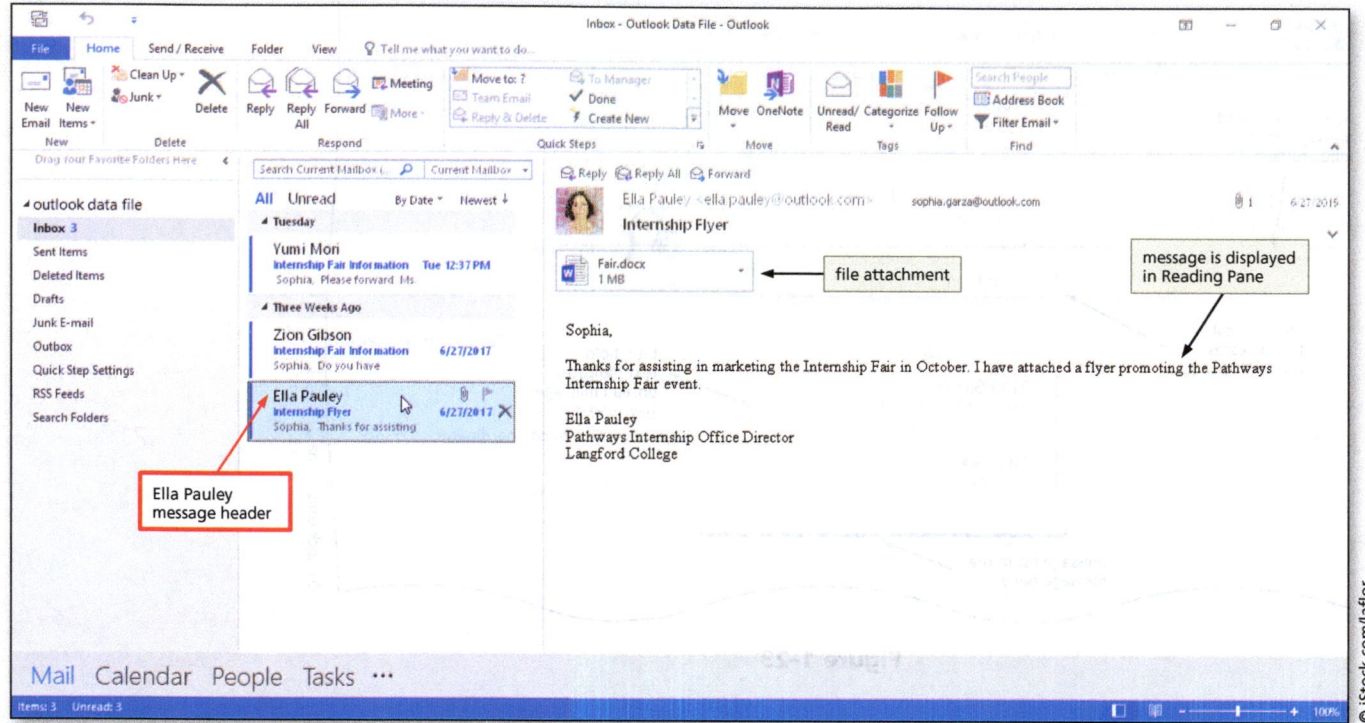

Figure 1–24

To Open an Email Message in a Window

1 CONFIGURE ACCOUNT OPTIONS | 2 COMPOSE & SEND | 3 VIEW & PRINT
4 REPLY | 5 ATTACH FILE | 6 ORGANIZE MESSAGES

Why? *To fully evaluate an email message and use additional Outlook tools for working with messages, you display the email message in a window.* The following step displays an email message from a sender in a window.

1

- Double-click the Ella Pauley message in the message list to display the selected email message in its own window (Figure 1–25).

Q&A Can I change the status of a message from unread to read without opening the message or displaying its contents in the Reading Pane?

Yes. Right-click the message you want to change, and then click Mark as Read on the shortcut menu.

Figure 1–25

Other Ways

1. Click message header, press CTRL+O

Opening Attachments

Email messages that include attachments are identified by a paper clip icon in the message list. Users typically attach a file to an email message to provide additional information to the recipient. An attachment in a message can appear in a line below the subject line or in the message body. To help protect your computer, Outlook does not allow you to receive files as attachments if they are a certain file type, such as .exe (executable) or .js (JavaScript), because of their potential for introducing a virus into your computer. When Outlook blocks a suspicious attachment in a message, the blocked file appears in the InfoBar at the top of your message. An **InfoBar** is a banner displayed at the top of an email message that indicates whether an email message has been replied to or forwarded.

The **Attachment Preview** feature in Outlook allows you to preview an attachment you receive in an email message from either the Reading Pane in an unopened message or the message area of an opened message. Outlook has built-in previewers for several file types, such as other Office programs, pictures, text, and webpages. Outlook includes attachment previewers that work with other Microsoft Office programs so that users can preview an attachment without opening it. These attachment previewers are turned on by default. To preview an attached file created in an Office application, you must have Office installed on your computer. For example, to preview an Excel attachment in Outlook, you must have Excel installed. If an attachment cannot be previewed, you can double-click the attachment to open the file.

To Preview and Save an Attachment

1 CONFIGURE ACCOUNT OPTIONS | 2 COMPOSE & SEND | **3 VIEW & PRINT**
4 REPLY | 5 ATTACH FILE | 6 ORGANIZE MESSAGES

Why? *When you receive a message with an attachment, you can preview the attached file without opening it if you are not sure of the contents.* A common transmission method of viruses is by email attachments, so be sure that you trust the sender before opening an attached file. The following steps preview and save an attachment without opening the file. You should save the attachment on your hard disk, OneDrive, or a location that is most appropriate to your situation. These steps assume you already have created folders for storing your files, for example, a CIS 101 folder (for your class) that contains an Outlook folder with a Module 01 folder (for your assignments). Thus, these steps save the attachment in the Module 01 folder in your desired save location. For a detailed example of the procedure for saving a file in a folder or saving a file on OneDrive, refer to the Office and Windows module at the beginning of this book.

1
- Click the Fair.docx file attachment in the message header of the opened email from Ella Pauley to preview the attachment within Outlook (Figure 1–26).

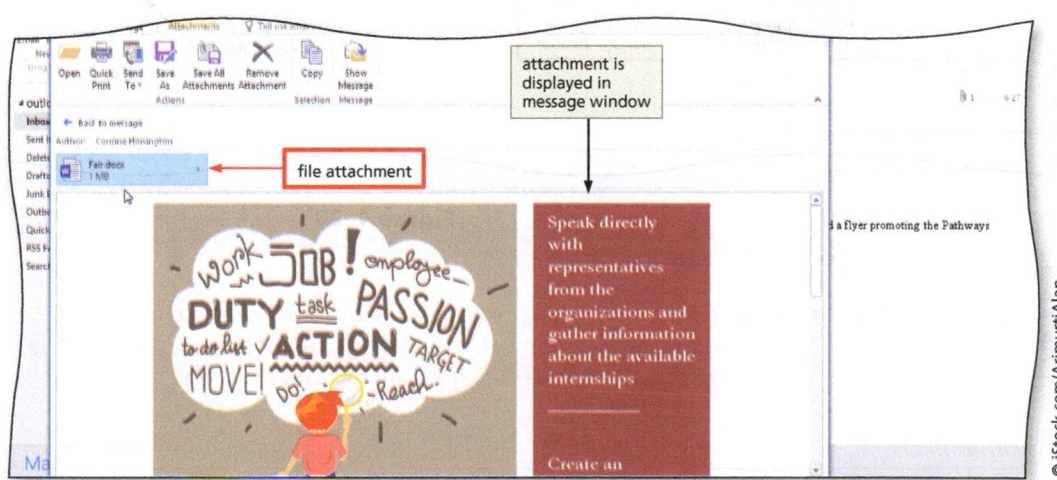

Figure 1–26

2

- Click the Save As button (Attachment Tools Attachments tab | Actions group) to display the Save Attachment dialog box.

- Navigate to the desired save location (in this case, the Module 01 folder in your Outlook folder or your class folder on your computer or OneDrive).

- If requested by your instructor, add your last name to the end of the file name (Figure 1–27).

Figure 1–27

3

- Click the Save button (Save Attachment dialog box) to save the document in the selected folder in the selected location with the entered file name.

- Click the Close button to close the attachment preview window and email message (Figure 1–28).

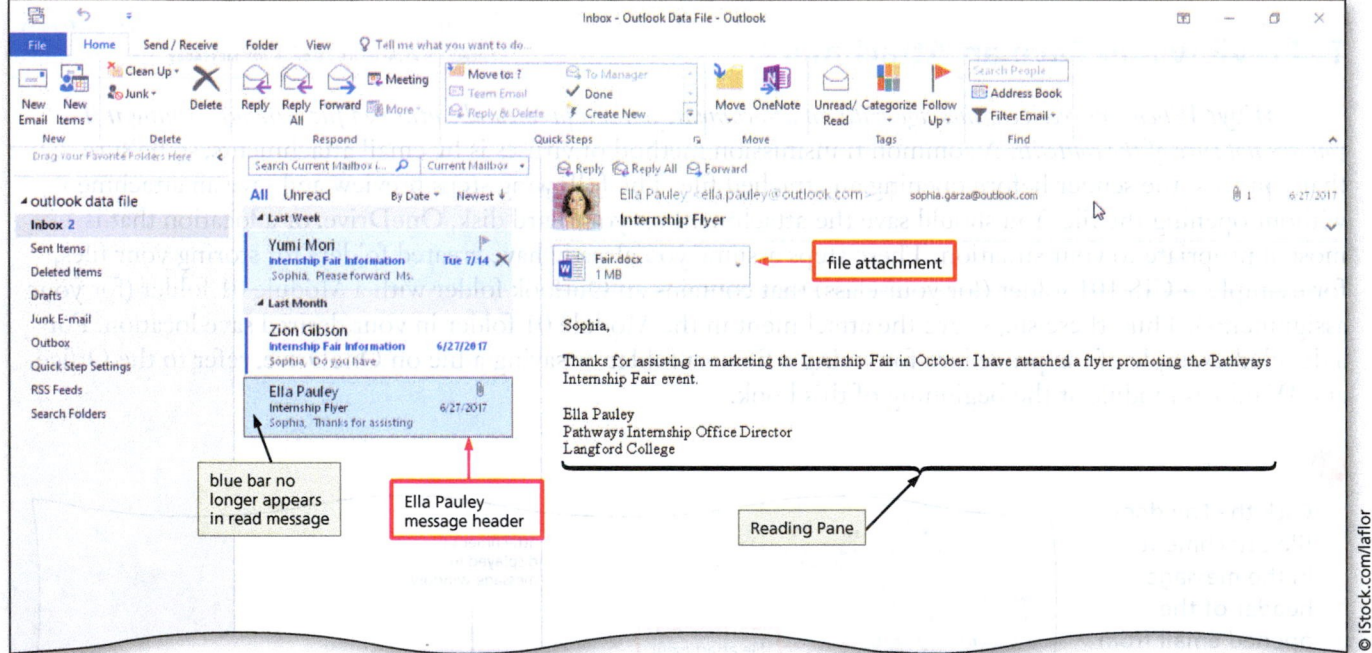

Figure 1–28

Q&A After I save the attachment, can I keep the email message but not the attachment?

Yes. Click the attachment in the Reading Pane, and then click the Remove Attachment button (Attachment Tools Attachments tab | Actions group) to remove the attachment from the email message.

Other Ways

1. Right-click attachment, click Save As

To Open an Attachment

If you know the sender and you know the attachment is safe, you can open the attached file. The following steps open an attachment. **Why?** *By opening a Word attachment in Microsoft Word, you can edit the document with the full features of Word.*

1

- If necessary, click the message header from Ella Pauley in the Inbox message list to select the email message and display its contents in the Reading Pane.

- Double-click the attachment in the Reading Pane to open the file attachment in Microsoft Word in Protected View (Figure 1–29).

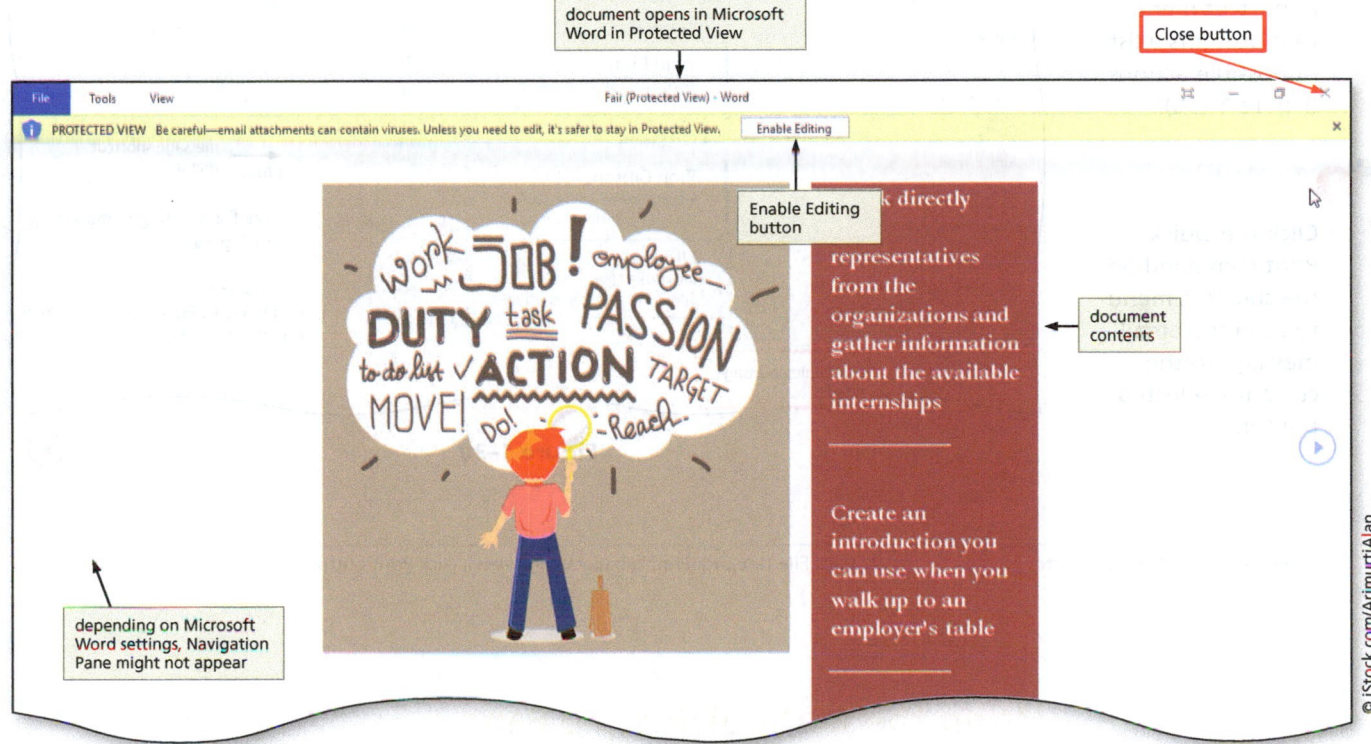

Figure 1–29

Q&A Why does the attachment open in Protected View in Microsoft Word?
File attachments can contain viruses, worms, or other kinds of malware, which can harm your computer. To help protect your computer, Microsoft Office apps open files from these potentially unsafe locations in Protected View. Click the Enable Editing button if you trust the sender to edit the document.

2

- Click the Close button to close the Word file.

To Print an Email Message

Occasionally, you may want to print the contents of an email message. **Why?** *A hard copy of an email message can serve as reference material if your storage medium becomes corrupted and you need to view the message when your computer is not readily available.* A printed copy of an email message also serves as a **backup**, which is an additional copy of a file or message that you store for safekeeping. You can print the contents of an email message from an open message window or directly from the Inbox window.

You would like to have a hard copy of Ella Pauley's email message for reference about the upcoming internship fair. The following steps print an email message.

1

- If necessary, click Home on the ribbon to display the Home tab.

- In the message list, right-click the Ella Pauley message header to display a shortcut menu that presents a list of possible actions (Figure 1–30).

2

- Click the Quick Print command on the shortcut menu to send the email message to the currently selected printer.

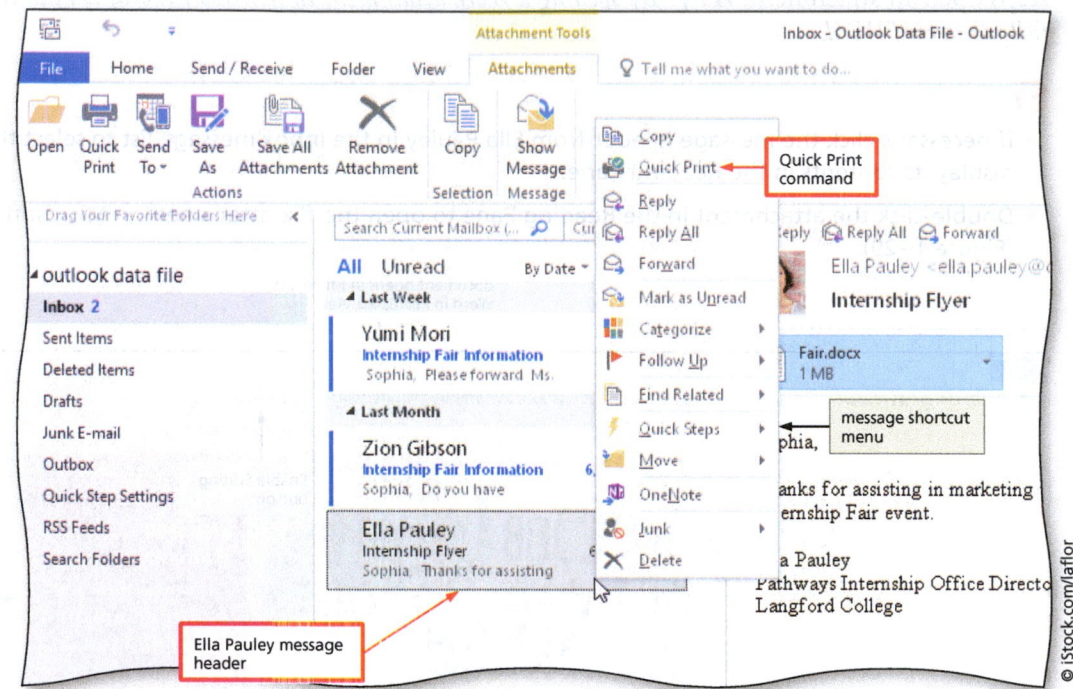

Figure 1–30

Other Ways

1. Press CTRL+P, click Print button
2. Click File tab, click Print tab (Backstage view), click Print button

Using the Outlook People Pane

Outlook provides a means of viewing email history, attachments, and meetings associated with each sender in the Reading pane. The **People Pane** accesses information about each of your contacts. The People Pane can display the photos and contact information of the email sender and recipient at the bottom of the Reading Pane in one location.

1 CONFIGURE ACCOUNT OPTIONS | 2 COMPOSE & SEND | **3 VIEW & PRINT** | 4 REPLY
5 ATTACH FILE | 6 ORGANIZE MESSAGES

To Change the View of the People Pane

By default, the People Pane is not displayed in the Reading Pane. By changing the People Pane to the Minimized setting, the contact information is displayed as a one-line bar below an open email message and does not take up a lot of room in the Reading Pane or open message window. To view more details, you can change the People Pane view to Normal. ***Why?*** *When you are reading a message in Outlook, you can use the People Pane to view more information about the contacts associated with the message, such as the senders and receivers of the message.* The following steps change the view of the People Pane.

1

- Click View on the ribbon to display the View tab.

- Click the People Pane button (View tab | People Pane group) to display the People Pane gallery (Figure 1–31).

Figure 1–31

2

- Click Normal in the People Pane gallery to display the People Pane in Normal view below the email message in the Reading Pane (Figure 1–32).

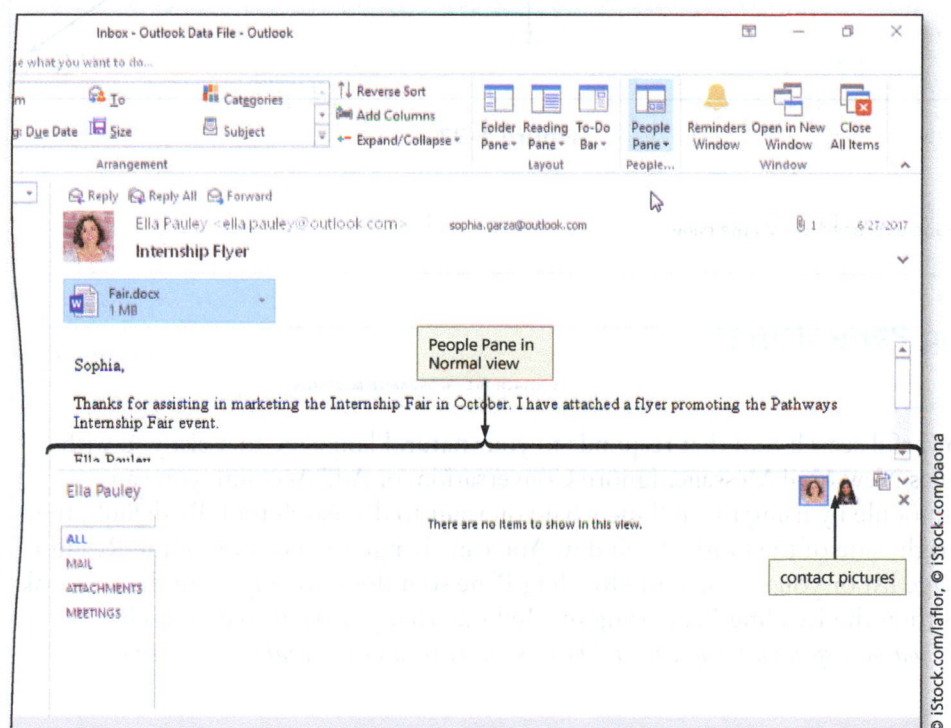

Figure 1–32

If you are using your finger on a touch screen and are having difficulty completing the steps in this module, consider using a stylus. Many people find it easier to be precise with a stylus than with a finger. In addition, with a stylus you see the pointer. If you still are having trouble completing the steps with a stylus, try using a mouse.

P **Experiment**

- Double-click the first contact picture in the People Pane. A contact card opens that displays the contact information. When you are finished, click the Close button to close the contact card.

Q&A

When the People Pane expands to Normal view, should messages from this sender be listed below the sender's name?
Yes. Email messages appear in the People Pane if you have previously corresponded with the sender.

A yellow message appears below Ella Pauley's name in the People Pane. How should I respond to the message?
Close the message by clicking its Close button.

3

- Click the People Pane button (View tab | People Pane group) to display the People Pane gallery.

- Click Minimized on the People Pane gallery to collapse the People Pane into a single line below the Reading Pane (Figure 1–33).

Q&A Does the People Pane update contact information automatically?
The People Pane automatically updates information about your professional and social network contacts while Outlook is running.

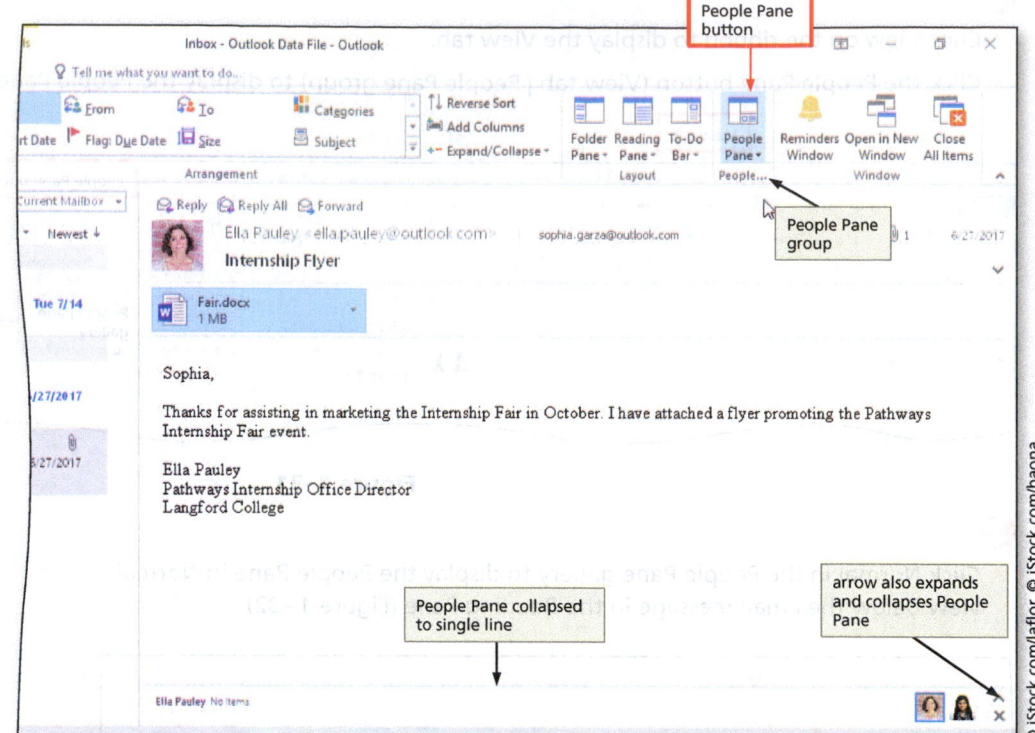

Figure 1–33

Other Ways

1. Click arrow to the right of the People Pane to expand or collapse pane

To Reposition the Reading Pane Using the Tell Me Search Tool

1 CONFIGURE ACCOUNT OPTIONS | 2 COMPOSE & SEND | **3 VIEW & PRINT** | 4 REPLY
5 ATTACH FILE | 6 ORGANIZE MESSAGES

Outlook 2016 includes a powerful search tool that responds to your natural language to assist you with most tasks. By typing phrases such as New Mail Message, Ignore Conversation, or Add Account, you can perform the previous tasks in this module by using the Tell me what you want to do search tool. By default, the Reading Pane is displayed on the right side of the Outlook window. You can change the position of the Reading Pane so it appears below the message list or you can hide the Reading Pane so it does not appear in the Outlook window. The following steps reposition the Reading Pane using the Tell me what you want to do search tool. *Why? In your work and personal life, you may spend a lot of time in Outlook, so create a layout that works best for your own needs.*

1

- Click the 'Tell me what you want to do' text box, and then type `Reading Pane` (Figure 1–34).

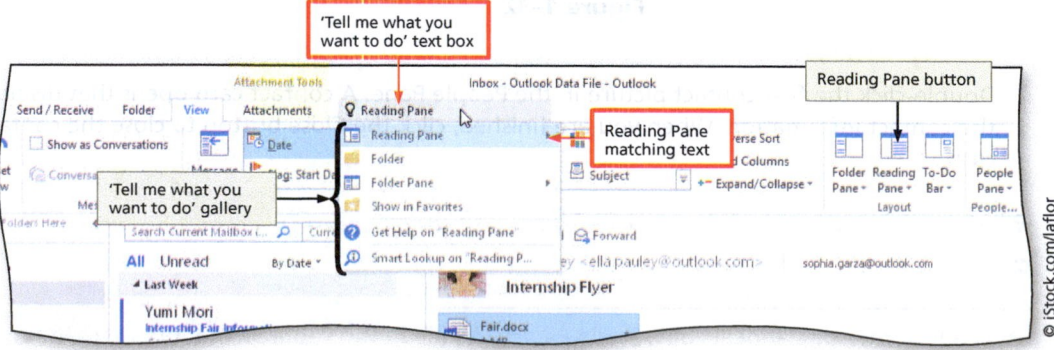

Figure 1–34

2

- Click the Reading Pane matching text option to display the Reading Pane options (Figure 1–35).

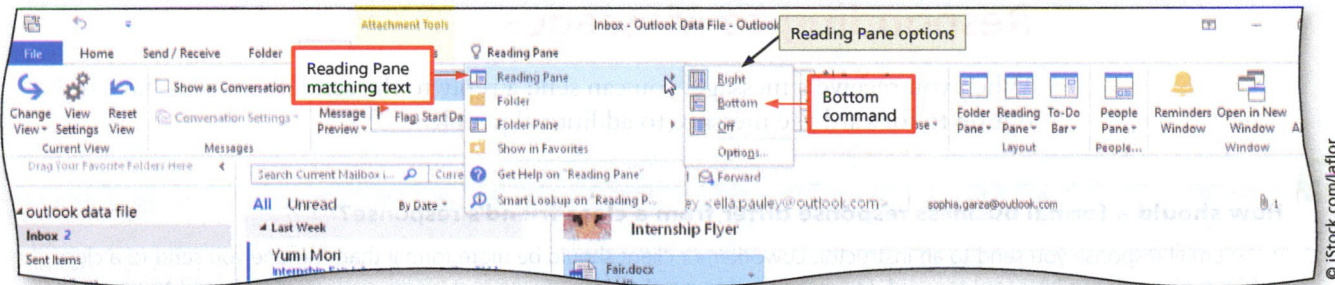

Figure 1–35

3

- Click Bottom in the Reading Pane options to place the Reading Pane for all mail folders at the bottom of the window (Figure 1–36).

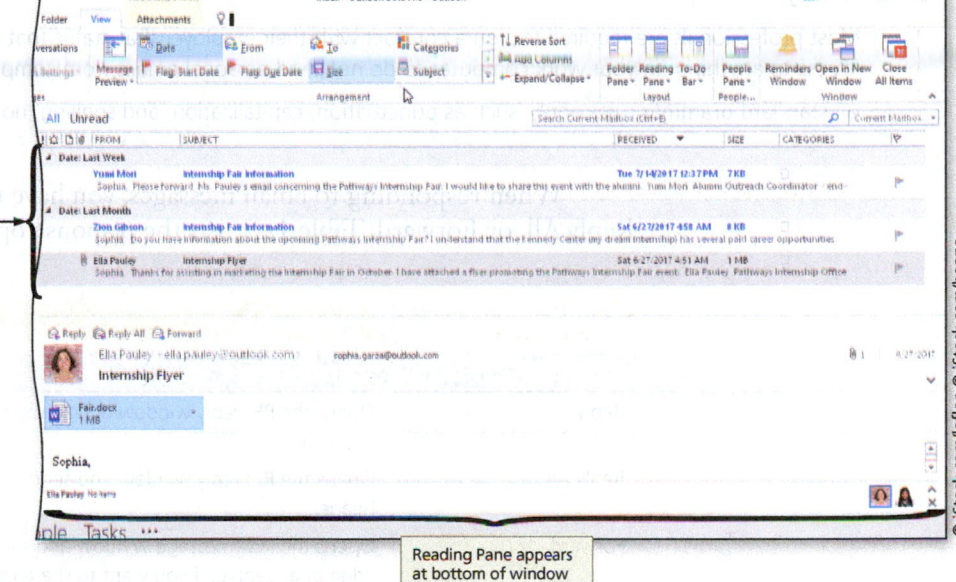

message list appears at top of window

Reading Pane appears at bottom of window

Figure 1–36

4

- Using the ribbon, click the Reading Pane button (View tab | Layout group) to display the Reading Pane gallery.

- Click Right on the Reading Pane gallery to return the Reading Pane to the right side of the Outlook window for all mail folders (Figure 1–37).

 Q&A Can you hide the Reading Pane completely?
Yes. Click the Reading Pane button and then click Off.

Figure 1–37

Responding to Messages

When you receive a message, you can send a reply to the sender. You also have the option to forward the message to additional people.

CONSIDER THIS

How should a formal business response differ from a close friend's response?

- An email response you send to an instructor, coworker, or client should be more formal than the one you send to a close friend placing your best foot forward. For example, conversational language to a friend, such as "Can't wait to go out!" is not appropriate in professional email messages.

- A formal email message should be business-like and get to the point quickly. An informal email is more conversational and friendly.

- Most professionals are required to sign a contract with their employer that states that the company has the right to have access to anything on your work computer so do not send personal emails from company email.

- All standard grammar rules apply, such as punctuation, capitalization, and spelling, no matter the audience.

When responding to email messages, you have three options in Outlook: Reply, Reply All, or Forward. Table 1–2 lists the response options and their actions.

Table 1–2 Outlook Response Options	
RESPONSE OPTION	**ACTION**
Reply	Opens the RE: reply window and sends a reply to the person who sent the message.
Reply All	Opens the RE: reply window and sends a reply to everyone listed in the message header.
Forward	Opens the FW: message window and sends a copy of the selected message to additional people, if you want to share information with others. The original message text is included in the message window.

© 2015 Cengage Learning

You reply to messages you already have received. You can forward an email message to additional recipients to share information with others. Based on the situation, you should request permission from the sender before forwarding a message, in case the sender intended the original message to remain private. When forwarding, you send the message to someone other than the original sender of the message. A reply sends the message to the person who sent the message.

To Reply to an Email Message

1 CONFIGURE ACCOUNT OPTIONS | 2 COMPOSE & SEND | 3 VIEW & PRINT | 4 REPLY
5 ATTACH FILE | 6 ORGANIZE MESSAGES

When you reply to an email message, the email address of the sender is inserted in the To box automatically. If you select Reply All, the To box automatically includes the sender and the other people who originally received the message (except for those who originally received a BCC message).

In an email message, a student named Zion Gibson has requested that Sophia send him information about the Pathways Internship Fair on campus. The following steps reply to an email message. *Why? When replying to a colleague, responding in a professional manner in an email message indicates how serious you are about your role and enhances your reputation within the organization.*

1

- Click Home on the ribbon to display the Home tab.
- Click the Zion Gibson message header in the message list to select it and display its contents in the Reading Pane (Figure 1–38).

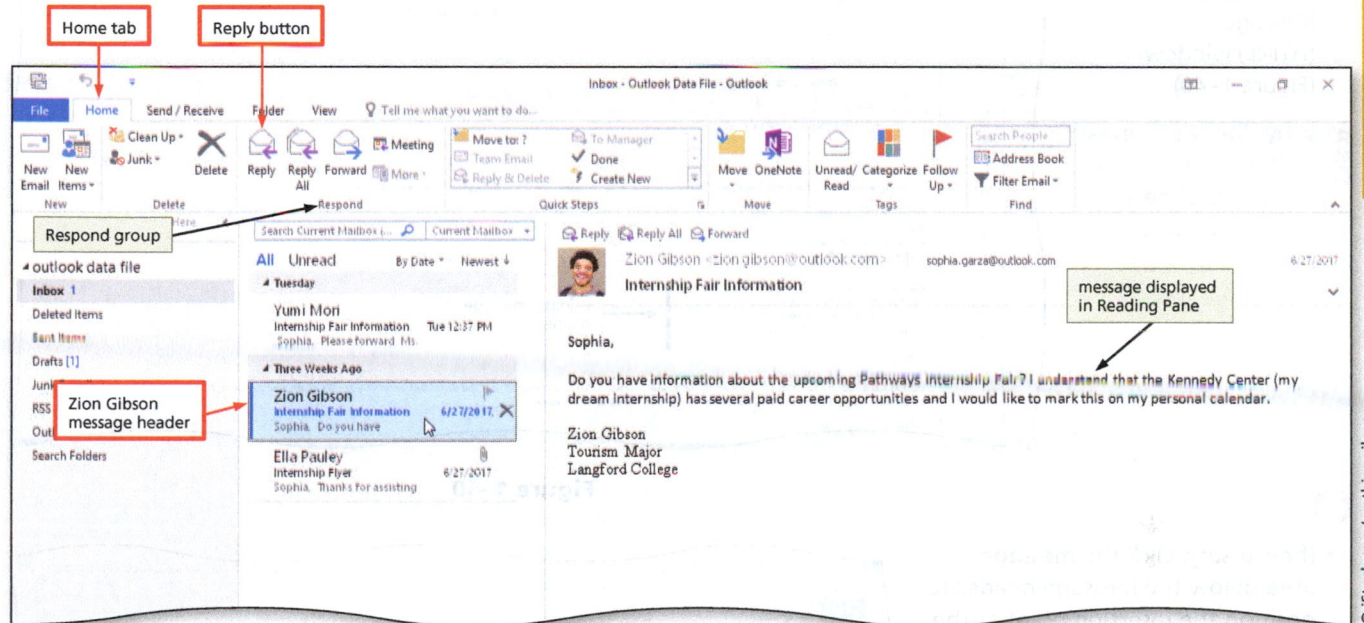

Figure 1–38

2

- Click the Reply button (Home tab | Respond group) to reply to the message in the Reading Pane (Figure 1–39).

Figure 1–39

3

- Click the Pop Out button to display the RE: Internship Fair Information – Message (HTML) window (Figure 1–40).

Q&A

Why does RE: appear at the beginning of the subject line and in the title bar?
The RE: indicates this message is a reply to another message. The subject of the original message appears after the RE:.

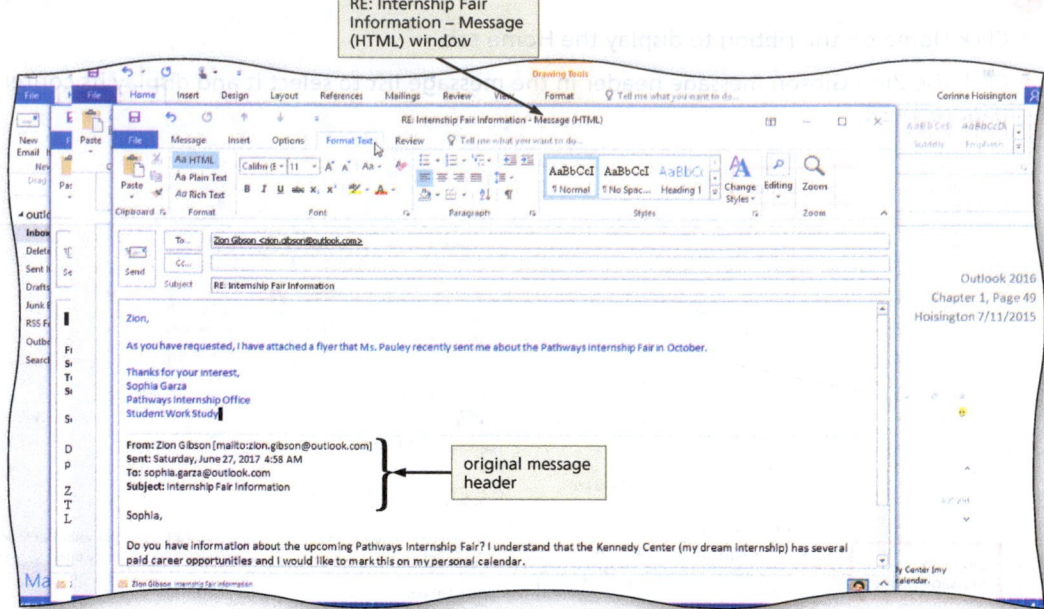

RE: Internship Fair Information – Message (HTML) window

original message header

Figure 1–40

4

- If necessary, click the message area below the message header to position the insertion point at the top of the message area.

- Type **Zion,** as the greeting line.

- Press the ENTER key two times to insert a blank line between the greeting line and the message text.

- Type **As you requested, I have attached a flyer that Ms. Pauley recently sent me about the Pathways Internship Fair in October.** to enter the message text.

- Press the ENTER key two times to insert a blank line between the message text and the closing.

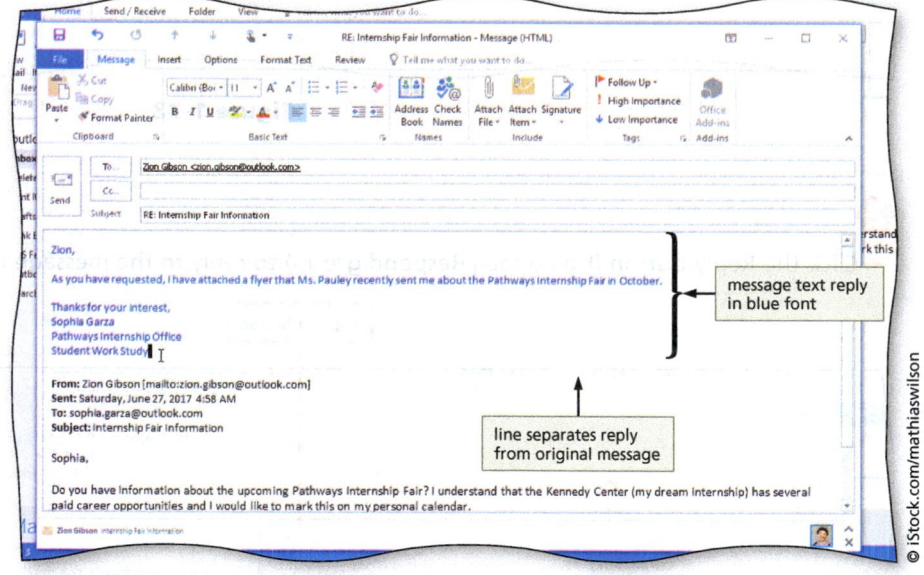

message text reply in blue font

line separates reply from original message

Figure 1–41

© iStock.com/mathiaswilson

- Type **Thanks for your interest,** as the closing, and then press the ENTER key to move the insertion point to the next line.

- Type **Sophia Garza** as signature line 1, and then press the ENTER key to move the insertion point to the next line.

- Type **Pathways Internship Office** as signature line 2.

- Type **Student Work Study** as signature line 3 (Figure 1–41).

Other Ways

1. Click Reply or Reply All in Reading Pane   2. Right-click message header, click Reply   3. With message selected, press CTRL+R

Message Formats

As shown in Figure 1–42, Outlook's default (preset) message format is **HTML (Hypertext Markup Language)**, which is a format that allows you to view pictures and text formatted with color and various fonts and font sizes. **Formatting** refers to changing the appearance of text in a document such as the font (typeface), font size, color, and alignment of the text in a document.

Before you send an email message, reply to an email message, or forward an email message, consider which message format you want to use. A **message format** determines whether an email message can include pictures or formatted text, such as bold, italic, and colored fonts. Select a message format that is appropriate for your message and your recipient. Outlook offers three message formats: HTML, Plain Text, and Rich Text, as summarized in Table 1–3. If you select the HTML format, for example, the email program your recipient uses must be able to display formatted messages or pictures. If your recipient does not have high speed connectivity, a Plain Text format is displayed quickly, especially on a device such as a smartphone. Reading email in plain text offers important security benefits, reducing the possibility of a virus within the email.

Table 1–3	**Message Formats**
MESSAGE FORMAT	**DESCRIPTION**
HTML	HTML is the default format for new messages in Outlook. HTML lets you include pictures and basic formatting, such as text formatting, numbering, bullets, and alignment. HTML is the recommended format for Internet mail because the more popular email programs use it.
Plain Text	Plain Text format is recognized by all email programs and is the most likely format to be allowed through a company's virus-filtering program. Plain Text does not support basic formatting, such as bold, italic, colored fonts, or other text formatting. It also does not support pictures displayed directly in the message.
Rich Text	Rich Text Format (RTF) is a Microsoft format that only the latest versions of **Microsoft Exchange** (a Microsoft message system that includes an email program and a mail server) and Outlook recognize. RTF supports more formats than HTML or Plain Text; it also supports hyperlinks. A hyperlink can be text, a picture, or other object that is displayed in an email message.

Can I use plain text formatting to guard against email viruses?
HTML-formatted messages can contain viruses. To minimize the risk of receiving a virus infected email message, change the format of messages you read. You can configure Outlook to format all opened messages in Plain Text. Click File on the ribbon to open the Backstage view. Click the Options tab. Click the Trust Center option in the Outlook Options dialog box, and then click the Trust Center Settings button to display the Trust Center dialog box. Click Email Security (Trust Center dialog box), and in the Read as Plain Text section, click the 'Read all standard mail in plain text' check box.

CONSIDER THIS

To Change the Message Format

1 CONFIGURE ACCOUNT OPTIONS | 2 COMPOSE & SEND | 3 VIEW & PRINT | **4 REPLY**
5 ATTACH FILE | 6 ORGANIZE MESSAGES

Why? *You want to make sure that your reply message is not blocked by an antivirus program, so you will change the message format to Plain Text.* The following steps change the message format to Plain Text.

1

- Click Format Text on the ribbon in the message window to display the Format Text tab (Figure 1–42).

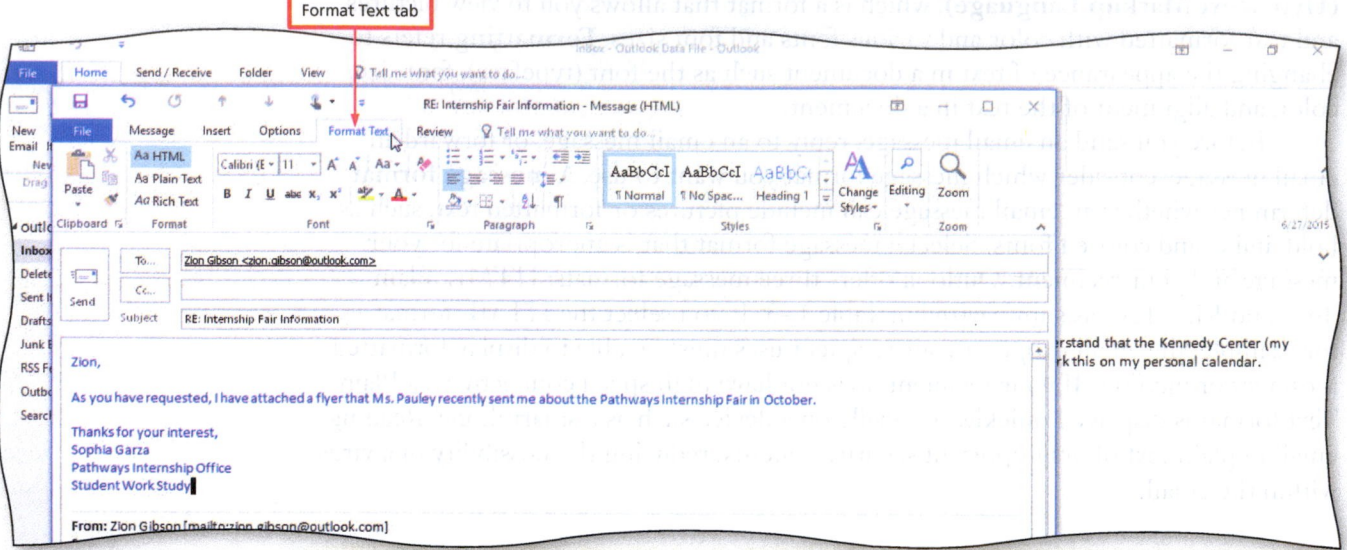

Figure 1–42

2

- Click the Plain Text button (Format Text tab | Format group) to select the Plain Text message format, which removes all formatting in the message.

- When the Microsoft Outlook Compatibility Checker dialog box is displayed, click the Continue button to change the formatted text to plain text (Figure 1–43).

© iStock.com/mathiaswilson

Figure 1–43

Q&A What happened to the line separating the existing message and the new message?

When Plain Text is selected as the message format, all formatting such as text color, font type, lines, themes, and size is removed.

Checking Spelling and Grammar

BTW

Misspelled Words in an Email Message

When you misspell words in a professional email message, your clients may think you are just sending a quick message and not giving the email your full attention when responding.

Outlook checks your message for possible spelling and grammar errors as you type and flags any potential errors in the message text with a red, green, or blue wavy underline. A red wavy underline means the flagged text is not in Outlook's main dictionary because it is a proper name or misspelled. A green wavy underline indicates the text may be incorrect grammatically. A blue wavy underline indicates the text may contain a contextual spelling error such as the misuse of homophones (words that are pronounced the same but have different spellings or meanings, such as one and won). Although you can check the entire message for spelling and grammar errors at once, you also can check these flagged errors as they appear on the screen.

A flagged word is not necessarily misspelled. For example, many names, abbreviations, and specialized terms are not in Outlook's main dictionary. In these cases, you instruct Outlook to ignore the flagged word. As you type, Outlook also detects duplicate words while checking for spelling errors. For example, if your email message contains the phrase *to the the store*, Outlook places a red wavy underline below the second occurrence of the word, *the*.

Should I remove the original message when replying?

Many email users prefer to reply to a message without including the original email message along with their response. To remove the original message from all email replies, click File to open the Backstage view, and then click the Options tab. Click Mail to display the Mail options. In the Replies and forwards section, click the 'When replying to a message box' arrow, select the 'Do not include original message' option, and then click OK.

1 CONFIGURE ACCOUNT OPTIONS | 2 COMPOSE & SEND | 3 VIEW & PRINT | **4 REPLY**
5 ATTACH FILE | 6 ORGANIZE MESSAGES

CONSIDER THIS

To Check the Spelling of a Correctly Typed Word

Sophia adds one more sentence to her email message, recalling that Zion is interested in an internship at the Kennedy Center. In the message, the Kennedy Center employer with the last name of Kolat has a red wavy line below it even though it is spelled correctly, indicating the word is not in Outlook's main dictionary. The following steps ignore the error and remove the red wavy line. *Why? The main dictionary contains most common words, but does not include most proper names, technical terms, or acronyms.*

 1

- Click after the first sentence in the email message to Zion to place the insertion point, and then press the SPACEBAR to insert a space.

- Type **I understand that Mr. Kolat, the marketing**

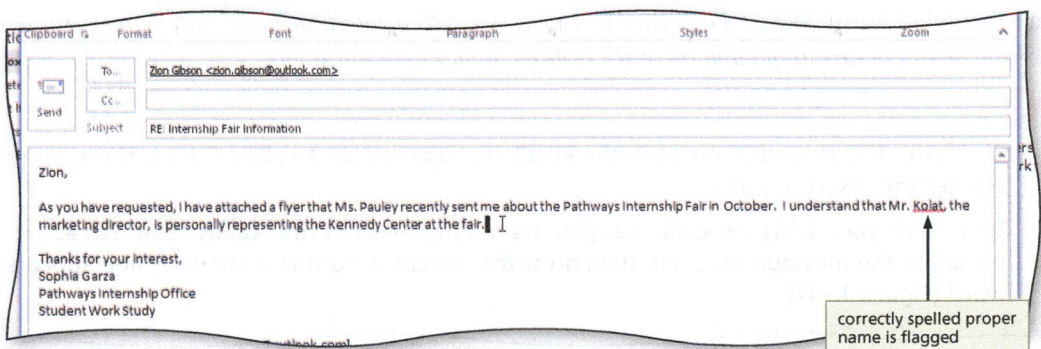

correctly spelled proper name is flagged

Figure 1–44

director, is personally representing the Kennedy Center at the fair. to enter a second sentence in the message text, and then click a blank spot in the window to have Outlook mark a spelling error (Figure 1–44).

Q&A | Why does a red wavy line appear below Kolat even though the last name is spelled correctly?
Outlook places a red wavy line below any word that is not in its main dictionary.

- Right-click the red wavy line below the proper name to display a shortcut menu that presents a list of suggested spelling corrections for the flagged word (in this case, the last name) (Figure 1–45).

Q&A

What if Outlook does not flag my spelling and grammar errors with wavy underlines?

To verify that the check spelling and grammar as you type features are enabled, click the File tab on the ribbon to open the Backstage view and then click Options to display the Outlook Options dialog box. Click Mail (Outlook Options dialog box) and click the Editor Options button to display the Editor Options dialog box. In the 'When correcting spelling in Outlook' section, ensure the 'Check spelling as you type' check box contains a check mark. Click the OK button two times to close each open dialog box.

Figure 1–45

- Click Ignore All on the shortcut menu to ignore this flagged error, close the shortcut menu, and remove the red wavy line beneath the proper name (Figure 1–46).

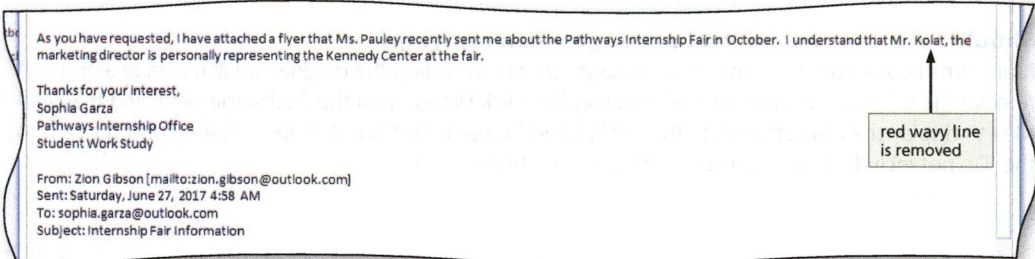

Figure 1–46

To Check the Spelling of Misspelled Text

1 CONFIGURE ACCOUNT OPTIONS | 2 COMPOSE & SEND | 3 VIEW & PRINT | **4 REPLY**
5 ATTACH FILE | 6 ORGANIZE MESSAGES

In the following steps, the word *event* is misspelled intentionally as *evnt* to illustrate Outlook's check spelling as you type feature. If you are performing the steps in this project, your email message may contain different misspelled words, depending on the accuracy of your typing. The following steps check the spelling of a misspelled word. ***Why?*** *The way you present yourself in email messages contributes to the way you are perceived, so you should be sure to proofread and check the spelling of all communications.*

- Click after the second sentence in the email message to Zion to place the insertion point, and then press the SPACEBAR to insert a space.

- Type `Let Ms. Pauley know if you have any questions about the internship fair evnt.` to complete the message text, and then press the SPACEBAR so that a red wavy line appears below the misspelled word (Figure 1–47).

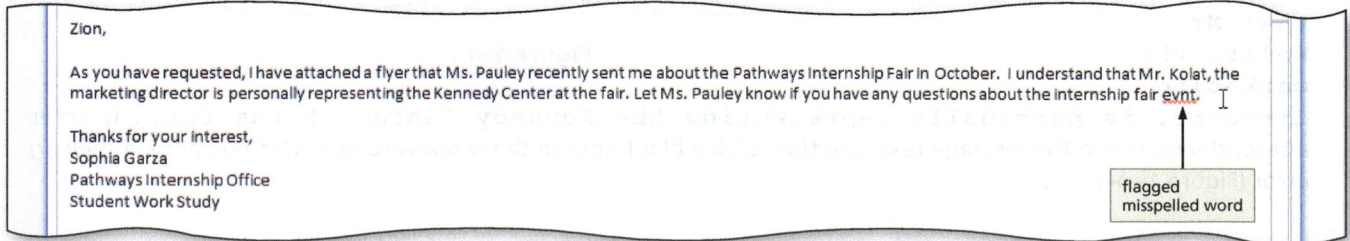

Figure 1–47

2

- Right-click the flagged word (evnt, in this case) to display a shortcut menu that presents a list of suggested spelling corrections for the flagged word (Figure 1–48).

Q&A What should I do if the correction I want to use is not listed on the shortcut menu? You can click outside the shortcut menu to close it and then retype the correct word.

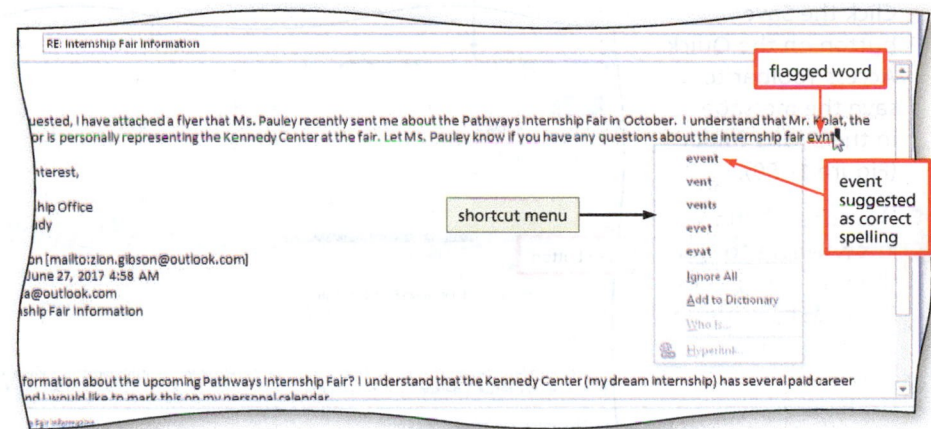

Figure 1–48

3

- Click the correct spelling on the shortcut menu (in this case, event) to replace the misspelled word in the email message with the correctly spelled word (Figure 1–49).

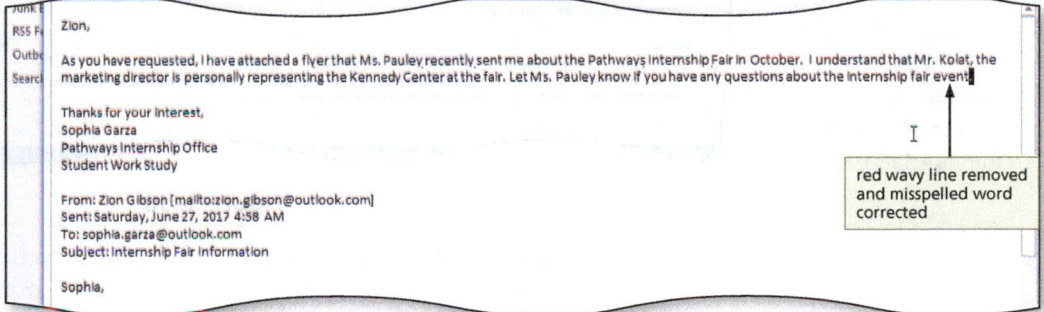

Figure 1–49

Other Ways

1. Click Review tab (message window), click Spelling & Grammar button (Review tab | Proofing group)
2. Press F7

Saving and Closing an Email Message

Occasionally, you begin composing a message but cannot complete it. You may be waiting for information from someone else to include in the message, or you might prefer to rewrite the message later after you have time to evaluate its content. One option is to save the message, which stores the message in the Drafts folder for your email account until you are ready to send it. The Drafts folder is the default location for all saved messages. Later, you can reopen the message, finish writing it, and then send it.

To Save and Close an Email Message without Sending It

1 CONFIGURE ACCOUNT OPTIONS | 2 COMPOSE & SEND | 3 VIEW & PRINT | 4 REPLY
5 ATTACH FILE | 6 ORGANIZE MESSAGES

The Internship Fair information that Zion Gibson requested has been drafted, but Sophia is not ready to send it yet. The following steps save a message in the Drafts folder for completion at a later time. *Why? If you are in the middle of composing a lengthy or important email and get called away, you can save your work so you can resume it later.*

1

- Click the Save button on the Quick Access Toolbar to save the message in the Drafts folder (Figure 1–50).

Q&A

How does Outlook know where to store the saved message?
By default, Outlook stores saved messages in the Drafts folder for your email account.

Can I save the message to a location other than the Drafts folder?
To save the message to the Outlook student folder, click the File tab on the ribbon to open the Backstage view, and then click Save As in the Backstage view to display the Save As dialog box. Navigate to the Outlook student folder. In the File name text box, type the name of the message file and then click the Save button. The message is saved with the extension .msg, which represents an Outlook message.

What should I do if Outlook did not save the message in the Drafts folder?
Click the Home tab, click the Move button, click Other Folder, select the Drafts folder for Sophia Garza's Outlook Data File, and then click the OK button.

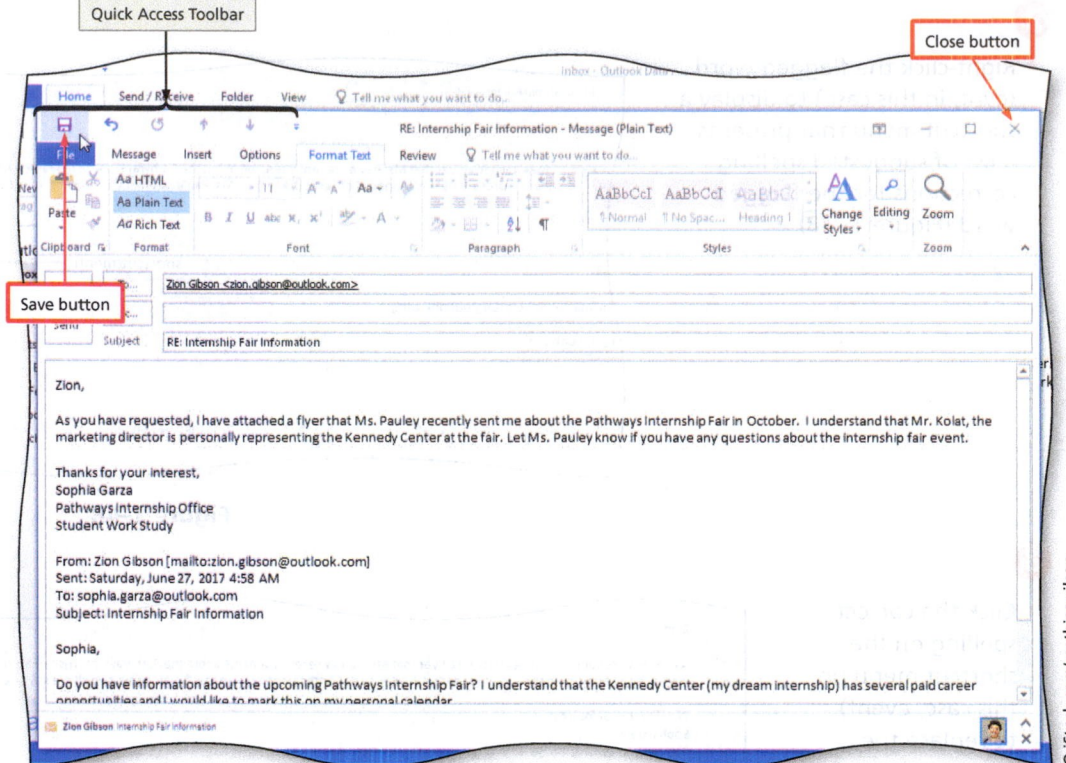

Figure 1–50

© iStock.com/mathiaswilson

2

- Click the Close button on the title bar to close the RE: Internship Fair Information – Message (HTML) window (Figure 1–51).

Q&A

How do I know when a message is a draft rather than an incoming message?
The message appears in the message list with [Draft] displayed in red.

What happens if I click the Close button without saving the message?
If you create a message and then click the Close button, Outlook displays a dialog box asking if you want to save the changes. If you click Yes, Outlook saves the file to the Drafts folder and closes the message window. If you click No, Outlook discards the email message and closes the message window.

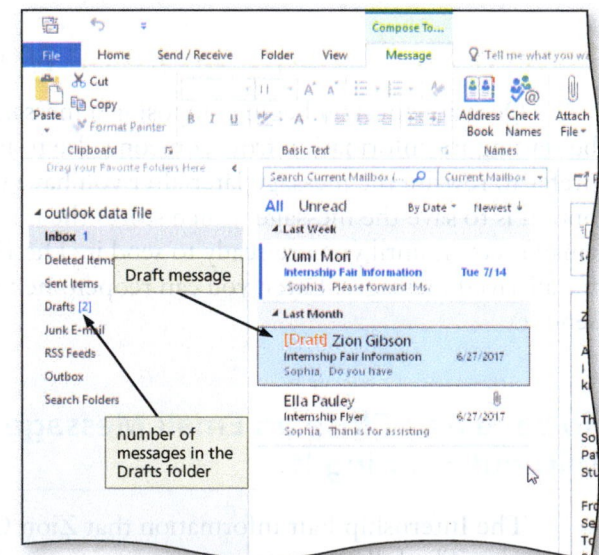

Figure 1–51

Other Ways

1. Click Close button and click Yes to keep saved draft of message   2. Press F12

To Open a Saved Email Message

The following steps open the message saved in the Drafts folder. *Why? By default, Outlook saves any email message in the Drafts folder every three minutes.* You can also save a message and reopen it later.

1

- Click the Drafts folder in the Navigation Pane to display the message header for the Zion Gibson email message in the message list (Figure 1–52).

Q&A What should I do if the message does not appear in my Drafts folder?
If the message does not appear in the Drafts folder, return to the Inbox, and then click the message header in the message pane.

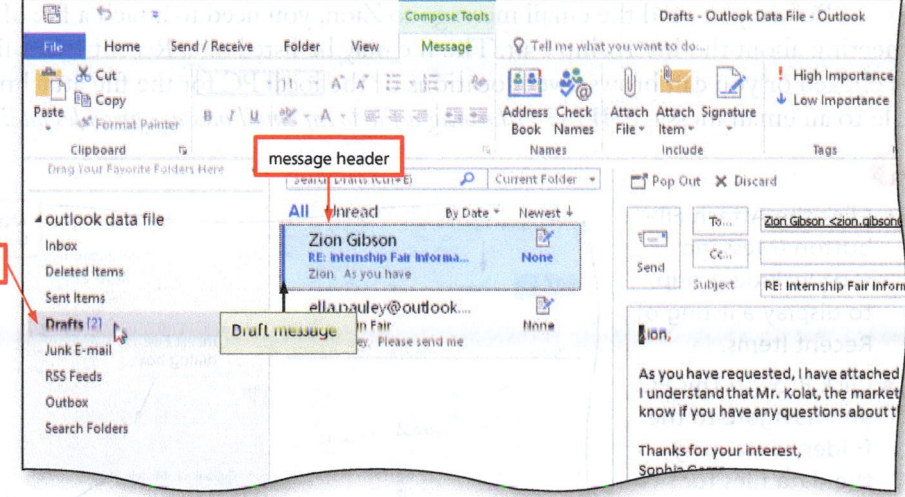

Figure 1–52

2

- Double-click the Zion Gibson message header in the Drafts folder to open the email message (Figure 1–53).

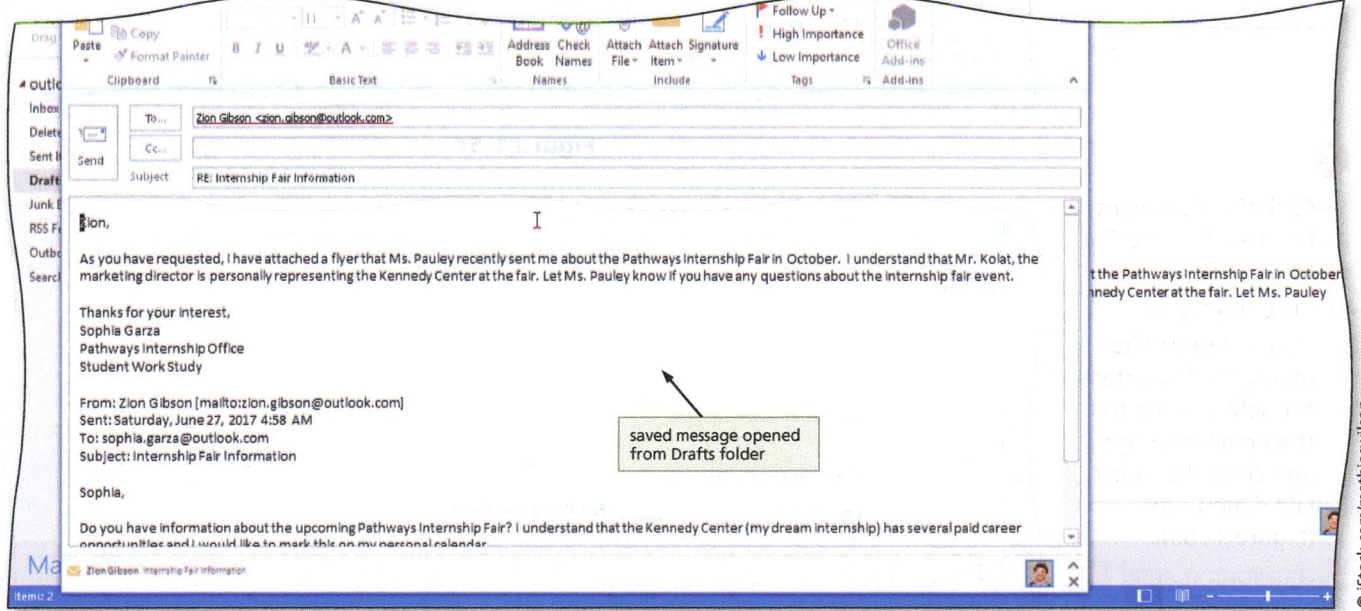

Figure 1–53

Other Ways

1. Right-click message, and click Open
2. With message selected, press CTRL+O

© iStock.com/mathiaswilson

To Attach a File to an Email Message

To share a file such as a photo, flyer, or business document through email, you attach the file to an email message. Outlook does not have a predefined file size limit for attachments, but an email service provider may restrict the size of incoming attachments or the size of the email mailbox. Very large email attachments may be rejected by the recipient's email service provider and returned to the sender as undeliverable. Consider storing large files in OneDrive and sharing a link to the file within an email.

Before you send the email message to Zion, you need to attach a file of a flyer describing the informational meeting about the Internship Fair. The file may be listed on a Recent Items listing when the Attach File button is clicked or you can browse web locations or the local PC for the file attachment(s). The following steps attach a file to an email message. *Why? Attaching a file to an email message provides additional information to a recipient.*

1

- Click the Attach File button (Message tab | Include group) to display a listing of Recent Items.

- Click Browse This PC and navigate to the folder containing the data files for this module (in this case, the Module 01 folder in the Outlook folder in the Data Files folder) (Figure 1–54).

Figure 1–54

2

- Click the document Fair to select the file to attach.

- Click the Insert button (Insert File dialog box) to attach the selected file to the email message and close the Insert File dialog box (Figure 1–55).

Q&A What should I do if I saved the Fair document to include my last name in the filename?
Select that document and then click the Insert button.

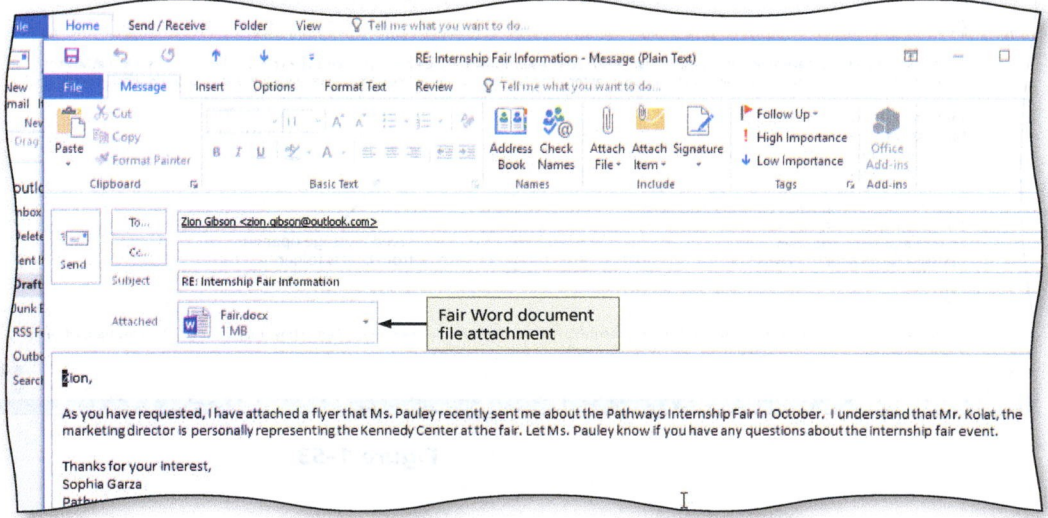

Figure 1–55

Other Ways

1. Click Insert tab, click Attach File button (Insert tab | Include group)
2. Drag file to message area
3. Right-click file attachment, click Copy, right-click message area, click Paste

To Set Message Importance and Send the Message

Why? *When you have a message that requires urgent attention, you can send the message with a high importance level.* Outlook provides the option to assign an **importance level** to a message, which indicates to the recipient the priority level of an email message. The default importance level for all new messages is normal importance, but you can change the importance level to high or low, depending on the priority level of the email message. A message sent with **high importance** displays a red exclamation point in the message header and indicates to the recipient that the message requires a higher priority than other messages he or she might have received. The **low importance** option displays a blue arrow and indicates to the recipient a low priority for the message. The following steps set the high importance option for a single email message and to send the message.

- Click the High Importance button (Message tab | Tags group) to add a high importance level (a red exclamation point) to the email message (Figure 1–56).

Figure 1–56

Q&A When does a red exclamation point appear in a message with high importance?
The red exclamation point appears in the message header when the message is received.

How would I set a low importance to an email message?
Click the Low Importance button (Message tab | Tags group).

- Click the Send button in the message header to send the email message.

- If necessary, click the Cancel button to close the Microsoft Outlook dialog box and then click the Close button to close the message window.

Q&A A message appeared that states 'No valid email accounts are configured. Add an account to send email'. What does this mean?
The Sophia.pst data file is an Outlook Data File, which cannot send an email message. If you are using the Sophia.pst data file, the sent message remains in the Drafts folder unless you configure an email account. You can set up and configure your own email address in Outlook to send an email message.

What happens to the actual email message after I send it?
After Outlook closes the message window, it stores the email message reply in the Outbox folder while it sends the message to the recipient. You might not see the message in the Outbox because Outlook usually stores it there only briefly. Next, Outlook moves the message to the Sent Items folder. The original message in the message list now shows an envelope icon with a purple arrow to indicate a reply was sent.

Can you place a tag in an email message that requests the recipient to respond within a certain time period?

- If you are sending an email message that requires a timely response, you can click the Follow Up button (Message tab | Tags group) to insert a flag icon indicating that the recipient should respond within a specified period of time.

- Based on your expected response time, you can select the Follow Up flag for Today, Tomorrow, This Week, Next Week, No Date, or Custom.

To Forward an Email Message

1 CONFIGURE ACCOUNT OPTIONS | 2 COMPOSE & SEND | 3 VIEW & PRINT | 4 REPLY
5 ATTACH FILE | 6 ORGANIZE MESSAGES

When you forward an email message, you resend a received or sent email message to another recipient. Yumi Mori, the Alumni Outreach coordinator, sent Sophia an email message requesting that she forward Ms. Pauley's email message about the Internship Fair to advertise on their website. Sophia adds Ms. Pauley as a courtesy copy (cc) recipient to make her aware that Yumi is receiving a copy of her email message. The following steps forward a previously received email message. *Why? Forwarding sends an email to someone who was not on the original recipient list.*

1

- Click the Inbox folder to display the Inbox messages.

- Click the Yumi Mori message header and read her message requesting information about the Pathways Internship Fair.

- Click the Ella Pauley message header in the message list to select the email message (Figure 1–57).

Why do my message headers show times instead of dates?
Outlook shows today's messages with times in the headers and messages prior to today with dates in the headers.

Figure 1–57

2

- Click the Forward button (Home tab | Respond group) to display the message in the Reading Pane (Figure 1–58).

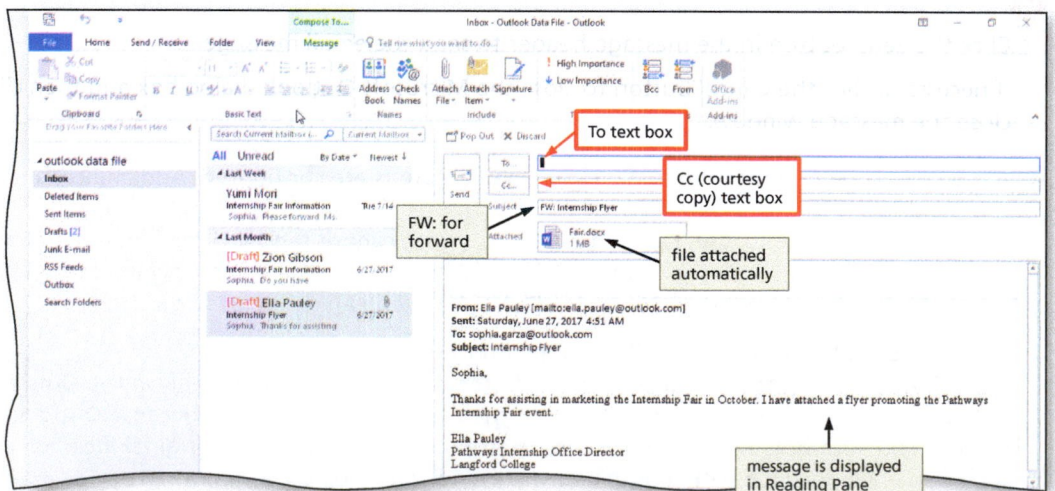

Figure 1–58

❸

- Click the To text box, and then type `yumi.mori@ outlook.com` (with no spaces) as the recipient's email address.

- Click the Cc text box, and then type `ella. pauley@outlook.com` (with no spaces) to send a courtesy copy to inform the original sender that you are forwarding her email message (Figure 1–59).

🔎 **Experiment**

- Click the Bcc button (Message tab | Show Fields group) to display the Bcc (blind carbon copy) text box. When you are finished, click the Bcc button (Message tab | Show Fields group) again to hide the Bcc text box.

Figure 1–59

Q&A Why does the original message appear in the message area of the window?

By default, Outlook displays the original message below the new message area for all message replies and forwards.

❹

- Click the message area above the original message text, type `Yumi,` as the greeting line and then press the SPACEBAR.

- Right-click Yumi and then click Ignore All to remove the red wavy line.

- Press the ENTER key two times to enter a blank line before the message text.

- Type `Per your request, I am forwarding the email and internship fair flyer from Ms. Pauley about the Pathways Internship event.` to enter the message text.

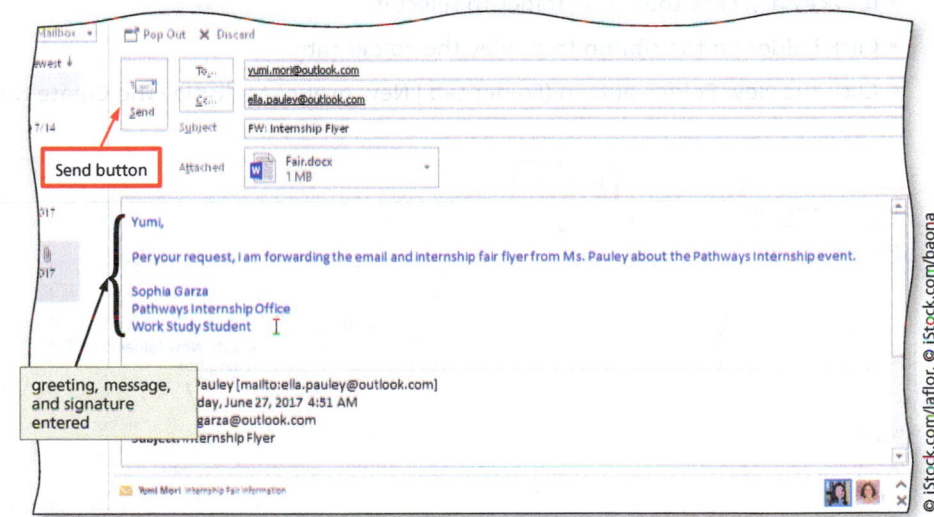

Figure 1–60

- Press the ENTER key two times to place a blank line between the message text and the signature lines.

- Type `Sophia Garza` as signature line 1, and then press the ENTER key to move the insertion point to the next line.

- Type `Pathways Internship Office`, and then press the ENTER key.

- Type `Work Study Student` as the third line of the signature to represent her title (Figure 1–60).

Q&A Does Outlook automatically forward the attachment to the recipient?

Yes. Outlook automatically adds the attachment to the forwarded message unless you choose to remove it.

❺

- Click the Send button in the message header to forward the message.

- If necessary, click the Cancel button to close the Microsoft Outlook dialog box.

Other Ways

1. Right-click message header, click Forward
2. Click message header, press CTRL+F

Organizing Messages with Outlook Folders

To keep track of your email messages effectively, Outlook provides a basic set of **folders**, which are containers for storing Outlook items of a specific type, such as messages, appointments, or contacts. Email is supposed to help you be more efficient and save time, but if you do not manage it effectively, you can quickly become overloaded with messages. The Inbox is an email folder that stores your incoming email messages. Instead of leaving all of your incoming messages in the Inbox, you can create additional folders and then move messages to these new folders so you can organize and locate your messages easily.

To Create a New Folder in the Inbox Folder

1 CONFIGURE ACCOUNT OPTIONS | 2 COMPOSE & SEND | 3 VIEW & PRINT | 4 REPLY
5 ATTACH FILE | **6 ORGANIZE MESSAGES**

By creating multiple folders within the Inbox folder, and then organizing messages in the new folders, you can find a specific email message easily. The following steps create a folder within the Inbox folder. *Why? Folders provide an efficient method for managing your email.*

- If necessary, click the Inbox folder to select it.
- Click Folder on the ribbon to display the Folder tab.
- Click the New Folder button (Folder tab | New group) to display the Create New Folder dialog box (Figure 1–61).

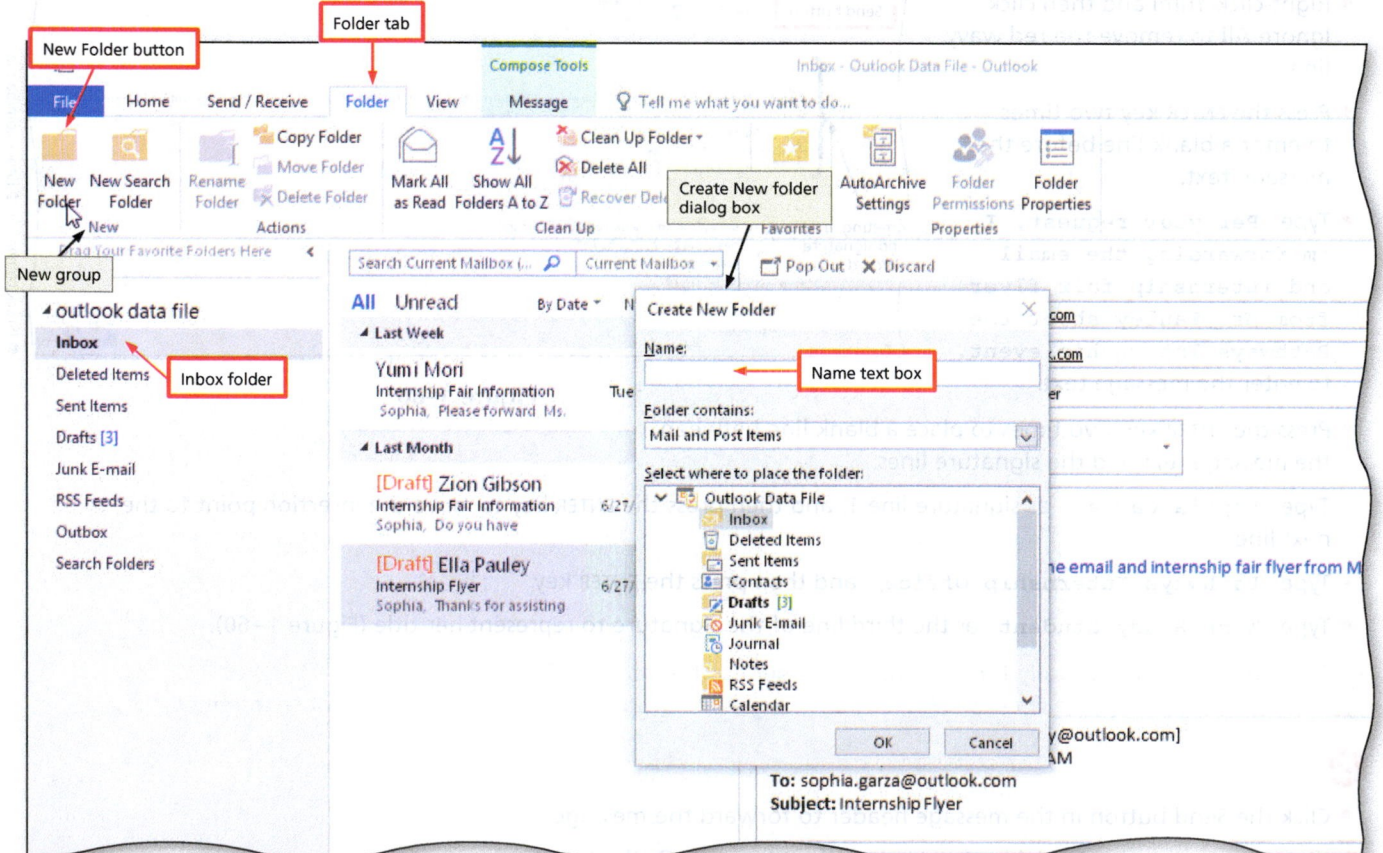

Figure 1–61

2
- Click the Name text box, and then type **Internship Fair** to name the folder within the Inbox folder.

- If necessary, click the Folder contains arrow, and then click 'Mail and Post Items' in the list to place only email messages in the new folder.

- If necessary, click Inbox in the 'Select where to place the folder' list to place the new folder within the Inbox folder (Figure 1–62).

Figure 1–62

3
- Click the OK button to create the Internship Fair folder within the Inbox and close the Create New Folder dialog box (Figure 1–63).

 Why is the Internship Fair folder indented below the Inbox folder? The Internship Fair folder is stored within the Inbox folder. Outlook indents the folder in the list to indicate that it is within the main folder.

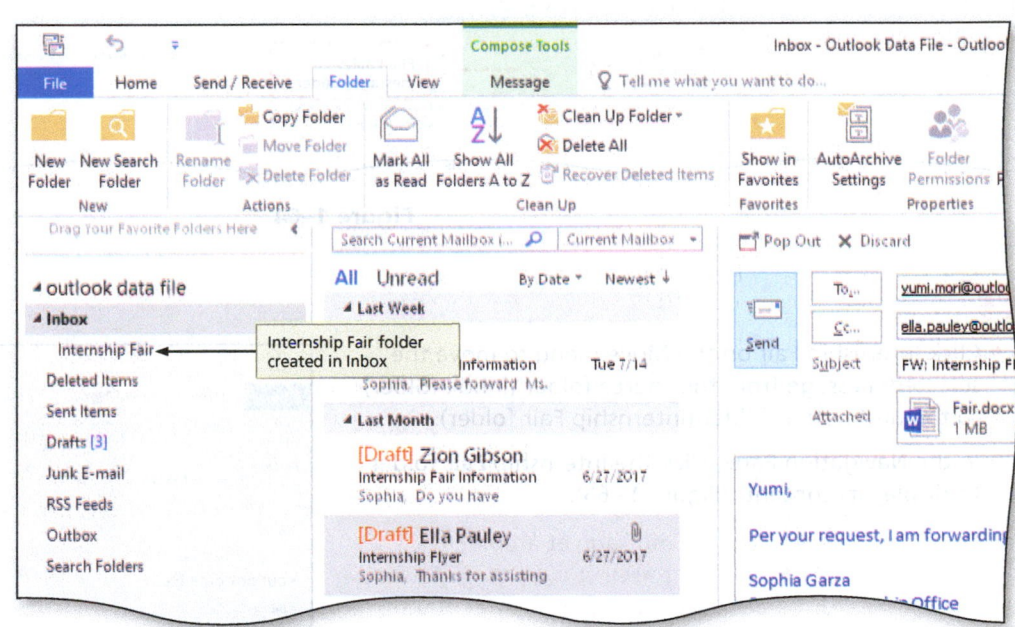

Figure 1–63

Other Ways

1. Right-click folder in Folder pane, click New Folder

1 CONFIGURE ACCOUNT OPTIONS | 2 COMPOSE & SEND | 3 VIEW & PRINT | 4 REPLY
5 ATTACH FILE | 6 ORGANIZE MESSAGES

To Move an Email Message to a Folder

Organizing important email messages about the Internship Fair event into the Internship Fair folder saves time when you search through hundreds or thousands of email messages later. Specifically, you will move the message from Ella Pauley from the Inbox folder to the Internship Fair folder. In this case, the Inbox folder is called the source folder, and the Internship Fair folder is called the destination folder. A **source folder** is the location of the document or message to be moved or copied. A **destination folder** is the location where you want to move or copy the file or message. The following steps move an email message into a folder. *Why? By organizing your emails into topical folders, you can access your messages easily.*

1

- In the Inbox folder (source folder), click the Ella Pauley message header in the Inbox message list to select the email message.
- Click Home on the ribbon to display the Home tab.
- Click the Move button (Home tab | Move group) to display the Move menu (Figure 1–64).

Figure 1–64

2

- Click Internship Fair on the Move menu to move the selected message from the source folder (Inbox folder) to the destination folder (Internship Fair folder).
- In the Navigation Pane, click the Internship Fair folder to display its contents (Figure 1–65).

Q&A

Can I move more than one message at a time?
Yes. Click the first message to select it. While holding the CTRL key, click additional messages to select them. Click the Move button (Home tab | Move group) and then click the destination folder to select it.

Can I copy the email messages instead of moving them?
Yes. Select the message(s) to copy, and then click the Move button (Home tab | Move group). Click Copy to Folder on the menu to display the Copy Items dialog box. Select the destination folder, and then click the OK button to copy the selected message to the destination folder.

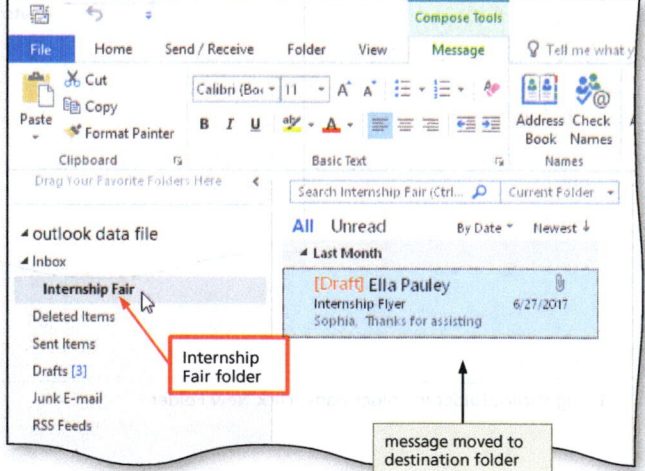

Figure 1–65

Other Ways

1. Right-click selected message, point to Move, click folder
2. Click selected message, drag message into destination folder

Outlook Quick Steps

An Outlook feature called **Quick Steps** provides shortcuts to perform redundant tasks with a single keystroke. For example, you can move an email message to a folder using a one-click Quick Step. You can use the built-in Quick Steps to move a file to a folder, send email to your entire team, or reply and then delete an email message.

To Move an Email Message Using Quick Steps

1 CONFIGURE ACCOUNT OPTIONS | 2 COMPOSE & SEND | 3 VIEW & PRINT | 4 REPLY

5 ATTACH FILE | **6 ORGANIZE MESSAGES**

If you frequently move messages to a specific folder, you can use a Quick Step to move a message in one click. The following steps create a Quick Step to move an email message into a specific folder. *Why? Quick Steps allow you to customize email actions that you use most often.*

1

- Click the Inbox folder In the Navigation Pane to select the Inbox folder.

- If necessary, click Home to display the Home tab.

- Click Move to: ? in the Quick Steps gallery (Home tab | Quick Steps group) to display the First Time Setup dialog box (Figure 1–66).

Figure 1–66

Q&A What should I do if Move to: ? does not appear on the Home tab?
Click the More button (Home tab | Quick Steps group), point to New Quick Step, and then click Move to Folder.

2

- Click the Move to folder arrow (First Time Setup dialog box) to display the list of available folders (Figure 1–67).

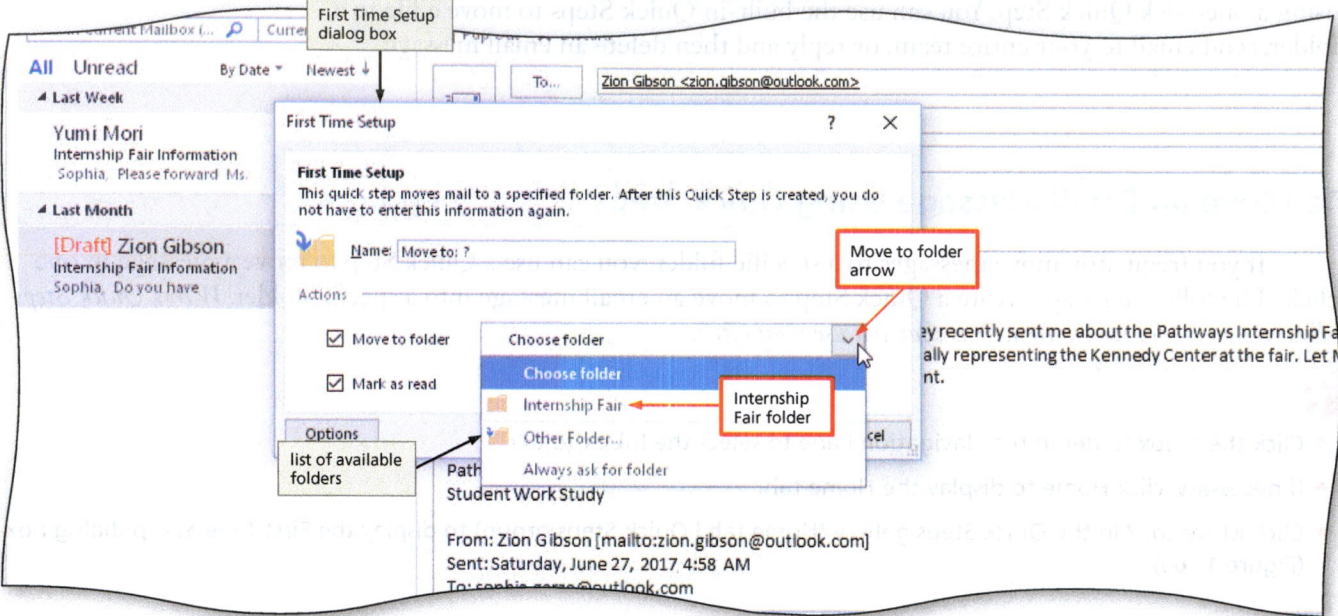

Figure 1–67

3

- Click the Internship Fair folder to create a Quick Step that moves a message to the specified folder.
- Click the Save button (First Time Setup dialog box) to save the Quick Step and display it in the Quick Steps gallery (Figure 1–68).

Q&A A Save button does not appear in my dialog box. What should I do?
Click the Finish button instead.

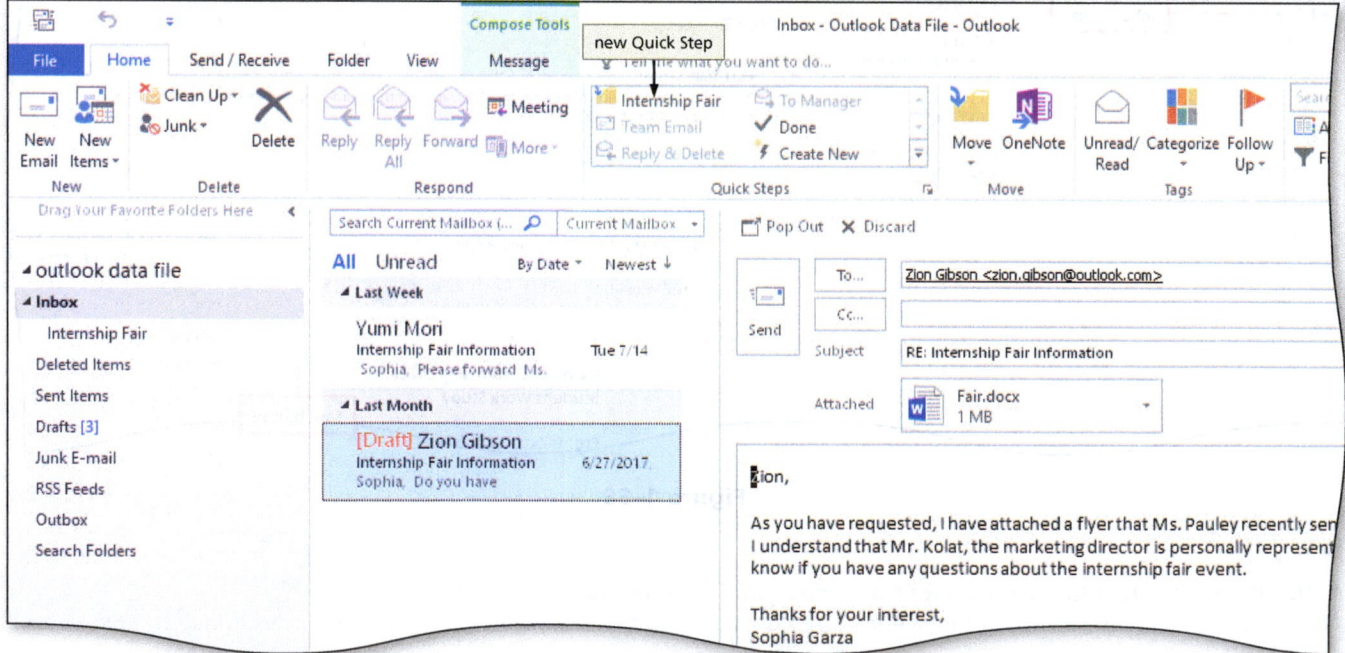

Figure 1–68

4

- In the Inbox folder, click the Yumi Mori message header in the Inbox message list to select the email message.

- Click Internship Fair in the Quick Steps gallery (Home tab | Quick Steps group) to move the message to the Internship Fair folder.

- In the Navigation Pane, click the Internship Fair folder to display its contents (Figure 1–69).

Figure 1–69

To Delete an Email Message

1 CONFIGURE ACCOUNT OPTIONS | 2 COMPOSE & SEND | 3 VIEW & PRINT | 4 REPLY
5 ATTACH FILE | 6 ORGANIZE MESSAGES

When you delete a message from a folder, Outlook moves the message from the folder to the Deleted Items folder. For example, Sophia no longer needs to keep the email message from Zion Gibson in the Inbox and has decided to delete it. The following steps delete an email message. *Why? Delete messages you no longer need so you do not exceed the limits of your mailbox.*

1

- Click the Inbox folder in the Navigation Pane to select the Inbox folder.

- Point to the Zion Gibson message header in the message list to display the Delete icon (Figure 1–70).

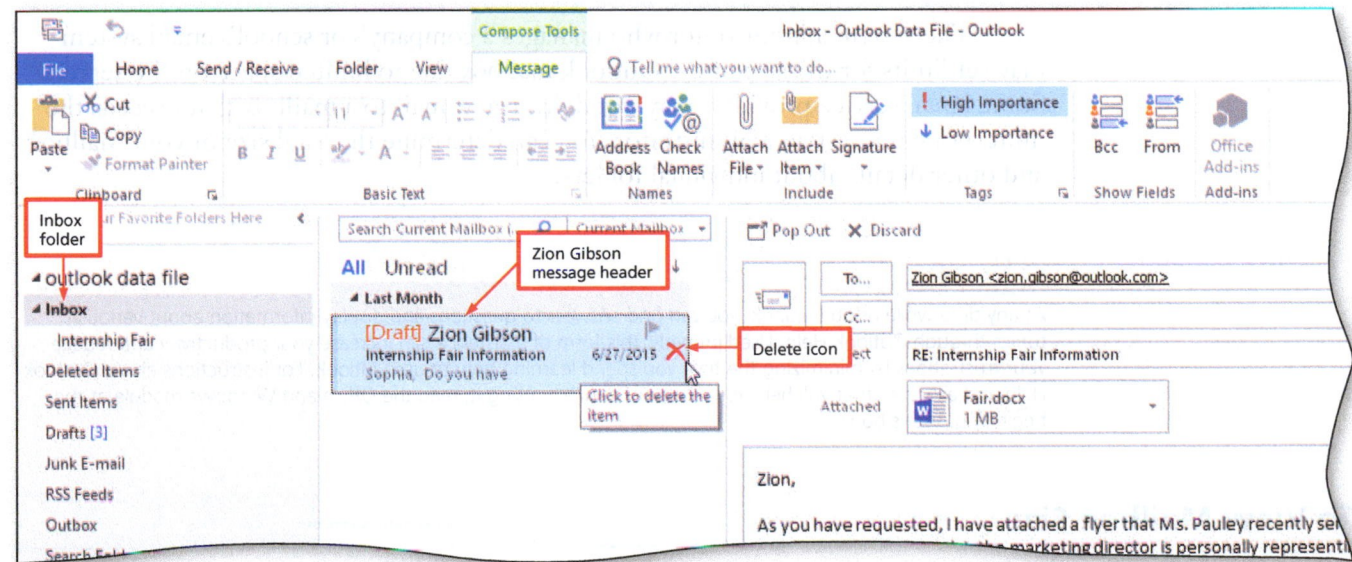

Figure 1–70

2

- Click the Delete icon on the message header to move the email message from the Inbox folder to the Deleted Items folder.

- Click the Deleted Items folder in the Navigation Pane to verify the location of the deleted message and display the Deleted Items message list in the message pane, which shows all deleted email messages (Figure 1–71).

Q&A

Is the email message permanently deleted when I click the Delete icon?

No. After Outlook moves the email message to the Deleted Items folder, it stores the deleted email message in that folder until you permanently delete the message. One way to permanently delete a message is to select the Deleted Items folder to view its contents in the message pane and then select the item to be deleted. Click the Delete icon on the message header and then click the Yes button in the Microsoft Outlook dialog box to permanently delete the selected item from Outlook.

Figure 1–71

Other Ways

1. Drag email message to Deleted Items folder   2. Click email message, press DELETE   3. Click email message, press CTRL+D

CONSIDER THIS

How can you ignore future messages in an email thread?

- You can ignore future messages in an email thread through the Ignore Conversation feature. An **email thread** is a message that includes a running list of all the follow-up replies starting with the original email.

- Select an email message header that you no longer wish to view future messages and click the Ignore Conversation button (Home tab | Delete group) to delete this message as well as future messages within the email thread.

Working with the Mailbox

The system administrator who manages a company's or school's email system may set limits for the size of the Outlook mailbox due to limited space on the server. Some email service providers may not deliver new mail to a mailbox that exceeds the limit set by the system administrator. You can determine the total size of your mailbox and other details about individual folders.

BTW

Outlook Help

At any time while using Outlook, you can find answers to questions and display information about various topics through Outlook Help. Used properly, this form of assistance can increase your productivity and reduce your frustrations by minimizing the time you spend learning how to use Outlook. For instructions about Outlook Help and exercises that will help you gain confidence in using it, read the Office and Windows module at the beginning of this book.

To View Mailbox Size

1 CONFIGURE ACCOUNT OPTIONS | 2 COMPOSE & SEND | 3 VIEW & PRINT | 4 REPLY
5 ATTACH FILE | **6 ORGANIZE MESSAGES**

The following steps view the amount of space available in the mailbox. **Why?** *You can determine if you are close to your mailbox size limit.*

1

- Click outlook data file in the Navigation Pane to select the mailbox.

- Click Folder on the ribbon to display the Folder tab (Figure 1–72).

Q&A What is the outlook data file in the Navigation Pane?

In this case, the outlook data file is the mailbox of Sophia Garza.

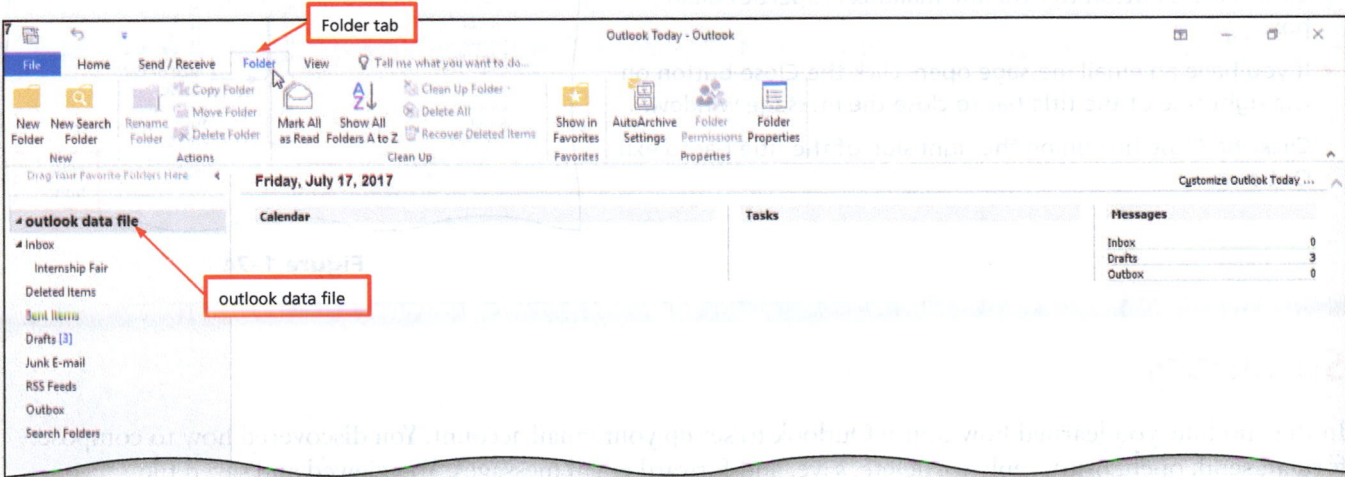

Figure 1–72

2

- Click the Folder Properties button (Folder tab | Properties group) to display the Properties dialog box for the mailbox (Figure 1–73).

Figure 1–73

- Click the Folder Size button (mailbox Properties dialog box) to display the Folder Size dialog box (Figure 1–74).

- After viewing the folder sizes, click the Close button to close the Folder Size dialog box.

- Click the OK button to close the mailbox Properties dialog box.

- If you have an email message open, click the Close button on the right side of the title bar to close the message window.

- Click the Close button on the right side of the title bar to exit Outlook.

Figure 1–74

Summary

In this module, you learned how to use Outlook to set up your email account. You discovered how to compose, format, send, open, print, reply to, delete, save, and forward email messages. You viewed and saved file attachments and attached a file to an email message. You learned how to add a courtesy copy to an email message and set the sensitivity and importance of email messages. Finally, you created a folder in the Inbox and moved an email message to the new folder.

CONSIDER THIS

Consider This: Plan Ahead

What future decisions will you need to make when composing and responding to email messages, attaching files, and organizing your Outlook folders?

1. Set up Outlook.

   a) Determine the language preferences and sensitivity level.

   b) Decide on the sensitivity level.

2. Compose the email message.

   a) Plan the content of your email message based on a formal or informal tone.

   b) Select an appropriate theme.

3. Open incoming email messages.

   a) Determine your preference for displaying messages.

   b) Save the attachment to the appropriate folder.

4. Respond to messages.

   a) Plan your response to the incoming message.

   b) Correct errors and revise as necessary.

   c) Establish which file you will attach to your email message.

   d) Determine the importance level of the message.

5. Organize your Outlook folders.

   a) Establish your folder names.

   b) Plan where each email message should be stored.

How should you submit solutions to questions in the assignments identified with a ✸ symbol?

Every assignment in this book contains one or more questions with a ✸ symbol. These questions require you to think beyond the assigned file. Present your solutions to the question in the format required by your instructor. Possible formats may include one or more of these options: write the answer; create a document that contains the answer; present your answer to the class; discuss your answer in a group; record the answer as audio or video using a webcam, smartphone, or portable media player; or post answers on a blog, wiki, or website.

Apply Your Knowledge

Reinforce the skills and apply the concepts you learned in this module.

Note: To complete this assignment, you will be required to use the Data Files. Please contact your instructor for information about accessing the Data Files.

Creating an Email with an Attachment

Instructions: Run Outlook. You are to send an email message addressed to your instructor with information about the French Club's Spring Break trip to Saint Martin. You also attach an Excel workbook called Apply 1-1 School Trip, which is located in the Data Files.

Perform the following tasks:

1. Compose a new email message addressed to your instructor and add your own email address as a courtesy copy address.
2. Type `French Club Spring Break` as the subject of the email message.
3. Type `Greetings,` as the greeting line. Check spelling as you type.
4. Enter the text shown in Figure 1–75 for the message text.
5. Type `Thanks,` as the closing line.
6. Enter your name as the first signature line.
7. Type `French Club Publicity Manager` as the second signature line.
8. If requested by your instructor, type your personal cell phone number as the third signature line.
9. Attach the Excel workbook called Apply 1-1 School Trip, which is located in the Data Files, to the email message.
10. Click the File tab, and then click Save As. Save the message on your hard drive, OneDrive, or a location that is most appropriate to your situation using the file name Apply 1-1 French Club Trip.
11. Submit the email message in the format specified by your instructor.
12. Exit Outlook.
13. ✸ The attachment in the email message contained an Excel workbook. What file types are typically not allowed as a file attachment? Name at least two file types and explain why they are not allowed.

Continued >

Apply Your Knowledge *continued*

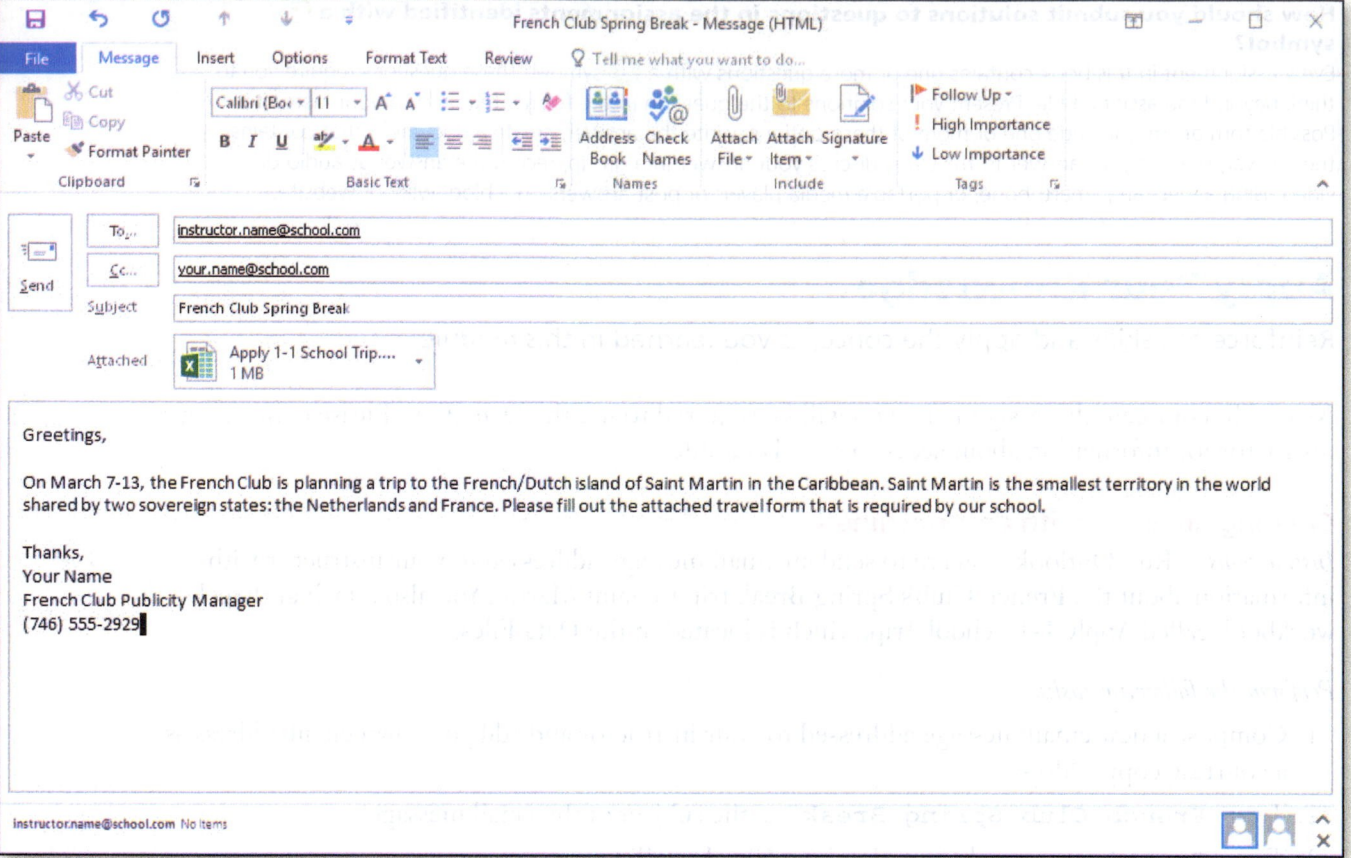

Figure 1–75

Extend Your Knowledge

Extend the skills you learned in this module and experiment with new skills. You may need to use Help to complete the assignment.

Organizing Email Messages

Note: To complete this assignment, you will be required to use the Data Files. Please contact your instructor for information about accessing the Data Files.

Instructions: Run Outlook. You are organizing a trip to Boston for you and your friends where you will participate as a group in an Escape Room activity and stay at a hostel. In the Extend 1-1.pst mailbox file, you will create two folders, add a folder in the Favorites section, and then move messages into the appropriate folders. You also will apply a follow-up flag for the messages in one of the folders. Use Outlook Help to learn how to duplicate a folder in the Favorites section, how to add a flag to a message for follow-up, and how to create an Outlook Data File (.pst file).

Perform the following tasks:

1. Open the Outlook mailbox file called Extend 1-1.pst, which is located in the Data Files.
2. Create two new folders within the Inbox folder. Name the first folder Escape Room and the second folder Hostels. Move the messages into the appropriate folders. Make sure that only mail items are contained in the new folders.
3. The Favorites section is at the top of the Folder Pane on the left. Display a duplicate of the Escape Room folder in the Favorites section.

4. Reply to the Boston Bay Hostel message indicating that you would like to book the hostel for the night of May 11. Sign your name to the email message. Assign high importance to the message.

5. Based on the message headers and content of the email messages in the Extend 1-1 mailbox, move each message to the appropriate folders you created. Figure 1–76 shows the mailbox with the messages moved to the new folders.

6. Export the Inbox mailbox to an Outlook Data File (.pst) on your hard drive, OneDrive, or a location that is most appropriate to your situation using the file name Extend 1-1 Boston.pst, and then submit it in the format specified by your instructor.

7. Exit Outlook.

8. ✸ Saving your mailbox as a .pst file provides a backup copy of your email messages to submit to your instructor. What are other reasons for saving your mailbox as a .pst file?

Figure 1–76

Expand Your World: Cloud and Web Technologies

Opening an Outlook.com Web-Based Email Message in the Outlook Client

Create a solution that uses cloud or web technologies by learning and investigating on your own from general guidance.

Note: To complete this assignment, you will be required to use the Data Files. Please contact your instructor for information about accessing the Data Files.

Instructions: In your Health class, you are presenting the topic, *Using a Health App to Track Your Workout.* Using Outlook, you compose an email message shown in Figure 1–77 and include a PowerPoint file attachment. Save the attachment from your outlook.com account to your OneDrive and edit the PowerPoint slides as a web app. Share the PowerPoint slides by providing a link to your OneDrive. Sharing files in the cloud as links can eliminate large attachments and saves email storage space.

Continued >

Expand Your World *continued*

Perform the following tasks:

1. If necessary, create a Microsoft account at outlook.com.

2. Compose a new email message from the client program, Outlook (not outlook.com). Address the email message to your Microsoft account with the message text shown in Figure 1–77. Select a theme of your choice. Replace the signature with your name and school name.

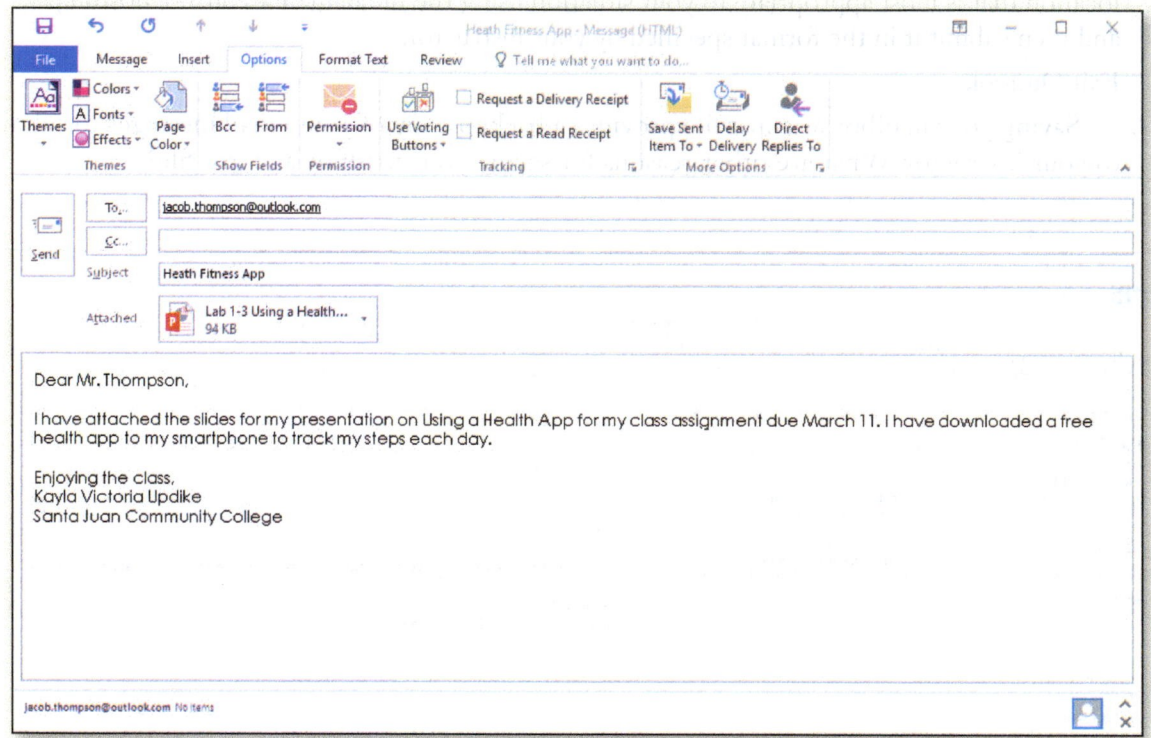

Figure 1–77

3. Attach the PowerPoint presentation called Lab 1-3 Using a Health App, which is located in the Data Files, to the email message.

4. Send the email message with high importance.

5. Open your Microsoft account at outlook.com. Open the email message that you sent from Outlook, click the attachment, and then click View online to view the PowerPoint file attachment.

6. Click Edit and Reply to edit the PowerPoint presentation in Microsoft PowerPoint Online.

7. If requested by your instructor, change the name on the first slide to your name on the first line and the name of your hometown on the second line.

8. Add a fourth slide to the PowerPoint presentation showing how far you have to walk to burn the calories in a typical slice of pizza. (*Hint:* Research this statistic on the web.)

9. Click the Insert tab, and then add a clip art image about walking to the fourth slide.

10. Click the File tab, and then click Share to share the PowerPoint file.

11. Click 'Share with people', and then type your instructor's email address and a short message describing how sharing a file by sending a link to your OneDrive can be easier than sending an attachment. Include your name at the end of the message.

12. Click the Share button to send the shared link of the completed PowerPoint file to your instructor.

13. Exit PowerPoint Online, and then exit Outlook.

14. ❋ In this exercise, you sent an email message from the Outlook client to your web-based email service provider at outlook.com. What are the advantages of using a Microsoft account with Outlook on your personal computer and checking the same email address at outlook.com when you are on a public computer?

In the Labs

Design, create, modify, and/or use files following the guidelines, concepts, and skills presented in this module. Labs 1 and 2, which increase in difficulty, require you to create solutions based on what you learned in the module; Lab 3 requires you to apply your creative thinking and problem-solving skills to design and implement a solution.

Lab 1: Composing an Email Message with Attachments

Note: To complete this assignment, you will be required to use the Data Files. Please contact your instructor for information about accessing the Data Files.

Problem: On a recent trip to Europe, your aunt took photos of castles using a digital camera. Because your aunt is new to technology, she asks you to extract the castle photos (provided in the Data Files) from her camera's memory card. She would like you to send them to her using email, because she is not on Facebook. Compose an email message to your aunt as shown in Figure 1–78 with the four picture attachments of castles.

Perform the following tasks:

1. Compose a new email message. Address the message to yourself with a courtesy copy to your instructor.

2. Enter the subject, message text, and signature shown in Figure 1–78. Insert blank lines where they are shown in the figure. If Outlook flags any misspelled words as you type, check their spelling and correct them.

3. Change the theme of the email message to the Integral theme.

4. If requested by your instructor, change the city and state from Zagreb, MN, to the city and state of your birth. Also change the signature to your name.

5. Attach the four image files called Lab 1-1 Castle1, Lab 1-1 Castle2, Lab 1-1 Castle3, and Lab 1-1 Castle4, which are located in the Data Files, to the email message.

6. Send the email message.

7. When you receive the message, open it, and then save the message on your hard drive, OneDrive, or a location that is most appropriate to your situation using the file name Lab 1-1 Castles. Submit the file in the format specified by your instructor.

8. ❋ Using one of your own email service providers, determine the maximum allowed mailbox size. Report the name of your email service provider, the maximum size, and whether you feel that is enough storage space.

Continued >

In the Labs *continued*

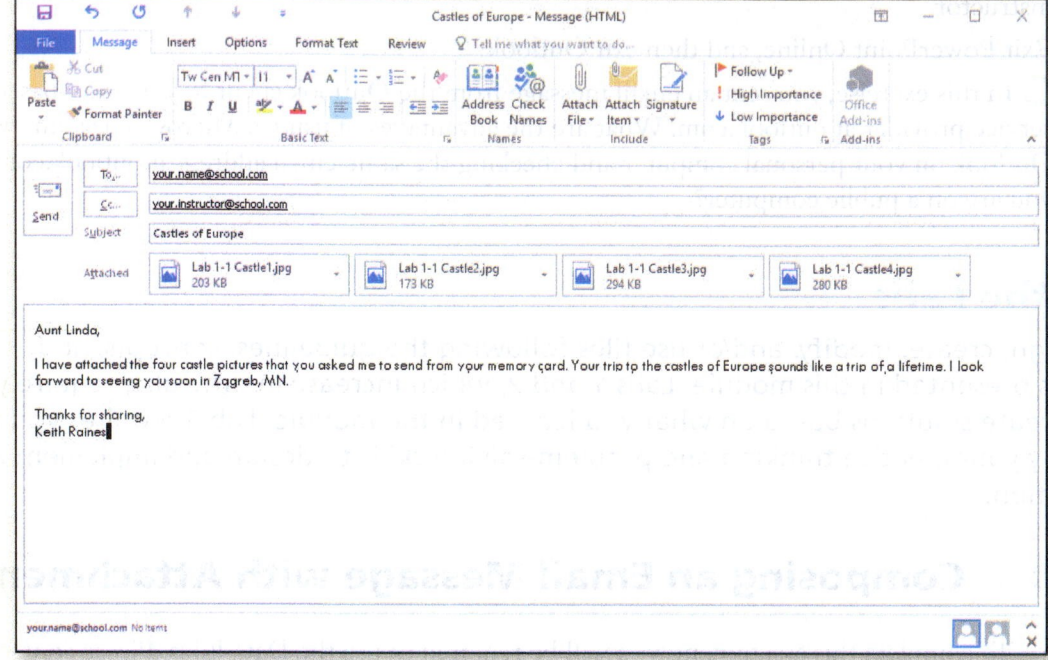

Figure 1–78

Lab 2: **Composing and Replying to an Email Message**

Problem: You recently moved into a new apartment. To turn on the electricity in your new apartment and place the bill in your name, you must fill out the request for electricity form. You need to send your completed form to the Compton Electric Company. First, you compose the email message shown in Figure 1–79a, and then you attach a file. Compton Electric Company responds to your email as shown in Figure 1–79b.

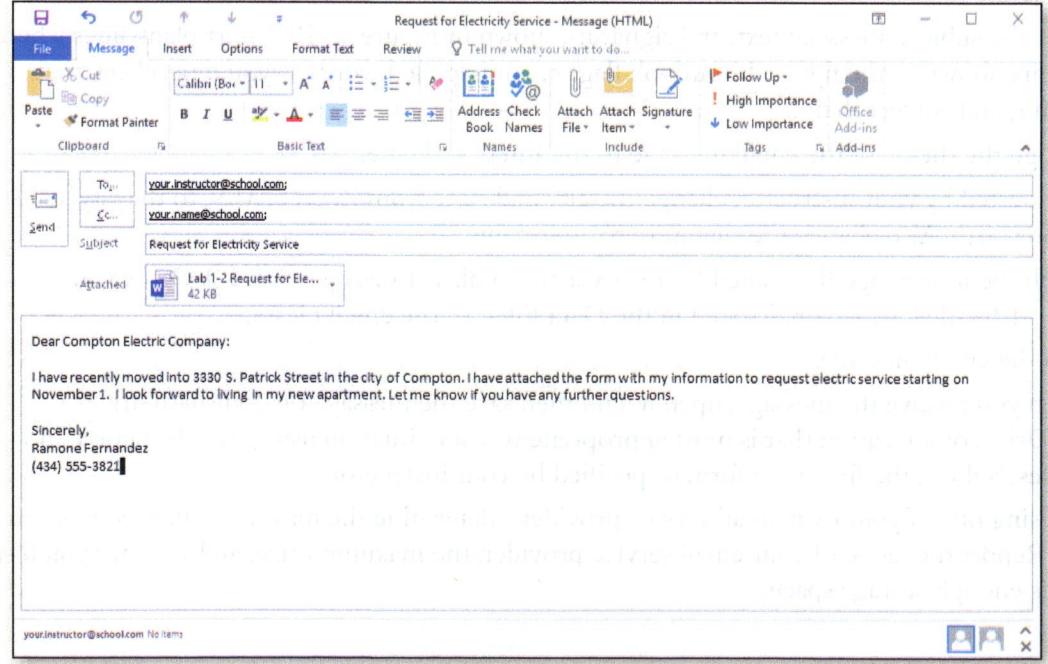

(a) Composed Email Message

Figure 1–79 (Continues)

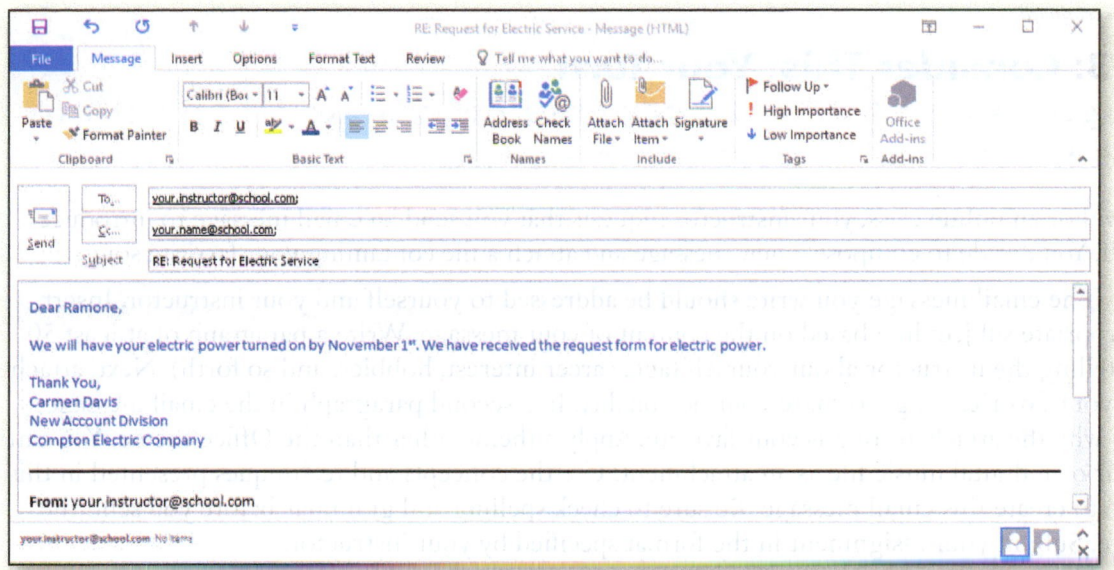

(b) Response to Email Message
Figure 1–79

Perform the following tasks:

1. Create a new email message. Address the message to your instructor with a courtesy copy to yourself.

2. Enter the subject, message text, and signature shown in Figure 1–79a. Check spelling and grammar.

3. If requested by your instructor, change the address in the email message to your own address.

4. Change the theme of the email message to the Slice theme.

5. Change the importance of this email to high importance because you would like to move in immediately.

6. Attach the document called Lab 1-2 Request for Electricity, which is located in the Data Files, to the email message. You do not need to fill out this form.

7. Send the email message and use the HTML format for the message.

8. When you receive the email message, move it to a new folder in your Inbox named Apartment.

9. Open the message in the Apartment folder, and then compose the reply. Figure 1–79b shows the reply from Compton Electric Company. Reply using the text in the email message shown in Figure 1–79b. If Outlook flags any misspelled words as you type, check their spelling and correct them.

10. If necessary, change the format of the email message to Plain Text, and then send the message to yourself.

11. When you receive the RE: Request for Electric Service message, move it to the Apartment folder in your Inbox folder.

12. Select the original Request for Electricity message in the Sent Items folder. Save the message on your hard drive, OneDrive, or a location that is most appropriate to your situation using the file name Lab 1-2 Electric. Submit the file in the format specified by your instructor.

13. ✳ Some company and utility websites do not include a phone number or a physical address. Why do you think that these business and utility sites only include an email address for correspondence?

Continued >

In the Labs *continued*

Lab 3: Consider This: Your Turn
Composing an Introductory Email Message to an Online Class Instructor and Attaching a File

Problem: For an online class, your instructor requests that you send an email message to introduce yourself. You decide to compose a new message and attach a file containing your favorite song.

Part 1: The email message you write should be addressed to yourself and your instructor. Insert an appropriate subject line based on the content of your message. Write a paragraph of at least 50 words telling the instructor about yourself (age, career interest, hobbies, and so forth). Next, attach one of your favorite songs to share your personality. In a second paragraph in the email message, explain why the attached song is your favorite. Apply a theme other than the Office theme. You can use your own digital music file as an attachment. Use the concepts and techniques presented in this module to create this email message. Be sure to check spelling and grammar before you send the message. Submit your assignment in the format specified by your instructor.

Part 2: ✹ You made several decisions while creating the email message in this assignment. When you decide on the subject of an email message, what considerations should you make? Why is it important that the email subject be eye-catching and informative? Why should you not use the following subject lines: FYI, Hey You, or Open This?

2 | Managing Calendars with Outlook

Objectives

You will have mastered the material in this module when you can:

- Describe the components of the Outlook Calendar
- Add a personal calendar to Outlook
- Add a city to the calendar Weather Bar list
- Navigate the calendar using the Date Navigator
- Display the calendar in various views
- Add national holidays to the default calendar
- Enter, save, move, edit, and delete appointments and events
- Organize your calendar with color categories

- Set the status of and a reminder for an appointment
- Import an iCalendar and view it in overlay mode
- Schedule and modify events
- Schedule meetings
- Respond to meeting requests
- Peek at a calendar
- Print a calendar
- Save and share a calendar

Managing Calendars with Outlook

This introductory module covers features and functions common to managing calendars in Outlook 2016.

Roadmap

In this module, you will learn how to perform basic calendar tasks. The following roadmap identifies general activities you will perform as you progress through this module:

1. CONFIGURE the CALENDAR OPTIONS
2. CREATE AND MANIPULATE APPOINTMENTS
3. SCHEDULE EVENTS
4. SCHEDULE MEETINGS
5. PRINT a CALENDAR
6. SAVE AND SHARE a CALENDAR

At the beginning of step instructions throughout the module, you will see an abbreviated form of this roadmap. The abbreviated roadmap uses colors to indicate module progress: gray means the module is beyond that activity, blue means the task being shown is covered in that activity, and black means that activity is yet to be covered. For example, the following abbreviated roadmap indicates the module would be showing a task in the Schedule Events activity.

1 CONFIGURE CALENDAR OPTIONS | 2 CREATE & MANIPULATE APPOINTMENTS | **3 SCHEDULE EVENTS**
4 SCHEDULE MEETINGS | 5 PRINT CALENDAR | 6 SAVE & SHARE CALENDAR

Use the abbreviated roadmap as a progress guide while you read or step through the instructions in this module.

Introduction to the Outlook Calendar

Plan your day, keep track of your deadlines, and increase your daily productivity. Whether you are a student, club organizer, or business professional, you can take advantage of the Outlook Calendar to schedule and manage appointments, events, and meetings. In particular, you can use Calendar to keep track of your class schedule and appointments and to schedule meetings. If you are traveling and do not have electronic access to your calendar, you can print a copy to keep with you. You can use Outlook to view a daily, weekly, or monthly calendar.

In addition to using Calendar in your academic or professional life, you will find it helpful for scheduling personal time. Most people have multiple appointments to keep each day, week, or month. Calendar can organize activity-related information in a structured, readable manner. You can create a calendar folder for a specific project and share it with your friends and professional colleagues.

Project — Appointments, Events, and Meetings in Calendar

By creating a daily time management schedule, you can stay organized and reduce your stress level. Managing your schedule using a calendar can increase productivity while maximizing free time. Outlook is the perfect tool to maintain both a professional and a personal schedule. The **Calendar** is the Outlook folder that contains your personal schedule of appointments, events, and meetings. In this project, Sophia Garza, the student work study employee for the Pathways Internship Office, sets up the basic features of Calendar to create her calendar for her appointments, classes, work schedules, and meetings (Figure 2–1).

People use a calendar to keep track of their schedules and to organize and manage their time. For students, a class list with room numbers and class times would be a good start toward managing their school schedule. For business professionals, the calendar is a dynamic tool that requires frequent updating to keep track of appointments and meetings. You also may want to keep track of personal items, such as doctor appointments, birthdays, and family gatherings.

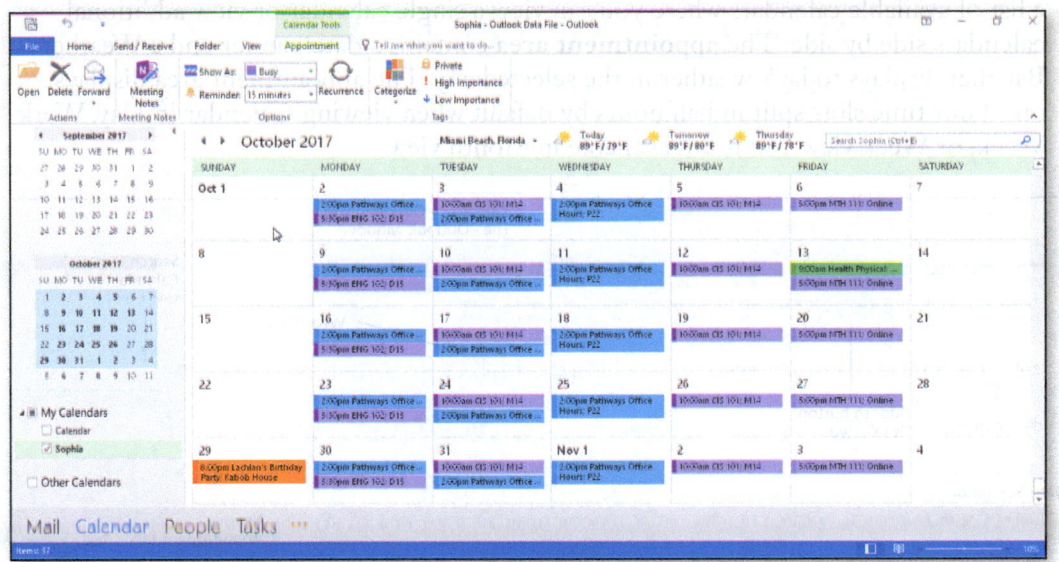

Figure 2–1

Configuring the Outlook Calendar

BTW

The Ribbon and Screen Resolution
Outlook may change how the groups and buttons within the groups appear on the ribbon, depending on the computer's screen resolution. Thus, your ribbon may look different from the ones in this book if you are using a screen resolution other than 1366 × 768.

When you start Outlook, the Mail view appears. The Navigation bar displays four views — Mail, Calendar, People, and Tasks. You changed the Navigation bar icons to text in Module 1. By selecting Calendar, you can create a customized calendar to assist in scheduling your day, week, and month. Before scheduling your first calendar appointment, you can add a personal calendar and customize your settings to fit the way you work. Each day as you check your calendar for the day's events, the Weather Bar displays your local weather so you can plan whether you need an umbrella or take other weather precautions. By adding national holidays to your Outlook calendar, you can make sure these dates are prominent in your calendar.

CONSIDER THIS

What advantages does a digital calendar like Outlook provide compared to a paper planner or wall calendar?
A digital calendar provides access from any location by synching your computer or smartphone with the cloud to view your appointments and meetings. You can view your schedule within an email meeting invitation. You can view more than one calendar at a time, share others' calendars, and overlay calendars to plan a meeting date with colleagues.

Calendar Window

The Calendar - Outlook Data File - Microsoft Outlook window shown in Figure 2–2 includes a variety of features to help you work efficiently. It contains many elements similar to the windows in other Office programs, as well as some that are unique to Outlook. The main elements of the Calendar window are the Navigation Pane and the appointment area.

The Navigation Pane includes two panes: the Date Navigator and the My Calendars pane. The **Date Navigator** includes the present month's calendar and the future month's calendar in Figure 2–2. The calendar displays the current month with a blue box around the current date, scroll arrows to advance from one month to another, and any date on which an item is scheduled in bold. The **My Calendars pane** includes a list of available calendars where you can view a single calendar or view additional calendars side by side. The **appointment area** contains a date banner and a Weather Bar that displays today's weather in the selected city. The appointment area displays one-hour time slots split in half hours by default when viewing Calendar in Day, Work Week, or Week view and is not available in Month view.

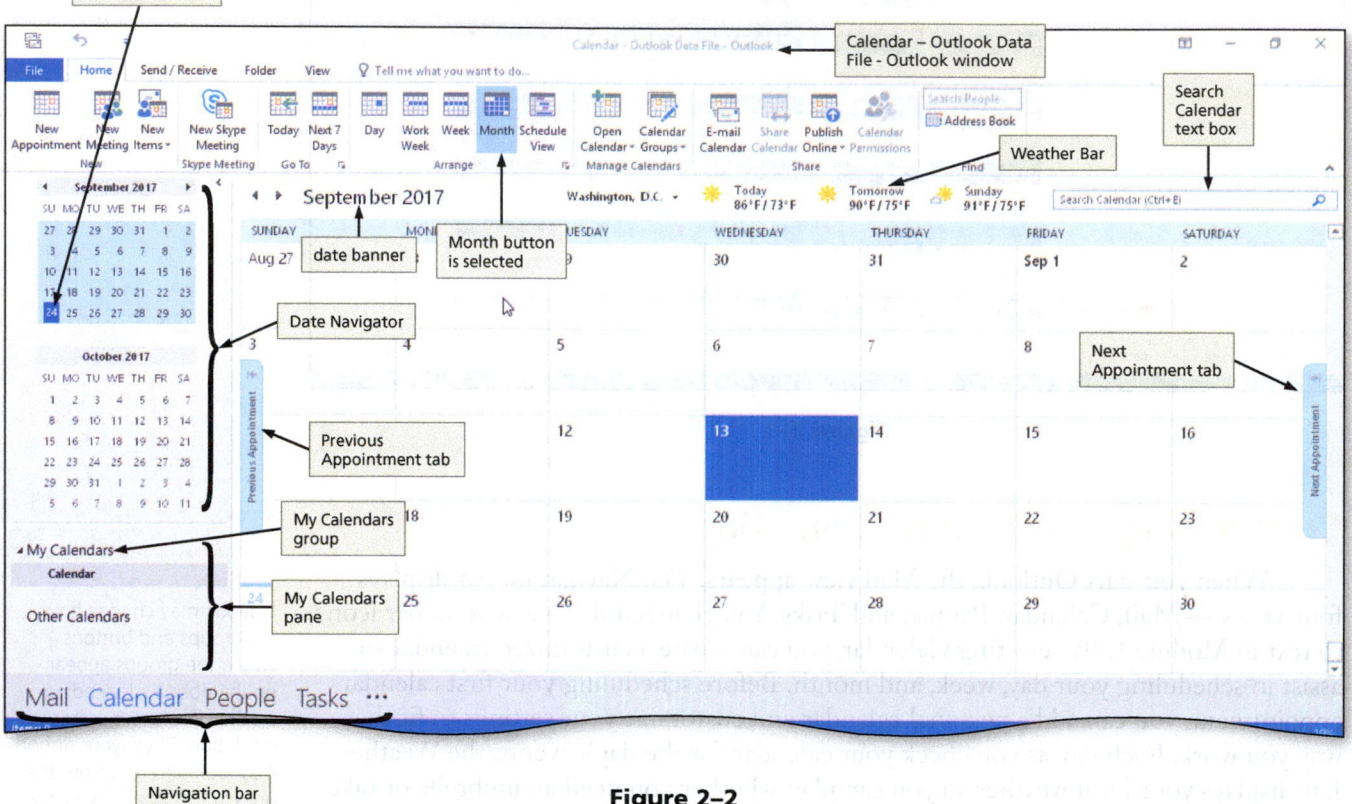

Figure 2–2

Calendar Items

BTW

Searching for Calendar Items

To find a calendar item, click the Search *Calendar Name* text box, and then type a word or phrase in the calendar item you are seeking. Items that contain the text you typed are listed with the search text highlighted. When you are finished, click the Close Search button (Search Tools Search tab | Close group).

An **item** is any element in Outlook that contains information. Examples of calendar items include appointments, events, and meetings. All calendar items start as an appointment. Outlook defines an **appointment**, such as a doctor's appointment, as an activity that does not involve other people or resources, such as conference rooms. Outlook defines an **event**, such as a seminar or vacation, as an activity that occurs at least once and lasts 24 hours or longer. An appointment becomes an event when you schedule it for the entire day. An annual event, such as a birthday, anniversary, or holiday, occurs yearly on a specific date. Events do not occupy time slots in the appointment area and, instead, are displayed in a banner below the day heading when viewing the calendar in Day, Work Week, or Week view. An appointment becomes a **meeting** when people and other resources, such as meeting rooms, are invited.

When you create items on your calendar, it is helpful to show your time using the appointment status information. You set the appointment status for a calendar item using the Show As button, which provides four options for showing your time on the calendar: Free, Tentative, Busy, and Out of Office. For example, if you are studying or working on a project, you might show your time as busy because you are unable to perform other tasks at the same time. On the other hand, a dental appointment or a class would show your time as Out of Office because you need to leave your home or office to attend. Table 2–1 describes the items you can schedule on your calendar and the appointment status option associated with each item. Each calendar item also can be one-time or recurring.

Table 2-1	Calendar Items	
Calendar Item	**Description**	**Show as Default**
One-time appointment	Default calendar item, involves only your schedule and does not invite other attendees or require resources such as a conference room	Busy
Recurring appointment	Occurs at regular intervals, such as weekly, biweekly, monthly, or bimonthly	Busy
One-time event	Occurs at least once and lasts 24 hours or longer, such as a vacation or conference	Free
Recurring event	Occurs at regular intervals, such as weekly, biweekly, monthly, or bimonthly, such as holidays	Free
One-time meeting	Includes people and other resources, such as meeting rooms	Busy
Recurring meeting	Occurs at regular intervals, such as weekly, biweekly, monthly, or bimonthly, such as staff meetings or department meetings	Busy

To Create a Calendar Folder

1 CONFIGURE CALENDAR OPTIONS | 2 CREATE & MANIPULATE APPOINTMENTS | 3 SCHEDULE EVENTS
4 SCHEDULE MEETINGS | 5 PRINT CALENDAR | 6 SAVE & SHARE CALENDAR

When you schedule an appointment, Outlook adds the appointment to the Calendar folder by default. Sophia Garza plans to keep track of her work study business tasks at the job at the Pathways Internship Office as well as her personal and academic items instead of creating separate calendars for every aspect of her life. Users often create multiple calendars to keep personal items separate from academic or business items. As in other Outlook folders, such as the Inbox, you can create multiple folders within the Calendar folder that each contains one or more calendars. The following steps create a calendar to store your personal and school-related information separate from your default Calendar within the same calendar group. *Why? In certain situations, you may need to keep more than one calendar, such as one for business items and another for personal items.*

- Run Outlook 2016.
- Click Calendar on the Navigation bar to display the Outlook Calendar.
- Click Folder on the ribbon to display the Folder tab (Figure 2–3).

Figure 2–3

For an introduction to Office and instructions about how to perform basic tasks in Office apps, read the Office and Windows module at the beginning of this book, where you can learn how to run an app, use the ribbon, save a file, open a file, exit an app, use Help, and much more.

One of the few differences between Windows 8 and Windows 10 occur in the steps to run Outlook. If you are using Windows 8, scroll the Start screen and then click the Outlook 2016 tile.

BTW

Outlook and Screen Resolution

If you are using a computer or mobile device to step through the project in this module and you want your screens to match the figures in this book, you should change your screen's resolution to 1366 x 768. For information about how to change a computer's resolution, refer to the Office and Windows module at the beginning of this book.

2

- Click the New Calendar button (Folder tab | New group) to display the Create New Folder dialog box.

- Type **Sophia** in the Name text box (Create New Folder dialog box) to enter a name for the new folder.

- Click the Folder contains arrow button to display a list of items the folder will contain.

- If necessary, click Calendar Items to specify what the folder will contain.

- If necessary, click Calendar in the 'Select where to place the folder' list to specify where the folder will be stored (Figure 2–4).

Figure 2–4

3

- Click the OK button to close the Create New Folder dialog box and add the new folder to the My Calendars group (Figure 2–5).

Q&A

Why is the named Sophia calendar not displayed in the Outlook window?
Outlook does not automatically display the newly created calendar until you select it.

I received an error message indicating that calendars cannot be created in Exchange ActiveSync accounts. What should I do?
Use a browser to sign into your email account at outlook.com. Use the Calendar feature at outlook.com to create a calendar. Restart Outlook 2016. After syncing, the new calendar should appear in Outlook 2016.

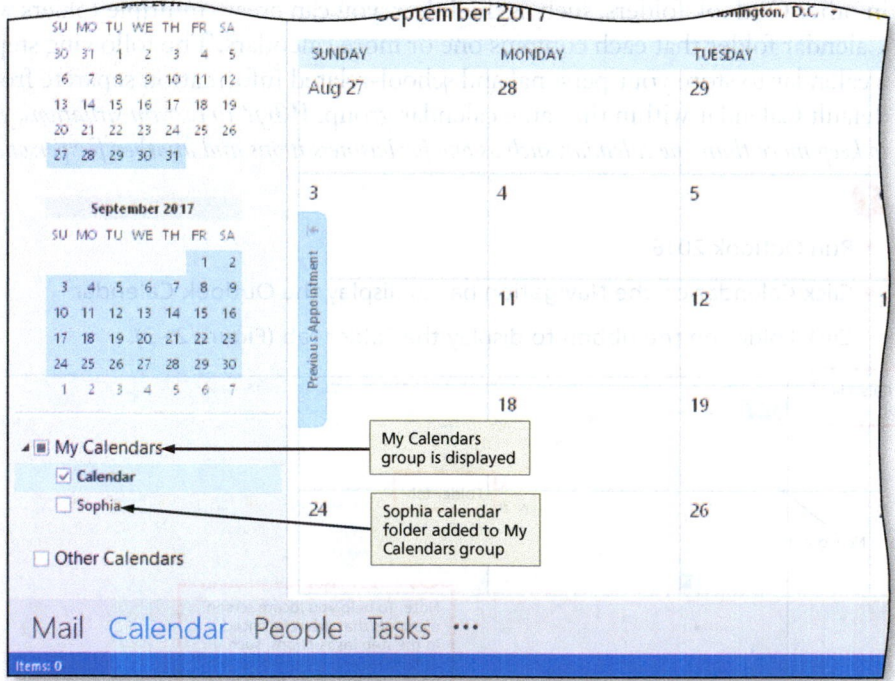

Figure 2–5

4

- In the My Calendars pane, click Sophia to insert a check mark in the check box, so that both the default Calendar and the Sophia calendars are selected and displayed in the appointment area of the Outlook window (Figure 2–6).

Q&A
Why is the default calendar displayed in a different color from Sophia's calendar?
Outlook automatically assigns a different color to each new calendar you create to make it easier to distinguish one calendar from the other. Your calendar colors might be different from those shown in Figure 2–6.

Can I select a color for the calendar?
Yes. Click the View tab, click the Color button (View tab | Color group), and then select a color from the Color gallery.

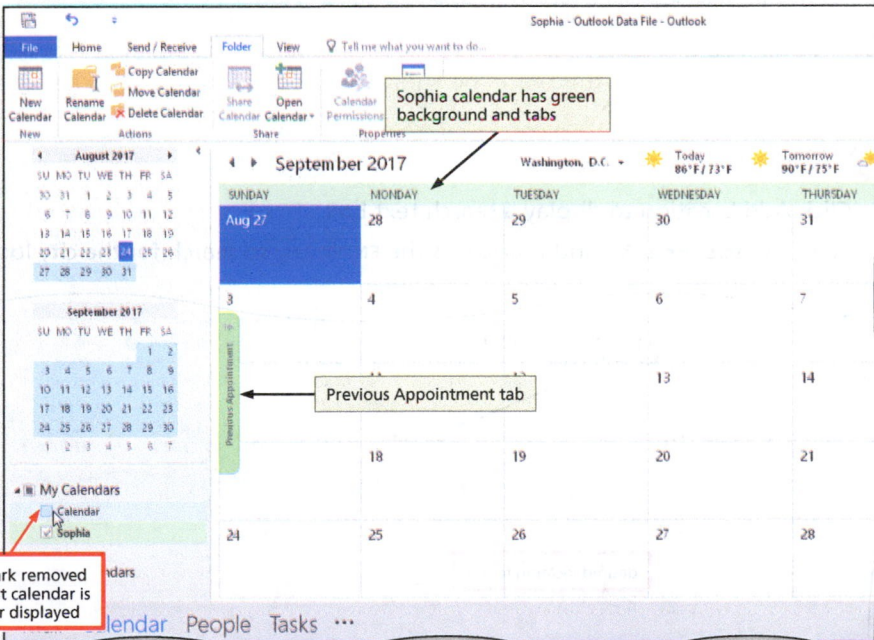

Figure 2–6

5

- Click Calendar in the My Calendars pane to remove the check mark from the Calendar check box so that the default calendar no longer is displayed in the appointment area (Figure 2–7).

Q&A
Why does my view look different from what is shown?
Figure 2–7 shows Month view, which is the default view for Calendar. If this is not the current view, click the Month button (Home tab | Arrange group).

What is the purpose of the colored tabs on each side of the appointment area?
The tabs are for navigating to the previous and next appointments.

Figure 2–7

Other Ways

1. Press CTRL+SHIFT+E

To Add a City to the Calendar Weather Bar

1 CONFIGURE CALENDAR OPTIONS | 2 CREATE & MANIPULATE APPOINTMENTS | 3 SCHEDULE EVENTS
4 SCHEDULE MEETINGS | 5 PRINT CALENDAR | 6 SAVE & SHARE CALENDAR

Outlook provides a Weather Bar so you can view the current three-day weather forecast when you open the calendar. By default, Washington, D.C. is displayed. You can customize the Weather Bar to display weather symbols such as cloud or snow symbols and today's high and low temperatures for your local weather conditions. When you click the forecast, further details appear such as the wind condition, humidity level, precipitation, and a link to a detailed weather forecast online. ***Why?*** *Each morning as you view your schedule, the Weather Bar informs you about the day's weather so you can plan your day accordingly.* The following steps add a city to the calendar Weather Bar to display the current forecast.

- Click the arrow button to the right of the current city in the Weather Bar to display the Add Location command (Figure 2–8).

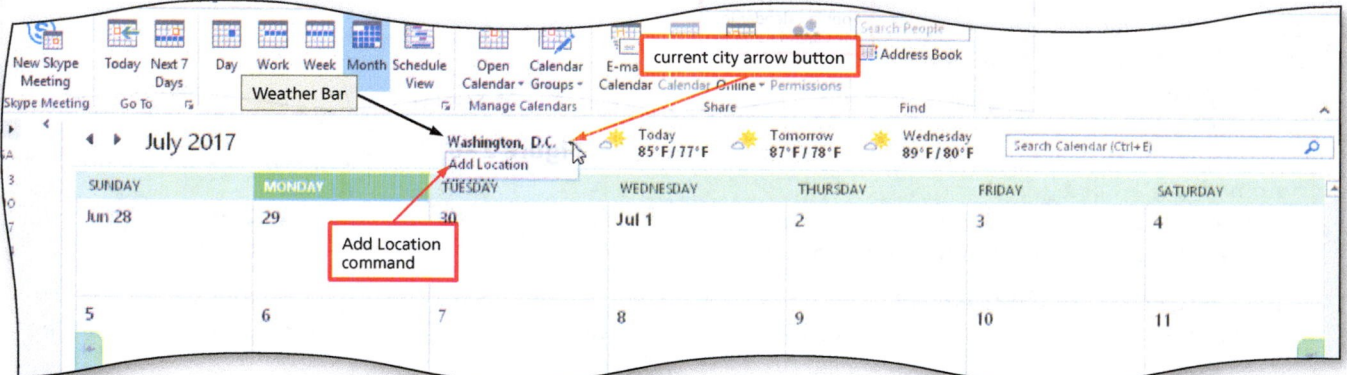

Figure 2–8

Q&A My Weather Bar does not appear in the calendar. What should I do?
Click the File tab to display Backstage View, click Options, and then click the Calendar category. Scroll down to the Weather section, and then click the Show weather on the calendar check box to insert a check mark.

- Click Add Location to display a search text box.
- Type **Miami Beach** and then press the ENTER key to search for the city location (Figure 2–9).

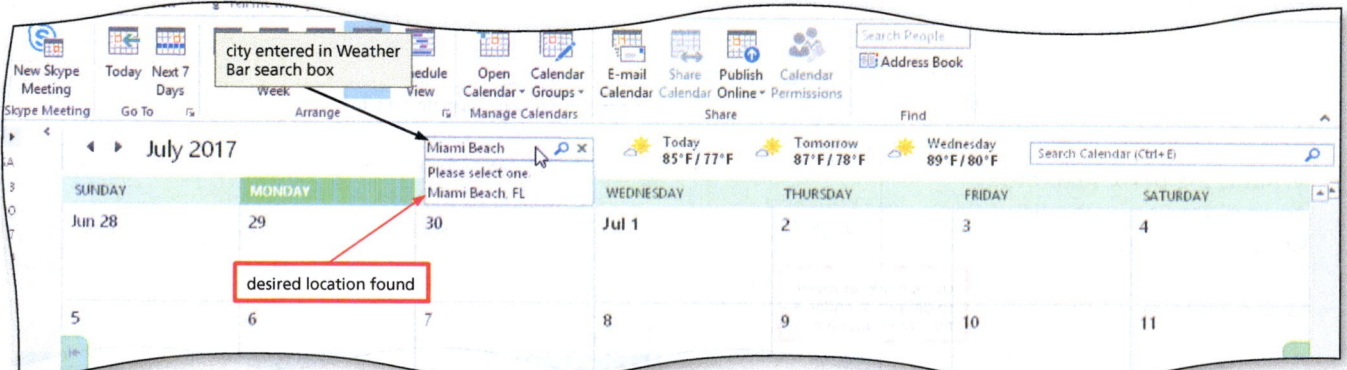

Figure 2–9

Q&A Can I search for a city using a postal code?
Yes. Type the postal code to search for the location in the Weather Bar search text box.

3

- Click Miami Beach, FL to select the location and display its three-day forecast in the Weather Bar.
- If requested by your instructor, replace Miami Beach, FL with your hometown in the Weather Bar (Figure 2–10).

Figure 2–10

Q&A Why does my Weather Bar display the message 'Weather service is not available'?
Most likely, you are not connected to the Internet. You must have Internet connectivity to display the weather forecast.

Navigating the Calendar

Each Microsoft Outlook folder displays the items it contains in a layout called a view. The **calendar view** is the arrangement and format of the folder contents by day, work week, week, month, or schedule, which is a horizontal layout. Recall that the default view of the Calendar folder is Month view. Some people prefer a different view of their calendar, such as weekly or daily. For instance, you might want to view all the items for a day at one time, in which case Day view would work best. Although the Outlook window looks different in each view, you can accomplish the same tasks in each view: you can add, edit, or delete appointments, events, and meetings.

For an introduction to Windows and instructions about how to perform basic Windows tasks, read the Office and Windows module at the beginning of this book, where you can learn how to resize windows, change screen resolution, create folders, move and rename files, use Windows Help, and much more.

To Go to a Specific Date

1 CONFIGURE CALENDAR OPTIONS | 2 CREATE & MANIPULATE APPOINTMENTS | 3 SCHEDULE EVENTS
4 SCHEDULE MEETINGS | 5 PRINT CALENDAR | 6 SAVE & SHARE CALENDAR

To display a date that is not visible in the current view so that you can view that date in the appointment area, one option is to use the Go to Date Dialog Box Launcher. The following steps display a specific date in the appointment area in a calendar. *Why? Rather than scrolling through your calendars in Outlook to find a specific date, you can quickly find a date in Outlook by using the Go To Date dialog box.*

1

- Click Home on the ribbon to display the Home tab.
- Click the Go to Date Dialog Box Launcher (Home tab | Go To group) to display the Go To Date dialog box (Figure 2–11).

Figure 2–11

2

- Type 10/2/2017 in the Date text box to enter the date you want to display in the current calendar.
- Click the Show in button, and then select Day Calendar to show the calendar in Day view (Figure 2–12).

Q&A Why did 'Mon' appear next to the date in the Date box?
Outlook automatically includes the day of the week (Monday, in this case) when you enter a date in the Date box.

Figure 2–12

3

- Click the OK button to close the Go To Date dialog box and display the selected date in Day view (Figure 2–13).

Figure 2–13

Other Ways

1. Press CTRL+G

To Display the Calendar in Work Week View

1 CONFIGURE CALENDAR OPTIONS | 2 CREATE & MANIPULATE APPOINTMENTS | 3 SCHEDULE EVENTS
4 SCHEDULE MEETINGS | 5 PRINT CALENDAR | 6 SAVE & SHARE CALENDAR

Why? In Outlook, you can display several calendar days at once so that you can see multiple appointments at the same time. **Work Week view** shows five workdays (Monday through Friday) in a columnar style. Hours that are not part of the default workday (8:00 AM – 5:00 PM) appear shaded when viewing the calendar in Day, Work Week, and Week view. The following step displays the calendar in Work Week view.

1

- Click the Work Week button (Home tab | Arrange group) to display the work week in the appointment area for the selected date (Figure 2–14).

Experiment

- Scroll up and down in Work Week view to see how the color changes to reflect hours outside the default workday.

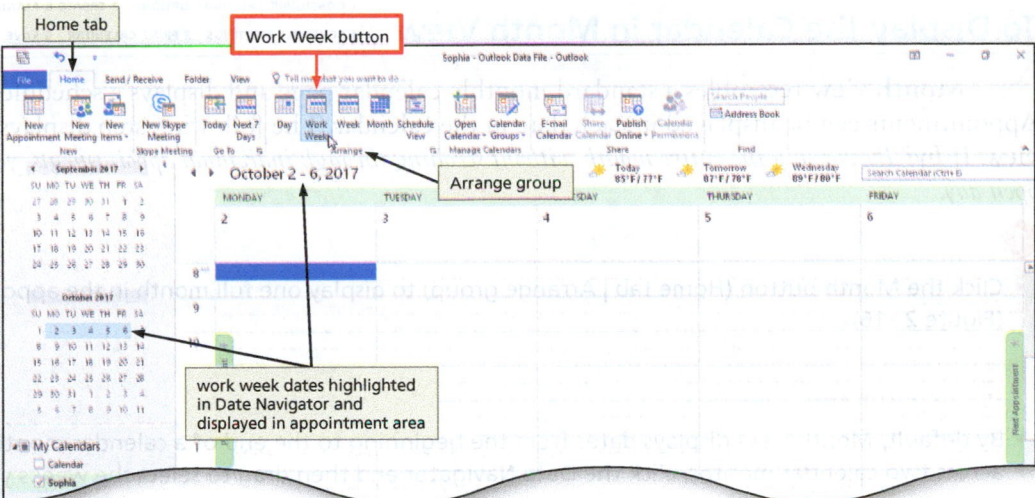

Figure 2–14

Q&A Why is Monday through Friday highlighted on the Date Navigator?

The calendar days displayed in the appointment area are highlighted on the Date Navigator.

Other Ways

1. Press CTRL+ALT+2

To Display the Calendar in Week View

1 CONFIGURE CALENDAR OPTIONS | 2 CREATE & MANIPULATE APPOINTMENTS | 3 SCHEDULE EVENTS
4 SCHEDULE MEETINGS | 5 PRINT CALENDAR | 6 SAVE & SHARE CALENDAR

Why? *The advantage of displaying a calendar in Week view is to see how many appointments are scheduled for any given week, including weekends.* In **Week view**, the seven days of the selected week appear in the appointment area. The following step displays the calendar in Week view.

1

- Click the Week button (Home tab | Arrange group) to display the full week, including weekends, in the appointment area (Figure 2–15).

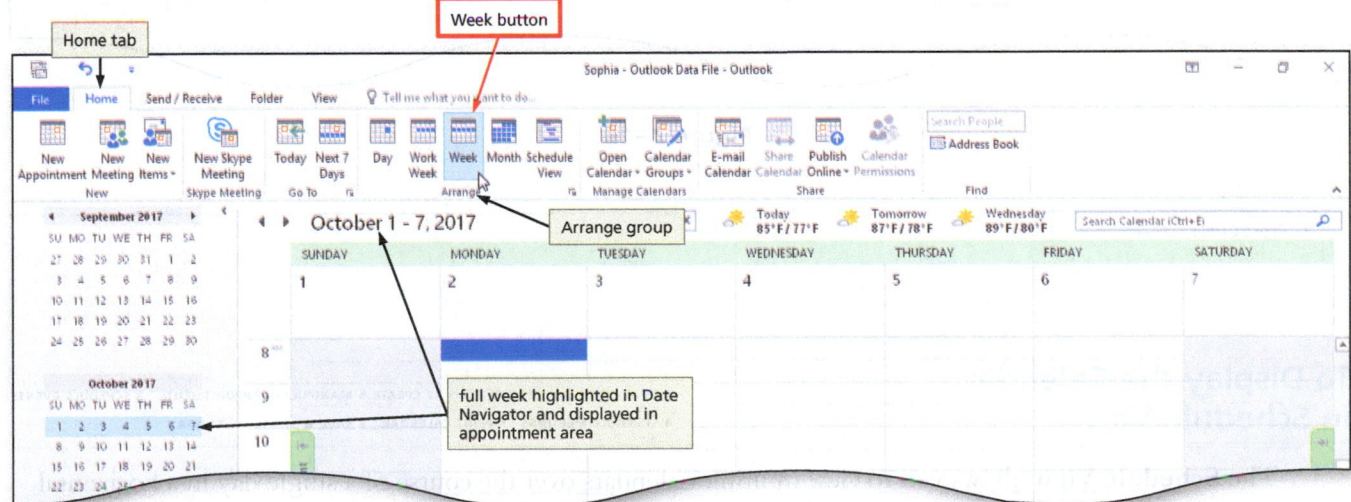

Figure 2–15

Other Ways

1. Press CTRL+ALT+3

To Display the Calendar in Month View

Month view resembles a standard monthly calendar page and displays a schedule for an entire month. Appointments can be displayed in each date in the calendar. The following step displays the calendar in Month view. *Why? By viewing the entire month without scrolling through individual appointments, you can see when you have an open day.*

 1

- Click the Month button (Home tab | Arrange group) to display one full month in the appointment area (Figure 2–16).

🔎 Experiment

- By default, Month view displays dates from the beginning to the end of a calendar month. To select several weeks across two calendar months, click the Date Navigator and then drag to select the weeks you want to view.

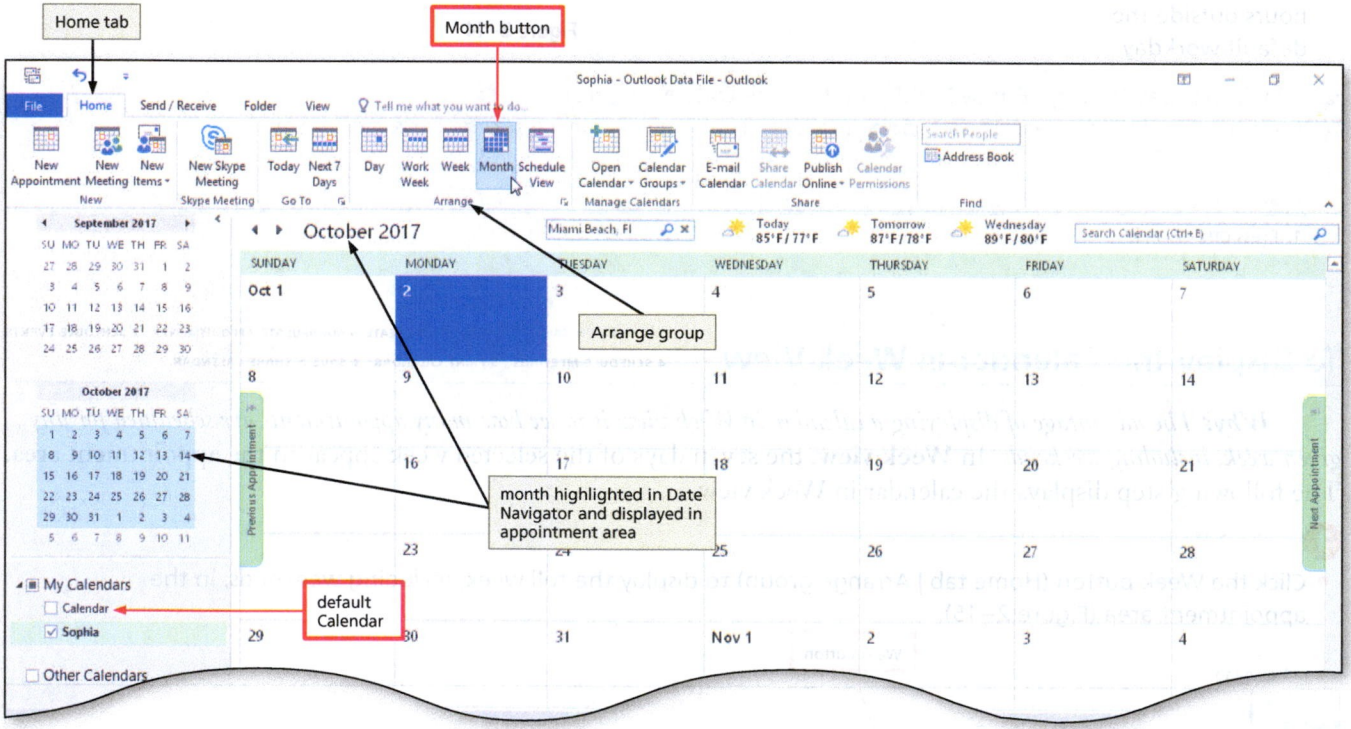

Figure 2–16

Other Ways

1. Press CTRL+ALT+4

To Display the Calendar in Schedule View

The **Schedule View** allows you to view multiple calendars over the course of a single day in a horizontal layout to make scheduling meetings easier. The following steps display the default Calendar and the Sophia calendar in Schedule View. *Why? Schedule View is useful when trying to see multiple calendars so that you can check for overlapping items.*

1

- Click Calendar (default Calendar) in the My Calendars pane to insert a check mark in the check box and to display both the default Calendar and Sophia's calendar in the appointment area (Figure 2–17).

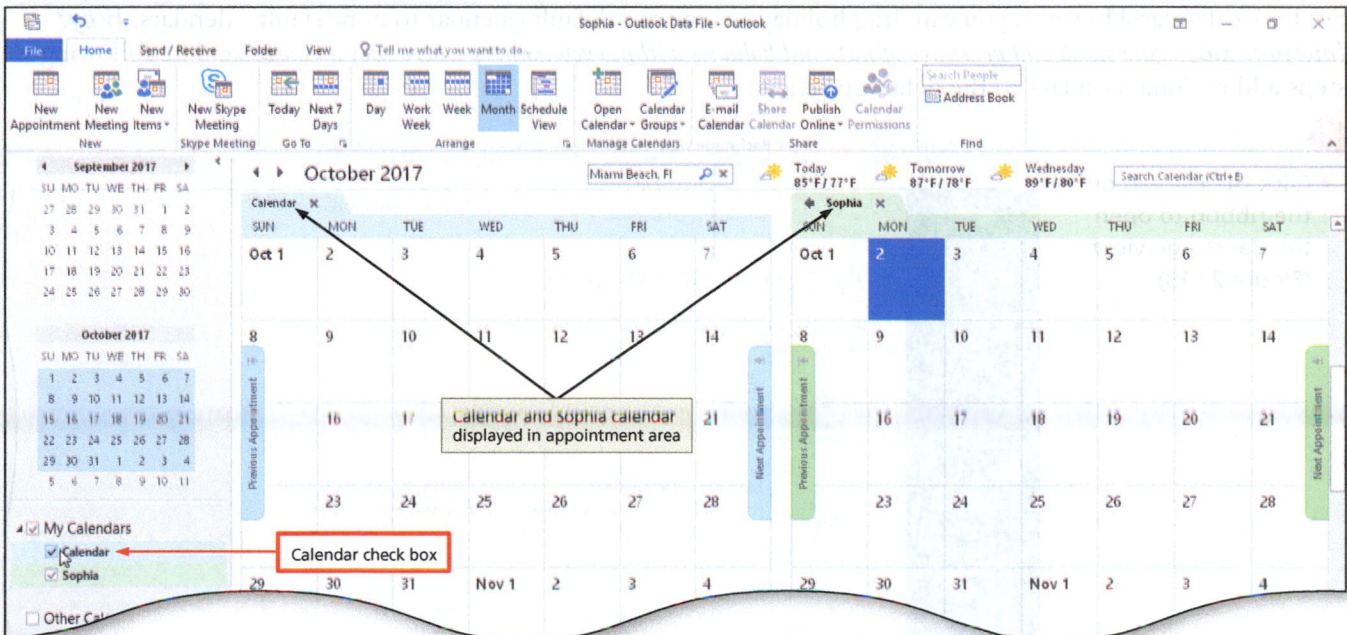

Figure 2–17

Q&A Why are both calendars displayed in Month view?

Outlook uses the view of the existing calendar for a newly displayed calendar. In this case, Sophia's calendar was displayed in Month view, so the default Calendar also is displayed in Month view.

2

- Click the Schedule View button (Home tab | Arrange group) to display both calendars in Schedule View (Figure 2–18).

Q&A Why does Schedule View show a single day instead of multiple days?

Schedule View displays one day at a time.

What does the dark blue shaded area in the calendar represent?

The dark blue shaded area represents the time slot selected in Day view.

Figure 2–18

Other Ways

1. Press CTRL+ALT+5

To Add Holidays to the Default Calendar

Before you add appointments to a calendar, you can mark the standard holidays for one or more countries. You can add holidays to your default calendar folder only, not to a public folder or nondefault calendar such as Sophia's calendar. However, you can drag holidays from your default calendar to nondefault calendars. *Why? International businesses should be aware of national holidays within each country where they do business.* The following steps add national holidays to the default calendar.

- Click the File tab on the ribbon to open the Backstage view (Figure 2–19).

Figure 2–19

- Click Options to display the Outlook Options dialog box.
- Click Calendar in the left pane to display the options in the Calendar category (Figure 2–20).

Figure 2–20

3

- Click the Add Holidays button to display the Add Holidays to Calendar dialog box (Figure 2–21).

Can I select multiple countries to display more than one set of national holidays?
Yes. You can select the holidays of multiple countries to display in the default calendar.

Figure 2–21

4

- If necessary, click the check box for your country of residence to add that country's national holidays to the default calendar.

- Click the OK button to close the dialog box, import the holidays, and display the confirmation message that the holidays were added to your calendar (Figure 2–22).

Figure 2–22

5

- Click the OK button to close the Microsoft Outlook dialog box and the Add Holidays to Calendar dialog box.
- Click the OK button to close the Outlook Options dialog box.
- Click the Month button (Home tab | Arrange group) to display both calendars in Month view in the appointment area (Figure 2–23).

Q&A

The national holidays do not appear in Sophia's calendar. Where are they displayed?
Holidays are displayed only in the default calendar.

Why are the national holidays on my default calendar different from Figure 2–23?
Your default calendar holiday dates might differ from those shown in Figure 2–23 if you selected a different country.

Figure 2–23

 6

- Click Calendar in the My Calendars pane to remove the check mark from the Calendar check box so that the default calendar no longer is displayed in the appointment area.

Creating and Editing Appointments

BTW

Deleting a Calendar
If you no longer need one of the calendars, you can delete a calendar by clicking the Delete Calendar button (Folder tab | Actions group). Click the Yes button in the Microsoft Outlook dialog box to delete the folder. Outlook sends the deleted folder to the Deleted Items folder.

An appointment is an activity you schedule in your Outlook calendar that does not require an invitation to others. Recall that every calendar item you schedule in Outlook Calendar begins as an appointment. In Outlook, you easily can change an appointment to an event or a meeting. Scheduling a dental visit, your best friend's birthday, or a class schedule as recurring appointments helps you successfully manage your activities and obligations. To better organize your appointments and meetings in your Outlook calendar, you can add color categories that let you scan and visually associate similar items. For example, you can set the color blue to represent your academic classes and the color green for doctor's appointments.

Creating Appointments in the Appointment Area

A **one-time appointment**, such as a concert event, conference call, or course exam date, is an appointment that occurs only once on a calendar. A **recurring appointment**, such as a class throughout an academic course, repeats on the calendar at regular intervals. Appointments can be created in two ways: using the appointment area, where you enter the appointment directly in the appropriate time slot, or using the Untitled – Appointment window, where you can enter more specific details about the appointment such as the location or address of the activity.

BTWs
Touch Screen Differences
The Office and Windows interfaces may vary if you are using a touch screen. For this reason, you might notice that the function or appearance of your touch screen differs slightly from this module's presentation.

To Create a One-Time Appointment Using the Appointment Area

1 CONFIGURE CALENDAR OPTIONS | **2 CREATE & MANIPULATE APPOINTMENTS** | 3 SCHEDULE EVENTS
4 SCHEDULE MEETINGS | 5 PRINT CALENDAR | 6 SAVE & SHARE CALENDAR

When you click a day on the calendar in the Navigation Pane, Outlook displays the calendar for the date selected in Day view in the appointment area. Day view shows a daily view of a specific date in half-hour increments. The following steps use the appointment area to create a one-time appointment for Sophia's yearly health physical. *Why? If you are scheduling a one-time activity such as a doctor's appointment, you can type directly in the appointment area because you do not need a detailed description.*

- Click the month name October on the Date Navigator to display a list of months with the associated year (Figure 2–24).

Experiment

- View several dates that are not consecutive by clicking a date in the Date Navigator, holding down the CTRL key, and then clicking additional days.

Figure 2–24

- If necessary, click October 2017 on the Date Navigator to display the selected month in the appointment area.

- Click 13 in the October 2017 calendar on the Date Navigator to display the selected date in the appointment area in Day view (Figure 2–25).

Figure 2–25

3

- Drag to select two half-hour increments from the 9:00 AM to the 10:00 AM time slot in the appointment area (Figure 2–26).

Q&A What if I select more or less than two half-hour increments? If you incorrectly select the appointment time, repeat this step to try again.

9:00 AM – 10:00 AM time slot selected in appointment area

Figure 2–26

4

- Type **Health Physical: Dr. Bolton** as the appointment subject and then press the ENTER key to enter the appointment in the appointment area (Figure 2–27).

Q&A Do I have to perform another step to save the appointment entry? No, the appointment entry is saved automatically when you press the ENTER key.

appointment status shown as Busy

Calendar Tools Appointment tab

bold date means one or more appointments are scheduled on that day

white dots indicate appointment is selected

appointment entered

Figure 2–27

Why is Busy displayed in the Show As box (Calendar Tools Appointment tab | Options group)? When you create an appointment, Outlook assigns your time as busy by default.

Why does the date of the health physical appointment appear in bold on the Date Navigator? Outlook displays in bold any date with a time allocated on your calendar as busy to indicate that you have something scheduled on that day.

Other Ways

1. Select beginning time slot, hold down SHIFT, click ending time slot, type appointment name, press ENTER

Organize the Calendar with Color Categories

As you add appointments to the Outlook Calendar, you can use categories to color-code the appointments by type. Adding color categories allows you to quickly scan and visually group similar items such as classes or work-related appointments. For example, Sophia can assign her work tasks to a blue category, doctor's appointments to green, classes to orange, and all friends- and family-related activities to purple. After you associate each category with a color, she can categorize each appointment. The associated color is used as the item's background color on the calendar in the appointment area.

BTW

Adding a Calendar Group

To organize multiple calendars, you can create calendar groups. Click the Calendar Groups button (Home tab | Manage Calendars group) and then click Create New Calendar Group. Type a name for the new calendar group, and then click the OK button.

To Add Color Categories

1 CONFIGURE CALENDAR OPTIONS | **2 CREATE & MANIPULATE APPOINTMENTS** | 3 SCHEDULE EVENTS
4 SCHEDULE MEETINGS | 5 PRINT CALENDAR | 6 SAVE & SHARE CALENDAR

Why? *Color categories enable you to easily identify and group associated items in the Outlook Calendar.* The following steps add color categories in the calendar.

- Click the Categorize button (Calendar Tools Appointment tab | Tags group) to display the Categorize list of color categories (Figure 2–28).

Q&A
Can you use color categories for any type of email account?
You should use a Microsoft account as your Outlook email account to take advantage of categories and other special features.

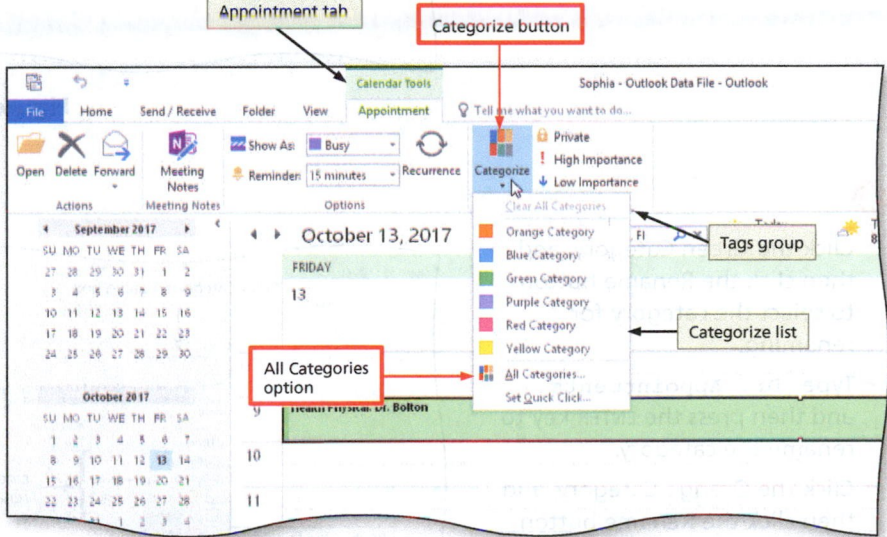

Figure 2–28

2

- Click All Categories to display the Color Categories dialog box (Figure 2–29).

Figure 2–29

- Click the Blue Category to select the category.
- Click the Rename button to select the category for renaming.
- Type **Work** and then press the ENTER key to rename the category (Figure 2–30).

Figure 2–30

- Click the Green Category, and then click the Rename button to select the category for renaming.
- Type **Dr. Appointments** and then press the ENTER key to rename the category.
- Click the Orange Category, and then click the Rename button to select the category for renaming.
- Type **Friends & Family** and then press the ENTER key to rename the category.
- Click the Purple Category, and then click the Rename button to select the category for renaming.
- Type **Classes** and then press the ENTER key to rename the category (Figure 2–31).

Figure 2–31

Q&A How many color categories can I set?
You can assign fifteen color categories in Outlook Calendar. Click the New button in the Color Categories dialog box to select colors not shown in the dialog box by default.

- Click the OK button to close the Color Categories dialog box.

To Assign a Color Category to an Appointment

1 CONFIGURE CALENDAR OPTIONS | 2 CREATE & MANIPULATE APPOINTMENTS | 3 SCHEDULE EVENTS
4 SCHEDULE MEETINGS | 5 PRINT CALENDAR | 6 SAVE & SHARE CALENDAR

The following steps assign a color category to a calendar appointment. *Why? By color coding your Outlook calendar appointments, you can quickly distinguish among your assigned categories such as class, work, or birthdays.*

- If necessary, click the Health Physical appointment at 9:00 AM to select the appointment.
- Click the Categorize button (Calendar Tools Appointment tab | Tags group) to display the Categorize list of color categories (Figure 2–32).

Figure 2–32

❷

- Click the green Dr. Appointments category to display the selected appointment with a medium-green background (Figure 2–33).

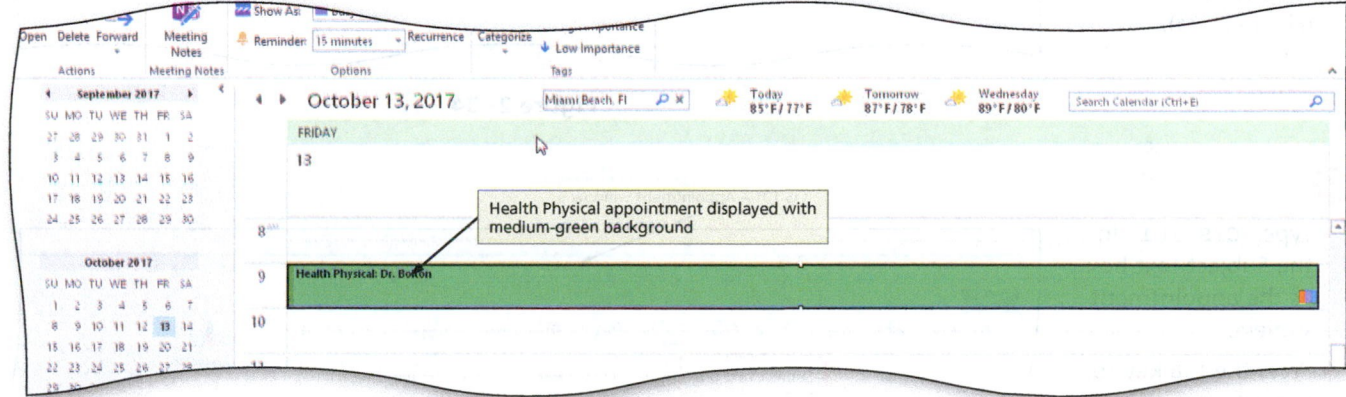

Figure 2–33

Creating Appointments Using the Appointment Window

Another way to create an appointment is by using the Appointment window, which provides additional options for entering an appointment, such as the location of the appointment and a recurrence pattern. When you set a **recurrence pattern**, Outlook schedules the appointment on the calendar at regular intervals for a designated period of time, such as a class that Sophia takes for an entire semester on Tuesdays and Thursdays.

Outlook also allows you to configure a **reminder**, similar to an alarm clock reminder, which is an alert window that briefly appears on your screen to remind you of an upcoming appointment. You also can set a chime or other sound to play as part of the reminder.

BTW
Entering Locations
As you enter calendar items, you can include location information by clicking the Location box arrow and selecting a location on the list.

Another option when creating an appointment is to set the **appointment status**, which is how the time for a calendar item is marked on your calendar. The default appointment status setting is Busy, as indicated in the previous steps, but you can change the status to reflect your availability as appropriate.

To Create an Appointment Using the Appointment Window

1 CONFIGURE CALENDAR OPTIONS | **2 CREATE & MANIPULATE APPOINTMENTS** | 3 SCHEDULE EVENTS
4 SCHEDULE MEETINGS | 5 PRINT CALENDAR | 6 SAVE & SHARE CALENDAR

Why? Instead of directly entering an appointment in the appointment area, you can specify various details such as the location by using the Appointment window. To schedule an appointment such as Sophia's CIS 101 computer class that meets repeatedly over the semester in a particular room on campus, you decide to use the Appointment window. The following steps create an appointment using the Appointment window.

1

- Click Home on the ribbon to display the Home tab.

- Click the New Appointment button (Home tab | New group) to open the Untitled – Appointment window (Figure 2–34).

Figure 2–34

2

- Type `CIS 101` in the Subject text box as the appointment subject.

- Press the TAB key to move the insertion point to the Location box.

- Type `M14` as the room number of the class (Figure 2–35).

Figure 2–35

Q&A

Why did the title of the window change from Untitled – Appointment to CIS 101 – Appointment?
The title bar displays the name of the appointment. Because the name of the appointment has changed, the name on the title bar also changes.

Why are the date and time already specified?
When you start to create a new appointment, Outlook sets the start and end times using the time selected in the appointment area.

3

- Click the Start time calendar button to display a calendar for the current month (Figure 2–36).

Figure 2–36

4

- Click 3 on the calendar to select the next CIS 101 class as October 3, 2017.
- Click the Start time box arrow to display a list of time slots (Figure 2–37).

Figure 2–37

5

- Click 10:00 AM to select it as the Start time for the appointment.
- Click the End time box arrow to display a list of time slots (Figure 2–38).

Q&A | Why did the End time change to the same date as the Start time?
Outlook automatically sets appointments to occur during a single day.

Figure 2–38

Why does the second end time list have a duration for each time?
Outlook automatically displays the duration next to the end time to help you set the length of the appointment.

6

- Click 11:30 AM (1.5 hours) to select it as the End time for the appointment (Figure 2–39).

Figure 2–39

Other Ways

1. Press CTRL+SHIFT+A

BTW

Time Zones
Use the Time Zones button (Appointment tab | Options group) to specify a time zone for the start and end times of an appointment.

Setting Appointment Options

When creating appointments on the Outlook calendar, you can set a number of options that determine how the appointment is handled. Table 2–2 lists the options available when creating an item on your calendar.

BTW

Room Finder
Some features in Outlook 2016 require a Microsoft Exchange Server account. **Exchange** is a collaborative communications server that many organizations use. Microsoft Office 365 includes Exchange Online, and some Internet hosting providers offer Exchange accounts. If you use a Microsoft Exchange account, you can click Rooms to check availability and reserve rooms when you select a location in the Location text box. A feature called the **Room Finder** assists you in locating times for your meeting when most attendees are available. To select a meeting time, click a time suggestion in the Room Finder pane in the Suggested times section, or pick a time on the free/busy calendar.

Table 2–2 Calendar Window Options	
Option	**Description**
Show As	Indicates your availability on a specific date and time; if you want to show others your availability when they schedule a meeting with you during a specific time, this must be set accurately
Reminder	Alerts you at a specific time prior to the item's occurrence
Recurrence	If an item on your calendar repeats at regularly scheduled intervals, sets the recurring options so that you only have to enter the item once on your calendar
Time Zone	Shows or hides the time zone controls, which you can use to specify the time zones for the start and end times of the appointment

Outlook provides five options for indicating your availability on the Calendar, as described in Table 2–3.

Table 2–3 Calendar Item Status Options	
Calendar Item Status Options	**Description**
Free	Shows time with a white bar in Day, Week, Work Week, or Month view
Working Elsewhere	Shows time with a white bar with dots in Day, Week, Work Week, or Month view
Tentative	Shows time with a slashed bar in Day, Week, Work Week, or Month view
Busy	Shows time with a solid bar in Day, Week, Work Week, or Month view
Out of Office	Shows time with a purple bar in Day, Week, Work Week, or Month view

To Change the Status of an Appointment

1 CONFIGURE CALENDAR OPTIONS | 2 CREATE & MANIPULATE APPOINTMENTS | 3 SCHEDULE EVENTS
4 SCHEDULE MEETINGS | 5 PRINT CALENDAR | 6 SAVE & SHARE CALENDAR

To make sure your time is displayed accurately on the calendar, you can change the appointment status from the default of Busy to Out of Office, meaning Sophia is not in the internship office during class time while attending CIS 101. The following steps change the status of an appointment. *Why? You can display time indicators such as Busy or Out of Office to show calendar entries that reflect your availability. If you share your calendar, others can see at a glance if you are available.*

- Click the Show As box arrow (Appointment tab | Options group) in the CIS 101 appointment to display the Show As list of appointment status options (Figure 2–40).

Figure 2–40

- Click Out of Office to change the appointment status (Figure 2–41).

Figure 2–41

To Set a Reminder for an Appointment

1 CONFIGURE CALENDAR OPTIONS | 2 CREATE & MANIPULATE APPOINTMENTS | 3 SCHEDULE EVENTS
4 SCHEDULE MEETINGS | 5 PRINT CALENDAR | 6 SAVE & SHARE CALENDAR

With the start and end dates and times for the class set and the appointment status selected, Sophia wants to schedule a reminder so that she does not forget class. *Why? Your Outlook Calendar can be your personal alarm clock by displaying reminders of your appointments with options such as snooze and dismiss.* When the reminder is displayed, you can open the appointment for further review. The following steps set a 30-minute reminder for an appointment.

- Click the Reminder box arrow (Appointment tab | Options group) to display the Reminder list of available reminder intervals (Figure 2–42).

Q&A

What does the Sound option in the Reminder list do?
In addition to a visual·reminder, Outlook allows you to set an auditory alarm, much like an alarm clock.

Figure 2–42

- Click 30 minutes to set a reminder for 30 minutes prior to the start time of the appointment (Figure 2–43).

Figure 2–43

Q&A

Why was the reminder time originally scheduled for 15 minutes?
By default, a Reminder is set to occur 15 minutes before the start of an appointment. However, you can increase or decrease the default reminder time.

Can you customize the sound that is played when a reminder is displayed?

- When you click the Reminder box arrow (Calendar Tools Appointment tab | Options group), click Sound to open the Reminder Sound dialog box.
- Click the Browse button, and then select the sound .wav file that you want played.
- Click the Open button. Click the OK button to select the custom reminder sound.
- A reminder time must be selected before the Sound command appears.

Creating Recurring Appointments

Many appointments are recurring appointments, meaning they happen at regular intervals for a designated period of time. The recurring appointment is configured with a recurrence pattern designating the rate of recurrence, for example, weekly, and on what day(s) of the week the appointment occurs.

To Set Recurrence Options for an Appointment

1 CONFIGURE CALENDAR OPTIONS | **2 CREATE & MANIPULATE APPOINTMENTS** | 3 SCHEDULE EVENTS
4 SCHEDULE MEETINGS | 5 PRINT CALENDAR | 6 SAVE & SHARE CALENDAR

The next CIS 101 class is on October 3 and is held every Tuesday and Thursday from 10:00 AM to 11:30 AM at regular intervals for the rest of the semester, making it a recurring appointment. The following steps configure a recurrence pattern for an appointment. *Why? By establishing a recurrence pattern, you do not have to enter each class into the schedule for the entire semester.*

- Click the Recurrence button (Appointment tab | Options group) to display the Appointment Recurrence dialog box (Figure 2–44).

Q&A Why are the start and end times and the duration already set in the Appointment time area of the Appointment Recurrence dialog box?
Outlook uses the settings you already selected for the appointment.

Figure 2–44

- If necessary, in the Recurrence pattern area, click the Weekly option button (Appointment Recurrence dialog box) to set the recurrence pattern.
- If necessary, in the Recur every text box (Appointment Recurrence dialog box), type 1 to schedule the frequency of the recurrence pattern.
- Click Thursday to insert a check mark in the check box and to schedule the class two times per week (in this case, Tuesday and Thursday) (Figure 2–45).

Figure 2–45

Why is the Tuesday check box already selected in the Recurrence pattern area?
Tuesday is already selected because the class starts on that day of the week.

Why does the Start box in the 'Range of recurrence' area contain a date?
When you display the Appointment Recurrence dialog box, Outlook automatically sets the range of recurrence with the date the appointment starts.

3

- In the Range of recurrence area, click the End by option button (Appointment Recurrence dialog box), and then press the TAB key two times to select the End by box.

- Type 12/14/2017 as the day the class ends to replace the displayed end date with a new date (Figure 2–46).

What if I do not know the end date, but I know how many times the class meets?
You can click the End after option button and then type the number of times the class meets in the End after text box.

Figure 2–46

4

- Click the OK button to close the Appointment Recurrence dialog box and set the recurrence pattern (Figure 2–47).

Why did the Appointment tab change to the Appointment Series tab?
When you set a recurrence pattern, the tab name changes to reflect that you are working with a series.

Figure 2–47

1 CONFIGURE CALENDAR OPTIONS | 2 CREATE & MANIPULATE APPOINTMENTS | 3 SCHEDULE EVENTS
4 SCHEDULE MEETINGS | 5 PRINT CALENDAR | 6 SAVE & SHARE CALENDAR

To Save an Appointment

With the details entered for the CIS 101 class, you can assign the appointment to a color category and then save the appointment. The following steps categorize the appointment, save the appointment series, and close the window. *Why? By changing the color-coded category and saving the appointment, your recurring appointment is scheduled.*

1

- Click the Categorize button (Appointment Series tab | Tags group) to display a list of color-coded categories (Figure 2–48).

Figure 2–48

BTW
Organizing Files and Folders

You should organize and store files in folders so that you easily can find the files later. For example, if Sophia is taking an introductory computer class called CIS 101, a good practice would be to save all Outlook files in an Outlook folder in a CIS 101 folder. For a discussion of folders and detailed examples of creating folders, refer to the Office and Windows module at the beginning of this book.

- Click the purple Classes category to assign this appointment to a category.
- Click the Save & Close button (Appointment Series tab | Actions group) to save the recurring appointment on the calendar and close the window.
- Click Home on the ribbon to display the Home tab.
- Click the Month button (Home tab | Arrange group) to display the calendar in Month view (Figure 2–49).

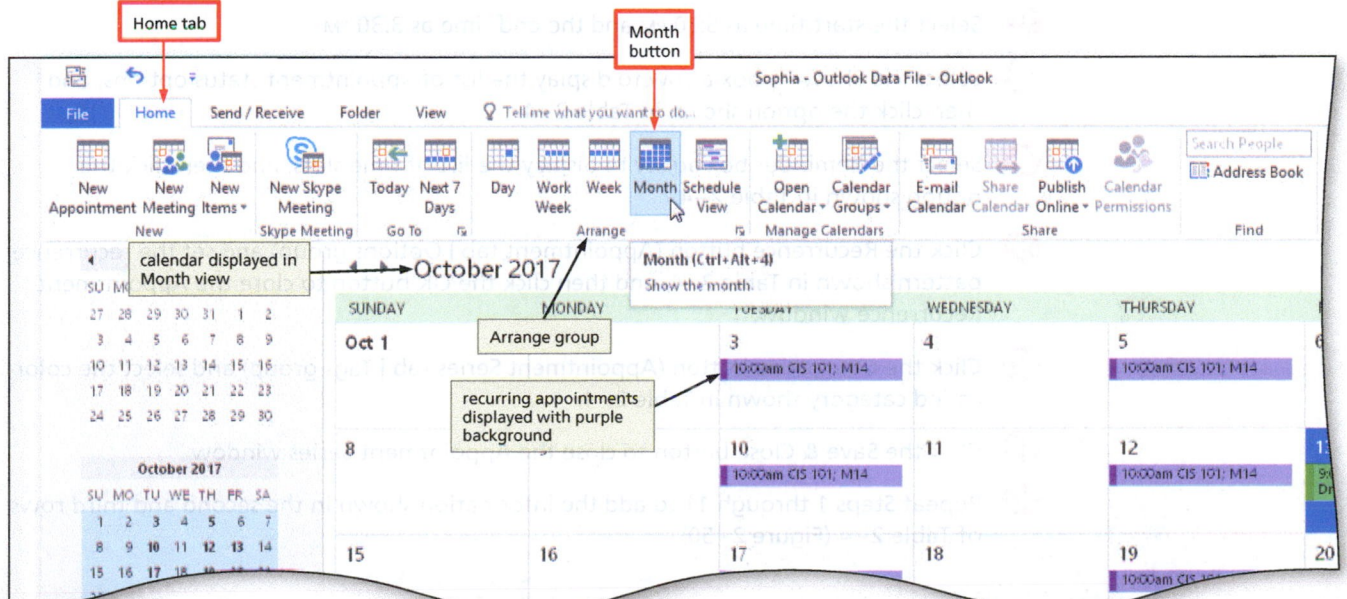

Figure 2–49

To Add More Recurring Appointments

1 CONFIGURE CALENDAR OPTIONS | 2 CREATE & MANIPULATE APPOINTMENTS | 3 SCHEDULE EVENTS
4 SCHEDULE MEETINGS | 5 PRINT CALENDAR | 6 SAVE & SHARE CALENDAR

With the CIS 101 class appointment series created, the next step is to create recurring appointments for the remainder of Sophia's class and work schedule using the appointment information in Table 2–4. The following steps create the remaining class schedule using the Appointment window. *Why? By adding your full schedule to the Outlook calendar, you will not miss any important appointments.*

Table 2–4 Recurring Appointments

Appointment	Location	Start Date	End Date	Start Time	End Time	Show As	Reminder	Recurrence	Category
ENG 102	D15	10/02/2017	Set in Recurrence	5:30 PM	8:30 PM	Out of Office	30 minutes	Weekly, every Monday; end by Monday, 12/11/2017	Classes
MTH 111	Online	10/06/2017	Set in Recurrence	5:00 PM	5:00 PM	Busy	1 hour	Weekly, every Friday; end by Friday, 12/08/2017	Classes
Pathways Office Hours	P22	10/02/2017	Set in Recurrence	2:00 PM	5:00 PM	Busy	15 minutes	Weekly, every Monday, Tuesday, & Wednesday; end by Wednesday 12/13/2017	Work

1 If necessary, click Home to display the Home tab.

2 Click the New Appointment button (Home tab | New group) to open the Appointment window.

3 Type **ENG 102** as the appointment subject.

4 Type **D15** as the location.

5 Select October 2, 2017 to set the start date.

6 Select the start time as 5:30 PM and the end time as 8:30 PM.

7 Select the Show As box arrow to display the list of appointment status options, and then click the option shown in Table 2–4.

8 Select the Reminder box arrow to display the list of time slots, and then click the option shown in Table 2–4.

9 Click the Recurrence button (Appointment tab | Options group) and set the recurrence pattern shown in Table 2–4, and then click the OK button to close the Appointment Recurrence window.

10 Click the Categorize button (Appointment Series tab | Tags group) and select the color-coded category shown in Table 2–4.

11 Click the Save & Close button to close the Appointment Series window.

12 Repeat Steps 1 through 11 to add the information shown in the second and third rows of Table 2–4 (Figure 2–50).

Q&A Why is the Calendar Tools Appointment Series tab displayed instead of the Calendar Tools Appointment tab?

The Calendar Tools Appointment Series tab is displayed when you select an appointment that is part of a series. This tab provides tools for working with recurring appointments.

What if I have appointments that recur other than weekly?

You can set daily, weekly, monthly, or yearly recurrence patterns in the Appointment Recurrence dialog box. A recurring appointment can be set to have no end date, to end after a certain number of occurrences, or to end by a certain date.

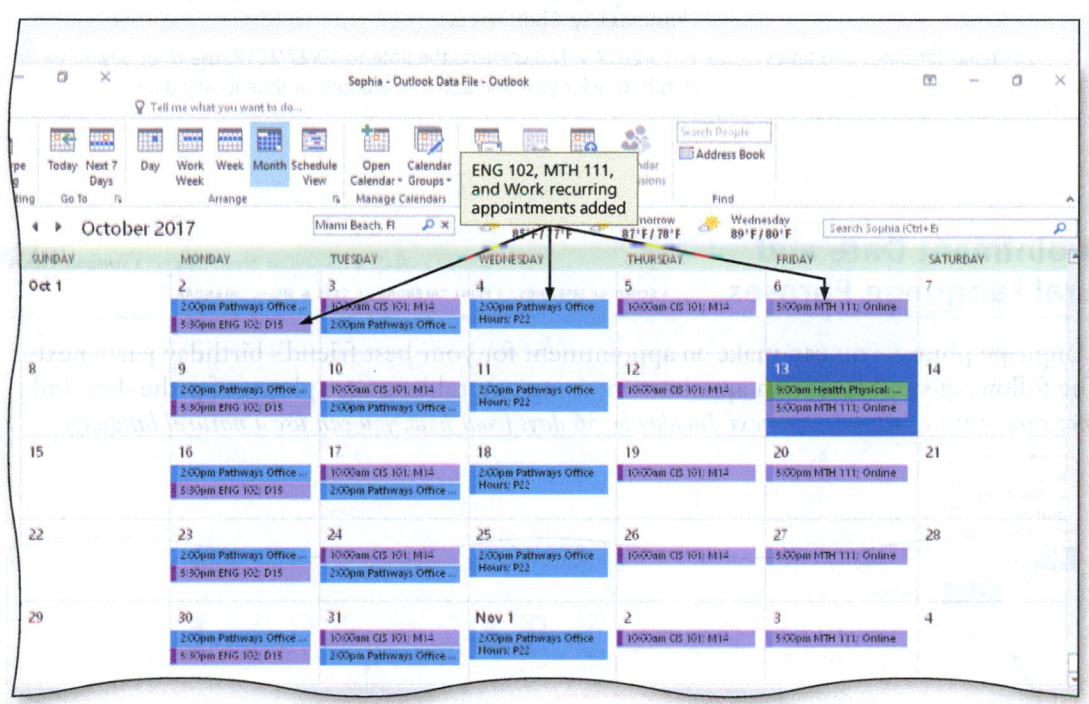

Figure 2–50

Using Natural Language Phrasing

In the previous steps, you entered dates and times in the Appointment window using standard numeric entries, such as 10/08/2017. You also can specify appointment dates and times using natural language. A **natural language phrase** is a phrase closely resembling how people speak during normal conversation. For example, you can type a phrase, such as "next Thursday" or "two weeks from yesterday," or you can type a single word, such as "midnight," and Outlook will calculate the correct date and time relative to the current date and time on the computer's system clock.

Outlook also can convert abbreviations and ordinal numbers into complete words and dates. For example, you can type "Feb" instead of "February" or "the first of May" instead of "5/1." Outlook's Calendar also can convert words such as "yesterday" and "tomorrow" and the names of holidays that occur on the same date each year, such as Valentine's Day. Table 2 – 5 lists various natural language options.

BTW
Outlook Help
At any time while using Outlook, you can find answers to questions and display information about various topics through Outlook Help. Used properly, this form of assistance can increase your productivity and reduce your frustrations by minimizing the time you spend learning how to use Outlook. For instructions about Outlook Help and exercises that will help you gain confidence in using it, read the Office and Windows module at the beginning of this book.

Table 2–5 Natural Language Options	
Category	**Examples**
Dates Spelled Out	July twenty-third, March 17th, first of May This Fri, next Sat, two days from now
Times Spelled Out	Noon, midnight Nine o'clock AM, five-twenty
Descriptions of Times and Dates	Now Yesterday, today, tomorrow
Holidays	Cinco de Mayo Christmas Day, Christmas Eve
Formulas for dates and times	10/15/2017 + 12d converts the date to 10/27/2017; use *d* for day, *m* for month, or *y* for year and add that amount of time to any date

To Create an Appointment Date and Time Using Natural Language Phrases

1 CONFIGURE CALENDAR OPTIONS | **2 CREATE & MANIPULATE APPOINTMENTS** | 3 SCHEDULE EVENTS
4 SCHEDULE MEETINGS | 5 PRINT CALENDAR | 6 SAVE & SHARE CALENDAR

Using a natural language phrase, you can make an appointment for your best friend's birthday party next Monday at 8:00 PM. The following steps create an appointment using natural language phrases for the date and time. *Why? If you are not sure of the exact date for next Tuesday or 36 days from now, you can use a natural language phrase.*

- Click the New Appointment button (Home tab | New group) to open the Untitled – Appointment window.

- Type **Lachlan's Birthday Party** in the Subject text box, and then press the TAB key to move the insertion point to the Location text box.

- Type **Kabob House** to add the location (Figure 2–51).

Figure 2–51

- Press the TAB key to select the first Start time text box, and then type **next sunday** to enter the start date.

Figure 2–52

- Press the TAB key to convert the phrase to a start date and to select the second Start time text box.

- Type **eight pm** as the time in the second Start time text box to enter the start time (Figure 2–52).

Q&A

Do I need to use proper capitalization when entering natural language phrases?
No. Outlook converts the text to the proper date or time, regardless of the capitalization.

Why did the text change to a numeric date when I pressed the TAB key?
If you enter the date using natural language phrasing, Outlook converts typed text to the correct date format when you click to move the insertion point to a different box.

3

- Press the TAB key two times to convert the Start time entry to 8:00 pm.

- Type **eleven pm** as the time in the second End time box.

- Press the ENTER key to convert the end time text to 11:00 pm.

- Click the Categorize button (Appointment tab | Tags group) to display the Categorize list.

- Click the orange Friends & Family category to assign this appointment to a category.

- Click the Save & Close button (Appointment tab | Actions group) to save the appointment and close the window.

- If necessary, scroll to next Sunday's date (Figure 2–53).

Figure 2–53

Editing Appointments

Schedules often need to be rearranged, so Outlook provides several ways to edit appointments. You can change the subject or location by clicking the appointment and editing the information directly in the appointment area. You can change the subject, location, date, or time by double-clicking the appointment and making corrections using the Appointment window. You can specify whether all occurrences in a series of recurring appointments need to be changed, or only a single occurrence should be altered.

BTW

Emailing Calendar Items

To send a calendar item to someone else, click the item, such as an appointment, and then click the Forward button (Calendar Tools Appointment tab | Actions group). Enter the email address of the recipient and send the message.

To Move an Appointment to a Different Time on the Same Day

1 CONFIGURE CALENDAR OPTIONS | **2 CREATE & MANIPULATE APPOINTMENTS** | 3 SCHEDULE EVENTS
4 SCHEDULE MEETINGS | 5 PRINT CALENDAR | 6 SAVE & SHARE CALENDAR

Suppose that you cannot attend the Health Physical appointment at 9:00 AM on October 13, 2017. The appointment needs to be rescheduled to 11:00 AM for the same amount of time. **Why?** *Instead of deleting and then retyping the appointment, you can drag it to a new time slot.* The following step moves an appointment to a new time slot.

- If necessary, click a scroll arrow on the Calendar in the Navigation Pane until October 2017 is displayed in the calendar on the Date Navigator.

- Click 13 in the October 2017 calendar on the Date Navigator to display the selected date in the appointment area.

- Drag the Health Physical appointment from 9:00 AM to the 11:00 AM time slot on the same day to reschedule the appointment (Figure 2–54).

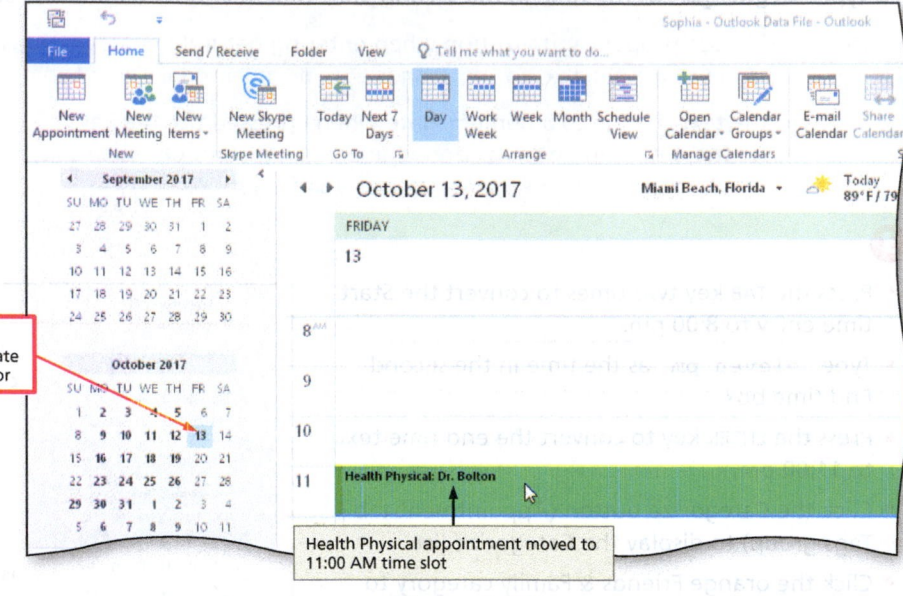

Figure 2–54

Other Ways

1. Double-click appointment, change time   2. Press CTRL+O, change time

BTW

Moving a Recurring Appointment

If you move a recurring appointment, you move only the selected instance of the appointment. To move all instances of a recurring appointment, open the appointment, click the Recurrence button (Appointment Series tab | Options group), and then change the recurrence pattern.

To Move an Appointment to a Different Date

1 CONFIGURE CALENDAR OPTIONS | **2 CREATE & MANIPULATE APPOINTMENTS** | 3 SCHEDULE EVENTS
4 SCHEDULE MEETINGS | 5 PRINT CALENDAR | 6 SAVE & SHARE CALENDAR

Why? *If you are moving an appointment to a new date at the same time, you can drag the appointment to the new date on the Date Navigator instead of retyping it.* The following step moves an appointment to a new date in the same time slot.

- Drag the Health Physical appointment on October 13, 2017 to October 20, 2017 on the Date Navigator to move the appointment to a new date (Figure 2–55).

Figure 2–55

To Delete a Single Occurrence of a Recurring Appointment

Because your school is closed for a Fall Break holiday on November 6, 2017, no classes will meet during that day. The following steps delete a single occurrence of a recurring appointment. *Why? Occasionally, appointments are canceled and must be deleted from the schedule.*

1

- Click the forward navigation arrow in the Date Navigator until November 2017 is displayed.
- Click **6** in the November 2017 calendar on the Date Navigator to display the selected date in the appointment area.
- If necessary, scroll down and click the class, ENG 102, scheduled for November 6, 2017, to select the appointment and display the Calendar Tools Appointment Series tab (Figure 2–56).

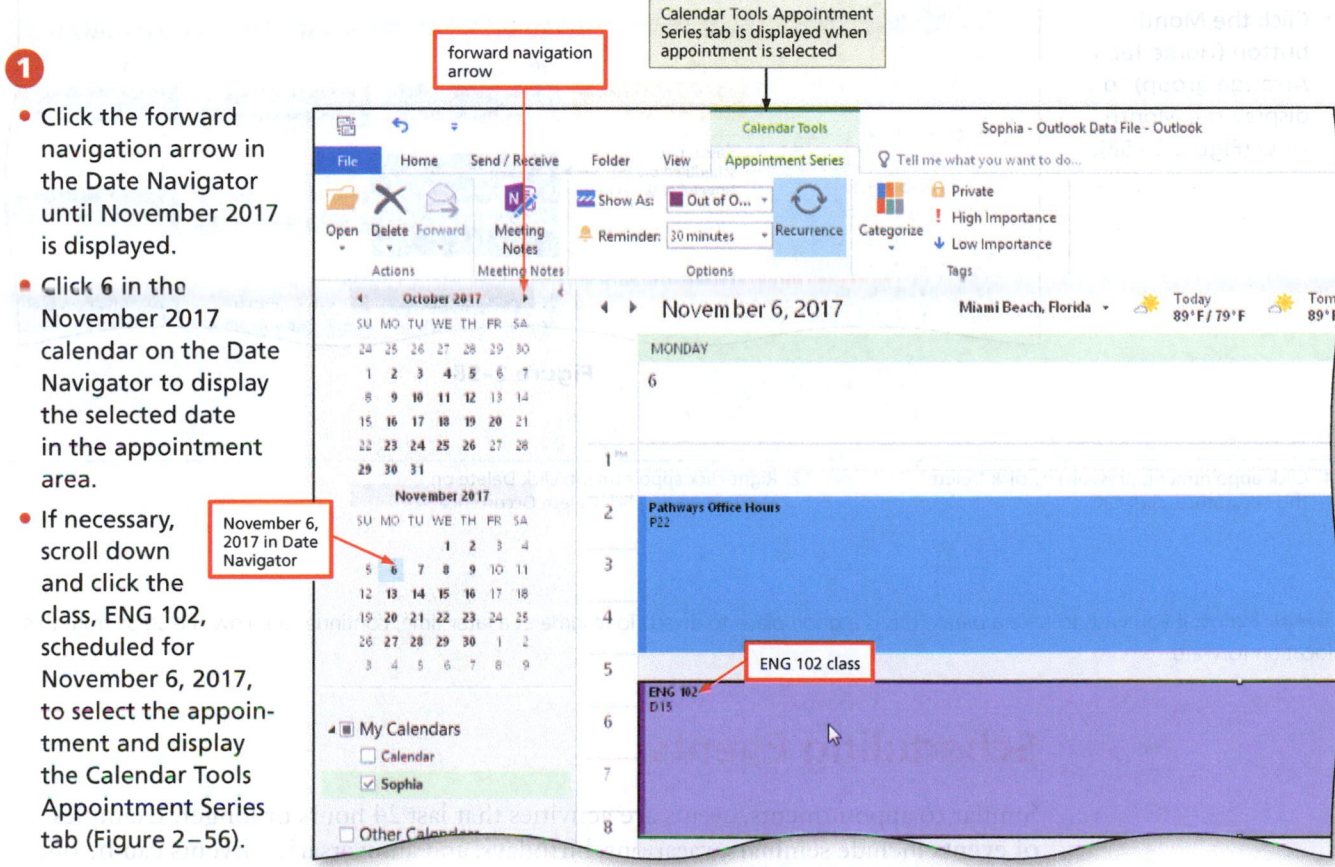

Figure 2–56

2

- Click the Delete button (Calendar Tools Appointment Series tab | Actions group) to display the Delete list (Figure 2–57).

Figure 2–57

3

- Click Delete Occurrence on the Delete list to delete only the selected occurrence (single appointment) from the calendar.
- Click the Month button (Home tab | Arrange group) to display the Month view (Figure 2–58).

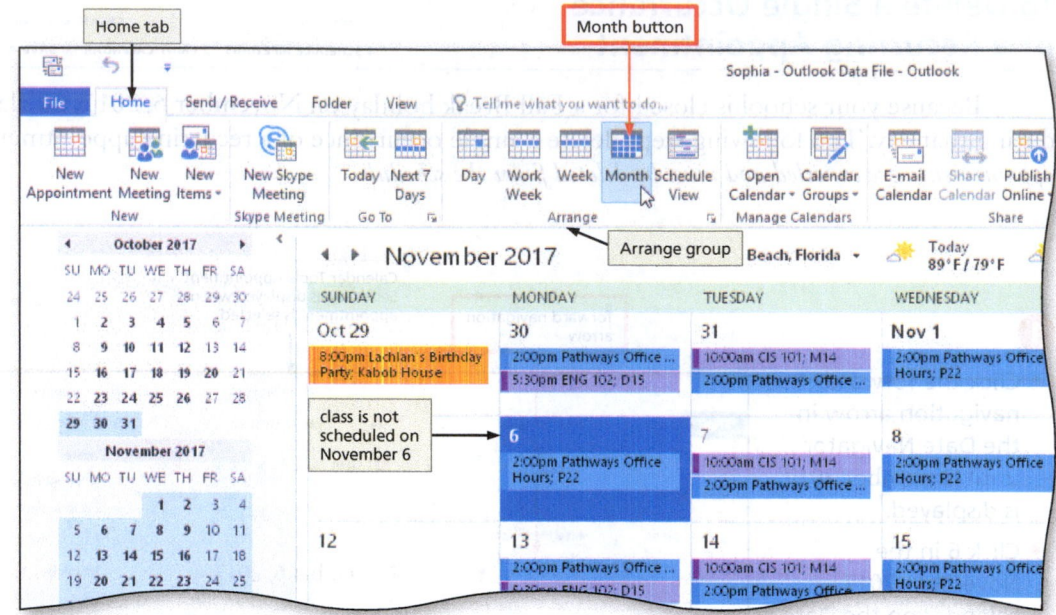

Figure 2–58

Other Ways

1. Click appointment, press DELETE, click Delete this occurrence, click OK

2. Right-click appointment, click Delete on shortcut menu, click Delete Occurrence

Break Point: If you wish to take a break, this is a good place to do so. To resume at a later time, continue to follow the steps from this location forward.

Scheduling Events

Similar to appointments, events are activities that last 24 hours or longer. Examples of events include seminars, vacations, birthdays, and anniversaries. Events can be one-time or recurring and differ from appointments in one primary way — they do not appear in individual time slots in the appointment area. Instead, the event description appears in a small banner below the day heading. As with an appointment, the event status can be free, busy, tentative, or out of the office and categorized according to the type of event. An all-day appointment displays your time as busy when viewed by other people, but an event or annual event displays your time as free. By default, all-day events occur from midnight to midnight.

To Create a One-Time Event in the Appointment Window

1 CONFIGURE CALENDAR OPTIONS | **2 CREATE & MANIPULATE APPOINTMENTS** | 3 SCHEDULE EVENTS
4 SCHEDULE MEETINGS | 5 PRINT CALENDAR | 6 SAVE & SHARE CALENDAR

Why? *An event represents an appointment that is scheduled over a period of days such as a conference.* The Pathways Internship Fair is being held at Hamblen Hall on October 6 but Sophia is assisting with the setup starting on October 5, so she wants to block out both days for the event. Because the Internship Fair will last for a couple days, Outlook will schedule the conference as an event. Sophia will be at Hamblen Hall both days, so she decides to show her time for the event as Out of Office. The following steps create an event on the calendar.

1

● Click the New Items button (Home tab | New group) to display the New Items list (Figure 2–59).

Figure 2–59

2

● Click 'All Day Event' to open the Untitled – Event window.

● Type **Internship Fair** in the Subject text box, and then press the TAB key to move the insertion point to the Location text box.

● Type **Hamblen Hall** as the location of the event.

● Click the Start time calendar button to display the Start time calendar.

● If necessary, display the October 2017 calendar.

● Click 5 in the October 2017 calendar to display Thu 10/5/2017 as the day the Internship Fair setup begins (Figure 2–60).

Figure 2–60

Q&A | Can I create an event by checking the 'All day event' check box in an appointment?

Yes. Click the New Appointment button (Home tab | New group) and then click 'All day event' to create an event.

③

- Click the End time calendar button to display the End time calendar.
- Click 6 in the October 2017 calendar to set the end date.
- Click the Show As box arrow (Event tab | Options group) to display the Show As list of event status options.
- Click Out of the Office to set the event status.
- Click the Categorize button (Event tab | Tags group) to display the Categorize list of color categories.
- Click Work to assign the event to a category (Figure 2–61).

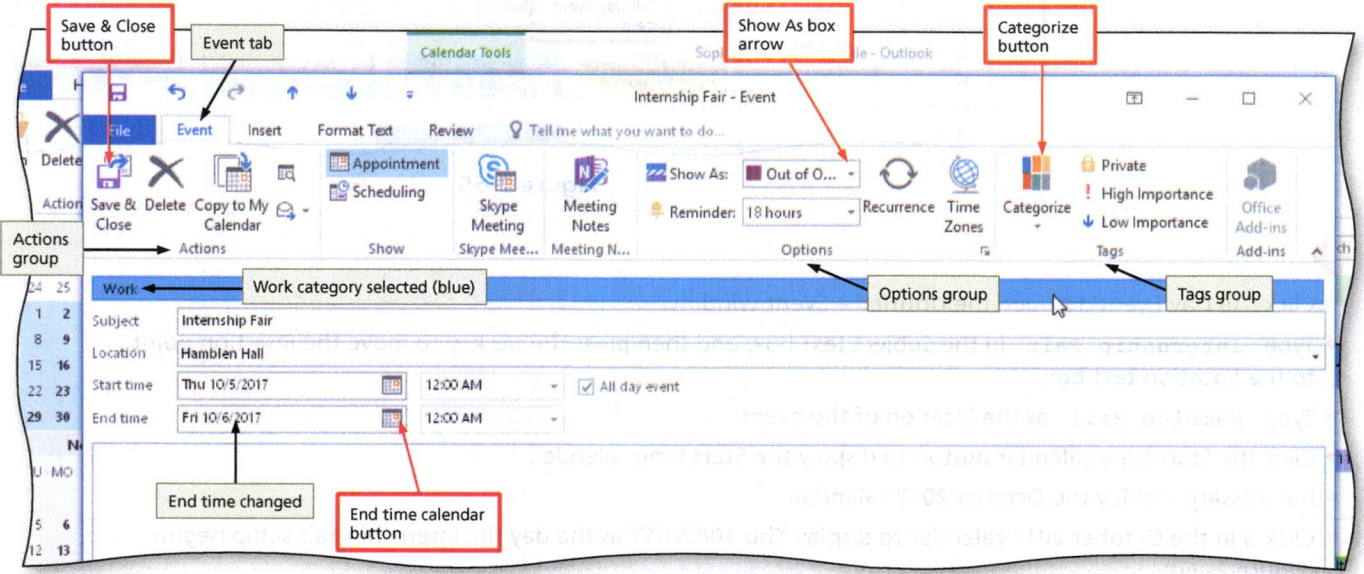

Figure 2–61

Why does the Show As box originally display the time as Free?
The default Show As appointment status for events is Free because events do not occupy blocks of time during the day on the calendar.

④

- Click the Save & Close button (Event tab | Actions group) to save the event and close the window.
- Click 5 in the October 2017 calendar on the Date Navigator to display the selected date in the appointment area (Figure 2–62).

Figure 2–62

Why is the Internship Fair event displayed at the top of the Day view of the calendar?
Events do not occupy time slots on the Day view of the calendar, so they appear as banners at the top of the calendar on the day they occur.

To Delete a One-Time Event

1 CONFIGURE CALENDAR OPTIONS | 2 CREATE & MANIPULATE APPOINTMENTS | 3 SCHEDULE EVENTS
4 SCHEDULE MEETINGS | 5 PRINT CALENDAR | 6 SAVE & SHARE CALENDAR

Ms. Pauley, the Internship Office director, decides that the Internship Fair must be cancelled due to a conflict with another event in the local area. *Why? Because the schedule has changed, the Internship Fair event is cancelled but will be rescheduled later in the semester.* The following step deletes an event from your calendar.

- Click the Internship Fair event banner in the appointment area of the calendar to select it and to display the Calendar Tools Appointment tab on the ribbon.

- Click the Delete button (Calendar Tools Appointment tab | Actions group) to delete the Internship Fair event from the calendar (Figure 2–63).

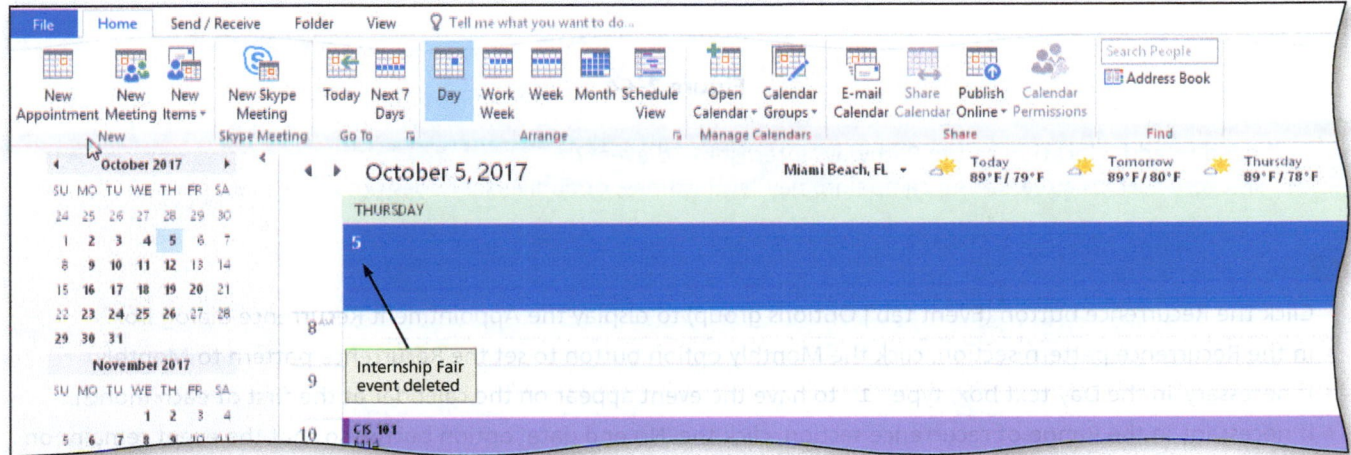

Figure 2–63

Other Ways

1. Select event, press DELETE

To Create a Recurring Event Using the Appointment Window

1 CONFIGURE CALENDAR OPTIONS | 2 CREATE & MANIPULATE APPOINTMENTS | 3 SCHEDULE EVENTS
4 SCHEDULE MEETINGS | 5 PRINT CALENDAR | 6 SAVE & SHARE CALENDAR

A recurring event is similar to a recurring appointment in that it occurs at regular intervals on your calendar. However, editing a recurring event is slightly different from editing one-time events. You can specify whether all occurrences in a series of recurring events need to be changed or if a single occurrence should be altered.

On the first day of each month, the college highlights an internship opportunity that Sophia wants to add to the calendar to keep track of when to prepare the marketing campaign for the internship. The following steps create a recurring event for the internship opportunity. *Why? To keep up with a periodic event such as your monthly or weekly occasion, the recurring event feature gives you a way to remind yourself of important dates.*

- Click the New Items button (Home tab | New group) to display the New Items list.
- Click 'All Day Event' to open the Untitled – Event window.
- In the Subject text box, type `Pathways Internship Ad` as the subject.
- In the first Start time text box, type `10/01/2017` as the date, and then press the ENTER key (Figure 2–64).

Figure 2–64

Do I need to add a location to the Pathways Internship Ad event?

No, an event such as a marketing campaign, payday, birthday, or anniversary does not have a location.

2

- Click the Recurrence button (Event tab | Options group) to display the Appointment Recurrence dialog box.
- In the Recurrence pattern section, click the Monthly option button to set the Recurrence pattern to Monthly.
- If necessary, in the Day text box, type 1 to have the event appear on the calendar at the first of each month.
- If necessary, in the Range of recurrence section, click the 'No end date' option button so that the event remains on the calendar indefinitely (Figure 2–65).

Figure 2–65

3

- Click the OK button to accept the recurrence settings and close the Appointment Recurrence dialog box.
- Click the Reminder box arrow (Recurring Event tab | Options group) to display the Reminder list of reminder time slots.
- Click None to remove the reminder from the event.
- Click the Categorize button (Recurring Event tab | Tags group) to display the Categorize list of color categories.
- Click the blue Work category to assign the event to a category (Figure 2–66).

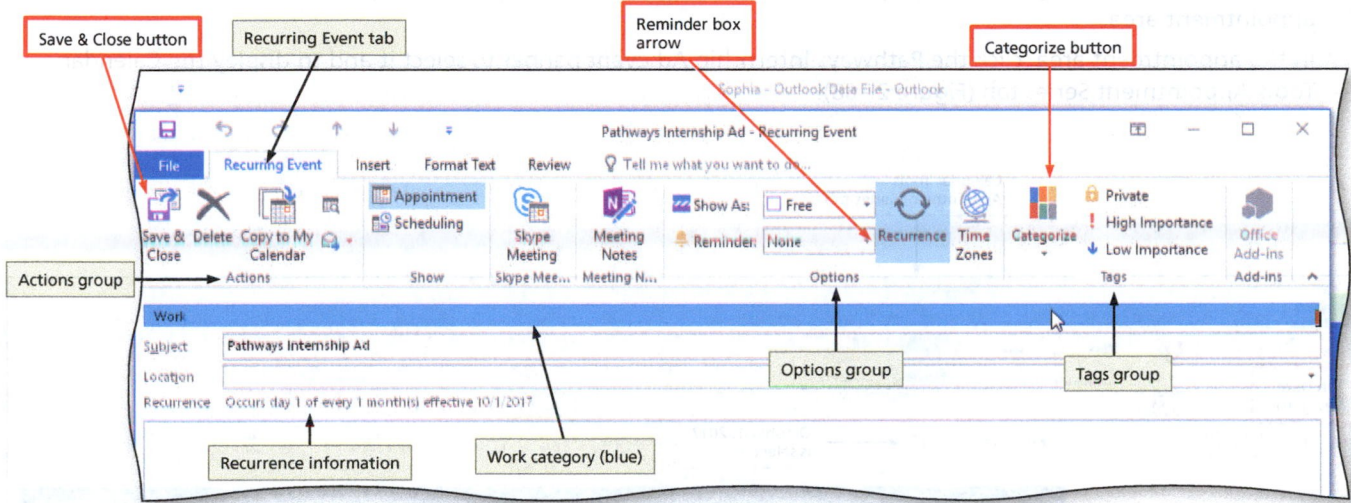

Figure 2–66

4

- Click the Save & Close button (Recurring Event tab | Actions group) to save the event and close the window.
- Click the Month button (Home tab | Arrange group) to view the Pathways Internship Ad event on the calendar (Figure 2–67).

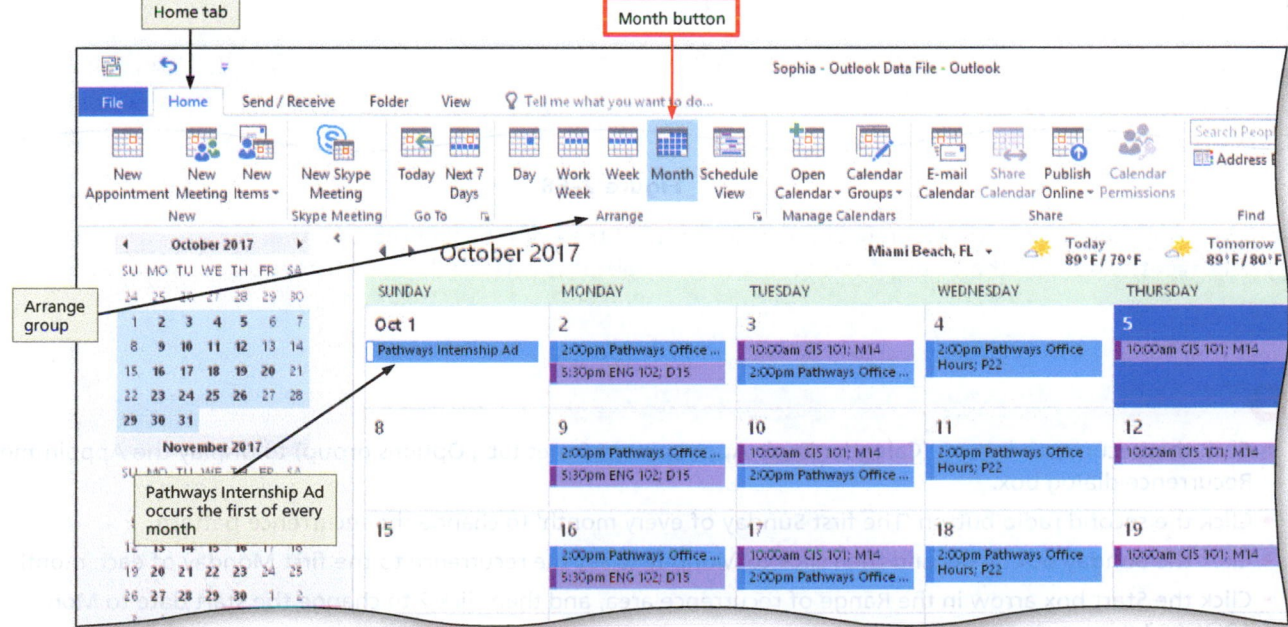

Figure 2–67

To Move a Recurring Event to a Different Day

Why? *A recurring date may change to a different day or duration.* The Internship Office Sophia works for is changing the internship ad rollout to the first Monday of each month. The recurring Pathways Internship Ad event must be changed for the entire series. The following steps change the date for all occurrences in a series.

- Click the Day button (Home tab | Arrange group) to display the Day view.
- Click 1 in the Date Navigator to display October 1, 2017 and the Pathways Internship Ad event banner in the appointment area.
- In the appointment area, click the Pathways Internship Ad event banner to select it and to display the Calendar Tools Appointment Series tab (Figure 2–68).

Figure 2–68

Q&A | What does the double arrow symbol on the right side of the event banner represent?
The event appears in the Outlook calendar with a double arrow symbol to show that it is a recurring appointment.

②

- Click the Recurrence button (Calendar Tools Appointment Series tab | Options group) to display the Appointment Recurrence dialog box.
- Click the second radio button 'The first Sunday of every month' to change the recurrence pattern.
- Click the Sunday box arrow and then click to Monday to set the recurrence to the first Monday of each month.
- Click the Start box arrow in the Range of recurrence area, and then click 2 to change the start date to Mon 10/2/2017 (Figure 2–69).

Figure 2–69

❸

- Click the OK button to close the Appointment Recurrence dialog box and change the event day.
- Click the Month button (Home tab | Arrange group) to view the full month calendar (Figure 2–70).

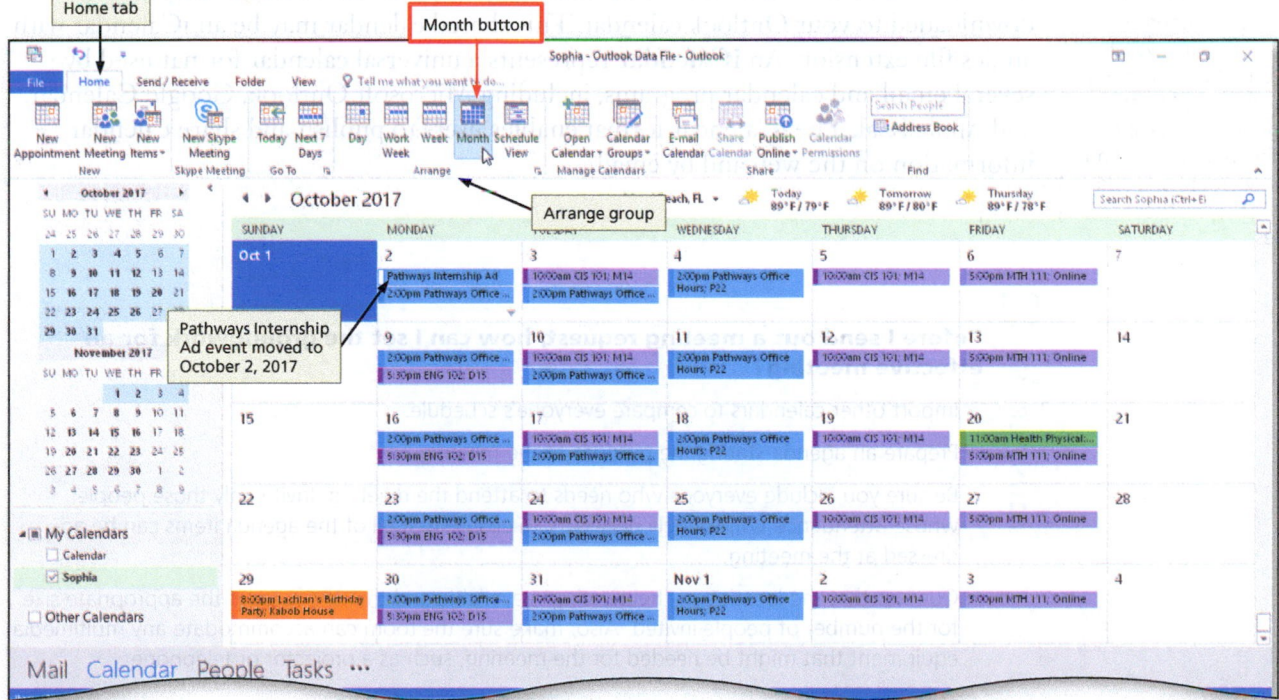

Figure 2–70

Other Ways

1. Double-click event, click entire series option button, click Recurrence button

2. Click event, press CTRL+O, click entire series option button, click Recurrence button

TO DELETE A RECURRING EVENT

Deleting a recurring event is similar to deleting a recurring appointment. If you choose to delete a recurring event, you would use the following steps.

1. Click the scroll arrow on the Date Navigator to display the date of the event.
2. Click the event to display the Calendar Tools Appointment Series tab.
3. Click the Delete button (Calendar Tools Appointment Series tab | Actions group) to display the Delete menu.
4. Click Delete Series on the Delete menu to delete the event from the calendar.

Scheduling Meetings

As defined earlier, a meeting is an appointment that you invite other people to attend. Each person who is invited can accept, accept as tentative, or decline a meeting request. A meeting also can include resources such as conference rooms. The person who creates the meeting and sends the invitations is known as the **meeting organizer**. The meeting organizer schedules a meeting by creating a **meeting request**, which is an email invitation to the meeting and arrives in each attendee's Inbox. Responses to a meeting request arrive in the Inbox of the meeting organizer. To create a meeting request, you use the Untitled – Meeting request window, which is similar to the Untitled – Appointment window with a few exceptions. The meeting request window includes the To text box, where you enter an email address for **attendees**, who are people invited to the meeting, and the Send button, which sends the invitation for the meeting to the attendees. When a meeting request arrives in the attendee's Inbox, it displays an icon different from an email message icon.

Before you invite others to a meeting, confirm that the meeting date and time are available. Your school or business may have shared calendars that can be downloaded to your Outlook calendar. This shared calendar may be an iCalendar with an .ics file extension. An **iCalendar** represents a universal calendar format used by several email and calendar programs, including Microsoft Outlook, Google Calendar, and Apple iCal. The iCalendar format enables users to publish and share calendar information on the web and by email.

If you are using your finger on a touch screen and are having difficulty completing the steps in this module, consider using a stylus. Many people find it easier to be precise with a stylus than with a finger. In addition, with a stylus you see the pointer. If you still are having trouble completing the steps with a stylus, try using a mouse.

BTW

Scheduling Assistant
If you have an Exchange account, you can use the **Scheduling Assistant** to find a meeting time when attendees and resources, such as rooms, are available. When you set up a meeting and are connected to an Exchange server, click the Scheduling button (Meeting tab | Show group) and add attendees to view their schedules.

CONSIDER THIS

Before I send out a meeting request, how can I set the groundwork for an effective meeting?

• Import other calendars to compare everyone's schedule.

• Prepare an agenda stating the purpose of the meeting.

• Be sure you include everyone who needs to attend the meeting. Invite only those people whose attendance is absolutely necessary to ensure that all of the agenda items can be addressed at the meeting.

• Confirm that the location of the meeting is available and that the room is the appropriate size for the number of people invited. Also, make sure the room can accommodate any multimedia equipment that might be needed for the meeting, such as a projector or telephone.

To Import an iCalendar File

Before scheduling a meeting, you can open your school's calendar to view your availability. Your school has a shared calendar in the iCalendar format that contains the school's master schedule. The following steps import an iCalendar file into Outlook. *Why? By importing another calendar, you can compare available dates for a meeting.*

- Click the File tab on the ribbon to open the Backstage view.
- Click Open & Export to display the Open gallery (Figure 2–71).

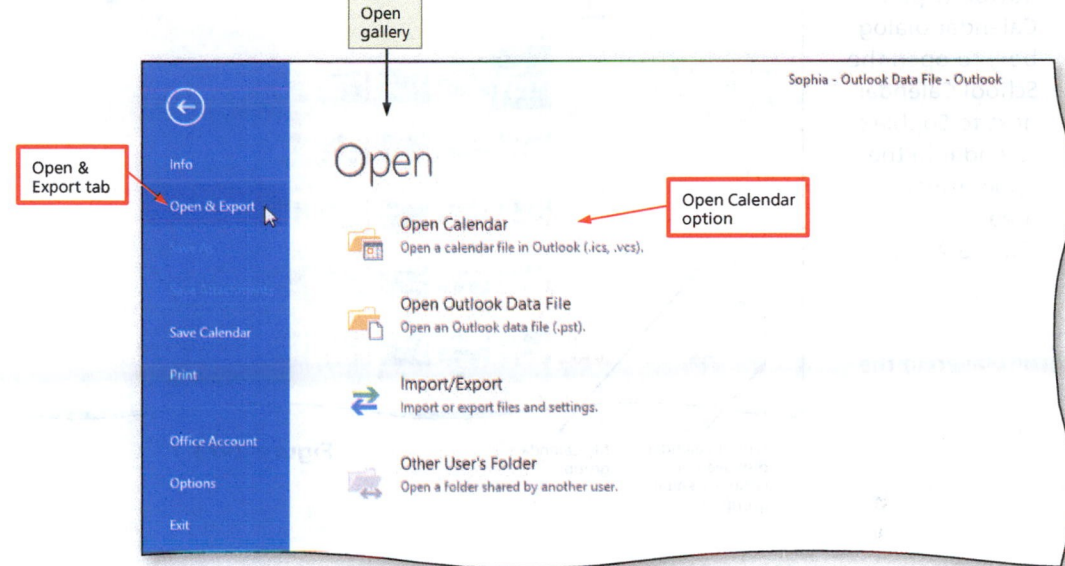

Figure 2–71

❷

- Click Open Calendar in the Open gallery to display the Open Calendar dialog box.
- Navigate to the mailbox location (in this case, the Module 02 folder in the Outlook folder) (Figure 2–72).

Figure 2–72

3

- Click School Calendar to select the file, and then click the OK button (Open Calendar dialog box) to open the School Calendar next to Sophia's calendar in the appointment area (Figure 2–73).

Why is the School Calendar not displayed in the My Calendar group?
Outlook organizes multiple calendars in groups. If you frequently work with a set of calendars, you can view them in groups. When you open an iCalendar, it initially might appear in an Other Calendars group.

Figure 2–73

To View Calendars in the Overlay Mode

1 CONFIGURE CALENDAR OPTIONS | 2 CREATE & MANIPULATE APPOINTMENTS | 3 SCHEDULE EVENTS
4 SCHEDULE MEETINGS | 5 PRINT CALENDAR | 6 SAVE & SHARE CALENDAR

Why? *Before Sophia schedules a meeting on her calendar, she may want to review her school's official calendar to avoid scheduling conflicts.* You can view multiple calendars at the same time side-by-side or combined into an overlay view to help you see which dates and times are available in all calendars. The following steps display both calendars in overlay mode and make the Sophia calendar the active calendar.

1

- Click the School Calendar arrow on the School Calendar tab to view the two calendars in overlay mode (Figure 2–74).

Figure 2–74

2

- Click the Sophia tab to display the Sophia calendar in front of the School Calendar (Figure 2–75).

Q&A

What happens if I click the arrow on Sophia's calendar at this point?
Outlook again displays the calendars side by side.

Figure 2–75

To View and Dock the Peek Calendar

1 CONFIGURE CALENDAR OPTIONS | 2 CREATE & MANIPULATE APPOINTMENTS | 3 SCHEDULE EVENTS
4 SCHEDULE MEETINGS | 5 PRINT CALENDAR | 6 SAVE & SHARE CALENDAR

The Outlook Navigation bar provides a **Peek** feature, a pop-up window that provides access to email, calendar, people, and tasks. **Why?** *Using the Peek feature, you can take a quick glance at your schedule without having to rearrange windows or lose your train of thought.* When you hover over Calendar in the Navigation Pane, a Peek calendar of the current month opens and the current date is highlighted with a blue background. The Peek calendar can be docked in the right pane of the calendar. Appointments and meetings scheduled for today appear below the calendar. The following steps view, dock, and remove the Peek calendar.

1

- Click the School Calendar check box in the Navigation Pane to remove the School Calendar from the Outlook window.

- Point to Calendar on the Navigation bar to display the Peek calendar with today's appointments or meetings (Figure 2–76).

Q&A

Why do I not see any appointments or meetings in the Peek calendar?
If you do not have any appointments or meetings today in the default Calendar, the Peek calendar does not display any calendar items.

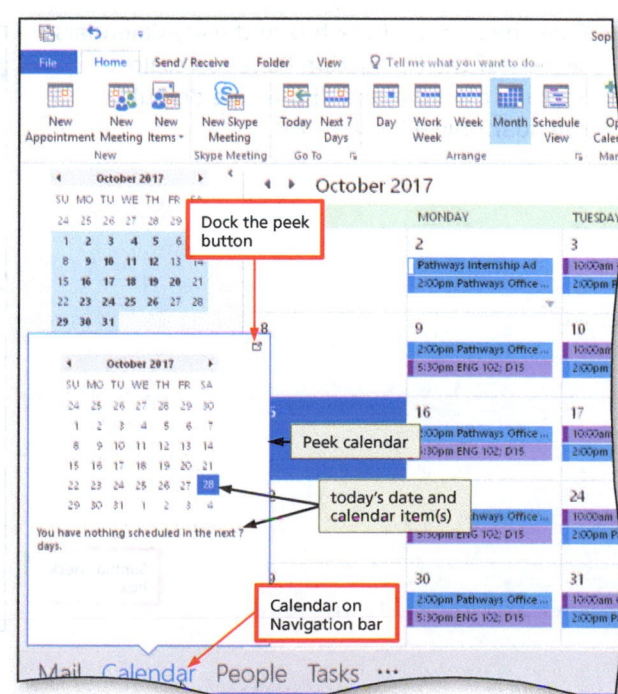

Figure 2–76

2

• Click the 'Dock the peek' button to dock the Peek calendar in the right pane of the Outlook window (Figure 2–77).

3

• Click the 'Remove the peek' button on the docked Peek calendar to remove the Peek calendar.

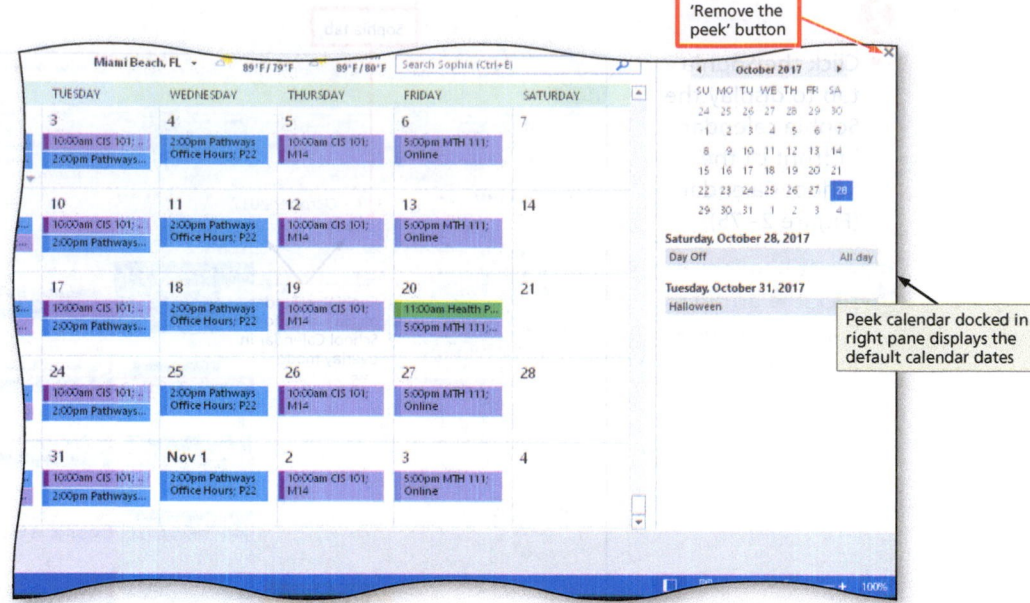

Figure 2–77

To Create and Send a Meeting Request

1 CONFIGURE CALENDAR OPTIONS | 2 CREATE & MANIPULATE APPOINTMENTS | 3 SCHEDULE EVENTS
4 SCHEDULE MEETINGS | 5 PRINT CALENDAR | 6 SAVE & SHARE CALENDAR

Why? *To find the best time to meet with other people, request a meeting, and keep track of the meeting date in your Inbox, you can send a meeting request in Outlook.* Sophia needs to meet with Ms. Pauley to discuss rescheduling the Pathways Internship Fair. Rather than send an email message requesting the meeting, she decides to use Outlook Calendar to create this meeting. Meetings can be scheduled on your default calendar or supplemental calendars. The following steps display the default calendar, create a meeting request, and send an invitation to the financial aid office. If you are completing this project on a personal computer, your email address must be set up in Outlook (see Module 1) so you can send an email meeting invitation. Use the email address of your instructor instead of the Ms. Pauley's email address.

1

• Click the Sophia check box in the My Calendars section of the Navigation Pane to deselect Sophia's calendar and display the default calendar only (Figure 2–78).

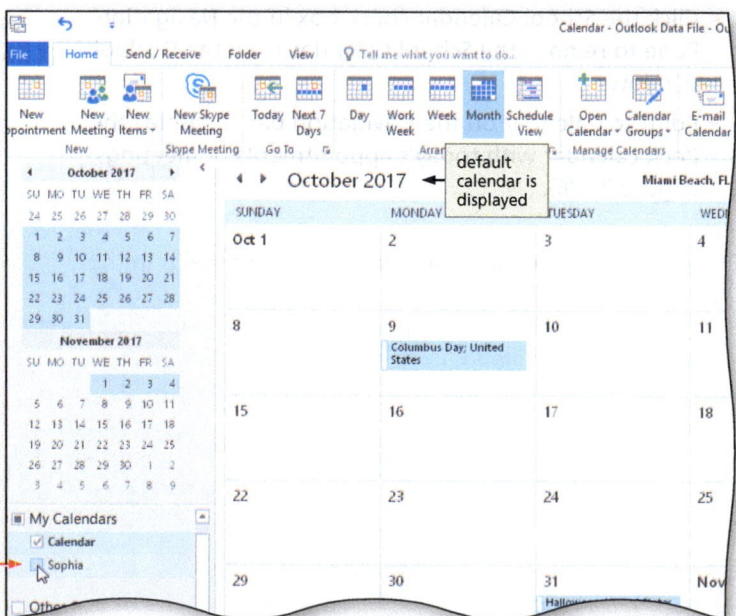

Figure 2–78

2

- Click the New Meeting button (Home tab | New group) to open the Untitled – Meeting window.
- Click the To text box and then type `ella.pauley@outlook.com` (substitute your instructor's email address for the email address) as the invitee to this meeting.
- Press the TAB key to move the insertion point to the Subject text box.
- Type `New Date for Pathways Internship Fair` as the subject of the meeting.
- Press the TAB key to move the insertion point to the Location text box.
- Type `P22` as the location of the meeting (Figure 2–79).

Figure 2–79

Q&A Why does the message header include the text, "You haven't sent this meeting invitation yet"?
This notice reminds you that you have not yet sent the invitation to the meeting. If you review this invitation after sending it, the notice no longer appears.

3

- Press the TAB key to select the date in the first Start time box.
- Type `10/2/2017` as the start date of the meeting, and then press the TAB key to select the time in the second Start time box.
- Type `1:30 PM` as the start time for the meeting, and then press the TAB key two times to select the time in the second End time box.
- Type `2:30 PM` as the end time for the meeting (Figure 2–80).

Figure 2–80

4

- Click the Send button to send the invitation and add the meeting to the calendar.

- If necessary, add an email account to Outlook to send the invitation to view the meeting on the calendar (Figure 2–81).

Q&A

When I sent the meeting request, an error message appeared that states "No valid email accounts are configured." Why did I get this error message?

A meeting request sends an email to each of the invitees. You must have an email account set up in Outlook to send the meeting request.

Figure 2–81

CONSIDER THIS

Is it possible to connect with my contacts using video or audio within Microsoft Outlook?

- Skype Meetings are integrated within Outlook by clicking the New Skype Meeting button (Home tab | Skype Meeting group). Using your Outlook contact list, you can call someone on their mobile, landline, or computer using video and audio capabilities. You do not need to be friends within Skype.

- Skype requires credit or subscription to reach landlines.

To Change the Time of a Meeting and Send an Update

1 CONFIGURE CALENDAR OPTIONS | 2 CREATE & MANIPULATE APPOINTMENTS | 3 SCHEDULE EVENTS
4 SCHEDULE MEETINGS | 5 PRINT CALENDAR | 6 SAVE & SHARE CALENDAR

Your schedule has changed, which means you need to change the time of the meeting about the Pathways Internship Fair and send an update about the change. Though the invitee can propose a new time, only the originator can change or delete the meeting. *Why? You can update any meeting request to add or remove attendees or resources, change the meeting to a recurring series, or move the meeting to a different date or time.* The following steps change the time of the meeting and send an update to the attendee. If you are completing this project on a personal computer, your email account must be set up in Outlook (see Module 1) to be able to view the meeting request.

1

- Double-click the meeting with Ms. Pauley (or your instructor) in the default calendar to open the New Date for Pathways Internship Fair – Meeting window.

- Click the Start time box arrow to display a list of times.

- Click 3:30 PM as the new start time for the meeting (Figure 2–82).

Figure 2–82

2

- Click the Send Update button in the message header to send the new information, close the meeting request, and view the updated meeting in the appointment area (Figure 2–83).

Q&A What if I need to cancel the meeting?
To remove a meeting, click the meeting in the appointment area to display the Calendar Tools Meeting tab, click the Cancel Meeting button (Calendar Tools Meeting tab | Actions group), and then click the Send Cancellation button to send the cancellation notice to the attendee and remove the meeting from the calendar.

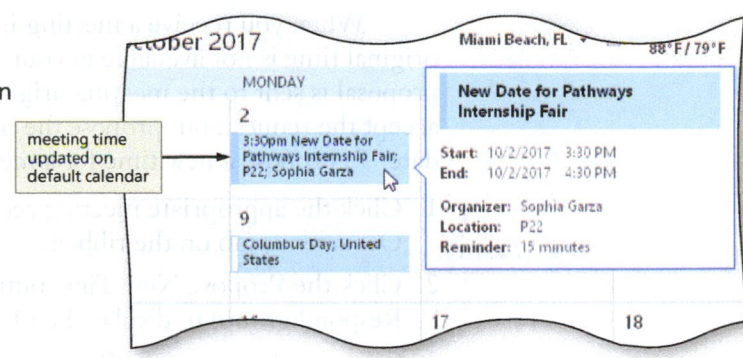

Figure 2–83

Other Ways

1. Drag meeting to new time, click 'Save changes and send update', click OK, click Send Update

To Reply to a Meeting Request

1 CONFIGURE CALENDAR OPTIONS | 2 CREATE & MANIPULATE APPOINTMENTS | 3 SCHEDULE EVENTS
4 SCHEDULE MEETINGS | 5 PRINT CALENDAR | 6 SAVE & SHARE CALENDAR

Ms. Pauley has received Sophia's meeting request in an email message and wants to respond. *Why? Outlook allows invitees to choose from four response options: Accept, Tentative, Decline, or Propose New Time.* The following steps accept the meeting request. If you have a meeting request in your personal email that is set up using Outlook, substitute your meeting request in the following steps. If you do not have any meeting requests, read these steps without performing them.

1

- Click Mail on the Navigation bar to display the Inbox folder.

- Double-click the email message header to open the meeting invitation (Figure 2–84).

Figure 2–84

2

- Click the Accept button (Meeting tab | Respond group) to display the options for accepting the meeting (Figure 2–85).

3

- Click Send the Response Now to send the accept response and add the meeting to the calendar.

Q&A What happened to the meeting invitation in the Inbox?
When you accept or tentatively accept a meeting request, the invitation is deleted from the Inbox and the meeting is added to your calendar. The meeting response is in the Sent Items folder.

What happens when I decline a meeting request?
When a meeting request is declined, it is removed from your Inbox and the meeting is not added to your calendar. The reply is placed in the Sent Items folder.

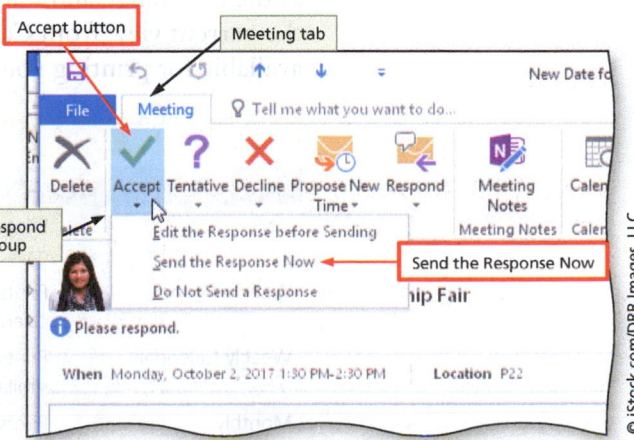

Figure 2–85

To Propose A New Meeting Time

When you receive a meeting invitation, you can propose a new time if the original time is not available in your calendar. When you propose a new time, a proposal is sent to the meeting originator via email, indicating that you tentatively accept the request, but propose the meeting be held at a different time or on a different date. To propose a new time for a meeting, you would perform the following steps.

1. Click the appropriate meeting request to display the Calendar Tools Meeting Occurrence tab on the ribbon.
2. Click the Propose New Time button (Calendar Tools Meeting Occurrence tab | Respond group) to display the Occurrence menu.
3. Click the Tentative and Propose New Time option to display the Propose New Time dialog box for the selected meeting.
4. Drag through the time slot that you want to propose, or enter the appropriate information in the Meeting start and Meeting end boxes (Propose New Time dialog box).
5. Click the Propose time button to open the New Time Proposed – Meeting Response window.
6. Click the Send button.

To Cancel A Meeting

To cancel a meeting, you would perform the following steps.

1. Click the meeting request in the appointment area to select the meeting and display the Calendar Tools Meeting tab on the ribbon.
2. Click the Cancel Meeting button (Calendar Tools Meeting tab | Actions group) to open the window for the selected meeting.
3. Click the Send Cancellation button in the message header to send the cancellation notice and delete the meeting from your calendar.

Printing Calendars in Different Views

All or part of a calendar can be printed in a number of different views, or **print styles**. You can print a monthly, daily, or weekly view of your calendar and select options such as the date range and fonts to use. You also can view your calendar in a list by changing the current view from Calendar view to List view. Table 2–6 lists the print styles available for printing your calendar from Calendar view.

Table 2–6 Print Styles for Calendar View	
Print Style	**Description**
Daily	Prints a daily appointment schedule for a specific date including one day per page, a daily task list, an area for notes, and a two-month calendar
Weekly Agenda	Prints a seven-day weekly calendar with one week per page and a two-month calendar
Weekly Calendar	Prints a seven-day weekly calendar with one week per page and an hourly schedule, similar to the Daily style
Monthly	Prints five weeks per page of a particular month or date range
Tri-fold	Prints a page for each day, including a daily task list and a weekly schedule
Calendar Details	Prints a list of calendar items and supporting details

To Print the Calendar in Weekly Calendar Style

Why? *Printing a calendar enables you to distribute the calendar to others in a form that can be read or viewed, but cannot be edited.* Sophia can print her calendar to create a hard copy of her first week of classes. The following steps print a calendar in a weekly calendar style.

1

- Click Calendar on the Navigation bar to display the Outlook calendar.

- If necessary, click the Sophia check box to display Sophia's calendar.

- If necessary, click the other check boxes to close the other calendars.

- Click the Go to Date Dialog Box Launcher (Home tab | Go To group) to display the Go To Date dialog box.

- Type 10/1/2017 in the Date text box to select that date.

- If necessary, click the Show in button, and then click Month Calendar to show the month view in the appointment area.

- Click the OK button to close the Go To Date dialog box (Figure 2–86).

Figure 2–86

2

- Click File on the ribbon to open the Backstage view.

- Click the Print tab in the Backstage view to display the Print gallery.

- Click Weekly Calendar Style in the Settings list to preview how the printed calendar will look in Weekly Calendar Style (Figure 2–87).

Figure 2–87

 Experiment

- Click the other settings to preview the different print styles. When finished, select Weekly Calendar Style.

3

- If necessary, click the desired printer to change the currently selected printer.
- Click the Print button in the Print gallery to print the calendar on the currently selected printer (Figure 2–88).

Q&A

How can I print multiple copies of my calendar?
Click the Print Options button to display the Print dialog box, increase the number in the Number of copies box, and then click the Print button to send the calendar to the printer and return to the calendar.

What if I decide not to print the calendar at this time?
Click File on the ribbon to close the Backstage view and return to the calendar window.

October 1, 2017 - October 7, 2017

Figure 2–88

Other Ways

1. Press CTRL+P, press ENTER

To Change the Calendar View to List View

1 CONFIGURE CALENDAR OPTIONS | 2 CREATE & MANIPULATE APPOINTMENTS | 3 SCHEDULE EVENTS | 4 SCHEDULE MEETINGS | 5 PRINT CALENDAR | 6 SAVE & SHARE CALENDAR

By default, the Outlook calendar is displayed in Calendar view, but other options include a List view, which displays the calendar as a table with each row displaying a unique calendar item. *Why? To display all of your calendar appointments, events, and meetings, change the current Calendar view to List view.* The following steps change the view from Calendar view to List view.

1

- Click View on the ribbon to display the View tab.
- Click the Change View button (View tab | Current View group) to display the Change View gallery (Figure 2–89).

Figure 2–89

2

- Click List in the Change View gallery to display a list of calendar items in the appointment area (Figure 2–90).

Sophia's calendar displayed in List view

Figure 2–90

To Print the Calendar in List View

To print a list of your calendar items in a table, print the List view display. The following steps print the calendar in Table style.

1 Click File on the ribbon to open the Backstage view.

2 Click the Print tab in the Backstage view to display the Print gallery.

3 Click the Table Style option in the Settings list to preview the calendar in Table Style.

4 If necessary, click the Printer box to display a list of available printer options, and then click the desired printer to change the selected printer.

5 Click the Print button to send the list of appointments to the selected printer (Figure 2–91).

Q&A When I changed the view from List view to Calendar view, why did the Calendar display the current date and not the date I printed?

The calendar always displays the current date when you change from List view to Calendar view.

BTW

Changing Settings before Printing
To change the margins, page orientation, or paper size before printing, click the Print Options button in the Print gallery and then click the Page Setup button to display the Page Setup: Table Style dialog box.

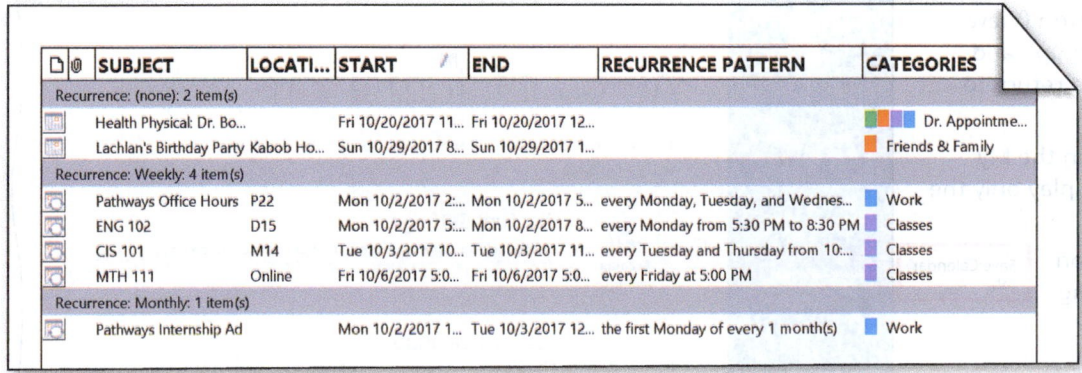

		SUBJECT	LOCATI...	START	END	RECURRENCE PATTERN	CATEGORIES
		Recurrence: (none): 2 item(s)					
		Health Physical: Dr. Bo...		Fri 10/20/2017 11...	Fri 10/20/2017 12...		Dr. Appointme...
		Lachlan's Birthday Party	Kabob Ho...	Sun 10/29/2017 8...	Sun 10/29/2017 1...		Friends & Family
		Recurrence: Weekly: 4 item(s)					
		Pathways Office Hours	P22	Mon 10/2/2017 2:...	Mon 10/2/2017 5...	every Monday, Tuesday, and Wednes...	Work
		ENG 102	D15	Mon 10/2/2017 5:...	Mon 10/2/2017 8...	every Monday from 5:30 PM to 8:30 PM	Classes
		CIS 101	M14	Tue 10/3/2017 10...	Tue 10/3/2017 11...	every Tuesday and Thursday from 10:...	Classes
		MTH 111	Online	Fri 10/6/2017 5:0...	Fri 10/6/2017 5:0...	every Friday at 5:00 PM	Classes
		Recurrence: Monthly: 1 item(s)					
		Pathways Internship Ad		Mon 10/2/2017 1...	Tue 10/3/2017 12...	the first Monday of every 1 month(s)	Work

Figure 2–91

Other Ways

1. Press CTRL+P, click Print

BTW
Distributing a Calendar
Instead of printing and distributing a hard copy of a calendar, you can distribute the calendar electronically. Options include sending the calendar via email; posting it on cloud storage (such as OneDrive) and sharing the file with others; posting it on a social networking site, blog, or other website; and sharing a link associated with an online location of the calendar. You also can create and share a PDF or XPS image of the calendar, so that users can view the file in Acrobat Reader or XPS Viewer instead of in Outlook.

Saving and Sharing the Calendar

For security and convenience, you can save your Outlook calendar by backing up your entire Outlook personal folder files (.pst) or an individual calendar (.ics). As a reminder, in Module 1 you saved the Outlook .pst file, which contained a backup of your email, calendar, and contacts. Saving your calendar file allows you to back up your appointments, events, and meetings in a single file. You can then move your calendar to another computer, for example, and continue to schedule items there. Besides saving your calendar, you can share it with others, whether they use Outlook or not. Finally, scheduling a meeting with someone who cannot see your calendar can be difficult, so you can share your calendar through email.

With Outlook, each appointment, task, or contact can be saved as a separate iCalendar file or you can save the whole calendar to your local computer or external storage device. An iCalendar file with the .ics file extension can be imported by other programs such as Google Calendar. Instead of emailing an iCalendar file as an attachment to share your calendar, you can share portions of your entire calendar through a built-in function in Outlook.

To Save a Calendar as an iCalendar File

1 CONFIGURE CALENDAR OPTIONS | 2 CREATE & MANIPULATE APPOINTMENTS | 3 SCHEDULE EVENTS
4 SCHEDULE MEETINGS | 5 PRINT CALENDAR | **6 SAVE & SHARE CALENDAR**

You have performed many tasks while creating this calendar and do not want to risk losing work completed thus far. Accordingly, you should save the calendar on your hard disk, OneDrive, or a location that is most appropriate to your situation.

The following steps assume you already have created folders for storing your files, for example, an Outlook folder (for your class) that contains a Module 02 folder (for your assignments). Thus, these steps save the calendar in the Module 02 folder in the Outlook folder in your desired save location. For a detailed example of the procedure for saving a file in a folder or saving a file on OneDrive, refer to the Office and Windows module at the beginning of this book.

Why? *By saving a copy of your calendar to an iCalendar format, you can back up or share your calendar with your business colleagues or friends.* The following steps save a calendar. They assume you already have created folders for storing your files, for example, an Outlook folder (for your class) that contains a Module 02 folder (for your assignments).

- Click View on the ribbon, click the Change View button (View tab | Current View group), and then click Calendar to return to Calendar view.
- Use the check boxes in the My Calendars pane to display only the Sophia calendar.
- Click File on the ribbon to display the Backstage view (Figure 2–92).

Figure 2–92

2

- Click the Save Calendar tab to display the Save As dialog box.
- Navigate to the desired save location (in this case, the Module 02 folder in the Outlook folder or your class folder) (Figure 2–93).

Figure 2–93

3

- Click the More Options button to display the Save As dialog box.
- Click the Date Range arrow to display the Date Range list (Figure 2–94).

4

- If necessary, click Whole calendar on the Date Range list to save the calendar's full details.
- Click the OK button (Save As dialog box) to specify the whole calendar date range.
- Click the Save button to save the calendar as an iCalendar file in the selected location.

Figure 2–94

1 CONFIGURE CALENDAR OPTIONS | 2 CREATE & MANIPULATE APPOINTMENTS | 3 SCHEDULE EVENTS
4 SCHEDULE MEETINGS | 5 PRINT CALENDAR | 6 SAVE & SHARE CALENDAR

To Share a Calendar

Ms. Pauley, the director of the Pathways Internship Office, needs to meet with Sophia to reschedule the fair. She requests a copy of Sophia's calendar. *Why? Sophia can send a copy of her calendar in an email message directly from Outlook to inform Ms. Pauley when she is available for a meeting.* The following steps share a calendar by forwarding the selected calendar. These steps assume you have an email account set up in Outlook.

1

- Click Home on the ribbon to display the Home tab.
- Click the E-mail Calendar button (Home tab | Share group) to open the Untitled – Message (HTML) window and display the Send a Calendar via E-mail dialog box (Figure 2–95).

Figure 2–95

2

- Click the OK button to attach the Sophia calendar to the email message.
- Click the To text box, and then type `ella.pauley@outlook.com` (substitute your instructor's email address for Ms. Pauley's address) as the recipient's email address (Figure 2–96).

3

- Click the Send button to send your iCalendar to share with the email message recipient.
- Exit Outlook.

Q&A

When I sent the email with the calendar attachment, an error message opened stating that "No valid email accounts are configured." Why did I get this error message?
You must have an email account set up in Outlook to send the calendar.

Figure 2–96

Summary

In this module, you have learned how to use Outlook to create a personal schedule by entering appointments, creating recurring appointments, moving appointments to new dates, and scheduling events. You also learned how to invite attendees to a meeting, accept a meeting request, and change the time of a meeting. To review your schedule, you learned to view and print your calendar in different views and print styles. Finally, you learned how to save your calendar and share your schedule with others.

What decisions will you need to make when configuring the Outlook calendar; scheduling appointments, events, and meetings; printing calendars; and saving and sharing your calendar in the future?

1. Configure the Outlook Calendar:
    a. Determine the purpose of your calendar — personal, professional, or for a group.
    b. Determine the city displayed on the Weather Bar and if you prefer holidays in your default calendar.

2. Schedule appointments, events, and meetings:
    a. Determine if each calendar item is an appointment, event, or a meeting.
    b. Determine which appointments and events are one-time or recurring.
    c. Plan which color-coded categories would best organize your calendar items.

3. Edit appointments, events, and meetings:
    a. Update the details of your calendar items as your schedule changes.
    b. Respond to meeting requests.

4. Print your calendar:
    a. Plan which calendar style would best fit your needs.

5. Save and share your calendar:
    a. Plan where your calendar should be stored.
    b. Determine how you will share your calendar with friends and colleagues.

How should you submit solutions to questions in the assignments identified with a ✺ symbol?

Every assignment in this book contains one or more questions identified with a ✺ symbol. These questions require you to think beyond the assigned file. Present your solutions to the questions in the format required by your instructor. Possible formats may include one or more of these options: write the answer; create a document that contains the answer; present your answer to the class; discuss your answer in a group; record the answer as audio or video using a webcam, smartphone, or portable media player; or post answers on a blog, wiki, or website.

Apply Your Knowledge

Reinforce the skills and apply the concepts you learned in this module.

Note: To complete this assignment, you will be required to use the Data Files. Please contact your instructor for information about accessing the Data Files.

Updating a Calendar

Instructions: Run Outlook. You are updating the Athletic Boosters iCalendar named Apply 2-1 Athletic Boosters Calendar, which is located in the Data Files, by revising the scheduled activities.

Perform the following tasks:

1. Open the Apply 2-1 Athletic Boosters Calendar.ics file from the Data Files.

2. Display only this iCalendar in the Outlook Calendar window. Use Month view to display the calendar for March 2017.

3. Add a monthly Athletic Boosters Meeting appointment for the first Wednesday of each month starting at 2 PM and lasting for one hour from March through December 2017.

4. Change the color category of the monthly Athletic Boosters Meeting to orange.

5. Change the Senior Night appointment from March 10 to March 17. Move the appointment to one hour later with the same duration.

6. Change the location of the Ladies Basketball Awards appointment on March 18 to Hanel Hall.

Continued >

Apply Your Knowledge *continued*

7. Reschedule the Fundraising Meeting appointment from Thursdays starting on February 23 until April 13 to meet at the same time on Mondays starting on March 6 until April 17.

8. Change the starting and ending time of the Athletic Booster Picnic on May 6 to two hours later.

Figure 2–97

9. If requested by your instructor, change the location of the picnic from Morristown Park to a park named after your birth city.

10. Save the Calendar as Apply 2-1 Athletic Boosters Updated and submit the iCalendar in the format specified by your instructor.

11. Print the final calendar in Month view, shown in Figure 2–97, and then submit the printout to your instructor.

12. Delete this calendar from Outlook and exit Outlook.

13. ✳ Most calendar programs save files with the .ics format. Why is it convenient that most calendar programs use the same format?

Extend Your Knowledge

Extend the skills you learned in this module and experiment with new skills. You may need to use Help to complete the assignment.

Creating and Sharing a Calendar

Instructions: Run Outlook. You are volunteering at a local animal shelter a couple days a week. Create a new calendar to share your availability to help at the shelter. Use Outlook Help to learn how to create a calendar group, change the color of the calendar, and create a private appointment.

Perform the following tasks:

1. Create a new calendar group called Pet Shelter.

2. Create a blank calendar named Volunteers and then move it to the Pet Shelter calendar group.

3. Change the color of the entire calendar to brown.

4. Add a recurring Feed Animals appointment from 5:00 PM to 6:30 PM on Monday and Wednesday beginning on June 5, 2017 and continuing for 20 occurrences at the Laredo Animal Shelter.

5. Create an event named Adoption Week starting on June 26, 2017 at the Laredo Animal Shelter lasting 7 days from this Monday to next Monday.

6. Add a recurring Post Animal of the Week Online as an All Day event starting on June 2 and lasting for 12 months on the first Friday of each month.

7. If requested by your instructor, change the Weather Bar to display weather information for your hometown. The completed calendar is shown in Figure 2–98.

8. Save the Calendar file as Extend Your Knowledge 2-1 Pet Shelter and submit the iCalendar in the format specified by your instructor.

9. Exit Outlook.

10. ☀ Think about the reason you might share your Outlook Calendar. In the case of sharing your schedule and other volunteer's calendars with the animal shelter, why would a digital calendar be more helpful to the director of the shelter instead of a paper schedule?

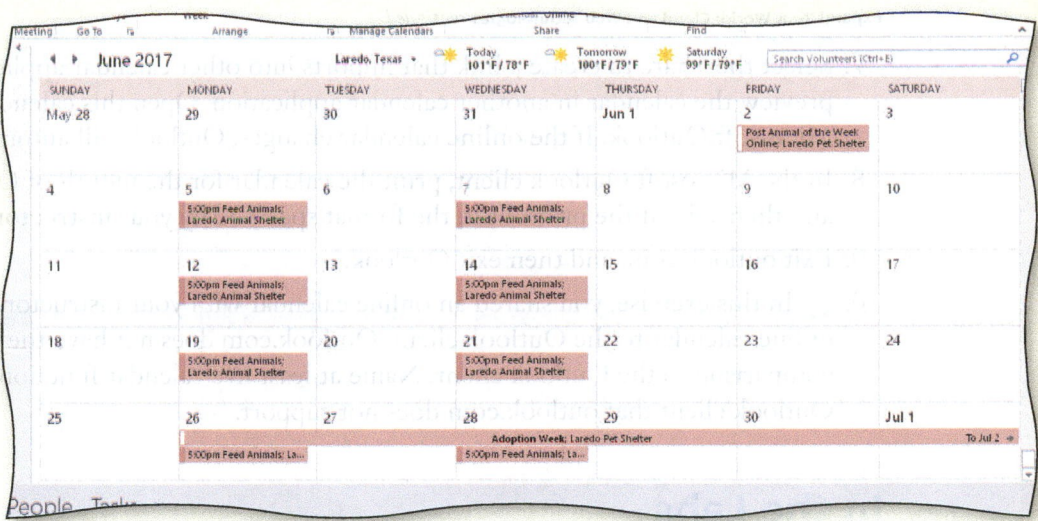

Figure 2–98

Expand Your World: Cloud and Web Technologies

Opening a Web-Based Calendar in the Outlook Client

Instructions: In your role as a barista at a new local coffee shop, you have been asked by the manager to assist with marketing the café on social media by posting to Facebook and Twitter. Use the calendar dates shown in Table 2–7 to create an online calendar at Outlook.com using your Microsoft account. Share the online calendar with your instructor. Using Outlook, open the online calendar and print the calendar in the Outlook client. Sharing your calendar in the cloud as a link allows anyone to see your calendar such as the café's manager, even if they do not have their own calendar established.

Perform the following tasks:

1. If necessary, create a Microsoft account at outlook.com.

2. Open the calendar option at outlook.com and add a calendar named Social Media for Coffee Shop Calendar with the description, `Online Marketing`.

3. Open the Social Media for Coffee Shop Calendar only and add the items shown in Table 2–7 to the online calendar.

4. If requested by your instructor, add a promotional calendar item on your birthday in 2017 titled Barista's Birthday — 1 Free Scone per Coffee Order.

5. Click the Share button to view the sharing options for this calendar. Select the option to send people a view-only link to access this calendar online. Select the ICS option to import into another calendar application to show event details.

6. Submit the outlook.com calendar link to view in a web browser in a format specified by your instructor.

Table 2–7 Social Media for Coffee Shop Calendar Items			
Description	**Recurrence**	**Due Date**	**Availability**
Pumpkin Latte Promotion	None	First Sunday in October 2017 at 5 AM	Free
Join the Jolt Frequent Customer Program	Monthly	First day of each month starting in October 2017 at midnight, never ends	Free
Happy Caffeine Hours	Mondays	Every Monday in October 2017 from 4:00 PM for 2 hours	Busy
Halloween Coffee Roasters 20% Off	None	October 31, 2017 All Day Event	Busy

Continued >

7. Select the 'share to create a link that imports into other calendar applications (ICS)' option to preview the calendar in another calendar application. Open this calendar link in the calendar in Microsoft Outlook. If the online calendar changes, Outlook will automatically update.

8. In the Microsoft Outlook client, print the calendar for the month of October in Monthly style, and then submit the printout in the format specified by your instructor.

9. Exit outlook.com, and then exit Outlook.

10. In this exercise, you shared an online calendar with your instructor and also imported the online calendar to the Outlook client. Outlook.com does not have the full functionality in comparison to the Outlook client. Name at least five calendar functions that are part of the Outlook client that outlook.com does not support.

In the Labs

Design, create, modify, and/or use files following the guidelines, concepts, and skills presented in this module. Labs 1 and 2, which increase in difficulty, require you to create solutions based on what you learned in the module; Lab 3 requires you to apply your creative thinking and problem-solving skills to design and implement a solution.

Lab 1: **Creating Recurring Events**

Problem: You would like to set up a calendar to remember to take care of your car scheduled maintenance, loan, cleaning, and, inspection as shown in Figure 2–99.

Figure 2–99

Perform the following tasks:

1. Create a Calendar named Lab 2-1 Car Maintenance Calendar in Outlook.

2. Create the events in the calendar in the year 2017, using the information listed in Table 2–8.

3. For each event, enter the location as local auto shop for the category Schedule Maintenance, otherwise leave the location blank.

4. For each event, show the time as Free.

5. For each event, set the reminder to one day.

6. For each monthly event, set the event to recur every month during 2017.

7. Each event should be an All Day event.

8. If requested by your instructor, add your favorite car model as a car show (for example, Mustang Car Show) on your birthday as an event in your 2017 Calendar.

9. Save the calendar as an .ics file and submit it in a format specified by your instructor.

10. Print the month of May using the Monthly Style and submit it in a format specified by your instructor.

11. ✳ A calendar can keep you organized. In the case of scheduling your car payment, how can a digital calendar assist in increasing your credit score?

Table 2–8 Car Maintenance Schedule			
Calendar Item	**Due Date**	**Category**	**Color Code**
Car Wash	First Saturday of each month	Cleaning	blue
Change Oil	Starting on January 2 and occurring every 120 days	Scheduled Maintenance	yellow
Car payment	5th day of the month	Payment	green
Add Antifreeze	October 15th	Scheduled Maintenance	yellow
Tire Rotation	January 2 and July 2	Scheduled Maintenance	yellow
New Tires	August 1	Scheduled Maintenance	yellow
Car inspection	May 30th	Tax and Scheduled Maintenance	red, yellow

Lab 2: **Creating a Calendar**

Problem: You were recently hired part-time by your local news station as a restaurant and events reviewer. By taking the time to develop a plan for your restaurant and event visits, as shown in Figure 2–100, you will remember to produce regular reviews for the news station.

Figure 2–100

Instructions: Open Outlook. Perform the following tasks:

1. Create a calendar named Lab 2-2 Event Reviewer Calendar in Outlook.

2. Create the appointments in the calendar, using the information listed in Table 2–9.

Table 2–9 Local Restaurant and Events Table				
Restaurant or Event	**Location**	**Event Date**	**Category**	**Color Code**
The Noodle Room	256 Adams Ave	May 6, 2017	Restaurant	red
Zig-Zag Concert	Pine Lake Stadium	May 11, 2017	Concert	green
Lori's Pizzeria	7800 Forest Lane	May 17, 2017	Restaurant	red
Forest Craft Festival	Crater Park	May 20, 2017	Festival	purple
Kelly's Irish Pub	129 45th St	May 22, 2017	Restaurant	red
Hall Pass Band	Pine Lake Stadium	May 26, 2017	Concert	green
Bingo Under the Stars	Crater Park	May 27, 2017	Other	yellow

Continued >

In the Labs *continued*

3. For each event in the table, set the reminder as 2 hours.

4. For each event, show the time as Tentative.

5. Set each restaurant dinner for 7:30 PM for one hour, concerts at 8 PM for two hours, festivals at noon for two hours, and other events at 7 PM for 2.5 hours.

6. For each Monday and Wednesday throughout the month of May 2017, add a recurring appointment. Enter **Write Reviews** as the subject. For location, enter **My Office**. Show the time as Busy. The appointment should start at 9:00 AM and end two hours later. Add all four color-coded categories and set a 10-minute reminder.

7. Delete the one occurrence of the recurring appointment on May 17.

8. If requested by your instructor, change your Weather Bar to show the weather for your hometown.

9. Save the calendar as an .ics file and submit it in a format specified by your instructor.

10. Print the calendar for the month of May in Monthly style, and then submit the printout in the format specified by your instructor.

11. ✳ What are the advantages of syncing your Outlook Calendar to a mobile phone?

Lab 3: **Creating a Personal Calendar and a Meeting Invitation**

Problem: You are meeting with your school advisor to plan next year's course schedule. She has requested that you create a personal calendar of the present semester listing your present classes, time, room numbers. In addition, add five other events that are scheduled with work, hobbies, or other activities.

Instructions: Open Outlook. Perform the following tasks:

1. Create a calendar named Lab 2-3 Personal Calendar in Outlook.

2. Create the appointments in the calendar based on your present class schedule with class names, locations, times, and a 10-minute reminder for each class.

3. Create at least four categories for your class types and associate each class type to the category.

4. Add the following meetings to the calendar and then send invitations for upcoming meetings to your instructor, as shown in Table 2–10. All the meetings are held in the Advisor's Office. Send a meeting invitation to yourself.

Table 2–10 Advisor Calendar Meetings				
Description	Date	Time	Show As	Reminder
Discuss Career Interest	June 3	1:00 PM – 2:00 PM	Out of Office	30 minutes
Class Schedule Selection	June 8	12:00 PM – 2:00 PM	Tentative	30 minutes

5. If requested by your instructor, add a third meeting titled **Class Performance** on June 2nd at 9:00 AM for one to meet with your instructor; include a one-day reminder and show as working elsewhere.

6. Save your calendar as an iCalendar named Lab 3-3 Personal Calendar. Submit your assignment in the format specified by your instructor.

Part 2: ✳ If you receive a meeting request, you can respond in several ways. What are the four ways to respond to a meeting request? You can add comments with each of these responses. Provide comments to each of the four meeting requests responses explaining why you can or cannot attend the meeting with your advisor.

Index

Note: **Boldfaced** page numbers indicate key terms

A

Access, **OFF 8**, **OFF 59**, OFF 59–60
creating databases, OFF 61–62
running, OFF 59–60
unique elements in, OFF 60–63
Access work area, **OFF 60**
accounts
email. See email accounts
Microsoft. See Microsoft accounts
signing in, OFF 6–7
active cell, **OFF 57**
active tab, **OFF 16**
add-in software, **PA-10**
address bar, **OFF 27**
Adobe Reader, OFF 23
animation emphasis effects, **PA-8**
app(s), **OFF 2**
exiting Office, OFF 41–42, OFF 53, OFF 59, OFF 63
Office Mix, PA-12
running and using. See running apps
switching between, OFF 30–31
appointment(s), **OUT 60**
changing status, OUT 81
creating in appointment area, OUT 73–74
creating using Appointment window, OUT 77–78
creating using natural language phrases, OUT 88–89
deleting single occurrence, OUT 91–92
moving, OUT 89–90
one-time, **OUT 73**, OUT 73–74
recurring. See recurring appointments
setting reminder, OUT 81–82
appointment area, **OUT 60**
appointment status, **OUT 78**
Appointment window
creating appointment using, OUT 77–78
creating one-time events, OUT 92–94
creating recurring events, OUT 95–97
attachment(s), **OUT 17**

attaching files to messages, OUT 36
opening, OUT 19, OUT 21
previewing and saving, OUT 19–20
Protected View in Microsoft Word, OUT 21
Attachment Preview, **OUT 19**
attendees, meetings, **OUT 100**
Augmented reality with Office Mix, teaching, PA-13
Auto Account Setup feature, OUT 15

B

BACKSPACE key, error correction, OFF 21
Backstage view, **OFF 22**
account information in, OUT 9
closing, OFF 31
closing Office using, OFF 52
creating new documents from, OFF 50–51
Info tab in, OFF 50
opening recent files using, OFF 52–53
backups, **OUT 21**
blank space between paragraph, OFF 21
blinking bar, OFF 21
blue wavy underline, OUT 31

C

Calendar, **OUT 58**
adding cities to Weather Bar, OUT 64–65
adding group, OUT 75
adding holidays to default, OUT 70–72
advantages of digital, OUT 59
appointments. See appointment(s)
color for, OUT 63
configuring, OUT 59
creating folder, OUT 61–63
deleting, OUT 72
deleting items permanently, OUT 58
distributing, OUT 112
entering locations, OUT 78

events. See events; one-time events; recurring events
in Exchange ActiveSync accounts, OUT 62
items, **OUT 60**. See also appointment(s); events; meeting(s); one-time appointments; one-time events; recurring appointments; recurring events
meetings. See meeting(s)
Month view, **OUT 68**
multiple copies, OUT 110
natural language phrasing, OUT 87–89
navigating to specific dates, OUT 65–66
overview, OUT 58
printing. See printing calendars
saving as iCalendar file, OUT 112–113
Schedule View, **OUT 68**, OUT 68–69
School, OUT 102
sharing, OUT 113–114
using, OUT 58
Week view, **OUT 67**
Work Week view, **OUT 66**, OUT 66–67
Calendar Tools Appointment Series tab, OUT 87, OUT 98, OUT 100
calendar view, **OUT 65**
Calendar window, OUT 59–60
options, OUT 80
card, **PA-6**
cell, worksheet, **OFF 56**
cell reference, **OFF 57**
cell reference C6, OFF 57
Change Account dialog box, OUT 15
charts, **OFF 53**
clip, **PA-11**
color categories, organizing calendar, OUT 75–77
adding, OUT 75–76
assigning to appointment, OUT 77
for email account, OUT 75
column heading, **OFF 56**
command, **OFF 9**
composing email messages, OUT 2, OUT 11–13

configuring Outlook Calendar, OUT 59
'Connect to Internet' button, OFF 6
contextual tabs, OFF 14
Cortana, **OFF 74**, **PA-14**
in Microsoft Edge, PA-14–16
Creative Commons license, **PA-7**

D

database(s), **OFF 59**
creating Access, OFF 60–61
database management system, **OFF 59**
Date Navigator, **OUT 59**, OUT 67
default calendar, adding holidays to, OUT 70–72
default language, setting, OUT 9
desktop (Windows 10), OFF 7
destination folder, **OUT 42**
Dialog Box Launcher, **OFF 15**
dialog boxes, navigating in, **OFF 34**, OFF 34–37
digital calendar, advantages of, OUT 59
Docs.com, Microsoft, **PA-8**
document(s)
electronic image of, OFF 24
method for distributing, OFF 23
printing, OFF 23–24
document properties, **OFF 22**
changing, OFF 22
purpose, OFF 22
document window, **OFF 12**
domain name, **OUT 4**
Drafts folder, OUT 33–35
drawing canvas, **PA-3**

E

'Ease of access' button, OFF 6
email (electronic mail), **OFF 64**, **OUT 2**, OUT 11–16
attachments. *See* attachment(s)
capital letters, OUT 12
checking spelling and grammar, OUT 31–33
composing, OUT 2, OUT 11–13
deleting messages, OUT 45–46
forwarding messages, OUT 38–40
hard copy of, OUT 21

importance level, OUT 37–38
message area parts, OUT 11
message formats, OUT 29–30
misspelled words in, OUT 31
moving messages, OUT 41–45
opening attachments in, OUT 21
opening messages in window, OUT 18–19
opening saved messages, OUT 35
printing messages, OUT 21–22
replying to message, OUT 26–28
responding to messages, OUT 26–39
saving and closing messages without sending, OUT 33–34
from sender to receiver, OUT 15–16
sending messages, OUT 2, OUT 15–16
Sensitivity level, **OUT 10**, OUT 10–11
signature, OUT 13
tag in, OUT 38
themes, OUT 14
typing error, OUT 13
viewing messages in Reading Pane, OUT 17–18
working with mailbox, OUT 46–48
email accounts, **OUT 2**
adding account to Outlook, OUT 5
removing, OUT 6
email address, **OUT 2**
parts of, OUT 4–11
email client, **OUT 2**
email service provider, **OUT 2**
email thread, **OUT 46**
error correction, BACKSPACE key, OFF 21
events, **OUT 60**. *See also* one-time events; recurring events
Excel, **OFF 8**, **OFF 53**, OFF 53–56
charts, OFF 53
creating new documents from File Explorer, OFF 54–55
entering worksheet titles, OFF 57–58
exiting, OFF 59
formula bar, **OFF 57**
ribbon, OFF 57

running from File Explorer, OFF 55–56
saving files, OFF 58–59
tables, OFF 54
unique features of, OFF 56–59
web support, OFF 54
workbook, **OFF 53**
worksheets, **OFF 53**, OFF 56–57
Exchange server, OUT 80

F

file(s), **OFF 7**, OFF 23
closing, OFF 62
deleting, OFF 69
moving, OFF 68–69
opening existing, OFF 63
organizing, OFF 25
renaming, OFF 68
saving, OFF 31–34, OFF 49–52
type, OFF 23
File Explorer
creating new documents from, OFF 54–55
running apps from, OFF 55–56
window, OFF 27
file management, **OFF 67**
file names, **OFF 23**
saving existing files with same file name, OFF 58
saving with new file name, OFF 59
File tab, OFF 36
fixed formats, OFF 23
flagged word, OUT 31
folder(s), **OUT 40**
collapsing, OFF 29–30
copying to OneDrive, OFF 42–43
creating, OFF 26–28
creating in Inbox folder, OUT 40–41
Drafts, OUT 33–35
expanding, OFF 29–30
within folders, creating, OFF 28
moving email messages to, OUT 41–42
OneNote, **OFF 67**
organizing, OFF 25, OUT 19, OUT 85
saving files, OFF 31–34, OFF 49–52
scrolling through contents, OFF 29–30

folder windows, **OFF 27**
Formatting, email messages,
 OUT 29
formula bar, **OFF 57**
free-response quiz, **PA-12**
Full Screen mode, **OFF 17**

G

gallery, **OFF 14**
gesture, **OFF 3**
grammar, checking in email
 messages, OUT 31–33
green computing, **OFF 23**
green wavy underline, OUT 31
gridlines, **OFF 57**
group (ribbon), **OFF 14**

H

hard copy (printout), **OFF 23**,
 OUT 17
high importance, email messages,
 OUT 37
HTML (Hypertext Markup
 Language), **OUT 29**
 in title bar, OUT 12
Hub, **PA-14**
hyperlink, **OUT 17**
 inserting, OUT 11

I

iCalendar, **OUT 100**, OUT 112
 .ics (individual calendar) file
  format, OUT 112
 importing files, OUT 101–102
 saving calendar as, OUT 112–113
importance level, email messages,
 OUT 37
Inbox folder, OUT 8, OUT 40–41,
 OUT 61
Info tab in Backstage view, OFF 50
InfoBar, **OUT 19**
Ink to Math tool, **PA-3**
Ink to Text tool, **PA-3**
Inked handwriting, **PA-3**
Inking toolbar, **PA-15**
insertion point, OFF 21
Internet service provider (ISP),
 OUT 2

item, Calendar, **OUT 60**.
 See also appointment(s);
 events; meeting(s); one-time
 appointments; one-time events;
 recurring appointments;
 recurring events
 emailing, OUT 89
 status options, OUT 80

J

junk email, **OUT 17**

K

keyboard shortcut, **OFF 5**
KeyTips, **OFF 16**

L

landscape orientation, **OFF 48**
language preferences, OUT 9
layouts, **OFF 48**
lecture in OneNote, recording,
 PA-4
List view, Calendar
 changing calendar view to,
  OUT 110–111
 printing in, OUT 111
live preview, **OFF 14**
lock screen, **OFF 5**
low importance, email messages,
 OUT 37

M

mailbox, working with, OUT
 46–48
maximizing windows, **OFF 11**,
 OFF 11–12
meeting(s), **OUT 60**
 cancelation, OUT 107–108
 changing time, OUT 106–107
 creating and sending meeting
  requests, OUT 104–106
 importing iCalendar files,
  OUT 101–102
 Peek feature, OUT 103–104
 replying to meeting requests,
  OUT 107–108
 viewing calendars in overlay
  mode, OUT 102–103

meeting organizer, **OUT 100**
meeting request, **OUT 100**
 creating and sending,
  OUT 104–106
 declining, OUT 107
 error message, OUT 106
 invitation in Inbox, OUT 107
 proposing new meeting time,
  OUT 108
 replying to, OUT 107–108
menu, **OFF 9**
message area, **OUT 11**
message format, **OUT 29**,
 OUT 29–30
message header, **OUT 11**,
 OUT 18, OUT 38, OUT 105
message list, **OUT 16**
message pane, **OUT 16**
Microsoft Access 2016. *See* Access
Microsoft accounts
 area, OFF 16
 signing out of, OFF 37
Microsoft Edge, PA-14
 annotating webpages, PA-15
 browsing web with, PA-14
 inking with, PA-16
 locating information with
  Cortana, PA-14–15
 tools, PA-14
 using Cortana in, PA-16
Microsoft Excel 2016. *See* Excel
Microsoft Office 365. *See* Office
 365
Microsoft Office 2016. *See* Outlook
 2016
 apps. *See* Office apps
 Help window, OFF 70–74
 suites, OFF 8
Microsoft Office Online, **OFF 8**
Microsoft OneNote 2016. *See*
 OneNote 2016
Microsoft OneNote Mobile app,
 PA-2
Microsoft Outlook 2016, **OFF 8**
Microsoft Outlook 2016 app,
 OUT 2
Microsoft PowerPoint 2016. *See*
 PowerPoint
Microsoft Sway. *See* Sway
Microsoft Word 2016. *See* Word
mini toolbar, **OFF 15**
 turning off, OFF 16

minimized window, **OFF 34**, OFF 34–35
Month view, Calendar, **OUT 68**
mouse operations, OFF 4
My Calendars pane, **OUT 60**

N

Name box, **OFF 57**
natural language phrase, **OUT 87**, OUT 87–89
 capitalization, OUT 89
 creating appointment date and time using, OUT 88–89
navigating Calendar, OUT 65–72
navigating in dialog boxes, **OFF 34**, OFF 34–37
Navigation bar, changing options, OUT 6–7
Navigation Pane, **OFF 28**, OUT 8
note, PA-2
notebook, OneNote, **OFF 67**

O

object tabs, **OFF 60**
Office 365, **OFF 8**
Office apps, OFF 7–8, OFF 45–63
 exiting, OFF 41–42, OFF 53, OFF 59, OFF 63
 Help in, OFF 73–74
 opening Help window, OFF 70
Office Help
 opening window, OFF 70
 using Search text box, OFF 72–73
 using Tell Me box, OFF 74
 while working in apps, OFF 73–74
Office Mix, PA-10
 adding to PowerPoint, PA-10
 capturing video clips, PA-11
 inserting quizzes, live webpages, and apps, PA-12
 marketing travel destination with, PA-13
 for OneNote, PA-13
 sharing presentation, PA-12
 teaching augmented reality with, PA-13
on-screen keyboard, OFF 7
one-time appointments, **OUT 73**, OUT 73–74
one-time events

creating in Appointment window, OUT 92–94
deleting, OUT 95
OneDrive, **OFF 8**
 account, unlinking, OFF 44–45
 copying folder to, OFF 42–43
 saving on, OFF 32, OFF 35–36
OneNote 2016, **OFF 8**, **OFF 66**, OFF 66–67
 converting handwriting to text, PA-3–4
 creating notebook, PA-2
 creating Office Mix for, PA-13
 organizing research paper, PA-5
 recording lecture, PA-4
 syncing notebook to cloud, PA-2–3
 taking notes, PA-3
 window, OFF 67
Online Sway Newsletter, creating, PA-9
opening attachment, email messages, OUT 21
operating system (OS), **OFF 2**
outgoing email server, **OUT 15**
Outlook 2016, **OFF 8**, **OFF 64**, **OUT 2**, OUT 57
 Calendar. *See* Calendar
 contact photo, OUT 8
 email. *See* email (electronic mail)
 expanding folder pane, OUT 6
 language preferences, OUT 9
 navigation bar options, OUT 6–7
 opening data file, OUT 7–8
 overview, OUT 2
 People Pane, OUT 22–25
 Quick Steps, OUT 43–45
 running, OUT 5–6
 and screen resolution, OUT 61
 Sensitivity level, **OUT 10**, OUT 10–11
 setting up, OUT 3–11
 window, OFF 64–65
Outlook Help, OUT 46, OUT 87
Outlook window, OUT 2
overlay mode, viewing calendars, OUT 102–103

P

pages, OneNote, **OFF 67**
paragraphs, black space between, OFF 21

password, **OFF 5**
path, **OFF 25**
Peek feature, Outlook, **OUT 103**, OUT 103–104
People Pane, **OUT 22**
 to change view of, OUT 22–24
 updating contact information, OUT 24
personal storage table (.pst file), **OUT 7**
Picture Tools Format tab, OFF 14
placeholders, **OFF 48**
Plain Text format, OUT 29–30
pointer (touch screen), OFF 4
POP3, **OUT 15**
Post Office Protocol (POP), **OUT 15**
postal code, searching city, OUT 64
PowerPoint, OFF 46–48
 adding to Office Mix, PA-10
 closing using Backstage view, OFF 52
 creating new documents from Backstage view, OFF 50–51
 entering content in title slides, OFF 49, OFF 51
 exiting, OFF 53
 opening recent files using Backstage view, OFF 52–53
 saving files in folders, OFF 49–50
 window and ribbon, OFF 48–53
presentation (PowerPoint), **OFF 46**
 creating Sway, PA-6–7
 sharing Office Mix, PA-12
Previous Locations arrow, **OFF 27**
Print Layout view, **OFF 12**
print styles, **OUT 108**
printing calendars, OUT 108–111
 changing Calendar view to List view, OUT 110–111
 changing settings before, OUT 111
 in List view, OUT 111
 in weekly calendar style, OUT 109–110
printout, **OFF 23**
publication types, **OFF 65**
Publisher, **OFF 65**
 running, OFF 65
 window, OFF 65–66

Q

Quick Access area, **OFF 28**
Quick Access Toolbar, **OFF 16**
  customizing, OFF 20–21
  relocating, OFF 19–20
Quick Steps, **OUT 43**
  moving email messages using,
    OUT 43–45

R

Reading Pane, **OUT 17**
  hiding, OUT 25
  repositioning, OUT 24–25
  viewing email messages in,
    OUT 17–18
Reading view, **PA-14**
  viewing online news with, PA-16
recurrence pattern, **OUT 77**
recurring appointments, **OUT 73**,
    OUT 83–87
  adding, OUT 86–87
  deleting single occurrence,
    OUT 91–92
  moving, OUT 90
  saving, OUT 84–85
  setting recurrence options,
    OUT 83–84
recurring events
  creating in Appointment window,
    OUT 95–97
  deleting, OUT 100
  double arrow symbol, OUT 98
  moving, OUT 98–100
Recycle Bin, **OFF 7**
red wavy underline, OUT 31–32
Refresh button, **OFF 27**
reminder, Calendar, **OUT 77**
  customizing sound, OUT 82
  default time, OUT 82
  setting, OUT 81–82
responding to email messages,
    OUT 26–39
  business *vs.* friend's response,
    OUT 26
  options, OUT 26
responsive design, **PA-6**
Restart command, OFF 6
restoring windows, OFF 34–35
ribbon, OFF 12–15, **OFF 28**
  Access, OFF 61
  collapsing and expanding,
    OFF 17–19

customizing, OFF 57
  displaying tabs, OFF 16–17
  Excel, OFF 57
  in PowerPoint, OFF 48
  screen resolution, OUT 6,
    OUT 59
  to stay open, OUT 11
Room Finder, OUT 80
router, **OUT 15**
row heading, **OFF 56**
running apps, OFF 9–12
  Access, OFF 59–60
  from File Explorer, OFF 55–56
  using Search box, OFF 47–48
  using Start menu, OFF 9–11

S

sandbox, PA-15
saving files
  existing files with same file name,
    OFF 58
  in folders, OFF 31–34,
    OFF 49–52
  naming, OFF 32
  on OneDrive, OFF 32,
    OFF 35–36
  purpose, OFF 34
Schedule View, Calendar,
    OUT 68, OUT 68–69
Scheduling Assistant, **OUT 100**
School Calendar, OUT 102
screen clipping, PA-15
screen recording, **PA-11**
screen resolution, **OFF 38**,
    OFF 38–45, OUT 6
  changing, OFF 39–41
ScreenTip, **OFF 14**
scroll arrows, **OFF 4**
scroll bar, **OFF 4**, OFF 12
scroll box, **OFF 4**
search box, **OFF 27**
  running apps using, OFF 47–48
  Windows, OFF 74
Search text box, Office Help using,
    OFF 72–73
section tab, **PA-2**
sections, OneNote, **OFF 67**
sending email messages, OUT 2,
    OUT 15–16
Sensitivity level, **OUT 10**,
    OUT 10–11
sheet tab, **OFF 56**

shortcut menu, **OFF 19**
  commands, displaying, OFF 39
Show As box, OUT 94
Shut down command, OFF 6
sign-in screen, **OFF 5**
signing out of Microsoft accounts,
    OFF 37
Sleep command, OFF 6
slide, **OFF 48**
Slide Notes, **PA-11**
slide recording, **PA-11**
slide show, **OFF 46**
SMTP (Simple Mail Transfer
    Protocol), **OUT 15**
solid state drive (SSD), OFF 23
source folder, **OUT 41–42**
spam, **OUT 17**
spelling, checking in email
    messages, OUT 31–33
  correctly typed word, OUT 31–32
  misspelled text, OUT 32–33
Start button, **OFF 9**
Start menu, **OFF 9**
  running apps using, OFF 9–11
starting Windows, OFF 5–7
status bar, **OFF 12**
storage medium, OFF 23
Storyline, **PA-6**
stylus, OUT 23
subject line, **OUT 11**
suite, **OFF 8**
Sway
  adding content to build story,
    PA-7
  creating presentation, PA-6–7
  creating Sway resume, PA-9
  designing, PA-8
  presentation, PA-9
  publishing, PA-8
  sharing, PA-8
Sway site, **PA-6**
sync, **PA-2**

T

tab (ribbon), **OFF 14**
tables, **OFF 54**
task pane, **OFF 15**
Tell Me box, **OFF 15**
  Office Help in, OFF 74
templates, PA-2
text, **OFF 57**
text box, OFF 6

text entry in documents, OFF 21
Time Zones, setting, OUT 80
title bar, **OFF 11**
Title Slide, **OFF 48**
  entering contents in, OFF 49,
    OFF 51
To Do tag, PA-2
tool tabs, **OFF 14**
Touch Keyboard button, OFF 12
touch mode, OFF 15
touch screen, OFF 3–4, OUT 6
  differences, OUT 73
  gestures, **OFF 3**
  pointer, OFF 4

U

user account, **OFF 5**
user icon, **OFF 5**, OFF 6
user name, **OFF 5**, **OUT 4**

W

Weather Bar, adding cities to,
    OUT 64–65
Web Note, **PA-15**
web support, Excel, **OFF 54**
Week view, Calendar, **OUT 67**
weekly calendar style, printing
    calendars, OUT 109–110
windows, **OFF 11**
  dragging to move, OFF 70–71
  dragging to resize, OFF 71
  maximizing, **OFF 11**, OFF 11–12
  minimizing, OFF **34**, OFF 34–35
  OneNote, OFF 67
  Outlook, OFF 64–65
  PowerPoint, OFF 48–53
  Publisher, OFF 65–66
  restoring, OFF 34–35
  worksheet size and, OFF 56
Windows 10, **OFF 2**, OUT 5

desktop, OFF 7
keyboard shortcuts, OFF 5
overview, OFF 2
scrolling, OFF 4
search box, OFF 74
starting, OFF 5–7
touch screen and mouse,
    OFF 3–4
Word, **OFF 7**, OFF 9–12
Work Week view, Calendar,
    OUT 66, OUT 66–67
workbook, **OFF 53**
worksheet, **OFF 53**,
    OFF 56–57
  size and window, OFF 56
  titles, OFF 57–58